CONTENTS

Acknowledgements VII
List of Images and Copyright Notices IX
Introduction to the Irish Aviators Series XIII
Introduction to Volume I: Irish Aces XLIX

Part I – Irish Aces

ATKINSON, Edward Dawson 'Spider' 1
BETTS, Eric Bourne Coulter 7
BLENNERHASSET, Giles Noble 17
BYRNE, Patrick Anthony Langan 23
CAIRNES, William Jameson 29
CARBERY, Douglas Hugh Moffat 33
CASEY, Francis Dominic 41
COOPER, Maurice Lea 47
COWAN, Sidney Edward 51
COWELL, John J 57
CROWE, Henry George 61
CRUESS-CALLAGHAN, Joseph 77
GREGORY, William Robert 85
GRIBBEN, Edward 111
HARTIGAN, Edward Patrick 117

HAZELL, Tom Falcon 121
HEGARTY, Herbert George 131
HERON, Oscar Aloysius Patrick 139
HUSTON, Victor Henry 149
KELLY, Edward Caulfield 157
LEATHLEY, Forde 163
MANNOCK, Edward 'Mick' 177
McCLINTOCK, Ronald St Clair 211
McCORMACK, George 217
McELROY, George Edward Henry 'McIrish' 221
McLAUGHLIN, Robert 237
MILLS, Alfred Stanley 243
MOLESWORTH, William Earle 'Moley' 247
O'GRADY, Conn Standish 263
POPE, Sydney Leo Gregory "Poppy" 271
PRICE, Guy William 285
PROCTOR, Thomas 291
SAUNDERS, Alfred William 295
TIDMARSH, David Mary 303
TYRRELL, Walter Alexander 313
TYRRELL, William Upton 321
WALLER, Albert Gregory 327

Part II – Unconfirmed Irish Aces

CASEY, Robert Francis 345
CATHIE, Archibald James 351
de BURGH, Desmond Herlouin 355

IRISH AVIATORS OF WORLD WAR I:

Volume I – Irish Aces

By
JOE C. GLEESON

Copyright © 2012 Joe Gleeson
All rights reserved.
ISBN: 1480082325
ISBN 13: 9781480082328
Library of Congress Control Number: 2012920117
CreateSpace Independent Publishing Platform
North Charleston, South Carolina

DICKEY, Robert Frederick Lea 361
DODD, Walter de Courcy 367
GRATTAN-BELLEW, William Arthur 373
HARVEY-KELLY, Hubert Dunsterville 383
MULHOLLAND, Dennis Osmond 395
ORR, John Richard 401
SCUTT, George Howard Homer 407
WORKMAN, Charles Service 411
APPENDIX I Data regarding Aerial Victories 417
APPENDIX II Excluded Aces—Persons of Irish parentage
 or Irish Ancestry 435
Bibliography 467

ACKNOWLEDGMENTS

A self-published work of this nature inevitably fails to adequately convey the range of people consulted in the course of preparing the material, e.g. whilst I can cite hundreds of sources from thousands of records examined it is nevertheless only a series of textual references: many of the most significant contributions came from engagement with other people. One further problem with the publication process is that one tends towards mentioning ingredients rather than ensuring that the cake is edible. However, I am hopeful to have struck a balance between referencing sources/ingredients appropriately whilst ensuring that the book is still in itself readable. There are nevertheless a wide range of people and institutions without whom the book would be inestimably poorer.

I am deeply grateful for the assistance of the Royal Aero Club Trust in sourcing images of the aces at the early stages of their flying careers and would like to specifically mention Andrew Dawrant for helping track down these and other likely sources of images.

The RAF Museum kindly scanned a number of casualty cards, of which I have gratefully included Robert Gregory's card in this volume.

The Imperial War Museum provided a number of aircraft images through their prompt and courteous service. The Sandhurst Collection provided an excellent service for obtaining both enrolment register details of a number of cadets – and also photographs of two of these – for the Royal Military College, Sandhurst and the Royal Military Academy, Woolwich.

The UK National Archives have been the source of thousands of records, only a fraction of which are referenced in the text. Their online service facilitated the copying of a number of records that had not been digitised.

IRISH AVIATORS OF WORLD WAR I

The website of the Commonwealth War Graves Commission proved to be quite useful in providing reference to squadron and regimental service history details of the fallen. However, full praise must go to Geoff Sullivan for providing a search engine facility that enables additional criteria for querying the CWGC data.

I thank Limerick City Council for providing me with a copy of correspondence concerning David Mary Tidmarsh. The National Library of Ireland has always been quite informative and helpful. The Irish military archives were a source of a wealth of information, and the photograph of Captain Heron is from their collection. For first-hand accounts of various IRA operations, including the ambushes and raids in which Robert Gregory's widow, David Mary Tidmarsh and Albert Gregory Waller survived, the Bureau of Military History proved to be an excellent resource, although I freely admit I have not traced all operations in which Irish RAF personnel were affected, e.g. incidents to which reference was made by Henry George Crowe and so forth.

I would like to mention Graeme Neale for confirming several aerial victories that I was unable to track down between my trawls of the available combat reports and squadron operations record book files.

However, it should be emphasised that none of the foregoing persons or institutions in any way endorse the views contained in this volume. Further, any mistakes, errors or inadequacies are wholly the fault of the author.

In September 2009 I took a career break from the Irish civil service with quite some trepidation, the primary purpose being to retrain in IT. My research efforts were intended to be of a secondary nature, to provide data for pattern matching and validation of results. As so often happens in these cases the research became something worthwhile in its own right and continued to expand and develop whilst my IT studies shifted direction. I am delighted to have had the opportunity to prepare this work, which hopefully will be the pathfinder from which others may improve upon my sometimes limited combination of hyperbolic navigation and dead reckoning.

Joe Gleeson
January 2013

ACKNOWLEDGMENTS

List of Images and Copyright Notices

Every effort has been made to contact the original copyright holders of the photographs.

Page I
Image 1 **Airco D.H.2 'Pusher'** (Crown Copyright, Imperial War Museum, Q 67534)
Image 2 **Sidney Edward Cowan** (Royal Aero Club Trust)
Image 3 **Patrick Anthony Langan Byrne** (Royal Aero Club Trust)
Image 4 **David Mary Tidmarsh** (Royal Aero Club Trust)

Page II
Image 5 **F.E.2d 'Pusher'** (Crown Copyright, Imperial War Museum, Q 69650)
Image 6 **Giles Noble Blennerhasset**
Image 7 **Victor Henry Huston**
Image 8 **Joseph Cruess-Callaghan** (Royal Aero Club Trust)

Page III
Image 9 **Nieuport 17 C1 scout** (Crown Copyright, Imperial War Museum, Q 45379)
Image 10 **Edward Dawson Atkinson** (Royal Aero Club Trust)
Image 11 **William Earle Molesworth** (Royal Military Academy, Sandhurst)

Page IV
Image 12 **S.E.5A fighter** (Crown Copyright, Imperial War Museum, Q 12051)
Image 13 **Edward 'Mick' Mannock** (Imperial War Museum, Q 60800)
Image 14 **George Edward Henry McElroy** (Royal Military Academy, Sandhurst)

IX

IRISH AVIATORS OF WORLD WAR I

Page V
Image 15 **Sopwith F1 Camel** (Crown Copyright, Imperial War Museum, Q 67556)
Image 16 **Maurice Lea Cooper** (Royal Aero Club Trust)
Image 17 **Guy William Price** (Royal Aero Club Trust)
Image 18 **Oscar Aloysius Patrick Heron**

Page VI
Image 19 **Airco D.H.4 bomber** (Crown Copyright, Imperial War Museum, Q 80861)
Image 20 **Forde Leathley** (Royal Military Academy, Sandhurst)
Image 21 **Albert Gregory Waller** (Royal Aero Club Trust)

Page VII
Image 22 **Robert Gregory** (Dublin City Gallery The Hugh Lane)
Image 23 **Robert Gregory's RAF casualty card** (RAF Museum)

Page VIII
Image 24 **Douglas Hugh Moffat Carbery** (Royal Aero Club Trust)
Image 25 **Henry George Crowe** (Royal Aero Club Trust)
Image 26 **Edward 'Mick' Mannock** (Royal Aero Club Trust)
Image 27 **Alfred William Saunders** (Royal Aero Club Trust)

The images of the D.H.2, F.E.2d, S.E.5A, Nieuport 17 C1, Sopwith F1 Camel, and D.H.4 bomber are Crown Copyright, which were provided by the Imperial War Museum.

Images of Edward Dawson Atkinson, Patrick Anthony Langan Byrne, Douglas Hugh Moffat Carbery, Maurice Lea Cooper, Sidney Edward Cowan, Henry George Crowe, Joseph Cruess Callaghan, 'Mick' Mannock (in flying gear), Guy William Price, Alfred William Saunders, David Mary Tidmarsh and Albert Gregory Waller are copyright of the original image owners. Many of these images are now in the public domain, but I would be most grateful should any

ACKNOWLEDGMENTS

of the original copyright holders contact me. The images were kindly provided by the Royal Aero Club Trust.

The image of Giles Noble Blennerhasset remains copyright of the Blennerhasset family and was provided by Giles' son Brian to the Europeana project as part of a wider donation of papers and memorabilia.

The portrait of Robert Gregory by Charles Haslewood Shannon is copyright of the Collection: Dublin City Gallery The Hugh Lane.

The casualty card of Robert Gregory was one of several supplied to me by the RAF Museum. There are plans underway to digitize their entire collection of casualty cards. Copyright resides with the RAF Museum.

The image of Oscar Aloysius Patrick Heron was supplied by the Military Archives of the Irish Defence Forces. Copyright resides with them.

The image of Victor Henry Huston is in the public domain. (In his biography I supply several sources from where better quality images may be seen of his service in Chile: I refrained from including them in this work due to the uncertainty on their copyright status).

The images of Forde Leathley, George Edward Henry McElroy and William Earle Molesworth are copyright of the Royal Military Academy Sandhurst. The Leathley image was supplied from a private collection. The McElroy and Molesworth images were supplied through Tempest Photography.

The portrait image of 'Mick' Mannock is copyright of the Jim Eyles Trust, provided by the Imperial War Museum.

✦ ✦ ✦

INTRODUCTION TO THE IRISH AVIATORS OF THE GREAT WAR SERIES

The Great War had an enormous impact on Ireland. Over 240,000 volunteered to serve with the Allied forces. Almost 40,000 Irish died in the conflict.

The Irish contribution to the air war however, remains quite overlooked. Although a mere 6,000 served with the Royal Flying Corps, the Royal Naval Air Service and—following the merger of these bodies—with the Royal Air Force, at a cost of perhaps 500 casualties, the impact of the Irish was out of all proportion to their numbers.

The volumes in this series attempt to address the enormous contribution made by Irish aviators during the Great War.

Rationale behind a three-volume series

One problem with the Irish input to the air war effort has been the sheer diversity of the contributors. Unlike the Irish regiments of the British Army, for example it is not possible to talk of a geographical location in the manner one can when discussing the Connaught Rangers or Royal Munster Fusiliers. Similarly, there is no particular campaign associated in the public mind with the Irish aviators in the manner there is with the 36th (Ulster) Division at the Somme or the 10th (Irish) Division at Gallipoli.

Similarly, the RAF had several Training Depot Stations (TDS) based in Ireland, though they were not Irish as such. A related problem to the lack of a specifically Irish squadron is the fact that Ireland

XIII

was a base for the US Naval Air operations in the anti-submarine war but Ireland was the subject of Allied control (some would argue occupation) as much as being a contributor of manpower to the Allied war effort. In this context some accounts of Ireland's contribution to the war against the U-Boats can appear as if the island was nothing more than an unsinkable aircraft carrier, with perhaps some ungrateful islanders to sell overpriced goods and services to the Allies, and as being a source of disease, e.g. in June 1918 the influenza epidemic resulted in 65 cases of 2 weeks' duration at the US Naval Air Station, Wexford, and some 243 cases at Queenstown (Cobh) over the July to October 1918 period. In the aftermath of the General Election of 1918 the mandate for a continued military presence in Ireland became problematic, even before the military conflict of 1919-1922 erupted that would give rise to many Irish people disassociating themselves with their families' previous involvement with the British military. In these circumstances the role of Ireland as an integral part of the Allied anti-submarine war effort tends to be lost in Irish disassociation from any collaborationist connotations for the post-1918 period of upheaval.

If one is therefore faced with 6,000 individual stories, and almost as many reasons for serving with the RFC, RNAS and RAF, then it can be difficult to cover their contribution to different squadrons or to particular campaigns without being left open to the charge of selectivity or having an agenda to promote the contribution one political or religious group over another, or of forsaking proper military history for a random list of celebrities and personalities.

Consider a random selection of Irish aviators. Those with an interest in military history would wish to see those with a significant military role included. Inevitably this produces a "top brass" type hierarchy of senior officers who came through the war alive and who went on to serve in the inter-war years through World War II. Step forward Lieutenant-Colonel Arthur Stuart Bellingham, Air Marshal John Stanley Bradley, Air Marshal John Joseph Breen, Air Commodore Harold John Collins, Air Chief Marshal Francis Joseph Fogarty,

INTRODUCTION TO THE IRISH AVIATORS

Air Vice-Marshal William Foster MacNeece Foster, Air Commodore Arthur Willoughby Falls Glenny, Brigadier-General Cyril Francis de Sales Murphy, Air Commodore Henry Dunboyne O'Neill, Air Vice-Marshal Richard Saul, Air Vice-Marshal William Munro Yool and so forth.

Stepping down a few ranks from the "top brass" category there are many Irish aviators with a significant wartime contribution that didn't necessarily receive military plaudits commensurate with their efforts, e.g. the first Royal Flying Corps aircraft to land in France were flown by Irishmen such as Charles James Burke, Edward Roux Littledale Corballis, Hubert Dunsterville Harvey-Kelly and Francis Fitzgerald Waldron. In August 1914 Harvey-Kelly won the first aerial combat victory for the Royal Flying Corps. The colourful Thomas Westropp Mulcahy-Morgan was shot down and taken prisoner of war when attempting to land a Belgian spy behind German lines and became a famous escapee. Charles James Burke, the former commander of No.2 Squadron, was killed fighting on the ground with the Royal Irish Regiment on the first day of the Arras offensive. (He answered the call for senior officers to fill the depleted Irish regimental leadership after the mid-war battles had bled them dry).

Those with an interest in aviation history would demand the inclusion of the great Irish pioneers who served with the Royal Flying Corps in the war. Denys Corbett Wilson, who made the first successful crossing of the Irish Sea, would need to be included. Also eligible on this criterion would be the land and water speed record breaker Sir Henry O'Neil de Hane Segrave. The noted Times and Statesman correspondent, and founder of the Bengal Flying Club, William Arthur Moore, consequently warrants inclusion. Consider then that most Irish people would think of Fota House at the mention of the name Smith-Barry or perhaps Cork people would mention the market town Buttevant (named after the Smith-Barry family motto "boutez et avant") but for aviators it is indelibly associated with Robert Raymond Smith-Barry, the eccentric commander of No.60 Squadron who went on to found the "Gosport School" of training students how to cope with danger rather than avoiding it. Of specifically Irish interest, Samuel William Dunckley, after whom the Dunckley Cup is named, would also require inclusion, as would Francis Kennedy McClean. Consequently those who engaged in post-war aviation record attempts would also need to be addressed, e.g. Frederick Frank Reilly Minchin, who died in failed attempt to cross the Atlantic, as did Terence Bernard Tully; or indeed James Fitzmaurice, who succeeded on the 'Bremen' crossing, and "Paddy" Saul who managed a similar feat in the 'Southern Cross'.

However the inclusion of aviation pioneers would naturally lead to another category of inventor: many of the earliest advocates of the aeroplane were motorcar and motorbike enthusiasts, quite a number of whom had a string of patents to their names or records achieved. Immediately one faces calls for the inclusion of Lord Garvagh (Leopold Canning), Vernon Leslie Porter and so forth, all of whom served with the Royal Flying Corps. This would stretch to those who served in other capacities, e.g. William Ringrose Gelson Atkins was a brilliant Irish scientist, who served the Royal Flying Corps through experimenting with wood, fabric and other materials and the effect of sunlight on materials used in aeroplane construction, the stability of lubricants and so forth. (The conferral of an OBE to Atkins was a military, not a civilian award). When the Royal Aircraft factory was militarized the designer and engineer Mervyn O'Gorman held military rank with the Royal Flying Corps, notionally becoming a Lieutenant-Colonel. (O'Gorman was an easy scapegoat for the failure of the B.E.2c relative to the performance of the German Fokker E.III Eindecker, and the British designer Sir Geoffrey de Havilland always maintained his support for O'Gorman, who went on to serve as chairman of the Royal Aeronautical Society and chair of the Accident Investigation and Civil Air Transport Committee of the Air Ministry in the post-war years).

On a related point, many of those who served with the Royal Flying Corps in World War I were to become key personnel in the foundation and development of the Irish Air Corps, e.g. William Jasper McSweeney, William Percy Delamere, Charles F Russell and so forth.

INTRODUCTION TO THE IRISH AVIATORS

For those with an awareness of the human interest aspect of history would demand special mention of those who served in the Royal Flying Corps or Royal Air Force but in respect of which their achievements lay elsewhere. Consider in this category the Dublin-born nutritionist Wallace Ruddell Aykroyd, who fought with the Royal Flying Corps in World War I and who experienced the horrors first-hand of the Bengal Famine of 1943 in World War II, a major stain on the Allied record in the Far East. Similar to Aykroyd would be Dublin-born Daniel Francis Horsman Brickell, who fought in a relatively minor capacity with the Royal Flying Corps but who went on to become a well travelled British diplomat, serving in Cairo, Montevideo, San Salvador and Philadelphia. Also of interest is the Cork/Indian Walter Gerard Brind, a decorated night bomber who went on to serve as an administrator in Bechuanaland Protectorate for many years, being knighted twice and leaving a legacy of data regarding Lake Ngami that is still frequently quoted in scientific papers. (Brind also invented a water pumping apparatus, patenting it in 1934). The Dundalk-born geologist George Martin Lees warrants mention. Similarly, Maurice John Bernard Davy, the noted aeronautics author, served with the Royal Flying Corps, as did Thomas P Glennon, who worked with the Kilkenny People, the Wexford Free Press, the Irish Independent and was ultimately editor of Port of Spain Gazette, Trinidad, West Indies.

From low-profile Royal Flying Corps veterans with significant contributions to public life one inevitably gets drawn into the political quagmire of "statesmen" and those with delusions of same. In this regard one meets the Dublin-born Unionist George Panter, who becomes an MP at Stormont in Northern Ireland; James Godfrey MacManaway, clergyman and disqualified MP for Westminster; Henry George Hill Mulholland MP and so forth. Consider also for example Theodore Conyngham Kingsmill-Moore, a Dublin law student who served with Trinity College's OTC and was involved in the suppression of the Dublin Rising in 1916. Kingsmill-Moore failed on several separate occasions to pass an army medical before the Royal

Flying Corps obliged him. In the post-war years he was to become an expert on fly fishing—his book *A Man May Fish* still has a lingering popularity for salmon and trout fishermen—a two-term Senator, a High Court and later a Supreme Court judge, after whom a prize for Trinity College law students is named. His wartime contribution to the Royal Flying Corps is negligible, being invalided out on account of ill health, but like many political and legal personalities he is worthy of mention.

Similar to politicians are public personalities of various descriptions, e.g. the cricketer Augustine Patrick Kelly; the footballer Terence Michael 'Mick' O'Brien, who played for both the IFA and FAI 'Ireland' teams; Joe Keppel, the entertainer of Wilson, Keppel & Betty fame—a music hall act whose "outrageous" oriental style dances managed to provoke Goebbels to comment on degenerate, decadent Western civilisation; the young poet Paul Charles Stacpoole O'Longan, who was to write so much poetry of questionable quality at sixteen and seventeen, but who signifies so much lost potential; Herbert Sydney Wilcox, the film producer and director; brothers Gordon and Kenneth Murray from Wexford, who survived the war to strike gold in Canada in the 1920s.

There were many who served with the Royal Flying Corps in a non-aviator capacity, e.g. Sophie Catherine Theresa Mary Peirce-Evans (Mary, Lady Heath) who served as a Women's Royal Air Force despatch rider during the war and became a major female aviation pioneer after the war. Similarly, the dentist, Lionel Wigoder, served with the Royal Flying Corps during the war but went on to become an important member of the Jewish community in Dublin and a benefactor of a large number of Irish bridge tournaments; the McWeeney brothers: —Dr EJT "Theo" served the RAF and went on to serve the UN and WHO, while Dr Cecil became a well liked editor of *Social and Personal* and *Irish Golf*; Group-Captain Quinnell, a Kerryman, who fought in the RAF and served with the Irish Times before and after the war; Dr Thomas Malcolm O'Neill of the RAF became a noted ophthalmic surgeon at various hospitals in the UK in

INTRODUCTION TO THE IRISH AVIATORS

the post-war years; Air Commodore Eric William Craig served in the RAF medical services but was also a Military Cross recipient.

As one may note from all the foregoing, we have mentioned perhaps 100 names yet are at a point at which any narrative coherence would be impossible. Further, it should be noted that Irish aviators do not turn a shade of off-green relative to their British counterparts and/or have a unique relationship with German bullets or anti-aircraft shells that would distinguish their fate as being any different from an American, Australian, French, New Zealand or South African aviator in the same squadron—or in the same aircraft in the case of two-seaters. The Irish fought in RFC, RNAS and RAF squadrons, and their story is one of contributing to that war effort; the significance lies in just how exceptional their input was relative to their numbers.

Consequently, it is proposed that the Irish efforts be recognized through publishing a volume on the Irish aces, as their role is one which bears a direct relationship to the number of aerial victories achieved, and therefore it is possible to combine biographical reference with military history. It is then proposed to address the role of the Irish in the Royal Naval Air Service and the naval squadrons of the RAF in a separate volume, as it is reasonably self-contained. It is then proposed that a broadly based military history of the air war be written, in which the Irish role in various squadrons and in particular significant operations can be seen in the wider context. In this final volume a 'casualty list' of over 500 dead and a 'roll of honour' of 1,000 people would briefly deal with individual combatants, as often a general history that mentions an Irish casualty in the context of a larger operation can often diminish rather than illustrate just how small the Irish numbers were relative to what their efforts achieved.

Volume I: Irish Aces

One obvious factor with the air war is the popular focus on (some would say 'cult' of) the aces. However, many of those who achieved ace status actually flew with bomber and reconnaissance squadrons.

An examination of the 37 Irish aces reveals just how diverse their military backgrounds were: many had served in the trenches, whilst many others had served as observers/gunners before becoming pilots. However, the contribution of Mannock, McElroy and Hazell to the Allied cause was extraordinary by any standards: only a handful of aces exceeded 40 aerial victories in World War I. Of the 7,500 aerial victories scored by the RFC, RNAS and RAF just 37 Irishmen accounted for over 430 of these. The old adage is that extraordinary claims require extraordinary evidence, and in this regard I had considered the inclusion of full details of each individual aerial victory in tabular form. However, this was impractical, as the sheer volume of tabular material would fragment and destructure the book into an almanac of tables and charts. Instead I have decided to include some basic aerial combat information in each biography, with some further levels of detail where relevant or necessary, e.g. the accompanying pilot or observer in the case of two-seaters, mention of shared claims where they arise and occasionally the name of their opponent.

However, for those with an interest in military history or aviation history, I have included some tables of information regarding the successes of Irish aces in particular aircraft types. I decided to include data by reference to aircraft type on the basis that it adds to the overall picture of the Irish contribution to the air war, and that an alternative classification by Squadron would not adequately reflect the transfer of personnel within squadrons. However, I have refrained from detailing each individual victory by ace across the different aircraft types: there is sufficient information in their profiles, and 37 individual tables would render a biographical approach redundant. For ease of reference I only refer to the Irish aces in the table, but in the individual biographies I often cite the pilot or gunner/observer who flew with a particular ace in the case of two-seater aircraft. Similarly, with shared claims I do not include the details in the tables, as the purpose of these tables is to give an easy visual reference across the different aces and squadrons the frequency and intensity of aerial combat operations.

INTRODUCTION TO THE IRISH AVIATORS

The Irish aces' victories by aircraft type were as follows:

B.E.2e	1
Bristol F2a/F2b	44
Airco D.H.2	20
Airco D.H.4	28
Airco D.H.5	5
F.E.2b/d	29[1]
F.E.8	3
Nieuport	61
R.E.8	5
S.E.5/5A	167
Sopwith 1 ½ Strutter	6
Sopwith Camel	42
Sopwith Dolphin	4
Sopwith Pup	9
SPAD	13
	437

---

[1] Blennerhasset and Huston's joint victories are counted only once.

IRISH AVIATORS OF WORLD WAR I

As one may note, there are a variety of fighters, bombers and reconnaissance aircraft listed. To further inform the reader there are some photographs of the main aircraft types included in this volume of the series.

However, there are also a considerable number of Irish pilots and observers who are frequently described as aces. I have examined the most plausible of these and included details in Part II of this volume. In most cases I do not entirely rule out the possibility that they were aces but I remain to be convinced in the absence of compelling evidence. The eleven aviators I chose to include in this section obtained at least 40 aerial victories between them. It should be emphasised, however, that this is in no way an exhaustive list, e.g. Captain Charles Edmund Ryan of No.6 Squadron is often credited with a half-dozen victories, whilst Captain John Crosby Halahan of No.4 Squadron is credited with several aerial victories even though his gallantry awards and his C.B.E. were conferred in respect of his bomber and reconnaissance successes.[2] There are dozens of Irish aviators with at least two aerial victories and scores with at least one aerial victory. This book is primarily about the Irish aces and therefore only examines the most plausible claims to ace status from among the others.

Given that there are quite a number of aces of Irish parentage who have either regularly or occasionally been categorized as Irish, I have included an additional Appendix for the reader to further examine their claims. I have refrained from including these as Irish aces out of respect to all concerned: I do not wish to be accused of grave-robbing through claiming persons to be Irish who were not so, nor do I wish to devalue the achievements of Irish aces by stretching the definition to reach some spurious predetermined objective (e.g. that over 750 or perhaps 1,000 of the RFC, RNAS and RAF aerial victories were by Irishmen). However, this section may prove contentious, e.g. the McCudden brothers, Charles Hickey, Denis Lat-

---

[2] It was actually Halahan's son, PJ "Bull" Halahan, who was to achieve success as a fighter pilot, in World War II.

imer and several other prominent aces of Irish parentage have been included in this appendix rather than the main part of the volume.

Volume II: the Royal Naval Air Service

The Irish contribution to the Royal Naval Air Service was a hugely important one. Quite apart from the Irish aces there were a large number of personnel who had a critical role in the development of the RNAS and in its many successes over the course of the war. Following the merger of the RNAS and RFC, quite a number of Irish played a prominent part in the naval squadrons of the RAF, some of which constituted the forerunner of Coastal Command.

History has not been kind to the RNAS, with all its petty rivalries with the Army's aviation wing, the RFC, it was often seen as inhibition to the successful prosecution of the air campaign against the Central Powers or as being an extension of the ego of Winston Churchill, but it made a difference to the development of lighter-than-air flight, to addressing the specific problems of maintaining an aerial coastal protection force, the development of an anti-shipping role, and the RNAS also expended much time, effort and many lives in the development of the aircraft carrier. Ireland contributed over 750 officers and other ranks to the Royal Naval Air Service, taking significant casualties in the process but having an impact far beyond the narrow metrics of kill: loss ratios through which—for example—the Irish aces can be measured.

It is beyond the scope of this introduction to the series to traverse the entire range of significant Irish contributions to the RNAS. However, there are several areas that would distinguish the Irishmen in the RNAS from a more general history of the Irish in the air war. In this regard the Irish role in the development of the airships, the Irish wartime achievements at Coastal Station level with flying boats and seaplanes in the anti-submarine war and the Irish contribution to the

Naval Squadrons are all areas for which there is sufficient material to warrant a separate volume.

Of those who served with airships there were a host of important innovators, e.g. Meath-born Claud Brabazon had been one of the founding members of the Royal Aeronautical Club, and had flown in hot air balloons before becoming involved in hydrogen-gas kite balloon types. Claud served as a Major in the Irish Guards. He became a Flight Officer 05 December 1912 and was promoted to Flight Commander on 30 May 1913, serving with No.9 Squadron before transferring back to airships during the war. Brabazon was the third son of Reginald, the 12th Earl of Meath (PC, KP, GCVO, GBE).[3] The Brabazon family are associated with Dublin's Liberties area: following the dissolution of the monasteries by Henry VIII the Anglo-Norman Liberty of Thomas Court and Donore was granted to the Earls of Meath; consequently the Meath Market, Meath Hospital and so forth. However, the Brabazons funded artisans' dwellings in the area, hence Brabazon Row, Brabazon Street. Meath Street and Ardee Street are named after the family. Brabazon's mother, the Countess of Meath, founded the Ministering Children's League, the Brabazon Employment Society, the Meath Home of Comfort for Epileptic Women at Godalming, the Sandford (Dublin) Brabazon House for Aged Ladies, the Brabazon and Hopkinson House Co for providing affordable accommodation for women in London, and the Workhouse and Hospitals Concert Societies. It was therefore no surprise that Claud Brabazon would be involved in a host of voluntary organizations after the war, holding the post of honorary secretary of the NSPCC in Dublin from the 1920s to the 1940s. Claud's eldest brother became Lord Ardee but his other brother Ernest was killed serving with the Coldstream Guards in 1915. His sister Lady Violet Brabazon, afterwards Countess of Verulam, lost both her sons in World War II, serving in the RAF. Brian and Bruce Grimston are

---

3   Claud is sometimes confused with "Brabazon of Tara", who is actually John Moore-Brabazon, related by marriage to a descendant of the Brabazon family but an Englishman through and through.

commemorated on a church panel at Christ Church, Bray, Co Wicklow. It is unclear if their uncle's feats of aviation pioneering inspired the young men to enlist in the RAF rather than follow in their father's family traditions in the British Army.

Squadron Commander Wyndor Plunkett de Courcy Ireland was born in Co Tipperary and was educated at Christ's Hospital 'Bluecoat School' (i.e. an "Old Blue") for less privileged Protestant children. He was one of the Royal Naval Air Service's earliest pilots, obtaining his Royal Aero Club certificate on a Bristol Biplane at the Naval School, Eastchurch on 01 November 1913. He had married Susan Myrtle Lloyd of Wexford but the family are most closely associated with Merton Hall, Cloughjordan, Co Tipperary (which has since been demolished). Air Mechanic Henry Allingham, the last Royal Navy survivor of the war, was to mention de Courcy Ireland favourably in several interviews over the decades. de Courcy Ireland was to die in a tragic crash as part of experimental works on launching aircraft from airships as a means of having aircraft airborne to meet the Zeppelin threat over London.

Also of significance was Wing Commander Neville Florian Usborne, a Cork-born innovator who died in the same crash as de Courcy Ireland. Usborne had served in the Royal Navy as a submariner before transferring to the select naval team that began the work on the Royal Navy's Airship No.1 (the 'Mayfly') in 1909. Although the airship was wrecked in a mishap in May 1911 Usborne went on to participate in the Naval Airships branch of the Royal Flying Corps in 1912 but also successfully obtained a Royal Aero Club certificate in April 1913 for heavier-than-air flight. Usborne was to be central in the development of the Royal Naval Air Service's Submarine-Scout (SS) class airship, which were proven to be an enormous success in the U-boat war. However, when pressed to develop solutions to combat the Zeppelin threat over London his experimental combination of aircraft and airship failed in test flight, killing Usborne and another Irish aviation pioneer, Wyndor Plunket de Courcy Ireland.

Usborne had married Elizabeth Monteith Hamilton, son of the artist Vereker Hamilton. Usborne's wife remarried and her son John Raymond Godley, 3rd Lord Kilbracken, was to become a decorated aviator of World War II, who controversially returned his 6 war medals and renounced British nationality in 1972 on account of British military policy in Northern Ireland at that time.

One of the most famous airship pilots of the war and afterwards was Herbert Carmichael Irwin. Dublin-born, he was the son of Frederick Irwin (a well known Dublin solicitor) and Elinor Carroll, the daughter of Rev Carroll, Rector of Dundrum. Irwin's uncles, Colonel Herbert Irwin and Major-General Sir James Murray were well known in the rowing world. Irwin was a successful athlete, on the track and as a cross-country runner, being an Irish record-holder and RAF mile and 3-mile champion in the post-war years. The recommendations for promotion detailed in Irwin's wartime service record[4] indicate that he was a very highly regarded airship officer. However, like many of the RNAS aircraft pilots the airship pilots were not immune to crashes and near-death experiences: on 20 December 1915 Irwin suffered a hard landing when control wires broke on the SS.31 but his reactions were recorded as "praiseworthy". On 12 May 1917 Irwin was discharged to Malta, suffering from shock arising from another incident. He competed as part of the last Great Britain and Ireland joint team, at the Antwerp Olympics of 1920. In the post-war years he transferred into the Imperial Airship Scheme, commanding the R-33 in 1924. In November 1929 he got to take the R-101 over Dublin—at an altitude of just 500 feet above Westmoreland St—as part of a 30-hour flight to test the prototype airship. However, although the media circus proclaimed an enormous success the designers were aware of the many failings in performance in terms of weight and range. The consequent revisions entailed a massively enlarged airship, which crashed near Paris on its maiden voyage to India on 05 October 1930, killing Irwin and 47 others, with just 7 survivors. Among the dead were Lord Thomson (Secretary of

---

4   ADM 273/7 HC Irwin, UK National Archives.

INTRODUCTION TO THE IRISH AVIATORS

State for Air), Sir W Sefton Brancker (Director of Civil Aviation) and Lt-Col V.C. Richmond (the designer of the airship). Britain's interest in the airship ended with this disaster. Irwin had trained under Tommy Burton at Clonliffe Harriers AC, and the club established the Irwin Cup in his honour in the 1930s, which was a cross-country event that nowadays has been incorporated into a club grand prix series.

As one may note, the role of Irishmen in the airship services could almost be worthy of a separate volume in its own right. However, their contribution would not in itself be remarkable when placed in comparison to the Irish involvement at naval air station level throughout the UK, from which many notable contributions to the anti-submarine war emerged. To give just one example I mention RNAS Felixstowe and the Irish contribution to the development of the RNAS' seaplane and flying boat capabilities.

It would be impossible to mention the RNAS and to fail to mention John Cyril Porte, from Bandon, Co Cork, one of the pioneers of the flying boat. Porte obtained a pilots' licence outside the Royal Navy, becoming a test pilot for a number of British companies. In April 1914 he joined the American company Curtiss as a pilot, helping redesign their H-1 flying boat 'America' and winning Admiralty orders for the type. Porte was appointed command of the RNAS training school at Hendon, later becoming commander of Felixstowe Naval Air Station, helping further refine the flying boat into what would become the inter-war trans-Atlantic workhorse we now know, e.g. the Felixstowe Fury was designed on a Porte hull. Porte did not get to see the outcome of his best work, dying in Brighton in October 1919 from tuberculosis he had contracted whilst serving with the Royal Navy a decade previously. The Commonwealth War Graves Commission do not commemorate him, presumably because his military-related illnesses were contracted prior to the 1914-1918 period, and because he left the RAF in August 1919 to act as designer for the Gosport Aviation Co Ltd. He remains one of the RNAS' best innovators and he is shamefully overlooked in many Irish accounts of World War I. There was a minor scandal involving Porte and some sub-contractors receiving commission on the number of orders placed by the RNAS, i.e. a breach of the principle of *nemo iudex in causa sua* (one can't adjudicate and advocate in a case), but it was not a case of Porte seeking financial gain—his was an evangelical zeal. Porte put his own life on the line, leading RNAS patrols from Felixstowe on occasion, e.g. on the 25 July 1917 Porte was on board his F.2C prototype in leading a 5-aircraft attack on the German mine-laying submarine UC-1, sinking it. The US President Woodrow Wilson awarded Porte the Distinguished Service Medal posthumously on 12 December 1919.

Monkstown-born Lieutenant-Colonel Owen Hugh Knox Maguire served with the RNAS at Felixstowe, winning the Distinguished Service Order in 1917 for his submarine-hunting exploits and enabling his commanding officer Cyril Porte to work on the development of experimental seaplane types. Maguire's role as "James the One" at the heart of the "Spider Web" grid of operations conducted via seaplane anti-submarine patrols also facilitated engagement with enemy aircraft. Although his service records[5] show that he was a Royal Navy veteran invalided out of service following the Somaliland campaign of 1908-1910, Maguire had rejoined for the duration of the war, serving not only with the RNAS but also continuing to become a Wing Commander in the RAF. The Canadian pilot Theodore Douglas Hallam recounts serving under Maguire:

"The First Lieutenant of the station was Lieutenant-Commander O.H.K. Maguire, R.N., known as James the one or Number One, who understood discipline, and reigned over an exceedingly fine mess. He ran the station under naval routine, the time being tapped off on a bell, the ship's company being divided into watches, anybody leaving the station "going ashore", and the men for leave, when marching out of the gate, were the "liberty boat"... As James the One had a shrewd tongue he was rather feared by the junior officers

---

5   ADM 196/50, AIR 76/330 OHK Maguire, UK National Archives.

… But he instilled discipline … And woe betide the defaulter, standing to attention outside the ship's office in full view of Number One as he sat in an easy-chair on the veranda of the mess, if the unfortunate so much as moved a little finger. The tiger roar which greeted such a disobedience to the order not to move, made every man with a guilty conscience on the station tremble".[6]

Maguire was not some latter-day version of Captain Bligh, however, and gave the RNAS the degree of latitude to make the difference in taking the initiative in the U-boat patrols, without having to channel the operational decisions at Felixstowe through Harwich. Using intercepted radio traffic, working the "Spider Web" through plotting the U-boat locations on the grid and keeping the anti-submarine war going, Maguire's station accounted for a dozen submarines, several aircraft and at least one Zeppelin. Towards the end of the war Maguire was assigned the notional title of Air Adviser to the Australian Commonwealth Naval Board but one can paper the walls with the number of energetic recommendations Maguire wrote for the Naval Board on the emerging threat from Japan, on the need for airship stations, kite balloon stations, seaplane and aeroplane schools and so forth. Maguire served as Australian Liaison Officer at the Air Ministry and was the key link between the Australian Navy and the Air Ministry. However, the evolution of the Australian Flying Corps of the RAF into the Royal Australian Air Force (RAAF) did not result in the Australian Navy being granted an Australian Fleet Air Arm. A vindication of Maguire's position though can be seen in the eventual establishment of an Australian Fleet Air Arm following the success of naval aviation in the Pacific theatre in World War II.

Despite what one way imagine from the foregoing, being Irish in the RNAS was not the exclusive preserve of Southern Protestants. Of the Ulstermen at Felixstowe there was Robert Frederick Lea Dickey, who memorably shot down the German airship L-43 from a Curtiss H-12 Flying Boat on 14 June 1917 using explosive ammuni-

---

6   P.I.X. "The Spider Web", pp.21-22 (Reprinted by Leonaur, 2009).

tion. Dickey was also a respected submarine-hunter, operating from Felixstowe.

Of the many varied contributions to the RNAS it is often easy to overlook the early casualties, e.g. Francis Annesley, the 6th Earl Annesley was killed in November 1914. In the early stages of the war in 1914 he allegedly helped check the German advance on Brussels and Antwerp. On 03 November 1914 the Irish Times carried details of "Lord Annesley's Thrilling Experience" in its 'Letter from the Front' pages. Dated 22 October 1914, it recounts a forced landing. "I shall never forget it as long as I live. This flying under shell and rifle fire must beat most things for pure unadulterated excitement". His aircraft was last seen on 06 November 1914, leaving from England for France. Later in the war a German POW claimed that the aircraft had been shot down by shellfire.

Also a casualty in the early weeks of the war was John Evans-Freke (Lord Carbery), injured in a crash at Antwerp. He was invalided from wounds on 24 November 1914. Lord Carbery had been an early aeroplane pioneer and—quite unusual for a member of the Munster landlord class—a supporter of the Irish Volunteers, who flew a tricolour over Castle Freke. Lord Carbery went on to sell everything to indulge in an alternative lifestyle in Kenya after the war.

The Royal Naval Air Service accepted people of all ages and abilities. Three interesting examples are Cecil Meares, René Bull and Erskine Childers.

Kilkenny-born Cecil Henry Meares was a fascinating character. His father was a major in the Indian Army, his mother died when he was a child. Having passed through a succession of schools and countries he became a "Great Gamer" of the 1890s, being involved in much British-Russian intrigue for influence on the frontiers of China and India. Serving in various shadowy roles in the Boxer Uprising, the Boer War and the Russo-Japanese war he ended up nearly losing his life as part of the misadventures of the explorer John Weston Brooke on the western frontiers of Szechwan and the Chinese/Tibetan borders. Brooke was killed by Lolo ("Yi") tribesmen in

INTRODUCTION TO THE IRISH AVIATORS

1908 but Meares survived to become part of Scott's second Antarctic Expedition. Meares was an expert dog-handler but was tasked with sourcing ponies. Although Lt Oates is often quoted regarding the poor quality of what Meares brought it should also be borne in mind that Oates was also deeply critical of Scott's refusal to adequately provision for feeding the animals and for being too sentimental when the time came to kill particular horses. Meares is sometimes scapegoated for the failure of Scott's expedition but he emerges with much credit. His service in World War I with the Royal Naval Air Service is an interesting one: he transferred from the corps of interpreters to become a Flight Commander with the RNAS. Later in the war he became an Air Attaché and working as Lieutenant Colonel from the Embassy in Rome, Meares would appear to have had a number of high-profile engagements. Of course the most significant military contribution he was to make in the inter-war years was one that ultimately proved detrimental to Allied interests: as part of a multi-disciplinary team stationed in Japan in the 1920s he was highly respected and was ultimately awarded the Order of the Sacred Treasure by the Japanese but the development of Japanese expertise in torpedo-bombing was to see the *HMS Repulse* and *HMS Prince of Wales* being the first capital ships to be sunk solely by air power in World War II.

Dublin-born René Bull was the son of an English father and French mother. His family firm on Dublin's Suffolk St for many years supplied church furniture and religious vestments. They were a creative family: his brother Lucien was to become the first man to record a million images per second in 1952. René Bull was unusual insofar as he was a strong supporter of the Union, if not a Catholic Unionist then certainly a Catholic imperialist. As a journalist he reported from many of the world's troubled hot-spots, being one of the few to have actually been present at the Battle of Omdurman. He went on to become war correspondent for *Black & White* weekly magazine, being the equivalent of an embedded reporter during the Boer War. His combination of photographs and sketches often helped bring home to the reading public the import of what was happening, even though photo-journalism was not yet a concept, and many of his sketches attempted to portray the mood rather than be a factual representation of what had transpired. His shrill pro-Empire apologias, often aimed at the reading public in the USA, for whom the Boer War was deeply unpalatable, do not take from his personal courage in being at the forefront of wartime journalistic investigation. Throughout his life Bull's wonderful illustrations and sketches graced many children's books, e.g. Joel Chandler Harris' "Uncle Remus", exceptionally elegant versions of "Arabian Nights" and "Carmen", and Edward Fitzgerald's translation of "The Rubaiyat of Omar Khayyam". Bull's journalism had coincided with the emergence of mass-circulation newsprint whilst his sketching had found a place in the golden era of children's illustration, before the advent of film reel was to render it obsolete. However, despite such a varied and accomplished career Bull presented himself for service with the Royal Naval Air Service, who deployed him to the experimental workshop at Battersea, the Repair Depot at Dunkirk and to the Naval Air Station there. He was mentioned in despatches and served with No.233 Squadron of the RAF after the RNAS was subsumed. Bull finished the war with the Armaments School.

Robert Erskine Childers was born to an Irish mother and English father. Because of the fame of his English father—the renowned scholar Robert Caesar Childers—and his English family generally (e.g. his uncle Hugh Childers served at the Admiralty and the War Office and later as Chancellor of the Exchequer) it is often overlooked that Childers' parents died of TB when he was quite young. It is also often not understood that the children were quarantined from their parents for their final years: Childers was actually raised in Ireland, by his mother's family on the Barton family estate in Glendalough, Co Wicklow.[7] Although Childers was raised in an orthodox Anglo-Irish unionist environment he had a strong affinity with

---

[7] The family also had connections with Bordeaux, through Chateau Léoville-Barton and Chateau Langoa-Barton, of Anthony Barton & Co, and also—more distantly—another company which is now known as Barton & Guestier.

INTRODUCTION TO THE IRISH AVIATORS

Ireland and spent his summers there, suffering a sciatic nerve injury when hiking to Connemara. Childers served as a parliamentary clerk in the House of Commons before joining the City Imperial Volunteers in the Boer War. His experiences led to a best-selling memoir. (His views on the Empire and its misadventures had begun to shift on foot of his wartime experiences). Childers' love of yachting and sailing were one beneficial consequence of his sciatic injury. In 1903 he wrote *The Riddle of the Sands*, a famous yarn about the threat of seaborne invasion, based loosely around his own sailing experiences of the Frisian Islands and North Sea. Childers' marriage to a Bostonian, Mary Osgood, was to further shake his Anglo-Irish unionist perspective. Childers wrote *The Framework for Home Rule* in 1911, in which he argued for Dominion status for Ireland instead of the more limited grand assembly status being considered. However, when the British government cowered before Unionist pressure and a threatened British military coup in March 1914 (serendipitously engineered to buy sufficient time to facilitate Unionist gun-running in April 1914, when they landed 35,000 German rifles), Childers became involved with a group of Anglo-Irish Protestants[8] who were sympathetic to Home Rule. They decided to provide weapons for the Irish Volunteers as a counterbalance to the Ulster Volunteer Force (UVF) and so hoped to restore the primacy of the parliamentary process. The purchase of 1,500 rifles was a token effort but symbolic, and Childers transported the majority of this consignment on his yacht, the 'Asgard', landing them successfully at Howth from where they were distributed by the Irish Volunteers.[9]

---

8   Childers liaised with Alice Stopford Green, Lord Ashbourne, Sir George and Lady Alice Young, Sir Alexander Lawrence, Captain George Fitzhardinge Berkeley and others, not exactly a cabal of lawless radicals.
9   A detachment of the King's Own Scottish Borderers travelled to Clontarf to intercept the Irish Volunteers but were too late. However, later that day on Bachelor's Walk when returning from their wild goose chase they fired into the jeering crowds, killing several. The contrasting treatment of the Unionist actions at Larne was not lost on Irish nationalists.

Childers, however, joined the RNAS when the war came. He was forty-four by this stage but, like Bull and Meares, the RNAS still found a use for his skill and talents. Childers was initially assigned to the *HMS Engadine*, an old cross-Channel steamer that was converted into an aircraft carrier. Childers had to teach coastal navigation to the RNAS pilots on the *HMS Engadine* and its sister ships, *Empress* and *Riviera*. He plotted charts and maps in meticulous fashion, making easy the training of pilots as to how to navigate by stars and landmarks of the enemy coast. On Christmas Day 1914 Childers flew as an observer in the RNAS raid on the German Zeppelin sheds at Cuxhaven. His disgust at the media for "making a fuss" and at the RNAS for overstating the raid's success was actually wide of the mark: they had been perilously close to scoring some direct hits, and the very fact of their actions caused the German High Seas Fleet to evacuate many of its ships to various locations on the Kiel Canal. Childers received a mention in despatches for his part in the raid.

Childers was subsequently posted to the aircraft carrier Ben-my-Chree (*Bean mo Chroí* for Gaelic readers of Manx). Childers' experiences of the disastrous Gallipoli campaign were tempered somewhat by the successes of his protégées. Following Bulgaria's declaration of war on the Allies in October 1915 Childers flew as observer in one attack on a key railway bridge over the Maritza River in Eastern Thrace as the RNAS attempted to disrupt the new land supply routes to the Ottoman Empire. Childers spent 1916 in reconnaissance operations against Ottoman Empire forces. It was Childers who photographed the new German airfield and hangers at Beersheeba in March 1916. He was awarded the DSC in 1917 for his reconnaissance work in 1916. Childers transferred to the Admiralty for strategic planning work. Childers' cousin, Robert Barton, resigned his British army commission in protest at the unfolding events in Ireland but Childers persisted with the RN and RNAS, serving with the Coastal Motor Boat section[10] on special duties before returning to reconnaissance patrols with the RNAS over Zeebrugge in spring

---

10   ADM 337/117 UK National Archives, E. Childers.

1917 until he was released to serve in the Irish Convention[11] of 1917-1918, an ill-fated talking shop that could do nothing to disguise that Ulster Unionists had already been promised all they wanted (e.g. the exclusion of 6 counties of Ireland from any 'Home Rule' arrangement, rather than the areas of the 4 counties in which they had a majority) and that the British government were still not yet prepared to countenance Dominion Status for Ireland. The Convention had been a fig leaf to help assuage King George V that the British government had a policy on Ireland and partially also as a means of pretending that the Irish 'Home Rule' Party was still relevant.[12]

Childers got to return to uniform with the newly founded RAF, and rather than return to a former RNAS squadron he was assigned to the RAF's Independent Force in September 1918, but—as a staff officer—was banned from operational flying. Childers' cousin Robert Baron was elected as a Sinn Féin MP for West Wicklow in the December 1918 general election, and was declared a *Teachta Dála* (TD) for *Dáil Éireann*, the new Irish parliament that was not recognized by the British. Consequently Barton was arrested and it fell to Childers to manage the family estate in Ireland upon recovering from influenza in the winter of 1918/1919. Ireland had little prospect of receiving the same status accorded to Czechoslovakia, Finland, Poland and so forth—Allied respect for national self-determination only extended to territories of defeated powers such as the Austro-Hungarian, German and Ottoman Empires or to the Russian Empire's successors outside the USSR—but Childers views gradually moved from his Dominion Status within the Empire to one of outright support for Irish independence. Childers was sent to Paris to act on behalf of the government of the Republic of Ireland (*Poblacht na hÉireann*) in seeking international recognition of Ireland or at least to get the British to pay lip service to Wilson's Fourteen Points as being applicable to the Irish situation but it was a futile exercise.

---

11 ADM 337/124; AIR 76/85 UK National Archives, E. Childers.
12 Sinn Féin had boycotted the convention, which turned into an 8-month fiasco, leaving all its participants discredited.

Childers was to eventually become a propagandist for the *Poblacht na hÉireann*, his sometimes overly melodramatic accounts of British atrocities devaluing the horrific truth of what was happening in many parts of Ireland. However, even the British couldn't disguise the gradual collapse of civil administration in Ireland, the sweeping electoral victory of Sinn Féin in the local elections of 1920, with many local authorities in what was later to be incorporated in Northern Ireland also affiliating themselves with Dáil Éireann. Childers served as secretary to the Irish delegation that negotiated the Anglo-Irish Treaty of 1921. Although he did not have plenipotentiary status, Childers was consistently on the side of the Republic in the negotiations, and the relationship between Childers and Arthur Griffiths became toxic over the ease with which the latter was bullied into compromise by the British negotiators.[13] Childers was to argue against the ratification of the Treaty, and continued to support the *Poblacht na hÉireann* over the Irish Free State and Northern Ireland. Eventually he was captured and executed by Irish Free State forces on the grounds of being in possession of a weapon (an ornamental gun given to him by the Free State's Commander-in Chief, Michael Collins). Childers shook hands with the members of his firing squad and his personal conduct did much damage to the Free State's propaganda value in their 'trophy' execution. Many decades later, in the Presidential election of 1973, Childers' son was to defeat Tom O'Higgins, who was the nephew of Kevin O'Higgins, the man who had signed Childers' death warrant.

Childers, like Bull and Meares, represents exactly the sort of wayward talent that the RNAS managed to channel in its prosecution of the war effort.

---

13 e.g. Childers' experience as a parliamentary clerk left him with the good sense to smell a rat on the proposed Irish Boundary Commission, which ultimately was to ignore nationalist majorities in many areas of Northern Ireland and was to propose to extend what nationalists regarded as the 'great Northern Ireland gerrymander' to include parts of East Donegal in exchange for reducing the overall length of the border to an easier-to-police 200 miles.

INTRODUCTION TO THE IRISH AVIATORS

The Royal Naval Air Service's Armoured Car Division was a wholly inappropriate development of a rival cavalry service to that operated by the British Army. In an Irish context it is often remembered for the Rolls Royce Silver Ghost chassis armoured cars, of which the Irish Free State acquired several, most notably Michael Collins' favourite *Sliabh na mBan* and General Seán Mac Eoin's *Ballinalee*. However the RNAS' Armoured Car Squadron attracted many motor sports enthusiasts and many who had worked as mechanics in civilian life. Inevitably industrial areas of Ulster were to feature heavily in its' ranks. Its casualty lists bear a huge number of Ulstermen, e.g. Joseph Donnelly, James Joseph Graham, Skeffington TC Graham, James Lindsay, John McFarland. Many others started with the RNAS Armoured Car Squadron but were ultimately to die with the RAF, e.g. Frederick James McCullough, and the ace Walter Alexander Tyrrell.

Of course there were those who left little by way of significant military contribution to the Royal Naval Air Service but who became persons of note in the post-war years. Galway-born John Sealy Edward Townsend was a well-respected mathematical physicist who served with the RNAS before transferring to the Experimental Establishment at Woolwich for research and development on the wireless. He was awarded the French Legion of Honour for his wartime service. Over the years he turned into a bitter old man and his refusal to assist the British war effort in World War II led to him being retired but made a Knight Commander of the British Empire (KBE) to lessen the prospect of any public scandal. Another famous Irish veteran of the RNAS was Professor Robert McCance. His wartime experiences on naval rations led him to re-train and become a prominent nutritionist; his invention of the "food pyramid" is an innovation that has undergone very little revision in the decades since its inception. Similarly, William Loftus Templeton emigrated from Co Tipperary to Canada in 1908. (He is often claimed by Co Antrim on account of giving a next-of-kin address of Bushmills, Co Antrim when enlisting in Canada). Templeton served with the RNAS as a submarine hunter, being mentioned in despatches. In the post-war years he returned to Canada, became a manager of Vancouver airport and wrote a song "Vancouver Calls Me" that helped fund municipal activities in the city.

Of course when mentioning the Irish in the Royal Naval Air Service it is impossible to refrain from mentioning those who do not warrant inclusion in the volume but in respect of whom many RNAS tales abound. Examples would be Charles Seropian and John Henry Ball.

Charles Dickron Déodat Seropian's mother was from Co Tipperary. His father was Armenian who had obtained a British naturalisation certificate in 1895 through claiming to be American. Raised in Ireland he went off to sea at a young age, rose through the ranks to reach that of Lieutenant during the war. He was awarded an OBE for his efforts in the anti-submarine war. However, the story goes, Seropian's interest in aircraft had rendered him unsuitable as potential officer material. On 29 June 1921 Lieutenant Commander Scott was to write of Seropian:

"For his age and seniority [he] knows astonishingly little about discipline, the right way to handle men etc and does not appear to have every had any sound fundamental training in the functions, principles and atmosphere of the Navy. Knows nothing of gunnery and does not attempt to educate himself ... Emphatically not recommended for a command".[14]

Seropian was to change his name by deed poll in September 1923, become Charles Foley, re-enlist and rise to the rank of Commodore with the Royal Navy's Fleet Air Arm in World War II, serving as the commanding officer of the RN Air Station in Sierra Leone and the No.14 Service Flying Training School in Canada during the later stages of the war.

This is a nice tale but the reality is somewhat different: although Seropian had an interest in aircraft and was to serve with the Royal Navy's Fleet Air Arm in World War II as told, his original service in

---

14 ADM 196/146 Foley, UK National Archives.

INTRODUCTION TO THE IRISH AVIATORS

the anti-submarine war was one that entailed the use of another newfangled device—the hydrophone (sonar)—that apparently caused Seropian to lose interest in naval pursuits beloved of Lt-Cdr Scott, like gunnery, discipline, making men walk the plank and so forth.

Another character that would be ineligible for inclusion in Volume II but who is regularly quoted as being an Irish RNAS officer is the chameleon Captain John Henry Ball. He was born in 1883 in Allesley, Warwickshire to English parents, John Henry Ball (b.1857, Lambeth) and Julia Ball, née Quarry, (b.1859, St Pancras). It would appear that his grandmother Elizabeth was Irish. Ball's connection with Ireland is an unusual one. It is believed that he spent part of his life in the employment of the Marquess of Londonderry at Mount Stewart, Co Down. He may have served as a chauffeur.[15] What is certain is that Ball served with the RNAS. His service record in the RNAS[16] and the RAF[17] reveal that Ball had served as a Warrant Officer in 1915 prior to being promoted to Lieutenant in June 1917. He was assigned to the aircraft carrier HMS Ark Royal on 18 October 1917. He eventually was discharged after several months of ill health, his medical board assessments on 26 February 1918 and 26 March 1918 certifying him as unfit for any service until late April 1918. Ball was promoted Captain. He transferred to No.255 Squadron and subsequently the Airship Station at Luce Bay before being eventually being transferred to the unemployed list on 20 May 1919.

It is known that in June 1918 he purchased quite a number of lots at the auction of the collection of the late Canon William Greenwell, to whom he had also sold some items. This was to be the nucleus of what became a significant collection of ancient gold and silver that Ball was to amass and display at Hertfordshire County Museum at St Albans. However, some years previously Ball had used ancient axehead moulds to create additional pieces. His set of forgeries,

---

15 Cahill, Mary "The Strange Case of the Strangford Lough Hoard", *The Journal of the Royal Society of Antiquaries of Ireland*, Vo..135 (2005), pp.5-118.
16 ADM 337/124 Ball, UK National Archives.
17 AIR 76/20 Ball, UK National Archives.

known as "the Strangford Hoard" cost Lord Iveagh £200 in acquiring material for the National Museum of Ireland. These pieces were eventually melted down, with a sum of £65 being realised for the exchequer. Although it is often suggested that Ball had engaged in the hoax to embarrass the antiques dealer Samuel Fenton and that it was all harmless fun, the continuing impact of his forgeries have been monumental: none of his collection can be safely regarded as being genuine, i.e. although the majority of the pieces are authentic their provenance may well not be so, e.g. these could be from Cornwall or Calais yet were passed off as being from Ireland.

Even if Ball's damage to Irish archaeology is significant, his role as an international arms dealer was far more detrimental to the common good. Ball started Soley Armaments from a one-bedroom flat, acquiring increasing quantities of British military surplus .303 inch (7.7 mm) rifles and re-working them via Belgian gunsmiths so that they could take continental 7.92 mm ammunition. This increased massively the range of odious regimes that could potentially buy the weaponry. However, it is clear from the UK Cabinet papers that Soley Armaments were pushing an open door. For example, the records of the Committee on the Private Armaments Industry of 1933[18] indicate that the problem was seen in terms of British industry. The Cabinet meeting of 12 April 1933 had agreed that a Committee should meet "to consider what action can be taken to remove the handicaps which are alleged to exist on the manufacture and export of armaments". The consequent report, of which Walter Runciman was committee chairman, recommended the extension of the Export Credits Guarantee legislation to the armaments industry, effectively making it a taxpayer-underwritten bet to supply any particular regime, and to provide an open licensing system.

Captain Ball's much-quoted proposals to the Nye committee in March 1934 were to the effect that the American government should buy weapons to arm the Chinese. "In spite of all the dreams of the idealist … Japan is going to take a still larger slice of China, and

---

18 UK National Archives, CAB 24/245.

comparatively shortly, while the getting is good. ... To place herself in a favourable position, Japan must either buy over the Soviet or fight them—and Japan will do one or the other before attending to some more of China. ... Such a move on Japan's part would seriously affect the United States interests in China, and we think that the United States would under the above circumstances support the Chinese, supply them with arms etc." Ball was affecting a stance of straight-taking realist, which some outsiders would have taken as urging the US government to "do the right thing" by China. In reality Soley Armaments had supplied the Japanese, and in seeking to have the US purchase from Solely Armaments to equip the Chinese the cynicism is simply breathtaking. (It would be another 5 years before the US government was to come to China's aid through financing the "American Volunteer Group"—the famous 'Flying Tigers' of the Chinese Air Force, led by Lieutenant-General Clair Chennault).[19]

A Memorandum to the Cabinet by Oliver Stanley, President of the Board of Trade of 21 January 1938 reiterated the Cabinet position of 17 November 1937, which officially stated "application by private firms for licences for export of war material to China Japan should be dealt with as hitherto". Unofficially, this policy was referred to as one of "masterly inactivity". On this occasion, however, Soley had an application outstanding for the supply of 130 Lewis guns (air type) with spare parts. The Secretary of the Board of Trade emphasised that there were no military grounds for rejection (e.g. Soley Armaments was disposing of Air Ministry surplus material) whilst "equally it is not practicable to withhold licences on commercial grounds." The Cabinet Decision (CAB 23/92) of 26 January 1938 decided to approve the applications, although some rhetoric on the continuation of the "go slow" position of neither approval or disapproval of export licences was endorsed. This is, of course, only weeks

---

19 Apart from the Irish-Americans in that group, the post-World War II Flying Tiger Line in 1962 was to be involved in one of Ireland's most serious air disasters, when Flight 923 crashed off the coast of Cork.

after the 'rape of Nanking' of 13 December 1937. Captain Ball and Soley Armaments did historians a favour in having export licences to odious regimes being so well documented.

Ball's will, dated 18 March 1938, amounted to an estate worth £221,381. This would amount to in excess of €15,000,000 in 2012. His son John Brayfield Ball was killed in 1940 whilst serving with the RAF in World War II. Ball's reputation seemed oddly undiminished in Ireland, i.e. although he was a chameleon who relied on an Irish identity as camouflage in antiquities dealing and occasionally to present himself as a neutral in his arms dealings, he nevertheless had plenty of sneaking regarders, e.g. the *Irish Times* of 22 October 1949 talks of the "mysterious Irishman". Under no circumstances can he be considered Irish or as being worthy of inclusion among the RNAS, but it would be impossible to publish a history of the Irish in the RNAS without mentioning Captain John Henry Ball.

Overall the Irish in the Royal Naval Air Service represent a hugely diverse group, including those from North and South, Roman Catholic and Protestant, from Anglo-Irish gentry to apprentice motor mechanics. Volume II of this series would hope to outline their achievements in the context the Irish involvement at every stage of the RNAS' existence, serving at every conceivable rank. The Irish in the RNAS also took casualties out of all proportion to their numbers.

Volume III—the Royal Flying Corps and Royal Air Force

Some commentators, e.g. on a selective reading of David Fitzpatrick in *Militarism in Ireland*, tend to talk down the Irish contribution to the war effort generally (e.g. to no more than 30,000 casualties) and to the air war in particular (e.g. a claim that just 4,000 served). There is a wide range of figures in circulation, based on several different methods of calculation, but also in some cases upon whether one wishes to make a particular point regarding Irish participation in the war. Recruitment in Ireland was voluntary, and in the absence of conscription it is meaningless to make comparisons with Great Brit-

INTRODUCTION TO THE IRISH AVIATORS

ain's contribution to the UK armies, (quite apart from the political arguments over whether more accurate comparisons for Irish in the UK armies would be with Poles in the Russian and German armies or Croatians in the Austro-Hungarian forces). However, there are some semi-official figures that may be used to put some context on the Irish recruitment to the Royal Naval Air Service, Royal Flying Corps and Royal Air Force.

A Parliamentary Question on 24 October 1918 from Major Newman to the Chief Secretary asked whether he would give the numbers recruited from 01 June 1918 to 15 October 1918. The reply stated that the enlistments in Ireland between the dates in question were as follows:

Royal Navy: 626

British Army: 4,712

RAF: 4,438

This is confirmed through numerous other academic sources that suggest the recruitment rate to the RAF in Ireland was approaching 50% of total enlistment in the final year of the war.

A further Parliamentary Question, on 18 November 1918, from Mr Boland to the Under-Secretary of State to the Air Ministry (Major Baird) requested information on the number of men of Irish birth in the Flying Services at the outbreak of the war and the number who enlisted subsequently. The reply was to the effect that there were just 42 at the outbreak of the war and 5,464 at the time the question was tabled. One may infer from the casualty rate of killed (500+), wounded (hundreds) and taken prisoner (c.100) the overall number of Irish who had served with the aerial services over the course of the war would easily exceed 6,000.

These figures make nonsense of suggestions that the number of Irish was 4,000 or so: it is at least 50% higher. Although 4,000 or 6,000 is statistically insignificant to the overall Irish contribution to the Allied war effort, it is important when attempting to calculate just how many casualties one would expect to find when researching attrition rates. (It must be remembered that Irish war dead of the RNAS, RFC and RAF are difficult to identify, as their squadrons don't have a readily identifiable geographical element such as the Royal Inniskilling Fusiliers or the Royal Irish Rifles). However, it may be borne in mind that a figure of 6,000 pilots, observers, ground-crew and other support staff is quite small and that the consequent "top to tail" ratio of air combatants to the overall number is much smaller. Further, it may also be remembered that nearly 50% of pilot casualties were at training squadron level, and the coroners' records of Wiltshire (i.e. for RAF Upavon, RAF Netheravon and so forth) contain extensive references to the Irish losses that never reached the front. In this regard it is easy for the focus to shift to a number of high-profile aces rather than the much broader input of reconnaissance pilots and observers, those on Army Co-Operation duties, guiding artillery and bombing strategic targets. However, a figure of 500 casualties from 6,000 participants seems somewhat lower than would be expected.

In comparison with the 500 RNAS, RFC and RAF losses, the approximate casualties suffered by the 8 Irish regiments are as follows: Connaught Rangers: 2,108; Leinster Regiment: 2,175; Royal Dublin Fusiliers: 4,948; Royal Inniskilling Fusiliers:5,935; Royal Irish Fusiliers: 3,570; Royal Irish Regiment: 2,778; Royal Irish Rifles: 7,343; Royal Munster Fusiliers: 2,938.

The cavalry regiment losses (North Irish Horse, South Irish Horse) are in the region of 100, as these were in effect reserve regiments, from which officers and men deployed elsewhere at an early stage of the war. If a general figure of 75% Irish-born is applied to these regiments then the Irish losses stand at approximately 24,000 of these regiments' 32,000 casualties.

Additionally there were several regiments of the British Army that recruited those of Irish origin. Following the heavy losses by Irish regiments in the Boer War the Irish were granted a Guards regiment.

INTRODUCTION TO THE IRISH AVIATORS

Many laugh nowadays at the peculiar ranking system, e.g. Lance-Sergeant and so forth, but—in its time and in the culture of militarism of the era—the Irish Guards would have been perceived as quite a prestigious regiment into which Irishmen and their descendants could join the colours. Additionally there were dozens of regiments which had a substantial Irish-born element in addition to recruiting from the Irish community in Great Britain. Their losses were as follows: Irish Guards: 3,106; London Regiment (London Irish Rifles): 1,092. Additionally the Liverpool Irish and Tyneside Irish would have had significant Irish losses prior to them being merged into larger units. The losses of all the foregoing would include a figure of 50% Irish, or approximately 3,000 Irish casualties.

There are also cavalry regiments with a once-distant connection to Ireland, e.g. regiments which had previously been headquartered in Ireland but had moved elsewhere, e.g. the 4th Royal Irish Dragoon Guards had their origins in the Earl of Arran's Cuirassiers but had swapped regimental establishment on countless occasions between Great Britain and Ireland. Similarly Henry Conyngham's Regiment of Dragoons evolved into the King's Royal Irish Regiment of Light Dragoons and eventually became the King's Royal Irish Hussars. Their casualties were as follows: 4th (Royal Irish) Dragoon Guards: 222; 5th (Royal Irish) Lancers: 180; 6th (Inniskilling) Dragoons: 192; 8th (King's Royal Irish) Hussars: 124. The Irish losses among their casualties would be no more than 30% in most cases.

This may naturally prompt the average American reader to wonder whether any battalion which contained the successor entities to the 63rd and 88th New York or 116th Pennsylvania regiments, let alone a few companies of the 69th New York or 28th Massachusetts infantry regiments ("Fighting Irish") would have a greater number of Irish casualties than a supposedly "Irish" cavalry regiment of the British army. The short answer is "yes", but in the context of the term "Irish" being taken to include the Irish-American community in general, which is something beyond the scope of this book. In World War I the 69th served as part of the 'Rainbow Division', with

William Joseph "Wild Bill" Donovan and Richard William O'Neill winning the Medal of Honor, but I have restricted the term "Irish" those born in Ireland or, in certain circumstances, those of Irish parents and so cannot traverse the Irish units of the US forces, of which are so many. Further, the Irish-American aviators did not just fight in American units, e.g. future US Secretary of the Naval James Vincent Forrestal served as a naval pilot with Canadian forces in World War I. Similarly, Patrick Alva O'Brien also reached the Western Front via Canada and the Royal Flying Corps, and not through the American armed forces.

Of the other cavalry and infantry regiments with notional Irish involvement, there were several in the British regiments of the Indian Army (e.g. Baluchis and Rajputs) that had Irish officers and some Irish units in the Canadian and South African forces that had a significant Irish contingent, but I would put the level of Irish in these at approximately 10% and their casualties as being in no way distinguishable from the vast number who served in other American, Australian, British, Canadian, New Zealand and South African regiments.[20] It should be noted, however, that most of these suffered heavy losses and were merged and restructured over the course of the war. The number of Irish in other general regiments was proportionately smaller but greater in absolute numbers, and this needs to be borne in mind when calculating Irish losses.

The Earl of Ypres' commission, which produced *Ireland's Memorial Records*, produced a figure of 49,400 Irish dead. As one can imagine, this has been subjected to severe criticism regarding those it included and those omitted. However, their figures included all Irish regimental casualties. On the other hand it also greatly underestimated the number of Irish in the American, Australian, Canadian, New Zealand and South African regiments. (Although not a World

---

20   For the record the Canadian battalions and regiments associated with Ireland were the 2nd Battalion (Irish Regiment of Canada), the 11th Regiment (Irish Fusiliers of Canada), the 55th Irish Canadian Rangers, the 121st (Western Irish) Battalion, 199th Battalion (Duchess of Connaught's Own) and the 208th (Canadian Irish) Battalion.

INTRODUCTION TO THE IRISH AVIATORS

War I casualty, of the 37 Irish aces, for example, Victor Henry Huston enlisted in Canada). I have conducted my own analysis of the records. There are 280 persons named in respect of whom reference to service in the RFC, RNAS and RAF is made. Of those I can only include just over 200 in my work, as many do not have a sufficiently strong connection to Ireland. This ratio (210/280) however, is 75%. However, I have identified 300 other Irish casualties outside of *Ireland's Memorial Records*.

Overall therefore one can take an Irish casualty figure in the region of 40,000 from the 240,000 who served. Accordingly a figure of 500 losses from 6,000 who served would seem quite underweight. I attempt to address the relatively smaller losses of the air services through the relatively high attrition rate at pilot and observer level, i.e. leaving aside relative calculations of "head to tail" ratios the Irish aviators were fully engaged in the air war and suffered losses at least as great a rate as any other nationality in the RFC, RNAS and RAF during the war.

By the end of the war nearly 300,000 had served in the RFC, RNAS and RAF. Their casualties amounted to approximately 11,000 dead. Consequently the Irish attrition rate would appear to be broadly comparable. However, the Irish kill: loss ratio remains completely out of proportion to the numbers involved.

As one may note from the foregoing, Volume III will attempt to address several broad themes regarding the extent of Irish participation in the flying services whilst also detailing the actual involvement in the air war, whether on land or at sea and at scout, reconnaissance and bomber squadron level.

Concluding Observations

It is hoped that the foregoing can explain the rationale behind a 3-volume series. However, one other issue that needs to be explained is the reference to particular forms of aerial victory, as these can often seem confusing. The air war was in effect fought over German-held territory. The very nature of these offensive operations gave the

RFC pilots a disadvantage when attempting to confirm a victory, as a German aircraft could be seen going down "out of control" following a drum of ammunition being emptied into it but they could not follow it down to confirm the destruction or indeed whether the German aircraft took anything other than minor damage. (Most enemy aircraft made it safely back to base, with varying degrees of damage and/or pilot or observer injury). However, the purpose of the RFC and RAF operations was to clear the skies of enemy aircraft, i.e. to facilitate British observation and reconnaissance or to prevent German aircraft doing the same, and therefore the category of aerial victory was not important to the RFC or RAF. Over the course of the war 'forced to land' victories were dispensed with, and by May 1918 the 'out of control' aerial victories were no longer being reported in the RAF Communiqués, although they were still being counted for individual pilot or observer aerial victories. In some squadrons an aerial victory may have been awarded to either the pilot or the observer, but in recent years it has been more common to respect their contributions equally when counting aerial victories. In this regard the number of aces will seem quite large relative to the number of French or German aces, given the differing methods of aerial victory classification. In comparison to the classification systems of later wars many of the "driven down", "out of control" and "forced to land" would be counted as "probables" as opposed to confirmed victories. In the tables that I have included as Appendices to Volume I the notation 'FTL' indicates a "forced to land", 'OOC' means "out of control", 'DES' denotes 'destroyed' and the similarly named 'DESF' denotes "destroyed in flames".

✦ ✦ ✦

VOLUME I
INTRODUCTION

The term 'ace' was not in common circulation in World War I. However, French newspapers took to describing Adolphe Pégoud as "l'as" ('the ace') when he became the first pilot to have shot down several enemy aircraft. Over the course of the war the term 'ace' was applied to those who shot down 5 or more enemy aircraft.

The British high command, however, discouraged praise of scout/fighter pilots over that of bomber and reconnaissance airmen. Also a consideration was respect for the overall contribution of airmen and groundcrew to the war effort. One factor in this was the concept of it being a team sport of sorts. Imagine it being akin to the game of rugby, in which all shapes and sizes play, and from which the try may be scored by either the forwards or the backs. Excessive praise for an individual try-scorer is not warranted, and the egotism of soccer strikers would appal many of the public school types of high command. A related factor was the public school system, which was oriented towards honours for one's house or school colours rather than an individual claim to glory. However, medal citations often made reference to the number of kills achieved though these were usually contextualised in terms of an overall operation in which bombing or reconnaissance are also mentioned.

One consequence of this was the general lack of public awareness of individual RNAS and RFC pilot or observer achievements in air-to-air combat engagements. This led to some exceptions, e.g. Albert Ball's family were well off Nottingham 'arriviste' new money, and happily publicized Albert's aerial successes, even though he personally was quite modest—almost the epitome of the public school character. With high command not in control of the message they allowed a number of selected individuals receive a measure of public recognition. One such pilot was James McCudden. He was the son of an Irish father—from Co Carlow—and English Catholic mother. Rising from the ranks of the Royal Engineers he became an expert pilot and a hugely respected ace. He was not a political animal, but was sufficiently clued-in to be deferential to his superiors and thus an authorised autobiography *Five Years in the Royal Flying Corps* was published shortly before his death. (He was careful to avoid criticism of high command or be drawn on Irish or British politics). Although the small drip-feed of individual tales and unauthorised brash success stories leaked haphazardly to the British public, one unintended consequence was that Manfred von Richthofen was to become a British war hero of sorts.

In the post-war years a whole genre of "hell in the heavens" wartime memoirs flooded out, and were avidly read by those looking for some positive or praiseworthy aspect of what had been otherwise a deeply traumatic experience in which every town and village had experienced grievous losses. Of course the poor quality of much of what was written did not necessarily mean that it was all wildly inaccurate but there was an element of publishers ensuring the audience got what they were looking for. In the build up to World War II there naturally came added agendas in the preparation of the next generation to do battle, e.g. Taffy Jones' biography of the Irish ace 'Mick' Mannock more or less turns the man into a Hun-hating killing machine, with various Kipling-like speeches about Imperial glory being ventriloquated through Mannock, who in real life had been a socialist who supported 'Home Rule' for Ireland.

The absence of Irish input into the post-war circus of aviation-related literary thrash tends to partially explain why their profile fell so quickly. However, 14 of the 37 Irish aces died in the war. Just 23 survived the war, two of whom were to die serving with the RAF in the inter-war years, whilst one was to die with the Irish Air Corps and another in a civilian flying accident. Two were to die in World War II as civilian casualties of war. Understandably, with these attrition levels there weren't too many around to contribute to the memoir genre. (Additionally, several were to serve in World War II with the RAF and the British Army. They were therefore unavailable to Ireland for any consciousness-building whilst also being outsiders in Great Britain). However, there were a number of broader factors in play that led to the diminishment of the Irish contribution to the air war of World War I.

World War I vs. World War II

It is impossible to escape the sheer contrast between the air war in both conflicts. In the British context this led to 'Battle of Britain' mania, with RAF Fighter Command immortalized in war films forever recycling images of Spitfires over Kent, with the role of RAF Bomber Command being side-stepped into plucky prison escapes and jolly bouncing bombs. In an Irish context the contribution to the RAF in World War II was enormous: over 25,000 served and 2,000 died. However, the nature of the contribution was much more diverse. If one may take Yeats' lines regarding "those I fight I do not hate/ those I defend I do not love" in this context it can perhaps partially explain why the Battle of Britain would not hold any greater a place than other aspects of the war in the air. Further, although Brendan "Paddy" Finuance was one of the highest-scoring Spitfire aces of the war, the most high profile Irish pilots in World War II were not in Fighter Command, e.g. Donald Garland from Co Wicklow won the Victoria Cross on a bombing mission, in a brave but futile attempt at preventing the Germans from securing the bridges over the Albert Canal; Cork-born David Lord won his VC in an astonishingly brave attempt to drop supplies to a designated zone over Arnhem, nursing a crippled aircraft long enough for one of the crew to bail out alive; English-born, Tipperary-raised Eugene Esmonde won his VC for the failed attempt at stopping the *Scharnhorst, Gneisenau* and *Prinz*

Eugen in their dash up the English Channel. (His death was particularly difficult: he led a flight of 6 aircraft to their doom in the slim chance of success but in a wider effort at allowing the RAF Coastal Command and Bomber Command, and RN's Fleet Air Arm, save face in having made a reasonable intervention and thus reassure the British public that the first successful enemy traversal of the English Channel since 1588 was a one-off event). All three VCs were posthumous. Two of the three (Lord, Esmonde) were former seminarians, and the sense of duty, suffering, self-sacrifice for the benefit of others and so forth all tend to play out a warped version of the Christian message rather than being military actions as such. Their worldview disappeared with the war, and an emerging sense that things need to be done differently, and that individual heroism or bravery was not a substitute for proper planning and organization, a view that was ultimately given expression in the Labour landside election victory in 1945 towards the end of the war. Quite apart from 3 VCs there were hundreds of DFCs won by Irishmen in every conceivable theatre of conflict, from the Atlantic to the Pacific, the Arctic to the Indian Ocean. At the highest echelons of the RAF there were Irish men who had made their mark in World War II, e.g. Rathdowney-born Marshal of the RAF, Sir Dermot Boyle, served with RAF Bomber Command, as did Air Chief Marshal Percy Bernard (5th Earl of Bandon), but overall the sheer number of Irish men and women who served in the RAF, Fleet Air Arm, WAAF and ATS results in their vast number of personal stories just dwarfing anything that arose from World War I, e.g. from traditional musicians such as the Clancy brothers to writers such as Patrick Galvin, (e.g. his *Song for a Fly Boy* in his 'raggy boy' trilogy) to broadcasters such as Cathal O'Shannon, there were a large number of distinctly anti-heroic tales to contrast with the more militaristic accounts. World War I aces just faded in comparison.

Another factor, however, was that the Irish Free State was subject to severe censorship in World War II. Further, any prospect of Northern Ireland celebrating the Irish aerial successes of World War II tend to be lost in the shadow of the Royal Inniskillings and the

Royal Ulster Rifles being part of a distinct Irish Brigade in the British Army's campaign in Italy. Despite the Northern Ireland Prime Minister's repeated exhortations to Churchill to invade the Irish Free State, the prospect of it being another Iceland-style occupation was not seriously entertained. Nevertheless Malahide-born Brian Inglis, journalist with the *Irish Times* and later the *Spectator*, was to write in his autobiography 'West Briton' of his discussion with another Irish RAF pilot as to what they would do in the event of a British invasion of Ireland. They decided they would present themselves for internment. Undoubtedly many other Irishmen had the same discussion. However, within the bubble of Irish censorship, every Irishman who joined the Allied forces was a potential invader, and this quasi-official "traitor in waiting" label remained affixed to many Irish war veterans for many years thereafter. In these circumstances, if the 12,000 Free State volunteers among the 25,000 Irish airmen/women of World War II were silenced then the prospects of 6,000 from a previous generation getting any sort of audience were also slim.

War of Independence 1919-1922

The Anglo-Irish conflict of the interwar years had an enormous impact upon the assessment of Irish contribution to the British war effort.

The United Kingdom of Great Britain and Ireland had come into existence less than a century after the formation of Great Britain, but the UK had never been a stable political entity. To some extent it was a constitutional fiction, as there was no such thing as UK public opinion: there was British public opinion and there was Irish public opinion. Further, the parliament almost invariably voted legislation in British interests, not the UK interests, and Westminster was essentially the British parliament, not the UK parliament. The position of Chief Secretary in Ireland was held by a succession of benign and menacing dictators, with Irish MPs in the UK parliament having little or no means of holding the Dublin Castle administration accountable. Legislation specifically passed in relation to Ireland was often in British interests, e.g. over 80 'coercion' Acts were passed in the 19th century and early 20th century, restricting freedom of speech or freedom of assembly in Ireland. However, the extension of a full measure of civil rights (in Ireland described as "Catholic emancipation") to Roman Catholics throughout the UK in 1829, combined with franchise extensions and the introduction of the secret ballot had, by the later part of the 19th century, given rise to an overwhelming number of the deputies elected for Ireland being supporters of some form of self-administration for Ireland. Although there had been some attempts in the 1880s and 1890s to introduce a Home Rule Bill, there was little prospect of success for any such measure given that the House of Lords had a veto over House of Commons' legislative proposals on constitutional matters. This had not stopped Lord Randolph Churchill stoking matters with inflammatory rhetoric, e.g. "Ulster will fight and Ulster will be right", whilst angling for internal British political advantage against the Liberal party.[21] (At this time it was still common for Irish people to be portrayed as simian-featured Neanderthals in the popular press and *Punch* magazine). It was only with the removal of the House of Lords' veto on Commons legislation in 1911 that enabled likelihood of the realisation of a measure of Irish self-government. However, the prospect of 'Home Rule' had triggered massive armed resistance in the north-eastern parts of the province of Ulster. Once again the British Conservative party ignored the outcome of the UK Election to seek political gain within Great Britain: Bonar Law was to make several inflammatory speeches which included phrases such as "I can imagine no length of resistance to which Ulster will go in which I shall not be ready to support them". Further, the British military in Ireland indicated that it would not assist the civil power in preventing any coup by Unionists in Ulster. The "Curragh Mutiny" was unusual:

---

21 Randolph Churchill privately spoke of "playing the Orange card". Encouraging sedition and damaging the UK of Great Britain and Ireland for internal British political gain was cynical and somewhat ironic that the party of "law and order" not to mention the one that purportedly supported the Union to be prepared to sacrifice it for short-term political advantage.

the crisis-ridden Liberal administration had no problem with force-feeding women suffragette prisoners of conscience or of turning the military into an armed wing of employers' cartels at Tonypandy in Wales in 1911, but suffered a political nervous breakdown when the British army refused to countenance deployment to guard ammunition depots that they had expected Ulster Unionists to seize. The Secretary of State for War, John Seely, went as far as cravenly writing down demands dictated to him by the military. Winston Churchill was one of the few members of the cabinet left to threaten to defend the UK, claiming he would deploy the Royal Navy if necessary, but ultimately Seely was forced to resign as was the Chief of the Imperial General Staff ('CIGS') John French, as the Cabinet rallied to disown any subservience to military rule and repudiated Seely's terms of obedience. The consequent and subsequent massive landing of German weaponry at Larne by Unionists led a significant minority of the Irish population to believe that the 40 years of parliamentary effort had been wasted. In this regard although people like Erskine Childers helped ferry a consignment of arms and ammunition to help restore the balance of power towards parliamentary politics, for many Irish people the impact of the exhaustion of the parliamentary process can be understood in the manner of the British 'winter of discontent' of uncollected rubbish and unburied bodies in 1978 that ended the post-war consensus for many British people.

In fact for many Irish people the disillusionment with the Irish Parliamentary Party (the 'Home Rule' party) in particular and the parliamentary process generally had led to a deeper questioning of the Union: the party had the epitomized the character of a servant, being required to be grateful to its English master for whatever was on the table and at whatever whim or generosity British public opinion had been willing to tolerate; decades of Irish majorities in that political system had been set at naught. The mirage of a political solution had passed: the 'Home Rule' movement, which had – in the 1870s and 1880s – managed to contain land agitation from agrarian violence and covert it to political activity such as 'boycotting' opponents and seeking legal mechanisms such as land courts, and in the 1890s had developed the modern parliamentary party whip system, had now been exposed. The Irish political system continued to disintegrate: despite talks about the geographical area which was to be included within any 'Home Rule' arrangements, the political process was now secondary to the threat of violence to back up a particular position. Even then there were varying degrees to which British politicians showed any grasp of the gravity of the situation, e.g. Churchill's reference to the dreary steeples of Fermanagh and Tyrone or to Asquith's observation (on negotiations surrounding these two counties) that what was in English eyes inconceivably small was in Irish eyes immeasurably large. The Easter Rising of 1916 and consequent upheavals of the subsequent five years led to an association of the British military with the murder of civilians, extra-judicial executions of suspected opponents, 'official reprisals' and the destruction of property. Consequently, Irish public opinion was not receptive to accounts of Irish achievements in the wartime British armed services.

In the immediate aftermath of the war 5 of the 8 Irish infantry regiments of the British Army (Connaught Rangers, Leinster Regiment, Royal Dublin Fusiliers, Royal Irish Regiment, Royal Munster Fusiliers) were disbanded, with their colours laid up in a ceremony at Buckingham Palace in 1922. However, there was a much deeper split, with the Irish Free State being accepted as a second-best by its supporters, an intolerable imposed settlement by its opponents, and for which a significant minority were trapped in a Northern Ireland that had been created on appeasement of Unionist demands rather than any attempt at ascertaining the legitimate right to national self-determination or the geographical jurisdiction to which it should have been applied. The rapid descent into a pointless Anglo-Irish 'economic war' in the 1930s and an Irish dismantlement of the Treaty via barely constitutional mechanisms led to a situation in which even the nadir of British-Irish relations still held an element of "unfinished business" and so previous military service with the British forces was held in deep suspicion; RAF veterans did not have a specific regimental depot upon which they could point to a local occasion of pride in the regiment in the manner of those who served in the Irish regiments of the British army.

Irish or from Ireland

One further problem encountered by the Irish aces was of the "they're not really Irish, are they?" variety. This arises on account of 'Mick' Mannock's birthplace most likely being outside Ireland, despite his protestations as to having been born in Ballincollig, Co Cork. Similarly, there is a tug-of-war over the McCudden brothers, e.g. they were English-born but their Irish father and his brothers had also settled in other parts of Great Britain, and so for every McCudden cousin born in Great Britain who claimed to be Irish there were others who did not. If the boundaries over who was Irish and who wasn't remained an open one then so too did the prospect of any post-war recognition in Ireland. Of the 37 Irish aces featured in this volume, only 31 were born in Ireland; however, the number of aces with Irish parents, and therefore potentially the subject of inclusion, is nearly half as large again—and so although I have taken the ultra-minimal approach to the Irish community abroad, many other historians include quite a number of these as being Irish.

An ugly cousin to the "un-Irish" argument is the stark fact that the vast majority of the Irish aces were Protestant. This leads to some unfair comparisons, e.g. of the aces of the Austro-Hungarian empire a large minority of the ethnic German aces were not from Austria but were 'Sudeten' Germans from Bohemia and Moravia, e.g. Eugen Bonsch, Andreas Dombrowski, Josef Friedrich, Otto Jaeger, Otto Jindra, Julius Kowalczik, Ernst Strohschneider, Karl Teichmann and so forth. This comparison seems to graft Catholicism onto Irishness and banish anyone not of perceived Gaelic heritage from being considered as Irish. This sort of thinking may be a convenient mechanism through which thousands of Irish soldiers, sailors and aviators can be written out of Irish history as "West Brits" but it cannot dispel the reality of these people not simply rolling over and relinquishing their

Irish identity. Of the 31 aces born in Ireland, 20 were from the area that was to become the Irish Free State, of whom 13 were Protestant. However, as these were regarded as being somewhat ambivalent in their relationship to the new Irish Free State, which was distinctly Roman Catholic in demographic profile, then they could expect little prospect of recognition there.

However, many Southern Irish Protestants seemed to confirm the Ulster Unionist view that they were different to some extent from their northern co-religionists, e.g. former Unionist MP Horace Plunkett founded the Irish Dominion League as an all-Ireland unionist body of sorts, seeking Dominion Status within the Empire for Ireland as an alternative to the British government's partition-based Government of Ireland Bill 1920, even going as far as having Thomas Rice, 2nd Baron Mounteagle of Brandon, introduce a version of their Bill into the House of Lords. There was a similar Unionist Anti-Partition League led by St John Brodrick, 1st Earl of Midleton. His was a particularly unrepresentative gathering of "Big House" unionism that would probably have been happy to see the torches-and-pitchforks grassroots demagoguery of the Presbyterian Ulster Unionist politicians subjected to a jolly good thrashing or judicious use of the whip-hand. (Despite their geographical title, many of the Unionist Anti-Partition League members were not even ordinarily resident in Ireland, or even the UK. The Earl of Midleton's niece Agathe was the first wife of Georg Johannes Ritter von Trapp, mother of their six children, about whom 'the Sound of Music' is based). Further, the Unionists of Northern Ireland had spent a decade claiming the unique nature of Ulster and therefore by implication the expendability of Southern Irish Protestants in any political solution which entailed a partitioning of the island. They were therefore unlikely to spend much time highlighting the achievements of those they had disowned once Northern Ireland and the Irish Free State had come into existence.

A related matter on the Northern Ireland situation was that the narrative of the wartime sacrifice centred almost entirely on the 36th

(Ulster) Division. This is understandable, as it was given to Carson as a vehicle through which the UVF could participate in the British army, and its battalions bore a direct relationship to UVF ones, as in many cases mass recruitment ceremonies were organised. This Ulster-at-the-Somme narrative was always unlikely to leave room for aviators, other than as exotic sights in the army veterans' memoirs. It also avoided the fact that, of the 11 Ulster-born aces, one was Roman Catholic (Oscar Heron) and three others had distinct connections with the rest of Ireland (Co Tyrone-born Forde Leathley's parents were from Dublin and Wexford, and he is recorded in the 1901 and 1911 census returns as being resident in Dublin and Meath; Co Down-born Sydney Cowan was the son of a Scottish father and Mayo mother, with one of his brothers being born in Co Mayo, and his parents being resident in Dublin in the 1901 and 1911 census returns; Co Down-born Guy William Price was the son of an English father and Dublin mother, with one of his brothers being born in Co Wicklow, and his parents being resident in Wicklow in the 1901 and 1911 census returns). If the 10 Ulster-born Protestant aces are a minority relative to their 13 Southern Protestant cousins and, on a per capita basis, a much smaller contribution to the British war effort then, rather than look at Irish aces, it was easier for many Unionists to squint a little and just see a distinct Ulster Unionist army at the Somme, uncontaminated by diverse elements.

In recent years the 'Good Friday' Agreement has given rise to improved British-Irish relations, and a set of North-South and internal power-sharing institutions to which all sides in Northern Ireland have pledged allegiance, and this has in turn facilitated an atmosphere of greater mutual respect and tolerance. One beneficial consequence has been that the wartime contribution of the 10th (Irish), 16th (Irish) and 36th (Ulster) Divisions have been accorded mutual recognition, with nationalist and unionist wartime combatants being given joint commemoration at memorial ceremonies. However, the focus is very much on the Irish regiments and therefore somewhat inward-looking in nature, e.g. Catholics from Belfast, Protestants from Munster and so forth are featured. Consequently, the aviators remain very much a secondary concern.

Concluding Observations

If the foregoing can help put a context within which the lack of recognition for the achievements of Irish aces has arisen, hopefully an account of each individual ace can help restore the balance.

❖ ❖ ❖

ATKINSON, EDWARD DAWSON 'SPIDER'

(**10 aerial victories**)

Born: 10 November 1891, India
Died: UNKNOWN
Awards: Distinguished Flying Cross, Air Force Cross
Religion: Church of Ireland

Captain Edward Dawson Atkinson is one of four Indian-born Irish aces. He was the second son of Joseph Henry Atkinson, of Calcutta (b.04 July 1840) and Elizabeth Mary Atkinson (née McCarthy).

On his mother's side, Edward's grandfather was Charles Vincent McCarthy, C.E. On his father's side, Edward was the grandson of Miles William Atkinson and Anne Mather. Edward's great grandparents were Captain William Atkinson, of Glennane, Co Armagh, who had served with the Portadown Yeomanry, and Anne Chamney of Ballyrahine, Co Wicklow.

Edward had four brothers and four sisters. His older brother Charles Vincent McCarthy Atkinson (b. 02 November 1879) became Assistant Superintendent of the Madras Police, whilst another older brother, Joseph Henry Atkinson (b. 05 May 1885) had served with the Royal Field Artillery.[22]

On 12 December 1915 the Royal Aero Club awarded Second Lieutenant Edward Dawson Atkinson (40th Pathans) the Aviator Certificate No. 2145.[23] Atkinson had graduated on an "L and P" [London and Provincial Aviation Company] biplane, at the London and Provincial School, Hendon[24]. Although his address is recorded as '7 Promenade, Warrenpoint, Co Down' it is unclear if Atkinson ever spent any significant length of time in Ireland.

Atkinson's transfer from the Indian Army Reserve to the Royal Flying Corps in 1916 saw him serve with No.1 Squadron. Indeed, the RAF Rugby Union team have a photograph on their website of Atkinson as part of the original No.1 Squadron Royal Flying Corps rugby union team. On 17 February 1917 Atkinson was promoted from Flying Officer to Flight Commander[25].

On 25 March 1917 he recorded his first aerial victory, destroying a balloon between Warneton and Wervicq. Atkinson obtained two further victories with No.1 Squadron, flying Nieuports during "Bloody April" when the Royal Flying Corps suffered grievous losses in a futile attempt to use its increasingly obsolete aircraft to support the major Allied offensive at Arras.

On 01 May 1917, he encountered Jasta 28 and was attacked by "an exceptionally good pilot" flying a red Albatros scout. The German pilot was Leutnant Karl Emil Schafer, scoring his second victory of that afternoon and the 25th of his 30 victories. Atkinson was forced down behind the safety of his own lines at Elverdinghe, but his Nieuport Scout was damaged beyond repair.[26]

---

22 Swanzy, Rev Henry Biddal "The Families of French of Belturbet and Nixon of Fermanagh and their Descendants", p.125. [Alex Thom & Co Ltd, 1908].
23 Flight Magazine, 17th December 1915, page 988.
24 Scan of original RAe Club index card available via ancestry.co.uk
25 Supplement to the London Gazette, 17 February 1917.
26 Christopher Shores, Norman Franks & Russell Guest- *Above the Trenches* [London: Grub Street, 1990].

On 24 July 1917 the London Gazette carried notice of promotions in the Indian Army Reserve of Officers, with Atkinson being promoted from 2nd Lieutenant to Lieutenant, dated to 9th April 1916.[27]

Atkinson returned to Home Establishment as an instructor. In April 1918 he returned to active service. Initially Atkinson served with No.56 Squadron, scoring two shared victories in May 1918 with SE5As. Atkinson served temporarily as squadron commander with No.56 Squadron due to their heavy losses.

Atkinson transferred to No.64 Squadron, where he scored 5 victories in less than a week. No. 64 Squadron, which claimed over 130 aerial victories, produced 11 aces, of whom 2 were Irish—Atkinson and Carlow man Ronald St Clair McClintock, MC. However, No .64 Squadron also had 2 other aces of Irish parentage: James Anderson Slater, (MC and Bar, DFC), had served in the Royal Irish Rifles but his mother was from Ardmore, Co Waterford, whilst the mother of Edmund Roger Tempest (MC, DFC)—Florence Helen O'Rourke—was from Dublin.

Atkinson returned to instructional duties. However, these were not his sole UK-based experiences. On 25th July 1918 his engagement was announced and on 14th August 1918 Atkinson married Nancy Rowan of Dunskaig, Ayr, in the Old Parish Church, Ayr, Scotland.[28]

On 3rd August 1918 the Supplement to the London Gazette carried the citation of Lt (temporary Captain) Edward Dawson Atkinson's Distinguished Flying Cross (DFC):

"A brilliant fighting pilot whose flight has proved very successful under his leadership, often in combats where the enemy formation was numerically superior. Capt Atkinson destroyed single-handed five enemy machines during May, and previously, whilst serving with another squadron, he brought down two enemy aeroplanes and one balloon".[29]

---

27   Gazette Issue 30199.
28   Flight Magazine, 25 July 1918; 22 August 1918, page 948.
29   London Gazette supplement. Gazette Issue 30827.

In a supplement to the London Gazette, dated 1ˢᵗ January 1919 Atkinson's award of the Air Force Cross (AFC) was gazetted.[30]

On 22 August 1920 Atkinson's cousin, District Inspector Oswald Ross Swanzy, was killed by the IRA. Swanzy had been blamed for being part of the Government-backed death squad that had killed the Lord Mayor of Cork, Tomás Mac Curtain. The death of Swanzy in Lisburn, Co Antrim triggered an anti-Catholic pogrom in the town, in which 1,000 Catholics were burned out from their homes. The American Committee for Relief in Ireland, via the Irish White Cross, helped re-house and resettle many of the refugees.

In the post-war era Atkinson served in various posts in Iraq. In January 1924 the Air Ministry included Atkinson in the list of promotions from Flight Lieutenant to Squadron Leader. Throughout the late 1920s Atkinson served as Squadron Leader of No.1 Squadron, mainly at RAF Tangmere, during which time he had flown a number of aircraft types including the Armstrong Whitworth Siskin. [31]

In 1930 Atkinson was placed on the half-pay list.[32] However, Atkinson was subsequently one of a number of officers restored to full pay on 16 March 1931.[33] However, some months later the Air Ministry announced that Atkinson had been placed on the retired list on account of ill health.[34]

The last public notice relating to Atkinson issued in the London Gazette on 03 April 1934 in respect of a company named R.J. Coley & Barnett Ltd. At an Extraordinary General Meeting a special resolution was passed to appoint Atkinson (then of 17 Upper Park Road, Kingston-upon-Thames, Surrey) and a Robert James Coley to be

---

30   London Gazette supplement. Gazette Issue 31098.
31   For example see *Flight* magazine 28 July 1927, p.526.
32   See London Gazette of 18 November 1930, Gazette Issue 33662, and the London Gazette of 09 December 1930, Gazette Issue 33668.
33   London Gazette 31 March 1931, Gazette Issue 33703.
34   London Gazette 19 January 1932, Gazette Issue 33791.

joint liquidators of the firm. Atkinson is described as Chairman of the company.[35]

Atkinson's legacy to Irish aviation is difficult to quantify: although a decorated pilot with a lengthy post-war career in the RAF, Atkinson—quite unlike at least two of the other Indian-born Irish aviators—would not appear to have had any significant presence in Ireland and thus would not have the recognition of many others. Atkinson's legacy perhaps lies in his service to the Allied cause, a formidable opponent and one of the few Irishmen who had—or ever will—succeed in obtaining 10 aerial victories.

✦ ✦ ✦

---

35   London Gazette 03 April 1934, Gazette Issue 34038.

BETTS, ERIC BOURNE COULTER

(**6 aerial victories**)

Born: 14 January 1897, Calcutta, Bengal, INDIA

Died: 30 October 1971

Religion: Church of Ireland

Commemorated: Great War Roll of Honour, St Patrick's Church of Ireland, Dalkey, Co Dublin.

Awards (in chronological order, not of precedence):

Distinguished Service Cross—21 April 1917; Croix de Guerre (France)—20 July 1917; Distinguished Flying Cross—21 September 1918; Croix de Guerre with Palme (France)—16 December 1919; Commander of the British Empire (CBE)—02 June 1943; Mentioned in Despatches—01 January 1945; Knight Commander of the Order of the Phoenix (Greece)—06 December 1946.

Air Vice Marshal Eric Betts was born in Calcutta to Cecil Coulter Betts and Louisa Alice Betts (née Toomey).

His father Cecil is described in the Irish Census 1911 as being a "Jute merchant" and was born in India. Eric's mother, Louisa Toomey, was from Dublin. Eric's grandmother Julia Toomey was living with them in 1911. Eric, his brother Conrad and sister Esther were all born in India, contrary to what most aviation publications state regarding the birthplace of Eric and Conrad.

The Betts family had a long-standing connection with India. It would appear that Anthony Bishop wrote an article for the journal of Military History Society of Ireland, *The Irish Sword*, on the memoir of Esther Anne Betts in respect of the Indian Rebellion of 1857, titled 'An Irishwoman's account of the Indian Mutiny'. This has been re-published in recent years in a collection of *Irish Sword* articles. The Betts and Bishop clans were intermarried Indian-based Irish families.

Betts started his career with the Royal Navy, joining the Public Service Schools Battalion on 19 January 1915, having previously served with the Officer Training Corps.[36] Betts was quite short, just 5' 4.5" and was described as having been a schoolmaster prior to enlistment.

On 06 February 1915 Betts was transferred to Signals School, then on 16 March 1915 was drafted to Chatham for Sea Service, obtaining his Service Certificate on 25 March 1915 as a Signalman.

From 28 April 1915 to 08 September 1915 Betts served on the HMS *Imperieuse*.[37] This can give rise to confusion: the name 'Imperieuse' had been used for a number of Royal Navy training ships over several generations. Betts served on what had once been the HMS *Audacious*, an old ironclad battleship that had been decommissioned in 1894 and stripped down for use as a training ship in the early 1900s. It had been re-named the *Imperieuse* in 1914 but reclassified from a training ship to a receiving ship, i.e. primarily to house new recruits prior to their reassignment.

From 09 September 1915 to 13 October 1915 Betts served on the HMS *Royal Arthur*. This ship was a cruiser with a long service history in the Pacific, Australia, North America and the West Indies. By the time of Betts' naval service the ship was a guardship for the Home Fleet at Scapa Flow. According to his service records, on 14 October 1915 Betts was granted a commission as a Sub-Lieutenant in

---

36   UK National Archives, ADM 339/1, EBC Betts.
37   UK National Archives, ADM 337/36, EBC Betts.

the Royal Naval Volunteer Reserve for the Royal Naval Air Service, which was widely reported.[38]

Betts was assigned to No.2 (Naval) Squadron and flew as an observer, undertaking long-range photographic reconnaissance missions. On 01 February 1917 Betts achieved his first aerial victory, driving down out of control an Albatros D.II that had engaged their Sopwith 11/2 Strutter whilst on a mission. Betts had flown as the observer and gunner to Flight Lieutenant Holden. On 28 February 1917 Betts was promoted to Temporary Lieutenant.[39]

Betts was awarded the Distinguished Service Cross (DSC). A supplement to the London Gazette of 20 April 1917 carried his citation:

"Sub-Lt. (now Lt.) E. B. C. BETTS, R.N.V.R.

In recognition of his services on February 1st, 1917, when he carried out a long reconnaissance and returned with extremely important information, shooting down an enemy scout machine which attacked him on his way back". [40]

The London Gazette of 26 June 1917 reported that Betts had been promoted to Temporary Observer Sub-Lieutenant, dated to 01 January 1916. *Flight* magazine of 26 July 1917 carried details of Betts being awarded the *Croix de Guerre* by the French.[41]

Betts was promoted from Observer-Lieutenant to Flight-Observer, with effect from 31 December 1917.

In April 1918 the Royal Flying Corps and the Royal Naval Air Service were merged to form the Royal Air Force (RAF). The former RFC squadrons retained their squadron numbers whilst the former RNAS squadrons were re-numbered through the addition of 200

---

38   London Gazette, 26 October 1915, Gazette Issue 29340, p.10508. Betts had been promoted from a Signalman to Sub-Lieutenant in the Royal Naval Volunteer Reserve.

39   *Flight* magazine of 05 April 1917 reported an Admiralty announcement of 29 March 1917, which stated that Betts had been promoted from Temporary Sub-Lieutenant to Temporary Lieutenant with effect from 28 February 1917.

40   London Gazette supplement, 20 April 1917, Gazette Issue 30029.

41   *Flight* magazine of 26 July 1917, p.752.

to their previous designation. Betts' No.2 (Naval) Squadron, RNAS, thus became No.202 Squadron, RAF.

Betts' brother Conrad was killed in World War I serving with the Royal Air Force on 17 April 1918. He was flying with "G" Squadron, 2 Wing, which had been formed at Imbros and was based at Mudros at the time of Conrad's death. Conrad was buried at East Mudros Military Cemetery, Lemnos, Greece.

Betts was awarded the Distinguished Flying Cross (DFC); the citation was gazetted on 21 September 1918:

"Capt. ERIC BOURNE COULTER BETTS, D.S.C, (Sea Patrol).—An observer officer of great skill who has carried out over 20 long-distance photographic reconnaissances during the past four months, and in conjunction with his pilot, has brought home about 1,000 photographs of enemy positions of inestimable value, in addition to destroying eight enemy machines."

The reference to the destruction of 8 enemy aircraft is inaccurate, as it is clear from the records available in respect of No. 202 Squadron that Betts had achieved 5 victories in the four-month period in question, flying as observer in a DH4 piloted by Flight Lieutenant Noel Keeble. Aerial photographic reconnaissance had always been the priority, not the destruction of enemy aircraft, and thus the granting of 5 or 8 claims would have been of secondary importance.

On 01 August 1919 the Air Ministry granted permanent commission to Betts at the rank of Lieutenant. In December 1919 it was reported that Betts had been awarded the Croix de Guerre with Palme by the French Republic.[42]

On 30 June 1921 Betts was promoted from Observer Officer to Flight Lieutenant. Betts transferred from HMS Pegasus to the RAF Depot (Inland Area), and subsequently to the RAF Staff College (Inland Area) in March and April 1922. Betts was part of the student intake of the RAF Staff College at Andover, i.e. he was not on the staff of the college, despite his demographic profile and experience. The purpose of the Staff College was—as may be gathered from its

---

42   London Gazette, Issue 31691, supplement of 16 December 1919, p.15615.

name—to train officers in staff duties. However, it also attempted to cover strategy and tactics in land, sea and air warfare; Army, Air Force and Naval organisation and structures; intelligence work and so forth. The idea was that the RAF could develop an institution similar to the Army Staff College at Camberley or the Naval Staff College at Greenwich, institutions which evolved over generations—the RAF was in a situation in which military aviation was only a decade old.

Upon completion of his training with the RAF Staff College (Inland Area), Betts was transferred to No.1 Flying Training School (Inland Area) with effect from 04 April 1923.[43] Betts was subsequently appointed to Headquarters (Inland Area) with effect from 17 September 1923, i.e. to a staff officer position from a training role.

However, Flight Lieutenant Betts was appointed to No.3 Flying Training School (Cadre) Spittlegate on 20 March 1928. Betts networked well, e.g. he is among those who attended the Royal Air Force Dinner Club's sixth annual dinner, at the Connaught Rooms on 29 June 1928. However, it was not until nearly a year later that Betts was eventually promoted from Flight Lieutenant to Squadron Leader, with effect from 29 May 1929.[44] Betts was certainly a career pilot at this stage, being among those participating in the RAF Rifle Meeting of 07 June 1929. However, on 16 November 1929 Betts was appointed to RAF HQ Aden Command. This was not a prestigious staff officer position but it was still useful for a man in his early thirties and at Squadron Leader rank.

With the topsy-turvy world of 1930s retrenchment in defence budgets and strategic readjustment it is often difficult to follow just exactly what is happening but it would appear that the London Gazette of 31 May 1932 stated that Squadron Leader Betts had been placed on the half-pay list, Scale A, with effect form 21 May 1932, whilst a subsequent Air Ministry notice issued in the London Gazette of 12 July 1932, which reported that Squadron Leader Betts was restored to full pay on 28 June 1932.

---

43   Widely reported, e.g. see Flight magazine of 29 March 1923.
44   London Gazette of 28 May 1929, Issue 33499, p.3520.

Betts was transferred to HQ Wessex Bombing Area, Andover on 08 August 1932 for Air Staff duties, but subsequently—on 21 December 1933—was transferred to No.101(B) Squadron, Andover. The (B) suffix to a squadron number denoted a Bomber Squadron, although there was much reorganization in the inter-war years of what were ultimately to become Bomber Command, Coastal Command and Fighter Command of the RAF. However, it was clear that Betts was still being bounced between air staff duties and squadron duties.

In April 1934 the King held at Levée at St James' Palace, and Betts was among those presented to the King. Betts and George V had further encounters prior to the latter's passing in 1936. The King reviewed the RAF in a Jubilee Year ceremony in July 1935, during the course of which he stopped at "Overstrands" bombers of No.101(B) Squadron, where Squadron Leader Betts "explained to the King the marvels of the revolving gun turret in the nose. Sergeant Thrussell was there presented to him as the best bomb aimer of 1934."[45]

In July 1935, in the annual exercise between fighter and bomber squadrons of the RAF, (divided into "Northlands" and "Southlands"), Squadron Leader Betts' No.101(B) Squadron was responsible for the Medium Bombers of the Central Area, consisting of Bicester, "Sidestrand" and "Overstrand" bombers. These exercises are generally thought of as being ones in which the bombers were useful fodder in training the RAF Fighter Command in how to win the Battle of Britain. However, the reality was the bomber squadrons gained much in terms of devising open formation tactics and in testing range, altitude and pilot stamina.

In January 1936 Betts was among the half-yearly promotions in the general duties branch, getting promoted from Squadron Leader to Wing Commander.

Wing Commander Betts was appointed Director of Operations, Department of Advanced Military Studies Course (AMSC), at the Air Ministry. Betts served in this role for several years. He was eventu-

---

45   *Flight* magazine of 11 July 1935 (p.43).

ally promoted from Wing Commander to Group Captain with effect from 01 April 1939.[46]

As one may expect from an ace who had been quite formidable as an observer/gunner, Betts was a good rifle shot. However, in the MacKinnon Match Trophy, Betts, an Indian-born and Dalkey-raised man, chose to represent India as Adjutant in 1939 and as a marksman in 1946. He also represented India in the Kolapore Match in 1946. However, Betts also represented Ireland at other international matches in 1929, 1934, 1935 and 1946.

Flight magazine of 23 January 1941 (p.81) reports Betts as among those commended by the King for the valuable services rendered in connection with the war.[47] Within weeks the Air Ministry announced that Betts had been promoted from Group Captain to Air Commodore (temporary) with effect from 01 March 1941.[48] Subsequently Betts was promoted from Air Commodore to acting Air Vice-Marshal with effect from 14 March 1943.

In June 1943 it was reported that "on the occasion of the Celebration of His Majesty's Birthday" Acting Air Vice-Marshal Betts was appointed Commander of the Most Excellent Order of the British Empire (Military Division).[49]

However, it was not until nearly a year later that Air Commodore (temporary)(Acting Air Vice-Marshal) Betts was granted the rank of Air Commodore, with effect from 14 March 1944. Further recognition was to follow: the King of the Hellenes conferred Betts with the Knight Commander of the Order of the Phoenix at the Greek Embassy on 27 August 1944.[50] However, in December 1944 Betts was

---

46   London Gazette, Issue 34613, p.2262.
47   Also Supplement to London Gazette of 01 January 1941, Gazette Issue 35029, p.41.
48   London Gazette of 11 March 1941, Gazette Issue 35102, p.1448.
49   Supplement to London Gazette of 02 June 1943, Gazette Issue 36033, p.2430.
50   *Flight* magazine of 05 September 1946 (p.259). See also London Gazette Supplement of 06 September 1946, p.4455 regarding King's permission to wear the decoration.

promoted from temporary acting Air Vice-Marshal to Air Vice-Marshal but was replaced by Air Vice-Marshal Charles Stafford as Air Officer, Administration at HQ Middle East.[51] On 01 January 1945 the Air Ministry announced that Acting Air Vice Marshal Betts had been mentioned in despatches.[52] Later that month the Air Ministry announced that Betts had relinquished the rank of Air Vice Marshal with effect from 16 December 1944.[53] However, subsequently it was announced that when Betts retired on 10 March 1946 he retained the rank of Air Vice-Marshal.[54]

'The Principles of War', a poem of doggerel by Betts, was included in a pamphlet *More Asp Ad Astra: the Lighter Side of Ten Years 'Hard', 1938-1948*, —it need not concern us here, and is available online from many sources—but one can be consoled with the knowledge that Betts embarked on military career rather than attempt to pursue an artistic one.

Betts would appear to have retired to London. However, an examination of passenger lists reveals that Betts arrived in Southampton on 28 January 1960 from Madeira on the *Venus*, with his wife Mary. Their UK address was given as 11 Hinchley Close, Esher, Surrey. Betts was by now a 'wine merchant', his nationality no longer 'Irish' or 'Indian' but 'British' in the nationality description. (Most likely he travelled on a UK passport). However, there is a marriage index record for Surrey in the first quarter of 1965 in which an Eric BC Betts gets married to a Margaret O'Dea.

Of the four Indian-born Irish aces, Betts is only one of two to have resided in Ireland but is the only one to have had long term residence in Ireland for any appreciable time. However, he was a man of the world and one of Ireland's few aces who attained senior rank in the RAF.

---

51   *Flight* magazine of 14 December 1944 (p.632), (p.648).
52   Supplement to London Gazette of 01 January 1945, Gazette Issue 36866, p.60.
53   Supplement to London Gazette of 23 January 1945, p.508.
54   Supplement to London Gazette of 26 March 1946, gazette Issue 37511, p.1533.

Further research or reading:

According to the records of the Centre of South Asian Studies, University of Cambridge, there are several boxes of papers given by the British Association for Cemeteries in South Asia (BASCA). Within this collection are the "Bishop Papers", lent by Mr A Bishop, and referring to Bengal, 1887-1916.

The UK National Archives have several of Betts' lecture papers on aeroplane co-operation with other armed forces on the Belgian Coast. (AIR 1/2393/249/1) for those interested in seeking staff college type papers.

The Imperial War Museum has some private papers of Betts, including an account of a flight from New York to Cairo during World War II.

✦ ✦ ✦

BLENNERHASSET, GILES NOBLE

(8 aerial victories)

Born: 16 April 1895, Co Sligo

Died: 04 December 1978

Awards: Military Cross

Commemorated: Great War Roll of Honour, Cathedral of St Mary and St John, Sligo, Ireland

Religion: Church of Ireland

Giles Noble Blennerhasset was born on 16 April 1895 in Leoville, Co Sligo to James and Selina Blennerhasset.

The Irish Census 1901 records the family as being resident at Finisklin, Sligo Town. (This is also recorded as Ardmachree, Larkhill, Co Sligo). Giles had 3 younger sisters by this stage: Kathleen, Eva and Oonah. Giles' father James is described as being a "bookkeeper" in the census return. Apparently James was originally from Gortalea, Ballymacelligott, Co Kerry. An apprentice in Revington's Drapery Store in Tralee, Co Kerry he moved to Omagh, Co Tyrone where he studied book-keeping, subsequently moving to Sligo where at Henry Lyons & Co Department Store he was the book-keeper/accountant, later becoming Managing Director. Apparently he was a good tenor. Giles' 84-year-old widowed grandmother Jane (b.1827, Kerry) was resident with the family in both census returns. Giles' mother was from Co Sligo.

Giles was educated at Sligo Grammar School. There seems to be confusion with regard to his military service history. However, his son Brian has recently provided Giles' logbook, together with photographs and other documentation, to the Europeana project. This information confirms that Giles joined the Inns of Court O.T.C. in 1914 at the rank of Private (No.6115). He served for 267 days as a soldier of the Territorial Force in London, being discharged upon being appointed a 2nd Lieutenant in the 4th Royal Irish Fusiliers on 09 September 1915.

Giles was not the only member of the family with a connection to the legal profession: his youngest sister Oonagh became a barrister, later marrying Justice Gardner Budd of the Supreme Court.

At the early stages of the war Blennerhasset served with the Royal Irish Fusiliers and fought in the trenches until 1916. According to his son's account to the Europeana project, Giles was very much in fear of rats until the end of his life following this experience.

On 24 March 1916 he transferred to the Royal Flying Corps, as an observer, being posted to No.18 Squadron on 31 December 1916, according to his service records.[55] However, the London Gazette Supplement of 30 May 1916 indicates that with effect from 02 June 1916 he was appointed 2nd Lieutenant from the Inns of Court Officers' Training Corps to the Royal Irish Fusiliers.[56]

On 04 February 1917 Blennerhasset achieved his first aerial victory, when flying as observer in an F.E.2b piloted by Second Lieutenant Robert Farquhar, they sent down out of control a German Albatros D.II north of Le Sars.

On 05 April 1917 when flying as observer to fellow Irishman Second Lieutenant Victor Huston they drove down out of control two German Albatros D.II scouts near Inchy when out on a photographic reconnaissance patrol. The next day, with a 2nd Lt Reid in F.E.2b

---

55 AIR 76/42 UK National Archives, Blennerhasset.
56 London Gazette Supplement, 01 June 1916, Gazette Issue 29605, p.5442.

(5468), Giles drove down a German aircraft that had attempted to interfere with 18 Squadron's photographic reconnaissance. According to RFC Communiqué No.82 "this machine fell completely out of control and anti-aircraft report that it crashed". However, in the "Combats in the Air" report submitted by Reid and Blennerhasset they suggest that the Albatros made an attack but that his guns jammed, enabling Reid to hit it with 60 rounds from the front Lewis gun. However, Blennerhasset was nevertheless becoming quite lethal at aerial gunnery. RFC Communiqué No.84 reported the following for 16 April 1917:

"A photographic patrol by 18 Squadron engaged six HA scouts over Cagnicourt. 2nd Lt S.J. Young and Lt. E.N. Blennerhasset attacked one HA which was engaging one of our machines and fired a whole drum into it. The HA fell completely out of control. They then attacked and downed a second HA … 426 photographs were taken during the day".[57]

In a strange parallel universe, the London Gazette of 16 April 1917 reported Blennerhasset's secondment to the RFC from 24 March 1917 with seniority from 31 December 1916.[58]

On 26 July 1917 Blennerhasset's citation for the Military Cross was gazetted:

"2nd Lt. Giles Noble Blennerhassett, R. Ir. Fus., Spec. Res., and R.F.C.

For conspicuous gallantry and devotion to duty. He has shown great skill and courage when, acting as escort in attacking hostile formations. On one occasion he attacked two hostile machines, driving down both out of control. Later, he forced three other machines down."[59]

Within a week Blennerhasset was promoted to Temporary Lieutenant whilst serving with the General List, quoting from London Gazette of 31 July 1917.

---

57 RFC Communiqué, 15-21 April 1917. Quoted in Chaz Bowyer "RFC Communiqués 1917-1918", p.39.
58 London Gazette Supplement, Gazette Issue 30021, p.3573.
59 London Gazette Supplement, Gazette Issue 30204, p.7623.

Blennerhasset returned to Home Establishment in August 1917, being posted to the School of Aeronautics on 09 August 1917 for further training. From Reading he was then posted to 198 Depot Squadron at Rochford on 25 September 1917. On 03 December 1917 Blennerhasset was assigned to No.78 Squadron upon appointment as Flying Officer. At this time No. 78 Squadron were based at Sutton's Farm (later called RAF Hornchurch), with a detachment stationed at Biggin Hill. Their role was the interception of German airships and Gotha bombers in the defence of London.

On 08 January 1918 he married Kathleen Maud Curry (b. 30 May 1898, Newbridge, Co Kildare) at Aldershot, Farnham, Hampshire.

In January 1918, in the half-yearly promotion lists, Blennerhasset was promoted to Flying Officer. However, the London Gazette Supplement of 04 March 1918 records Blennerhasset as being 2nd Lieutenant with effect from 02 December 1917 in the Special Reserve of Officers. It would appear that his temporary acting grade in the RAF and his home position in the Royal Irish Fusiliers were somewhat out of sync.

According to his service record, Blennerhasset was shuffled around quite a lot over the course of various home defence squadrons being restructured and reorganised. He transferred from No.78 Squadron to No.112 Squadron, subsequently moving to No.152 Squadron on 12 October 1918 but being attached to No.61 Squadron on occasion from No.152 Squadron. This marks quite a versatility in Blennerhasset: in World War I No.112 Squadron were on home defence duties (it was only in World War II they sported the famous 'shark's mouth' symbols on their engine nacelles), but No.152 Squadron were only formed in October 1918 as a night-fighter unit, flying Sopwith Camels.

Blennerhasset's appointment as acting Captain with effect from 08 November 1918 was gazetted on 26 November 1918. Blennerhasset's served the past the Armistice with No.152 Squadron, but on 03 March 1919 he was transferred to 11th (Irish) Group, being based at

RAF Baldonnell until 01 April 1919 when he was transferred to the 6th Brigade. Blennerhasset relinquished the rank of acting Captain with effect from 01 May 1919. Following a series of re-assignments in May 1919 Blennerhasset served with No.143 Squadron from 06 June 1919 onwards. This squadron was disbanded on 31 October 1919.

A qualified pilot, in October 1919 Blennerhasset was granted a short service commission as Flying Officer by the Air Ministry. On 01 November 1919 he was transferred to the notional strength of No.39 Squadron. On 18 December 1919, however, he was stationed in RAF HQ India, as a Corps Observer rather than pilot, from which he was assigned to No.48 Squadron in India on 12 January 1920. This squadron had distinguished service in France during World War I but was scheduled for disbandment on 01 April 1920 and merged into No.5 Squadron at Quetta for Army Air Co-operation on the North West Frontier.

On 30 April 1920 Kathleen Maud Blennerhasset and her son Brian sailed from Liverpool to Bombay on the 'City of Calcutta' to join Giles in Karachi.

Blennerhasset duly served with No.5 Squadron but his medical record indicates that on 16 August 1920 an assessment recommended that he be granted 6 months leave to England. On 14 October 1920 Blennerhasset was placed on board the ambulance transport ship "Vita", leaving Bombay on that date. A further assessment on 23 November 1920 recommended 4 weeks' leave with a requirement to report on 21 December 1920 for further assessment.

The London Gazette of 21 January 1921 indicates that Blennerhasset resigned his Short Service Commission and appointment as Captain with effect from 22 January 1921. By December 1921 Blennerhasset had relinquished his commission in the Royal Irish Fusiliers.[60]

There is a marriage recorded in Edmonton, Middlesex of a Giles N Blennerhasset to a Dorothy M Pinnock, in the first quarter of 1933, but I have no information as to how this transpired, nor is there any other information to link this event to the Irish ace Giles

---

60 London Gazette Supplement, Issue 32559, 23 December 1921, p.10568.

N Blennerhasset. (The name Dorothy M Pinnock features heavily in the marriage records of the Middlesex district over subsequent decades).

Giles was a lay representative for the Church of Ireland. He donated the Bishop's Throne at Sligo Cathedral in memory of his father James. Giles died on 04 December 1978.

❖ ❖ ❖

BYRNE, PATRICK ANTHONY LANGAN

(10 aerial victories)

Born: 12 November 1894, Clogherhead, Co Louth

Died: 17 October 1916, killed in action

Awards: Mentioned in Despatches, Distinguished Service Order (DSO)

Religion: Roman Catholic

Commemorated: Arras Flying Services Memorial, France; Great War Memorial, Drogheda, Co Louth, Ireland; Clongowes Wood College Great War Memorial (commemorated as "Langan Byrne").

According to the Commonwealth War Graves Commission records Patrick Anthony Laugan Byrne was the son of the late Dr. Byrne and of Mrs. J. V. Humphries (formerly Byrne), of Mayne, Clogherhead, Co. Louth, Ireland.

However, a deceased father and a re-married mother do not wholly preclude tracing his pre-war life in Ireland. The Irish Census 1911 records Patrick A Byrne from Co Louth as being a student at Clongowes, Co Kildare.

It is uncertain of his pre-war movements, but it is generally agreed that Byrne served with the 129th Battery, 30th Brigade, of the Royal Field Artillery. Byrne's next-of-kin details on his RFC service record indicate that his mother once resided at 53 Cadogan Square London, and at "Cowslip Lodge", Drogheda, Co Louth. (It is my understanding that Cowslip Lodge is closer to the villages of Bettystown or Mornington in Co Meath than Drogheda but this is irrelevant to Byrne's own circumstances). The mother's address in August 1931 was the "Standard Hotel, Dublin".[61]

Byrne would appear to have been posted to Oxford on 23 May 1916 upon transfer from the Royal Field Artillery. He transferred to No.2 Reserve Squadron on 03 June 1916, subsequently training with No.10 Reserve Squadron in July and August 1916. As may be noted at the time the Reserve Squadrons/Training Squadrons had not yet been re-structured into Training Depot Stations (TDS) for the formation of new squadrons. On 11 July 1916 Byrne was awarded Royal Aero Club Certificate No.3211 for succeeding at the Military School, Brooklands with a Maurice Farman biplane. His birthplace is given as Drogheda, Co Louth.

On 11 August 1916 Byrne was posted to No.24 Squadron. Of the 33 aces who served in this squadron, several were Irish, e.g. Sidney Cowan, Tom Falcon Hazell and George McElroy. On 31 August 1916 Byrne, flying an Airco DH.2 forced an enemy aircraft to land near Bapaume. As noted in *Above the Trenches*, most of Byrne's claims were 'forced to land' and other "soft" or essentially moral victories, which were granted in the early years of the war but were not awarded by the Royal Flying Corps after 1916.

Royal Flying Corps Communiqué No.52 of 1916 records Byrne's victory as attacking, driving down and damaging a hostile machine on 31 August 1916. On 02 September 1916 Byrne was involved in another encounter in which the claim was deemed to be an 'out-of-control' victory rather than a confirmed destruction:

---

61   AIR 76/71 UK National Archives, Patrick Anthony Byrne.

"Lt Byrne of the same patrol [No.24 Squadron with Captain Andrews] saw two F.E.s attacking three hostile machines near Villers. Another machine approached to join the enemy. Lt Byrne attacked it, firing 20 rounds at 50 yards range. The hostile machine banked steeply, offering a good target, and Lt Byrne fired the remainder of his drum at very close range. The German machine side-slipped, and went down in a very steep dive towards Beaulencourt. Owing to the continued fighting, Lt Byrne was unable to see whether it reached the ground".[62]

Byrne features in RFC Communiqué No.54 of September 1916. On 15 September 1916 he was in the thick of the action:

"Lieutenants Byrne, Mackay and Nixon, of 24 Sqdn, whilst on offensive patrol near Morval, encountered 17 hostile aeroplanes at various heights. They dived into the middle of the hostile formation and attacked. Lt Byrne got to very close quarters with one machine, which burst into flames and was seen to crash. He then attacked a second machine, which was driven down and crashed in a field".[63]

Byrne was only credited with one victory from this incident. In many of these cases several pilots can often see the same stricken plane crash after disappearing down through clouds, imagining it to be the one they had engaged in combat. In some cases what are imagined to be several additional enemy machines joining the fight are actually the same ones the pilots and observers thought they had accounted for with their previous fire. In the confusion it can sometimes even be an aircraft from their own squadron they see in the final stages of its destruction and confuse it with one they thought they had shot at and seen going down. The common perception is that the Royal Flying Corps granted claims massively in excess of actual German losses but the foregoing communiqué shows that often pilots were awarded one victory from several claims arising in a combat incident.

---

62   'Royal Flying Corps Communiqués 1915-1916', by Christopher Cole (ed), [Tom Donovan, 1990], p.242.
63   'Royal Flying Corps Communiqués 1915-1916', by Christopher Cole (ed), [Tom Donovan, 1990], p.258.

However, on 22 September 1916, although not credited with a double-victory, Byrne forced an enemy aircraft to land on two separate occasions that day, near Velu in the morning and at Grandcourt that evening. Although the majority of Byrne's victories were "forced to land" types this should not be taken as some sort of chivalry being exercised, as frequently the aircraft were strafed on the ground.

On 16 October 1916 when leading his flight into an attack Byrne was shot down by the famous early war German ace Oswald Boelcke, for the latter's 34th victory.

Langan-Byrne's DSO citation was gazetted on 14 November 1916:

"2nd Lt. Patrick Anthony Langan-Byrne, R.A. and R.F.C.

For conspicuous skill and gallantry. He has shown great pluck in attacking hostile machines, often against large odds. He has accounted for several. On one occasion, with two other machines, he attacked seventeen enemy machines, shot down one in flames and forced another to land."[64]

Given the large number of 'forced to land' victories credited to Byrne, it is ironic that the medal citation includes a 'forced to land' aerial victory that was not actually awarded to him.

According to his service record, on 18 October 1916 Byrne was mentioned in despatches by Sir Douglas Haig, which was gazetted on 04 January 1917. However, I have been unable to identify any such corresponding reference to this. It may have been a reference to the work of No.24 Squadron rather than the achievements of individual officers.

Byrne was one of Ireland's first aces, but—by the aerial victory standards of the later war years—perhaps just over half his 10 victories would have counted in comparison with Ireland's late-war aces. However, Byrne was one of those who showed just what was achievable in aerial combat and deserves a lot more respect than the cursory nod given when discussing aces. The Airco D.H.2 was a "pusher" aircraft, i.e. the engine was behind the pilot like that of a ship. They

---

64   London Gazette Supplement, Issue 29824, p.11041.

were quite unstable, with a tendency to spin easily and to stall. This also contributed to their manoeuvrability, and although they were useful in ending the "Fokker scourge" of the Fokker EIII Eindecker it should be pointed out that Byrne's No.24 Squadron engaged in 774 aerial combats to achieve 44 victories over German types. With the introduction of the Halberstadt DII and Albatros DI the D.H.2 was completely outclassed. Byrne's achievements need to be seen in this context. His score of 10 is the joint-highest achieved on this type. Several notable pilots who survived the early war engagements using the D.H.2, e.g. James McCudden, went on to fantastic service on more advanced types. Byrne, like VC-winner Lanoe Hawker, were unfortunate to be caught in the transitional period between the evolution of British and French types relative to German aeronautical advances.

✦ ✦ ✦

CAIRNES, WILLIAM JAMESON

(**6 aerial victories**)

Born: 07 June 1898, Co Louth

Died: 06 June 1918 (one day short of his 20th birthday)

Commemorated: Arras Flying Services Memorial, France; Great War Memorial, Drogheda, Co Louth, Ireland; Roll of Honour, St Peter's Church of Ireland, Drogheda, Co Louth, Ireland.

Religion: Church of Ireland

Also: Thomas Agar Elliott Cairnes (2 aerial victories)

Captain William J Cairnes was born at Stameen, Co Louth. One of his brothers, Francis Herbert Cairnes, served with the Royal Field Artillery in World War I. Another brother, Thomas Agar Elliott Cairnes, also served in the Royal Flying Corps, rising to the rank of Lieutenant-Colonel in the RAF.

They were the sons of William Plunket Cairnes and Alice Jane Algar. Their grandfather on their mother's side was Major-General James Sturgeon Hamilton Algar. Their grandfather on their father's side was William Elliot Cairnes, a director of the Great Northern Railway, chairman of the Cairnes family brewery and Governor of the Bank of Ireland.

All three brothers were born in Stameen, which is on the boundary between counties Louth and Meath. (Generally Louth is cited, as Drogheda is the family's main centre of interest). All three brothers were educated at Rugby, and both Tom and Francis went to the Royal Military College at Sandhurst.

In the Irish Census 1901 Cairnes was resident with his parents, two brothers, an uncle and six servants in a house at Stameen. Cairnes was educated at Rugby and Cambridge.

On 22 September 1914 Cairnes' promotion from Cadet to 2nd Lieutenant, 5th Battalion Leinster Regiment was gazetted. Subsequently in April 1915 Cairnes was confirmed in his rank as 2nd Lieutenant, 5th Bn Leinster Regiment.[65]

Cairnes transferred to the RFC in November 1916, being appointed Lieutenant (Flying Officer) with effect from 06 November 1916. He trained with No.62 Squadron and was transferred to No.19 Squadron, entering France with them on 21 February 1917.[66]

On 19 May 1917 Cairnes achieved his first two victories, when flying a SPAD, destroying an Albatros C east of Croisilles and an Albatros D.III north of Vitry. After scoring two further victories with No.19 Squadron, Cairnes was returned to Home Establishment in July 1917 to serve as a Flying Instructor. Initially he served with 7th Wing, in September 1917 becoming a Flying Instructor with No.56 Training Squadron in September 1917.

Cairnes was appointed Flight Commander in February 1918, transferring to No.74 Squadron on 14 March 1918 as Temporary Captain. There is a much-quoted conversation between Cairnes and 'Mick' Mannock as to what their final thoughts would be in the event of the aircraft catching fire. Cairnes did not wish to be drawn into another row over the absence of parachutes for pilots and confessed not to know what he would do. However, the question was actually an attempt at a joke by Mannock, who said "the last thing going through my head would be a bullet", as he would blow his own brains out!

On 01 June 1918 Cairnes was shot down by Lt Paul Billik of Jasta 52. Ira "Taffy" Jones witnessed the kill and reported that Cairnes' SE.5 had lost a wing in the engagement. However, Cairnes' service record reports him as "Missing" and is dated 01 June 1918. On

---

65 Supplement to the London Gazette of 21 April 1915, Issue 29137, p.3924.
66 AIR 76/72 UK National Archives, W Cairnes.

14 November 1918 this is updated to "Prisoner of War". Eventually, on 09 December 1919, his record was amended to read "[d]eath accepted for official purposes on or after 1.6.18". It is unclear from the information to hand as to whether it was a genuine error in recording Cairnes as missing and/or prisoner of war. (In some military services it is possible for the families to benefit from a measure of pay whilst the MIA is described as being a POW). However, it is a near-certainty that the Cairnes family would not have wished anything other than to have certainty on the fate of William, so it is likely that bureaucratic caution was being exercised.

Cairnes' probate is dated and sealed on 22 January 1920. He left £2,768 18s. 6d, which was quite a considerable sum for a young officer.

It would not be possible to conclude any discussion of Cairnes without reference his eldest brother Tom. Lieutenant-Colonel Thomas Agar Elliott Cairnes was the eldest of the three: the other brother was Major Francis Herbert Cairnes.

Overall it would appear that there may have been some confusion between the aerial victories attributed to William and Tom. Further, there are quite a number of officers with variations on the surname Cairns, Cairnes and/or Kearns. It is likely that any articles attributing ace status to Tom are the product of a misunderstanding, e.g. see local Louth historians Brendan and Donal Hall's material on the Cairnes family. (This is not intended as a criticism, merely an observation that in 2012 much of the painstaking local history research of non-digitized newspaper archives is still returning misunderstandings/mis-reportings of the previous generations).

Cairnes received his commission with the 7th Dragoon Guards in 1905. According to several accounts Cairnes had only one eye as a result of a pre-war polo injury. Cairnes served as an observer with No.15 Squadron. He obtained Royal Aero Club Certificate No.1811 on 2 October 1915 at the Military School Norwich, flying a Maurice Farman biplane. (In his Royal Aero Club Certificate photograph Cairnes' tunic features the RFC observer's "flying O" wing). Cairnes was to become a flight commander with No.27 Squadron.

As far as may be ascertained with any degree of certainty, according to RFC Communiqué No.34 of 1916, on 26 April 1916 Tom Cairnes, flying a Martinsyde G.100 'Elephant' of 27 Squadron, engaged a German aircraft near Souchez. "He fired half a drum at about 70 yards and then swerved to avoid collision. He attacked again from behind and below, firing the remainder of the drum. The observer of the hostile machine was apparently hit, as during the second attack he appeared to be kneeling in the turret doing nothing, and no shots were fired". A 2nd Lieutenant Arthur Henry William Tollemache, near Douvrin, then sent down this aircraft after firing a further drum into it from 50 yards. It would have been customary to share a kill of this nature.

RFC Communiqué No.36 of 1916 indicates that, on 19 May 1916, Cairnes and Tollemache combined once again to engage an enemy aircraft. They claim to have driven down an Albatros out of control between Festubert and Fournes.

Cairnes was to later command No.32 Squadron in July 1916 following the wounding of their commanding officer Major LWB Rees in an aerial engagement for which Rees was to receive the Victoria Cross. Tom returned to the 7th Dragoon Guards in 1919, but served with the RAF in World War II. An obituary in the Irish Times of 7 November 1960 outlined his post-war military and civilian career, including his occupations in civilian life. (Cairnes was a director of the family brewery but also served as a director in a number of companies). Cairnes was a member of the Kildare Street Club in Dublin and the Cavalry Club in London. He served as secretary to the Diocesan Council of Meath and was a member of the Representative Church Body. His wife, Katherine (née Hosken) predeceased him.

The *Drogheda Independent* also devoted a lengthy obituary to Cairnes. In more recent years the *Church News Ireland* gave a retrospective tribute to Cairnes on 15 December 2011. However, none of these disclose any further information that would give rise to any revision of the allocation of 8 aerial victories between the two brothers.

❖ ❖ ❖

CARBERY, DOUGLAS HUGH MOFFATT

(**6 aerial victories**)

Born: 26 March 1894, Ambala, India
Died: Apr-1959 Lanner, Cornwall, UK
Awards, Military Cross, Distinguished Flying Cross with Bar
Religion: Anglican

Not to be confused with Lord Carbery (John Evans-Freke), Brigadier Douglas Hugh Moffatt Carbery was born in India, the son of Lilian Eliza Louisa Moffatt (b.1874) and Hugh John Carbery (b.1863), a Corkman. His grandfathers were Charles Brown Carbery and Alexander Chisholm Moffatt. Douglas' parents were married on 26 December 1892 at Dehli, Bengal, India. Douglas was baptized at Ambala, Bengal on 11 June 1894. However, it would not appear that Douglas' parents lived to any great age—in *Above the War Fronts* it is suggested that Douglas travelled to the UK in 1913, the year in which his father died—and his service record indicates the next-of-kin address as being Sir William Austin, Bart, of Bardwell Manor, Suffolk. Sir William is described as Carbery's guardian. Ultimately Carbery married Violet Cecily Austin on 12 May 1932. She is described as being the daughter of Sir William Michael Byron Austin, 2nd Baronet, and Violet Irene Fraser, i.e. Carbery married into his guardian's family.

Sir William Austin does seem to have a connection with Ireland through the hunting, shooting and fishing set, e.g. he missed out on the Irish Red Setter Club Field Trials on 04 August 1914 at the Marquess of Waterford's shooting lodge, Glenbride, owing to the War Office requiring his services. (A Colonel Milner acted as judge in the field trials in Austin's absence).

Carbery was educated at the King's School, Bruton, Somersetshire. The UK Census 1911 records him as a boarder there. His birthplace is described as being Umbala, Punjab, India.

Norman Franks wrote a very comprehensive biography of Carbery for 'Cross & Cockade (International)', Volume 27, Issue No.4 (pp.212-214), although there are a number of omissions regarding his post-World War I service.

Carbery entered the Royal Military Academy at Woolwich in 1913, obtaining a commission in the Royal Horse Artillery. According to their registry details he was enrolled with the number 8754, was 18 years 8 months and 11 days old when joining and 20 years, 2 months and 17 days when leaving. His nationality was recorded as being Irish. Of the other Irish students enrolling at this time were John d'Arcy, son of the Bishop of Down, Connor & Dromore; [Captain] George Rivers Russell, son of a physician; [Major] Patrick Joseph Cliff Honner [MC-winner], son of a Major; William Frederick Hamilton Mallins, son of a Lt Colonel; Roderick Algernon Antony de Stacpoole, one of the few Roman Catholics there (educated at Downside), who was killed in action on 15 March 1915.

Carbery was 48th in the order of merit when joining, rising to 32nd on leaving.

He was commissioned in the Royal Field Artillery on 12 August 1914.[67] Carbery went to France with the 96th Battery in December 1914. He was wounded in the Second Battle of Ypres in May 1915. In July 1916 Carbery was again wounded, losing the top of an index finger.

---

67   London Gazette, Issue 28867, 11 August 1914, p.6304.

Carbery's service records indicate that he transferred from the Royal Artillery to the Royal Flying Corps on 20 May 1916. He was serving as a Lieutenant in France and was returned to the Home Establishment for training. Initially he was sent to Reading for preliminary training in June 1916, transferring to the 19 Reserve Squadron in July 1916, subsequently receiving training at the Central Flying School.[68]

On 04 August 1916 Carbery was appointed Flying Officer, initially being sent to No.52 Squadron, which was an army co-operation squadron (sometimes also referred to as being a bomber/corps squadron), and not a "scout" (fighter) squadron, although the distinctions were not great at this stage of the war insofar as engagement with enemy aircraft was becoming an expected outcome of any aerial activity such as reconnaissance, directing artillery and so forth. Carbery's duties were primarily in directing artillery rather than attacking hostile batteries.

On 07 September 1916 his appointment as Flying Officer was gazetted. Carbery served with No.52 Squadron, with an apparent brief return to Home Establishment duties in November 1916.

Carbery's first aerial victory was achieved in a R.E.8, with 2nd Lieutenant H MacKay as observer. On 25 January 1917 they succeeded in bringing down a German 2-seater, which was captured. Carbery obtained his second victory on 14 February 1917, flying a B.E.2e (6755) with 2nd Lieutenant M Vaile as observer. They sent down an Albatros D.III out of control near St Pierre.

Following these efforts, Carbery was granted leave from 28 February 1917 to 14 March 1917. Carbery was awarded the Military Cross, which was gazetted on 26 March 1917:

"Lt. Douglas Hugh Moffatt Carbery, R.F.A. and R.F.C.

For conspicuous gallantry and devotion to duty while engaged on artillery observation. He was attacked by four hostile machines, which he succeeded in driving off and continued to carry out his observations. Later, he was again, attacked by several hostile machines and

---

68 AIR 76/76 UK National Archives, DHM Carbery.

succeeded in bringing one of them down. He has previously done fine work."[69]

Carbery continued to serve with No.52 Squadron throughout the summer of 1917, obtaining 2 further victories. In May 1917 he was mentioned in despatches.

He was granted leave from 10 July 1917 to 24 July 1917, and shortly after his return Carbery was transferred from No.52 Squadron to No.9 Squadron, on 28 August 1917. This squadron had undergone two incarnations, originally being formed in December 1914 to develop the use of radio for reconnaissance missions, subsequently being re-formed in April 1915. The squadron had suffered heavy losses during the Battle of Passchendaele in 1917 when engaged in artillery spotting duties. Carbery was among a number of experienced personnel transferred to No.9 Squadron.

Carbery's promotion from Flying Officer to Temporary Captain (with effect from 26 August 1917) was gazetted on 12 September 1917. On 21 October 1917 Carbery was transferred to Home Establishment, being deemed suitable as a flying instructor. In terms of his army rank, Carbery was promoted to Temporary Captain in the Royal Artillery, with effect from 03 November 1917. However, as an RFC Flying Instructor, Carbery was sent to the Northern Training Brigade HQ, being assigned to No.15 Training Squadron on 21 November 1917.

Carbery served with 15 Training Squadron over the winter of 1917, being then transferred to HQ 27th Wing on 11 March 1918 for re-assignment. He was transferred to No.48 Training Squadron, but following an assessment by the Medical Board was granted 21 days leave on 14 March 1918. Carbery's Medical Board re-assessment of 16 April 1918 records him as being unfit for general service for 4 weeks, with a recommendation for a weeks' leave.

If Carbery's service with No.48 Training Squadron is somewhat inauspicious due to being on their notional strength whilst being out of action, his return saw him assigned to the Army Air Co-operation School on 24 April 1918, to serve as a Liaison Officer.

---

69   Supplement to the London Gazette, 26 March 1917 (30001/2983).

On 28 August 1918 Carbery returned to front-line action, being assigned to No.59 Squadron. He was immediately in the thick of the action, with an aerial victory over a Fokker D.VII on 30 August 1918. Over the course of September Carbery accounted for three more enemy aircraft when piloting an R.E.8 with a variety of different observers. No.59 Squadron had a more offensive role than No.52 Squadron, as the duties extended to ground attack in addition to the reconnaissance and artillery spotting roles. On 28 September 1918 Carbery, with Clements as his observer, in R.E.8 (C2537) scored his final aerial victory, a Halberstadt C over La Vacquerie. However, it was also on this day that a celebrated event occurred: they strafed and bombed a German artillery limber, leading to the abandonment of a 77 mm gun, which was captured by advancing British troops.

The gun was presented to Carbery, who gave it to RAF Staff College. According to Franks' article "for some years [it] became a target for raiding cadets from the Army College at Sandhurst, the RAF College's students then having to counter-attack and raid Sandhurst to get their gun back. The gun survived until WW2 when it appears to have been melted down for re-use. One of the gun's broken wheels was retained by Carbery as a souvenir.

Later, when 59 Sqn's crest was designed and presented for official recognition, Carbery's exploit was recalled. The badge was of a broken gun wheel, with the motto 'Ab Uno Disce Omnes' ('From one learn all'). There can be few men whose squadron badge came about from their own direct actions".[70]

Carbery was granted leave from 17 November 1918 to 01 December 1918. He was awarded the Distinguished Flying Cross (DFC), which was gazetted on 03 December 1918. The citation to award is quite similar to his Military Cross (MC) citation of 1917, i.e. facing numerically superior enemy and winning through:

"Capt. Douglas Hugh Moffatt Carbery, M.C. (R.F.A.). (FRANCE)

During recent operations this officer has displayed remarkable courage and skill in attacking hostile batteries, troops, etc., rendering

---

70 Cross & Cockade (International)', Volume 27, Issue No.4 (p.214).

valuable service in silencing the former and causing heavy casualties to the latter. In the air he is a bold and intrepid fighter. On 30th August he and his observer, attacked by seven Fokker biplanes, drove them off, shooting down one out of control.

(M.C. gazetted 26th March 1917)".[71]

However, Carbery's health was not improving. Upon returning from leave in December 1918 he was diagnosed with influenza on 15 December 1918. Carbery was hospitalized, eventually recovering in January 1919.

On 16 February 1919 Carbery was transferred from No.59 squadron to 52 Wing in the Middle East, subsequently transferring from the Suez and Egypt to No.31 Squadron at Bombay, India on 26 March 1919. Carbery fought in the 3rd Anglo-Afghan War in 1919. The RAF had a small but significant role in bombing Afghan positions, scattering tribesmen from gathering to viable combat formations and in the bombing of Kabul. The RAF used Handley-Page 0/400 bombers and a Handley-Page V/1500 long-range heavy bomber (one of only a handful in RAF service). Although there was no Afghan aerial opposition, at least one 0/400 bomber was lost to a storm.

In May 1919 Carbery's Armstrong Whitworth FK8 was brought down by sniper fire during an attack on Dakka, the aircraft a write-off. Carbery was involved in the bombing of Jelallabad, reaching his target via the Khyber Pass in the dark, as his bomb-laden aircraft could not clear the mountains.

On 01 August 1919 Carbery was granted a permanent commission as Captain in the RAF, which was gazetted in London Gazette of 01 August 1919. On 12 March 1920 Carbery switched from No.31 Squadron to No.5 Squadron, which had been re-formed at Quetta as an Army Air Co-operation squadron. (Another Irish ace, Giles Blennerhasset, also served with the reconstituted No.5 Squadron in India).

---

71 Supplement to the London Gazette, 3 December 1918 (31046/14319)".

Carbery was awarded a Bar to his DFC for his role in the Afghan War but there is no citation in the Supplement to London Gazette of 12 July 1920. Carbery was granted leave from 10 December 1920 to 19 December 1920. On 17 December 1920 the London Gazette carried a notice that Carbery's permanent commission at the rank of Captain had been cancelled. I have been unable to locate the relevant military police file but it would also appear that on 02 August 1920 Carbery had been charged with assault at Quetta but was acquitted. (Franks' article for 'Cross & Cockade' is also silent on the matter).

Carbery returned from India to the Middle East in January 1921, continuing on to the UK in February 1921. His time with the RAF was at an end. In the Supplement to the London Gazette of 22 March 1921 it was stated that Carbery, a "supernumerary" captain, had been restored to the establishment. However, in the London Gazette of 08 July 1921 a notification was published to correct the previous notification of March 1921. It was instead stated that Carbery had relinquished "his temporary commission on return to Army duty". In fact he was relinquishing a temporary commission on foot of a previous permanent commission that had been revoked. Carbery remains one of a select few to have won a Bar to the Distinguished Flying Cross (DFC). Since the award had been established in June 1918 it had only been awarded on less than 1,200 occasions, including the 80 occasions on which a Bar to those already awarded the medal. To have finished such a distinguished career with the aerial services on the same rank at which he held in April 1918 seems harsh.

However, Carbery continued to serve with the Royal Regiment of Artillery. On 26 October 1927 he was appointed Adjutant. This was gazetted on 23 December 1927. On 15 August 1933 the War Office issued a notice in the London Gazette of 15 August 1933 to the effect that Carbery was one of those in the Royal Regiment of Artillery promoted from Captain to Major.[72]

In World War II Carbery turned down a flying appointment but continued to serve with the Royal Artillery. He was promoted from

---

72   London Gazette, Issue 33969, p.5425.

Major to Lieutenant-Colonel in 1941. In 31 January 1941 the War Office announced that Carbery was to be allowed retain the rank of Regimental Lieutenant-Colonel on a supernumerary basis. He served as Commanding Officer, 14th West African Anti-Aircraft Brigade in Sierra Leone from May 1943 before transferred to Assam and Burma in command of Royal Artillery's Horse Batteries there. On 24 March 1944 Carbery was confirmed in rank as Colonel. The Supplement to the London Gazette of 02 July 1946 announced the retirement of Colonel Carbery (misspelled 'Carberry') with the honorary rank of Brigadier.[73]

He died in Lanner, Cornwall in April 1959.

✦ ✦ ✦

---

[73] Third Supplement to the London Gazette, Issue 37635, p.3361.

CASEY, FRANCIS DOMINIC

(9 aerial victories)

Born: 03 August 1890, Mitchelstown, Co Cork

Died: 11 August 1917.

Awards: Distinguished Service Cross, Mentioned in Despatches.

Commemorated: Adinkerke Military Cemetery, Belgium

Religion: Roman Catholic

Francis Casey was born in Mitchelstown, Co Cork. However, he is most generally associated with Co Tipperary on account of his father's position as Treasurer of Clonmel Borough Corporation.

The Irish Census 1901 records a Francis Casey as being the son of Maurice (b.1851) and Mary A Casey, née Ryan (b.1867), of 21 Parnell Street, Clonmel, Co Tipperary. Francis' grandmother, Eleanor Ryan, was resident there at the time, as was a servant. The census records Francis as having actually been born in Co Cork. His father was born in Co Limerick, his mother in Co Mayo and his grandmother in Co Galway.

The Commonwealth War Graces Commission records the next of kin names as being Son of Maurice J. and Agnes M. Casey, of Spring Garden, Clonmel, Co. Tipperary, Ireland. However, Casey's naval service records confirm his next-of-kin details. Presumably his mother was Mary Agnes Casey, variously recorded as 'Mary A' and 'Agnes M' in the different records.

Casey joined the Royal Navy as a Sub-Lieutenant, progressing to the Royal Naval Air Service. His Royal Naval Reserve service record[74] indicates that Casey served on the "Medina", a 12,350-ton P & O ship, with which he voyaged to Australia from January 1915, being discharged on 28 April 1915. Casey was subsequently with the "Excellent" after which he transferred to the RNAS via the notional "President".

Upon joining the Royal Naval Air Service Casey was originally assigned to No.1 Naval Squadron and subsequently flew as an observer with 2 Naval Wing. In June 1915 the Admiralty announced the assignment of Temporary Sub-Lieutenant F.D. Casey to the "President" for duty with the RNAS, dated to 30 May 1915. HMS President is largely an accounting category of a shore establishment, not a particular ship of that name. It was used for ships too small to have their own paymaster or for certain of those on shore-based duties.

Casey is listed in the September 1915 Navy List as:-

Temporary Sub-Lt. Francis Dominie Casey RNR, seniority 15.5.15, PRESIDENT for Air Service.

No.1 Naval Aeroplane Squadron [Foreign Service], as an Observer.

Casey's service record[75] indicates that the commission of Temporary Sub-Lieutenant F.D. Casey (Royal Naval Reserve) was terminated with effect from 27 May 1916 and he was entered as Probationary Flight Sub-Lieutenant (temporary) and appointed to "President" for the RNAS.

Casey was appointed to No.3 (Naval) Squadron, which was based at Dunkirk. According to Mike O'Connor[76] the assessment of Casey at Dover had been that he was "perhaps too dashing, always sets a good example to his fellow flyers". In his naval service records[77]

---

74   ADM 340/25 UK National Archives, Francis Dominic Casey.
75   AIR 76/79 UK National Archives, F.D. Casey.
76   O'Connor, Mike "Airfields and Airmen of the Channel Coast", pp.104-107, (Pen & Sword, 2005). See also ADM 273/9/103 at UK National Archives.
77   ADM 273/9, p.103, FD Casey, UK National Archives.

from Casey's time with No.3 (Naval) Squadron he is described as an "exceptionally daring pilot. Can handle men".

Air Vice-Marshal Leonard "Tich" Rochford's biography "I Chose the Sky" (1977) makes several references to Casey.

"Among our pilots the Irishman was an interesting and amusing character. Before becoming a pilot he had been an observer. As such he had flown for a considerable time with Red Mulock in the RNAS Dunkirk Command and there was a very close bond between them. Like many of his countrymen Casey had to have a particular pet grouse which, in his case was the delay in his promotion to the rank of Flight Lieutenant. At regular intervals, his temper reaching a high pitch, he would write out a letter of resignation and hand it to the CO's office, Mulock, who understood Casey through and through, would shelve the letter, or more likely tear it up and throw it in the fire. There the matter would rest until Casey's anger was roused again".[78]

Rochford deems most of Casey's stories unprintable but goes on to relate one incident when Casey was observer and kept jamming the control stick on his unsuspecting pilot when Casey decided the pilot wasn't taking sufficient risk in their photographic reconnaissance flight. On another occasion, as a pilot, Casey was alleged to have accidentally deliberately shorn the tail off a Bristol Scout when landing an Avro 504, as he and the Bristol pilot in question did not get along.

Casey was promoted from Flight Sub-Lieutenant to Flight-Lieutenant with effect from 01 April 1917. In May 1917 Casey was mentioned in despatches, which was gazetted on 12 May 1917, although named as "Francis Domine Casey". The London Gazette of 12 May 1917 is cited on his service record.

Casey's first aerial victory came on 17 March 1917 (St Patrick's Day), when he sent down a Halberstadt D.II out of control. He was to subsequently to claim 6 aerial victories for the month of April

---

[78] Also quoted in O'Connor, Mike "Airfields and Airmen of the Channel Coast", p.105, (Pen & Sword, 2005)

1917 when serving with 3 (Naval) Squadron. Casey was one of the leading aces flying the Sopwith Pup single-seat fighter.

RFC Communiqué No.85 of 1917 gives an idea of just how physically close victors and their victims came within each other in combat flight:

"Flight Sub-Lts FD Casey and HS Broad, 3 Squadron RNAS, attacked four Albatros scouts. Flight Sub-Lt Casey fired 80 rounds into one HA, finishing it at about 10 yards distance. The HA was seen to fall out of control. He then attacked and drove down a second HA out of control".[79]

Casey was awarded the Distinguished Service Cross (DSC), which was gazetted on 29 June 1917:

"Flight Lieutenant Francis Dominic Casey, R.N.A.S.

For conspicuous bravery and skill in attacking hostile aircraft on numerous occasions. On April 21st, 1917, he attacked a hostile two-seater machine at a range varying from 40 to 100 yards, and brought it down completely out of control. On April 23rd, 1917, on four different occasions during one flight, he attacked hostile machines, one of which was driven down in a spinning nose dive and another turning over on its side went down completely out of control. This Officer has driven down four machines completely out of control, and forced many others down."

Casey's death was reported in the *Irish Times* of 13 August 1917, *Flight* magazine of 16 August 1917 (p.835), and the *Weekly Irish Times* of 18 August 1917. Most recounted familiar details, e.g. that his father was a Justice of the Peace, Borough Treasurer of Clonmel and late manager of the National Bank Clonmel, and that Casey entered the merchant navy at an early age.

According to Norman Franks[80] Casey was killed when he crashed a newly delivered Sopwith Camel (B3805) while 'stunting' over the

---

79   Chaz Bowyer [ed] "Royal Flying Corps Communiqués 1917-1918", p.40 [London: Grub Street, 1998].
80   Norman Franks "Sopwith Pup Aces of World War I", pp18-19 [London: Osprey, 2005].

airfield at Furnes. Mike O'Connor[81] recounts a similar tale. O'Connor quotes Rochford, who claimed that Casey's friend Mulock brought two wreaths to the funeral—one from himself and another from Kathryn Martyn, a young London-based actress to whom Casey was apparently engaged. As Mike O'Connor notes, Casey epitomizes the idiom "there are old pilots and bold pilots but there aren't any old, bold pilots".

Presumably Casey's death would not have been an unusual one: there were no hard or fast rules on how the pilots should test their new mounts, and a degree of latitude would have existed on how pilots would have familiarized themselves with a new type. It's therefore not contradictory for official reports to make reference to Casey being killed on test flight duties whilst unofficial squadron accounts would have mentioned the actual aerial exploits that led to his death.

✦ ✦ ✦

---

81   Mike O'Connor "Airfields and Airmen of the Channel Coast", p.107 [Pen & Sword, 2005]

COOPER, MAURICE LEA

(6 aerial victories)

Born: 18 December 1898, Dublin

Died: 02 October 1918

Awards: Distinguished Flying Cross

Commemorated: Dadizeele New British Cemetery, Belgium; Mount Jerome Cemetery, Dublin, Ireland.

Religion: Presbyterian

Maurice Lea Cooper was born in Dublin, the son of John Hall Cooper and Gertrude Lea Cooper. The Irish Census 1901 records Maurice as being resident at Sunbury Gardens, Rathmines, Dublin with his father and his sister Nora Lea Cooper. Maurice's father is described as being a "match manufacturer". The UK Census 1911 records Cooper as being resident at Dalton House, Kendal, Westmorland—a boarder at the school.

Captain Maurice Lea Cooper—like Eric Betts, Francis Casey and Guy William Price—was a RNAS ace. A further Irish ace, Robert McLaughlin, achieved this status with a former RNAS squadron, whilst several other Irish aces, such as Thomas Proctor and Walter Tyrrell, had also served with the RNAS. However, Cooper would appear to have been less steeped in naval tradition that the other aces, his service being primarily in the RNAS, without any lengthy pre-war experiences in the RNVR.

IRISH AVIATORS OF WORLD WAR I

Cooper became a Temporary Reserve Flying Officer on 29 April 1917.[82] He was initially trained at Crystal Palace, but transferred to Redcar on 26 May 1917. On 16 July 1917 Cooper was awarded Royal Aero Club Aviator Certificate No. 5024. On 21 July 1917 Cooper transferred to Cranwell. He was promoted to Flight Sub-Lieutenant on 29 August 1917 with effect from 29 July 1917. His examination results of 29 August 1917 indicate that his flying abilities were first class, that his aerial engine and technical marks were 82.5%, while his navigation and gunnery skills were both well above 70%. His wireless, telegraphy and photography marks were his weakest, at just 66% but well over the required level. At Cranwell he was "recommended for scouts deck flying".[83] In the early days of military and naval aviation the scouts deck ships had the characteristics of cruisers with an aviation component. From Cranwell Cooper transferred to Manston on 02 October 1917. Cooper was transferred from Manston to Dunkirk on 27 October 1917. Cooper's other service records[84] indicate that he had 4 months' aero engine experience at Rolls Royce, Derby.

Cooper was posted to No.13 (Naval) Squadron, flying Sopwith Camels. In Geoffrey L Rossano's biography of Rear Admiral David Sinton Ingalls – *Hero of the Angry Sky*[85] – it's stated that Ingalls was roomed with Cooper, and described him as "a darn nice Irishman".

On 05 December 1917 Cooper secured his first victory, a 2-seater, shared with 3 other aces. On 29 January 1918 he achieved another joint aerial victory, destroying in flames a German 2-seater near Ostend. Following the merger of the Royal Flying Corps and Royal Naval Air Service, Cooper's squadron was re-numbered No.213 Squadron. The final entry on his naval service records state "Ability to command VG. A keen, reliable officer all round". On 01 April

---

82   AIR 76/104 UK National Archives, Maurice Lea Cooper.
83   ADM 273/13, p.122 UK National Archives.
84   AIR 76/103 UK National Archives, Maurice Lea Cooper.
85   Rossano, Geoffrey L. "Hero of the Angry Sky: The World War I Diary and Letters of David S. Ingalls, America's First Naval Ace" [Ohio University Press, 2013].

1918 Cooper destroyed a seaplane at Zeebrugge, killing Fl.Obmt M Behrendt and Lt D.R. Hauptvogel of *SeeFlug 1*.

On 03 June 1918 Cooper was awarded the Distinguished Flying Cross, gazetted on that date. However, the citation was not published. On 03 July 1918 Cooper was promoted to Temporary Captain, which was gazetted on 30 August 1918. On 31 July 1918 Cooper was 'slightly wounded', being hospitalized, but was discharged on 06 August 1918 to rejoin his squadron.

According to Shores et al[86], on 02 October 1918, while attempting to bomb an enemy troop train, Cooper's plane was hit by ground fire. He crashed near Gitsberg, Belgium. After the war his grave was identified near Ostend, Belgium. His service record dates this to 16 March 1921.

Cooper is also commemorated with the other members of his family at Mount Jerome Cemetery in Dublin. His mother Gertrude died on 27 January 1937, his father John on 16 November 1944.

✦ ✦ ✦

---

86   Christopher Shores, Norman Franks & Russell Guest "Above the Trenches", p.121 [London: Grub Street, 1990].

COWAN, SIDNEY EDWARD

(7 aerial victories)

Born: 23 August 1897, Downpatrick, Co Down
Died: 17 November 1916
Awards: Military Cross with 2 Bars
Commemorated: Cagnicourt British Cemetery, France.
Religion: Church of Ireland

Captain Sidney Edward Cowan was one of three brothers, two of whom died in the war whilst serving in the Royal Flying Corps.

Cowan was one of the earliest aces of the war and one of the most highly decorated. A note of caution, however, should be sounded in respect of awards to aviators in the early stages of the war, e.g. a Victoria Cross was often granted almost automatically for the destruction of a Zeppelin but as the war progressed this practice was discontinued. Similarly, Cowan's early aviation exploits, which would have been seen as so exceptional became more routine as the war continued. However, it is nevertheless quite an achievement to win the Military Cross three times, let alone over the period of just a few months, and at only 19 years of age. It should also perhaps be remembered that the early aces helped establish just what was possible in the exercise of air power generally and in the specific performance of particular machines.

Cowan's background is an interesting one: he is often claimed by Belfast, Dublin, Down and Mayo. His father was actually from Scotland. Peter Chalmers Cowan served in a number of senior engineering positions in Counties Mayo and Down, having worked as an assistant engineer to New York state and in a number of roles in railway engineering throughout Canada and the USA. In 1886 he was appointed County Surveyor of South Mayo. He met his future wife, Marion (née Johnston) of Westport, Co Mayo, whilst serving there. Additionally Peter served as Consulting Engineer to the Piers and Roads Commission. He was responsible for the Achill viaduct and swing-bridge. Cowan married in 1888. Their first son, Frederick Alex, was born in Co Mayo in 1889. In 1889 Cowan was promoted to County Surveyor of South Down, later being responsible for the entire county.[87] Cowan appears in Hansard on numerous occasions, as his position as Chief Engineering Inspector for the Local Government Board of Ireland led to his professional opinion being the subject of debate for the Great Northern Railway (Ireland) Bill in 1900.

Sidney's sister, Hilda Marion, was born in Belfast in 1894. His older brother, Philip Chalmers Cowan, was born in Belfast in 1896. Sidney was born at Downpatrick, Co Down. As one may expect from all the movement around Ireland, it is difficult to refer to the family as being from any particular locality such as Mayo, Down or Dublin. However, the Irish Census 1901 and 1911 both record Peter Chalmers Cowan and his wife Marion as being resident at Ailesbury Road, Dublin.

Sidney was educated at Castle Park, Dalkey, Co Dublin, and later at Marlborough College, Wiltshire. The UK Census 1911 records him as being resident there as a student. His older brother Philip is also present.

Both Sidney and Philip were also educated at Trinity College Dublin.

According to Jon Guttman,[88] Cowan was a founding member of No.24 Squadron when it formed in Hounslow on 01 September 1915 from a nucleus of personnel drawn from No.17 Squadron.

---

87 Institute of Civil Engineers, Minutes of Proceedings, Vol.231, Issue 1931, 01 January 1931, p.372. Citation: **E-ISSN:** 1753-7843
88 Jon Guttman "Pusher Aces of World War I", p.34 [London: Osprey, 2009].

On 25 April 1916 Cowan had an indecisive encounter with a number of Fokkers. Cowan's No.24 Squadron was on escort duty to No.27 Squadron, who were acting as the British IV Army's reconnaissance and artillery ranging aircraft. No.27 Squadron succeeded in ranging a 12-inch howitzer on Comines railway station. The work of the aces should often be seen in the context of the success of the army co-operation units rather than whether or not an enemy aircraft was shot down in the encounters: aerial superiority was the priority.

Cowan obtained his first victory on 04 May 1916, flying an Airco DH.2. For his exploits in May 1916 he was awarded the Military Cross:

"2nd Lt. Sidney Edward Cowan, R.F.C. (Spec. Res.)

For conspicuous gallantry and skill. He dived on to an enemy machine in the enemy's lines and drove it to the ground, where it was smashed, and then circled round and fired at the pilot and observer as they ran for shelter. Although forced to land through his engine stopping he contrived to restart it and got back under heavy fire".[89]

On 03 August 1916 Cowan achieved further success in aerial combat. For example RFC Communiqué No.46 of August 1916 records Cowan engaged several enemy aircraft in combat in several different encounters:

"On the IV Army front four de Havillands of 24 Sqn—piloted by Capt Andrews, Lts Cowan, Glew and Sgt Piercey, encountered 7 hostile machines near Flers. Capt Andrews fired a double drum into one at 100 yards range, which disappeared in a nosedive, but was unable to follow it owing to the proximity of other machines. The other pilots also attacked, and the hostile machines scattered east. Lt Cowan drove one down near Sailly, and pursued two others, driving them down at Velu aerodrome. Returning, he encountered another machine at which he fired several bursts from above and behind. The machine ceased fire and began to manoeuvre wildly. Lt Cowan saw the observer hanging head downwards over the side

---

89   Supplement to the London Gazette, 31 May 1916 (29602/5408).

of the fuselage. After he had fired a few more rounds it commenced to spiral, gradually descending more steeply and faster. Lt Cowan did not see it reach the ground, as he was engaged with another machine which he also drove away east".[90]

For this particular engagement Cowan was credited with an 'out of control' victory over the German LVG 2-seater.

On 09 August 1916 Cowan was slightly wounded, being temporarily blinded by wooden splinters after emptying a drum into an LVG over Bapaume, but he was back in action shortly thereafter. On 16 September 1916 he sent down a German 2-seater in flames between Sailly and Saillisel.

The award of a Bar to the Military Cross was gazetted on 20 October 1916:

"2nd Lt. Sidney Edward Cowan, M.C., R.F.C., Spec. Res.

For conspicuous gallantry and skill. He has done fine work in aerial combats, and has shot down four enemy machines.

(The Military Cross was awarded in the London Gazette dated 31st May 1916.)"[91]

The award of a 2nd Bar to the Military Cross was gazetted on 14 November 1916:

"2nd Lt. (temp. Capt.) Sidney Edward Cowan, M.C., R.F.C., Spec. Res.

For conspicuous gallantry in action. He fought a long contest with seven enemy machines, finally bringing one down in flames. He has displayed great skill and gallantry throughout.

(The Military Cross was awarded in London Gazette dated 31st May 1916. The 1st Bar was awarded in London Gazette dated 20th Oct 1916)".[92]

It should perhaps be remembered that at this time the land battles were raging, and artillery spotting was crucial. Cowan's squad-

---

90 Christopher Cole (ed) "Royal Flying Corps Communiqués 1915-1916", pp208-209 [Tom Donovan, 1990]
91 Supplement to the London Gazette, 20 October 1916 (29793/10196).
92 Supplement to the London Gazette, 14 November 1916 (29824/11083).

ron were a "scout" squadron, charged with interdiction of German artillery observation aircraft. Of the 33 aces who served with No.24 Squadron at various stages during their career, several were Irish, (e.g. Patrick Anthony Byrne, Tom Falcon Hazell and George McElroy), but it is the early pioneers such as Byrne and Cowan who perhaps have received less than is deserved, even if in Cowan's case there is much official recognition through his medal tally: less than a dozen aviators received a 2nd bar to the Military Cross.

Cowan was transferred to No.29 Squadron. On 27 November 1916 he drove down a Halberstadt D.II out of control but when maneuvering for a further kill he collided with another British pilot, William Spencer FitzRobert Saundby.

Cowan had been mentioned in articles in the *Irish Times* of 16 November 1916 and *Weekly Irish Times* 02 December 1916, the former in respect of the Bar to his Military Cross whilst the latter article categorized him as being missing in action.

Flight magazine of 26 April 1917 and the *Irish Times* of 02 May 1917 carried fine obituaries, the latter of which stated that "a letter from an officer at the front, also a Marlburian, states that he came across the grave of his schoolfellow in an old graveyard at Ablainzevelle, 12 miles south-east of Arras".

The actual correspondent was 2nd Lieutenant H.A. Freeman, who wrote "It is in very good condition with a rail round it and a cross at the head on which is written in German: "In memory of a gallant English Officer, Captain S.E. Cowan, killed in air combat"… The Germans always bury the dead well and put up crosses to them. Hoping I have not made a mistake or taken too great a liberty".[93]

Sidney's brother Philip was killed less than 1 year later, on 08 November 1917.

✦ ✦ ✦

---

93 Mike O'Connor "Airfields and Airmen: Cambrai", p.175 [Pen & Sword, 2003].

COWELL, JOHN J

(16 aerial victories)

Born: 1889, Limerick

Died: 30 July 1918

Awards: Distinguished Conduct Medal, Military Medal with Bar

Commemorated: Longuenesse (St Omer) Souvenir Cemetery, Pas de Calais, France

Religion: Roman Catholic

JJ Cowell is one of Ireland's most accomplished aces, yet receives so little recognition. He obtained 15 of his 16 aerial victories as an observer rather than a pilot, but it should be remembered that observers were gunners, not some exotic form of passenger burden upon the pilot. Too many German pilots underestimated Cowell and it is unfortunate that so many of his countrymen also do so.

One of 10 children to Michael and Kate Cowell, he was born at Carey's Road in the city of Limerick. However, some details of his childhood are unclear, e.g. the Irish Census 1911 only records 7 of the 9 children as being resident with the parents at Carey's Road, whilst the Irish Census 1901 does not record any of the family as being present in Limerick. (Some sources suggest that the Michael Patrick Cowell and Kate Benson who married in Philadelphia, Pennsylvania in 1888 were the Limerick Cowell clan but I am not convinced that this is the same family).

Initially Cowell served as a sapper with the 12th Field Company of the Royal Engineers. On 27 October 1916 he was awarded the Military Medal, as a Sapper (acting Corporal) in the Royal Engineers.[94]

JJ Cowell married on 20 December 1916 in Limerick. Upon transferring to the Royal Flying Corps he was initially posted to No.20 Squadron as a Sergeant mechanic. He became an observer/gunner in 1917, on the F.E.2.

On 05 May 1917 Cowell obtained his first aerial victory in a F.E.2b piloted by 2nd Lieutenant Reginald Conder. Throughout May 1917 Cowell secured several victories against a variety of types, including the much-vaunted Albatros D.III, i.e. the victories were against German fighters and not their artillery observation and reconnaissance aircraft.

In the build-up to the Battle of Messines the RFC stepped up the aerial offensive. Some squadrons were receiving the new Sopwith Camel, which helped tilt the balance towards the Allies. However, Cowell was still surviving with the F.E.2d, a "pusher"-type aircraft, which looked a little like a flying bedframe—the engine being mounted behind the pilot and propelling the contraption forward much in the way a ship's corkscrew operated. Although the F.E.2 had officially been withdrawn from offensive operations following the slaughter during "Bloody April" of 1917, it was still formidable if there were sufficient aircraft together to cover each other's blind spot. Like in most "pushers", the observer sat in front of the pilot and thus the aircraft had a wide angle of attack. RFC Communiqué No.91 indicates No.20 Squadron were still quite prepared to use the F.E.2d on offensive patrols, and that with Cowell as the gunner/observer it was still a lethal opponent, even against the superior Albatros DIII:

---

94   London Gazette Supplement, Issue 29805, p.10477.

"An Offensive Patrol of 20 Squadron engaged eight Albatros scouts, and Lt RM Trevethan and 2/AM JJ Cowell picked out the leader, whose machine burst into flames and crashed".[95]

Cowell was awarded the DCM, which was gazetted on 18 July 1917.[96]

"78171 Sjt. J. Cowell, R.F.C.

For conspicuous gallantry whilst assisting as an aerial gunner during bomb raids. He showed remarkable skill and judgment in the eight combats in which he has been engaged, and on several occasions has shot down hostile aircraft".

(Officers receive crosses, NCOs and other ranks receive medals, hence Cowell receiving a DCM).

In July 1917 Cowell accounted for 7 of the Luftstreitkrafte's new Albatros DV, including a double-victory over Polygon Wood on 17 July 1917, sending one of his victims down in flames.

Cowell was sent on pilot training in August 1917. Whilst training he received the Bar to the Military Medal on 27 September 1917. Initially Cowell was posted to 31 Training Squadron and subsequently 35 Training Squadron in December 1917.[97]

Upon completion of pilot training he re-joined No.20 Squadron as a pilot in the summer of 1918. Flying the Bristol F.2b Fighter he scored his only pilot victory on 29 July 1918, being shot down the next day by Oberleutnant Friedrich "Fritz" Ritter von Roth of Jasta 16, the latter's 17th of 28 victories during the war.

✦ ✦ ✦

---

95   Chaz Bowyer [ed] "RFC Communiqués 1917-1918", p.63 [London: Grub Street, 1998].
96   London Gazette Supplement, Issue 30188, pp.7262-7263.
97   AIR 76/109 UK National Archives, JJ Cowell.

CROWE, HENRY GEORGE "HAL"

(8 aerial victories)

Born: 11 June 1897, Co Dublin

Died: 26 April 1983

Awards: Military Cross (26 July 1918); Commander of the Order of British Empire (08 June 1944); Cloud and Banner Decoration with Special Cravat (25 June 1946)

Religion: Church of Ireland

In terms of his service in World War I, Air Commodore Henry George Crowe is one of the more remarkable Irish aviators: he survived being shot down 6 times in 11 days in April 1918.

Crowe was the son of John Joseph (b.1862, Dublin) and Florence Helen Crowe (b.1870, Dublin). His family lived at Simmonscourt, Donnybrook, Dublin and are recorded as being present there for the Irish Census 1901 and 1911. In the latter census Francis Howard (b.1903) and Cecil John (b.1910) were still living with the parents but Henry is recorded in the UK Census 1911 as being a boarder at Mydon, Old Colwyn, Colwyn Bay, Conway, Wales. (He was one of quite a number of Irish students—from Carlow, Dublin and Wicklow—resident at the school). Crowe was subsequently a student at Cheltenham. He studied at Trinity College Dublin, joining the OTC there, continuing to Sandhurst upon the outbreak of the war.

Crowe sought a commission as a 2nd Lieutenant to the Royal Irish Regiment in 1915. He enrolled in the Royal Military College [Sandhurst] in November 1915. Although Crowe was interested in aviation at an early age—serving as secretary of St Helen's school aviation club—and arranged his first flight at this time (in a Maurice Farman at Farnborough) Crowe served with the Royal Irish Regiment for some months until he managed to secure secondment to the Royal Flying Corps.

In William Sheehan's "The Western Front: Irish Voices from the Great War" (Gill & MacMillan, 2011) Crowe's letters home feature on a number of occasions but they are not significant contributions in an excellent work which helps convey the reality of life in the trenches through many accounts from the ranks of the infantry. Accordingly I do not intend to refer to Crowe's experiences from this source. However, in 'Cross & Cockade (International)', Volume 19, Issue Number 2, 1988, (pp.49-64), Stuart Leslie includes an extensive set of extracts from Crowe's unpublished memoirs, which provides a more comprehensive account of Crowe's military career.

On 18 July 1916 the War Office announced that Crowe was among those who had graduated from the Royal Military College [Sandhurst], Crowe's commission being as a 2nd Lieutenant to Royal Irish Regiment.[98]

Initially Crowe was posted to the Reserve Battalion in Dublin. However, the Royal Irish Regiment was badly mauled at the Somme, and in September 1916 Crowe was sent to the 6th Battalion near Kemmel. He fought in the Battle of Messines in 1917.

Crowe's posting to the Royal Flying Corps came through on 05 September 1917 and he returned to England via RFC Headquarters at Hesdin for air training. Crowe had been lucky to have survived a year on active service at the front, as the average life of a second lieutenant was a matter of days at certain stages of the Western Front campaigns of 1916 and 1917. Crowe was seconded to the RFC as an observer pending assessment of his suitability for training as a pilot. Crowe's initial training was at the School of Military Aeronautics at Reading, then to the School of Aerial Gunnery at Hythe.

---

98   London Gazette, Issue 29671, p.7103.

CROWE, HENRY GEORGE "HAL"

Crowe was assigned to No.20 Squadron in November 1917, which was based at St Marie Cappel near Cassel.

"During the winter of 1917 20 Sqn was employed on offensive patrols at about 17000 feet designed to establish air superiority for the Allies in the particular air space detailed. The pilot flew the aeroplane while the observer carried out the following. Operate the rear gun or guns. Navigate by map reading. Drop bombs 112lb and 20lb when carried. Operate camera for vertical photos. Compile recce reports. There was a spare joystick in the rear cockpit and a rudder control which would enable the observer to get the aeroplane down if the pilot was wounded. The observers flying badge, 'the flying 0' was almost a decoration. Before one could wear it one had to complete so many hours war flying; have had at least two successful air combats, and pass a viva exam in memorising a map of enemy aerodromes etc in a large area. I remember a lady asking me 'have you ever been up' as she examined my wing. And was I annoyed!"[99]

On actual aerial combat, Crowe's experiences as an observer in the Bristol Fighter are quite a universal one, echoed by many others, but interesting nonetheless:

"When the leader decided to attack he gave a pre-arranged signal and dived on the enemy firing his front gun. Then as he turned away, to repeat the attack perhaps, his observer engaged the enemy with his gun. This sort of air tactics would be carried out as opportunity presented by other aircrews. By then our own and enemy formations would get split up and the whole would develop into what was called a 'dog fight'. It was often very difficult for the observer in a scrap of this sort. The aeroplane would be flown into steep turns with excessive increases in the force of gravity, which often forced one down on one's knees on the floor of the cockpit. With no safety harness and an open cockpit one had to hold on tight with one hand to the gun mounting to avoid being thrown out. One small observer was

---

[99] Stuart Leslie, article in 'Cross & Cockade (International)', Volume 19, Issue Number 2, 1988. This extract is from p.48.

thrown out on to the top of the fuselage but was able to climb on board again.

Guns often developed stoppages during firing and this might force a crew to withdraw from the fight to clear the trouble. It was often very cold in the open cockpits with the wind howling around. We had no 'intercom' so observers used to hit the pilots over the head to draw attention to anything".[100]

Crowe scored his first victory on 13 January 1918 in a Bristol F.2b piloted by 2nd Lieutenant Thomas Colvill-Jones. Just over a week later, in a F.2b piloted by 2nd Lieutenant Douglas Cooke, Crowe achieved 2 further victories on 22 January 1918, one of which was an Albatos D.V that went down in flames. Crowe was not yet a Flying Officer, so it is clear that No.20 Squadron were throwing all they had to the fray.

On 21 February 1918 Crowe's appointment as a Flying Officer (Observer) was gazetted. Although No.20 were one of the RFC's premier scout (fighter) squadrons, the German offensive in the spring of 1918 required all squadrons to engage in fighter, reconnaissance, ground-attack and army support roles.

In March 1918 Crowe was engaged in dropping bombs and machine-gunning the advancing enemy. One occasion they were hit by ground fire and had to made a hard landing near Marieux aerodrome, but were fortunate to be in a position to avail of the services of a tank fitter from among the retreating ground forces, who was able to repair their damaged radiator and enable them get back to St Marie Cappel. In the confusion they had been posted 'missing'. On 27 March 1918 in a Bristol F.2b (B1191) piloted by the South African ace, 2nd Lieutenant Ernest Lindup, they sent down a Fokker triplane out of control over Albert when they were badly shot up. Their crippled aircraft made it back to Bruay but was so badly damaged it was stuck off the squadron's strength. On 29 March 1918, in a new Bristol F2b, Crowe was badly shot up again, with a damaged oil tank and were forced to land.

---

100 Cross & Cockade (International)', Volume 19, Issue Number 2, 1988, (p.50), Stuart Leslie.

On 02 April 1918 he was shot down by anti-aircraft fire:

"While doing an evening patrol at about 15000 feet in perfect clear weather with not a sign of trouble the pilot (my Flight Commander) was foolishly on a straight course. Suddenly a German anti-aircraft shell burst just below us and close enough for black smoke to be smelt. It was a lucky shot but German gunners were good and had good predictor instruments. We were at once covered in petrol, both tanks having been ripped open.

The pilot switched off and we did a steep dive combined with violent turns and made it to our side of the lines with a barrage of AA shells following us. We crash-landed among shell holes near a battery. Neither of us were hurt in the crash and we got out with the Lewis gun in double quick time, dashing to the shelter of the battery. German artillery had seen our landing and got the range, accurately destroying the aeroplane in minutes".[101]

Crowe had now been shot down several times during this period. On 12 April 1918 Crowe was observer to a Bristol F.2 fighter piloted by Captain Douglas Graham Cooke when they crash-landed at Boisdinghem after evacuating to there at night from St Marie Cappel, which had by that stage fallen within German artillery range and was being shelled. However, throughout March, April and May 1918 Crowe achieved a string of aerial victories, against Fokker Dr.I and Albatros D.V fighters.

On 22 April 1918 Crowe was promoted from 2nd Lieutenant to Lieutenant. By May 1918 Crowe's 6 months as an observer had been completed. His Commanding Officer, Major Johnson, acceded to his request to return to England for pilot training, which was facilitated through being sent back as a patient at Etaples to the RAF hospital at Hampstead.

Crowe's citation for the Military Cross was gazetted on 26 July 1918:

"Lt. Henry George Crowe, R. Ir. Regt. and R.A.F.

---

[101] Cross & Cockade (International)', Volume 19, Issue Number 2, 1988, (p.51), Stuart Leslie.

For conspicuous gallantry and devotion to duty when taking part in many low-flying bomb raids and reconnaissances as an observer. On every occasion he brought back very accurate and valuable information. On three occasions his machine was shot down by enemy fire, but he continued his work, and his great fearlessness and fine spirit have been an invaluable example to others. He has taken part in several air combats and been responsible for the destruction of many hostile machines".[102]

In August 1918 Crowe was posted to the Aircraft & Armament Experimental Establishment at Orfordness whilst awaiting his place on the pilots' course at Reading. At the time the Lewis guns was the subject of various 4-gun experimental mountings but none of Crowe's experiences were to have led to an operational version being adopted. In September 1918 Crowe started pilot training at Reading. He learned Morse code for artillery observation work purposes but during his time there radiotelephony was being developed but it was still transmission in one direction only and thus was not yet more than a navigational aid. By the time Crowe undertook training on the armaments course at Ealing the war was over.

In December 1918 Crowe was transferred to RAF Collinstown (the site of present-day Dublin Airport) for flying training on the Avro 504 biplane, a dual-control trainer in which the pupil sat in the rear seat. In March 1919 the IRA raided Collinstown, cutting telephone wires and making off with arms and ammunition. Crowe escaped censure, as he had turned out the guard correctly at 11pm before retiring that night. Collinstown was abandoned shortly thereafter, and flying training was transferred to RAF Baldonnel. At the end of April 1919 Crowe was posted to No.106 Squadron, one flight of which was based at Fermoy, Co Cork. Crowe was re-seconded for a 2-year period as Observer Officer, effective from 01 August 1919.[103] There are several photographs of Crowe in a D.H.9 at Fermoy, Co Cork in 1920.

---
102 Supplement to the London Gazette, 26 July 1918 (30813/8791).
103 London Gazette of 27 April 1920, Issue 31879 (p.4850).

CROWE, HENRY GEORGE "HAL"

Flight magazine, 17 February 1921 (p.114) reported Crowe being awarded Aviator's Certificate No.7911. However, an examination of the RAe Club index cards indicates that the certificate was awarded on 25 November 1920. His address in Ireland at the time was "Carahor", Shrewsbury Rd, Dublin. The British Army medal rolls index cards have "No.2 Squadron, RAF, 11 Irish Wing, Fermoy, Co Cork" as Crowe's address on 11 January 1921. It's also known from his RAF service records that Crowe was based at Baldonnel from April 1919 to November 1921. No.106 Squadron had flights at Oranmore, Co Galway, Castlebar, Co Mayo and Fermoy, Co Cork. Crowe's time in Fermoy entailed daily dropping of mail bags at army and police detachments and barracks, dropping baskets of carrier pigeons to police posts, passenger flights for VIPs, reconnaissance of road and railways for signs of damage, dropping British propaganda leaflets and acting as escort to road convoys.

If the Auxiliaries and 'Black and Tans' consisted largely of mercenary forces, the RAF in Ireland was also quite unsettled at this time, with many being long-serving veterans awaiting demobilization:

"We often saw the burnt out cars and buildings with dead and wounded lying about but never a sign of armed IRA. Bloodhounds were flown from England and taken to various points in Bristol Fighters in attempts to track the rebels but were not much use.

We were a cheery bunch of officers who came and went, some to be demobilised, others to return to their homelands in Canada, Australia and South Africa. I was the only one with a Regular Army Commission and I wanted to follow this up with a permanent commission in the RAF which I was granted later. There was much discontent after the war at the slowness of demobilisation. There were mutinies at aerodromes abroad and in England but at Fermoy we only had a refusal to go on parade which was quickly withdrawn when we officers paraded wearing our revolvers".[104]

---

104 Cross & Cockade (International)', Volume 19, Issue Number 2, 1988, (p.55), Stuart Leslie.

Crowe recalls instances of local girls' hair being shorn off for fraternizing with RAF officers. During his time with the RAF in Fermoy, Crowe had occasion to go on an operation with British troops.

"I had to give lectures at various times to the Army on air co-operation. One lecture was given in Cork Barracks and after it I went with the troops on a raid. The object of the operation was to capture several rebel leaders which were thought to be hiding in a house in the hills west of Cork city. We left the barracks at 2am in a column of open vehicles with armoured cars as escort. After 3am we debussed and marched several miles across country led by guides familiar with the area. Eventually we halted and police with troops crept up to a house which was just visible in the darkness. A knock at the door produced no answer and then we heard shouts saying that men were running away from the back of the building. We gave chase but lost them in the bushes. If we had had tracker dogs we might have caught them. It grew light as we advanced across the hills in open order in case we met up with any enemy. Then quite suddenly we came under machine gun fire. We took cover. I went over a high bank like a Grand National winner! It was in that burst of firing that we had three officers killed. But we could see columns of black smoke in the valley and thought another part of our forces had found a rebel hide-out and burnt some vehicles. We found later that by pure chance the rendezvous for our transport had been fixed just where the rebels had set up an ambush. It was our cars we had seen burning. We found the drivers' dead bodies lined up by the roadside. If the Army had asked for air co-operation from dawn this operation might not have ended so disastrously".[105]

Crowe perhaps failed to recollect that many military operations were notionally in aid of the civil power, e.g. the Auxiliaries were there in support of the police and not the military. Over time martial law was declared but for long periods the war was fought out with the military in a quasi-policing role but with unofficial extra-judicial

---

[105] Cross & Cockade (International)', Volume 19, Issue Number 2, 1988, (pp.55-56), Stuart Leslie.

killings by British forces, e.g. the Lord Mayor of Cork Tomás MacCurtain, combined with unofficial reprisals as part of a terror campaign to subdue the local population. This campaign, predictably enough, inflamed the local population whilst also alienated many of those who would otherwise have been supporters of the retention of the link between the UK and Ireland. Crowe recalls a rampage by British troops in Fermoy, in which windows were smashed and shops looted on foot of the kidnapping of a hapless British officer, Brigadier-General Lucas, who had been abducted whilst out fishing:

"I went into the town in mufti to see what would happen. Like all such situations it started quietly. The soldiers walked down into the town from barracks with their officers in mufti and we followed. Then someone shouted 'Put that bloody light out.' A brick shattered a street lamp, then it started. The troops ran into the town square. They threw bricks at shop windows shattering the plate glass with a noise like shrapnel. Householders came to their doors and were questioned without result. Then the soldiers started looting. Some stole from grocers' shops; some threw trays of trinkets from jewellers' shops into the river; some threw cycles into the river until one officer found he had thrown his own motorbike into the river! It had been down at the garage for repair. Some tried to set fire to draperies in the town centre while the owner watched from an upper window. The situation was now completely out of control and McKeever and I went back to camp. It really was a disgraceful affair. Every shop window smashed, and nearly every store looted. The end of it was that the IRA chased the troops out of the town, and the Army still did not know where their General was being held! Days later he escaped up a chimney and made his way to safety".[106]

As may be gathered, Fermoy was a garrison town, and the destruction meted out to those areas of Ireland in which a substantial proportion of the population supported the Crown was disastrous for the prospects of the UK's survival. James Burke Roche, 3rd Baron

---

106 Cross & Cockade (International)', Volume 19, Issue Number 2, 1988, (p.56), Stuart Leslie.

Fermoy, Princess Diana's great-great grandfather, took to living in London until his death in November 1920. (One Irish aviation connection with the family lies in Maurice Burke Roche, 4th Baron Fermoy and Conservative MP for King's Lynn in Norfolk, who served in the RAF during World War II). What Crowe neglects to mention is that in September 1919 the IRA had ambushed men of the King's Shropshire Light Infantry on their way to church services in the town. The intention had been to seize weaponry but a solider was killed and three were wounded in the course of seizing just 13 rifles. It should have been a propaganda disaster for the IRA but was turned into a minor recruitment tool when the British military were granted an unofficial reprisal/rampage; the KSLI, together with the Buffs (East Kent Regiment) were joined by RAF personnel in smashing of shop windows and attempting to set fires. Although it had none of the menace of the more structured unofficial reprisals, in which civilians were shot, it was part of a pattern in which much of the local population was permanently alienated from British rule.

British military history tends to record the number of British military personnel deaths as being in the region of 200 or so for the period of the Irish War of Independence while Irish newspapers of the period record at least 500 British military deaths (excluding Auxiliary troops), all these dead being quite apart from Irish servicemen in the British Army, Royal Naval or RAF who died of wounds or from pneumonia, influenza and so forth. By way of example in Cork one may consider some of the following deaths which occurred in Cork at the time Crowe was stationed in Fermoy. For example, in late November 1920 two deserters from the Essex Regiment made contact with the IRA in Bandon. On 03 December 1920, three IRA men were shot in an ambush at a rendezvous, at which they were to have met the brother of one of the deserters to arrange for procurement of British arms and munitions. It would appear that the relevant message may have reached the wrong person, a different soldier with the same surname, Taylor. Percy Taylor and Thomas Watling, the two deserters from the Essex Regiment, were executed as spies, a somewhat ridiculous action by the IRA, as why would two genuine spies have sacrificed their lives in this manner? However, the IRA point would have been that the two men could have been "useful idiots" and given some spurious promise that they would be rescued having delivered at least some IRA personnel to the British forces. The soldiers are not commemorated on the Commonwealth War Graves Commission records either, which suggests they were genuine deserters who had enough of the campaign in Ireland.

The local IRA in Cork extracted a grim tally, however, on what were notionally military personnel, e.g. an attack on a coastguard station at Ballygrovane on the Beara peninsula in West Cork had resulted in the death of Coastguardman (Grade I) Philip William Snewin and Coastguardman (Grade II) Charles Brown. (Both these deaths are commemorated by the Commonwealth War Graves Commission). In October 1920 two artillery officers stationed at Fermoy, Lt Bernard Loftus Brown and Lt David Alfred Rutherford, were killed when apparently off-duty, on a motorcycle trip to Killarney. In reality both men had previously engaged in reconnaissance work in conjunction with the security forces and therefore the IRA executions were probably on sounder ground than many of the more spurious killings in Cork, but it is unlikely that the men were on a spying mission: their trip coincided with the funeral of Terence MacSwiney, Sinn Féin Lord Mayor of Cork, who had died after 74 days on hunger strike. They may have simply been at the wrong place at the wrong time. On 15 November 1920 the IRA boarded a train at Waterfall, just outside Cork, abducting Captain Montague Henry William Green, Captain Stewart Chambers and Lieutenant William Spalding Watts. It's unclear as to why these men were removed and others left on board the train but all three were executed. It's quite likely that the IRA imagined they had gotten Lt George Edward Green, an Intelligence Officer in Cork, but the Captain MHW Green would appear to have been relatively harmless. Chambers was probably an Intelligence Officer, and had been responsible supplying the evidence for the court martial of an Australian military chaplain, Father O'Donnell, in October 1919.

However, there were often IRA executions of British military personnel in Cork who were suspected of being spies, regardless of how innocuous the situation, e.g. on 05 June 1921 three teenage boy musicians from a military band, Matthew Carson (aged 18), Charles Arthur Chapman (aged 17) and John Cooper (aged 16) were captured whilst out on an escapade from Ballincollig barracks. These boys had grown up in the pre-World War I Baden Powell delusion of scouts as something more than cannon fodder. The IRA shot all three as spies, even though Carson's father was Irish and that whatever the lads were up to it would be highly unlikely to have been sanctioned by British Intelligence. The British authorities did not seek the bodies, and it was not until the mid-1920s that they were exhumed and reinterred as military casualties. Similarly, in Charleville, north Cork, there were two soldiers of the Machine Gun Corps executed by the IRA as spies. They had apparently deserted to join a circus. It's likely that their story may have been true, as the British authorities had no interest in recovering the bodies, and they are commemorated (unnamed) in a joint grave in Charleville Cemetery, with no corresponding Commonwealth War Graves Commission commemoration. An Army Educational Corps officer and probable British Intelligence Officer, Captain Seymour Livingston Vincent, was captured near Fermoy by the IRA and executed, his body not being reinterred to Glenville, Co Cork until the late 1920s. (Vincent had apparently a notebook on his person with details of various local Protestant families, and it was therefore suggested that he was engaged in intelligence-gathering or at least attempting to engage local families in an intelligence network). As one may note from all the foregoing there was quite a grim tally outside regular ambush combat in Cork, and Crowe was lucky to avoid becoming an IRA target. However, Crowe did not have an uneventful time in Cork: he crashed a Bristol Fighter (H1590) at Fermoy on one occasion.

On 14 October 1921 Crowe's continued attachment to the RAF as Flying Officer, for a 2-year period with effect from 01 August 1921 was gazetted.[107] Crowe was transferred from Fermoy to No.39 (Bomber) Squadron at Spittlegate, Grantham in Lincolnshire. On 13 January 1922 Crowe was granted a permanent commission as Flying Officer with effect from 17 November 1921.[108] During this 2-year period secondment period Crowe served with No.39 Squadron in both the UK, later transferring to Farnborough for training in air photography.

Crowe's promotion from Flying Officer to Flight Lieutenant with effect from 30 June 1922 was gazetted on the same date. Crowe transferred from No.39 Squadron (Inland Area) to School of Photography (Inland Area) on a supernumerary basis with effect from 19 October 1922. At the end of 1924 he was posted to Air HQ in Baghdad.

Flight magazine, 12 March 1925 (p.153) reported Flight Lieutenant Crowe being assigned to HQ Iraq, 27 February 1925. Crowe's photographic reconnaissance was largely undertaken in D.H.9As, the flying time often being in support of the work of geologists in the oil exploration business. Although Crowe contracted sandfly fever on one occasion, his time in Iraq seems to have been a happy one, with weekend shooting parties in the ruins of Babylon, visits to Damascus and Beirut.

Crowe subsequently moved to Amman, Jordan for similar photographic reconnaissance duties. Overseas tours of duty with the RAF at this time entailed either 5 years in India, or 2 in Iraq plus 3 in Egypt or Palestine. Crowe's time in Jordan was served with No.14 (Bomber) Squadron for a 3-year period. During his time in Jordan Crowe flew bi-weekly sorties to assist in the monitoring of Wahabi raiders from Saudi Arabia. This work brought him south to Aqaba regularly and so he was quite fortunate to visit Petra twice. (Viewers of "Indiana Jones" will recognize the Siq of Petra, which leads to the

---

107 London Gazette, Issue 32487, p.8103.
108 London Gazette, Issue 32576, p.375.

Treasury, a magnificent edifice carved into the wall of the cliffs there and just one of hundreds of man-made caves in the valley).

Crowe was serving with No.14 Squadron at the time of the death of fellow Irish ace George McCormack, but he makes no reference to McCormack's death in 1928:

"In the Spring of 1928 Peake Pasha, chief of the Arab Legion, heard through agents that the Wahabis were planning to raid Jordan and so we increased our patrols of possible routes and wells that might be used. Then one midday we got a very bad meteorological report forecasting heavy rains which would have put Amman aerodrome out of action owing to mud. My flight was at standby so the CO decided to send it to Ramleh in Palestine which, being a grass aerodrome, would remain useable. We flew to Ramleh within the hour. The rains came and turned Amman into a bog.

The weather cleared after 48 hours and we did a desert patrol from Ramleh without seeing anything unusual. The third day was fine and we were all in the ground floor ante-room of Ramleh Mess having a pre-lunch aperitif with windows open and sun beating down on the lovely gardens when, with no warning sound, the pictures came off the walls and the whole place shook. Not a word was spoken but in a few seconds we had all gone through the windows to end up in the garden with our drinks still in our hands, looking at a great column of dust from Ramleh village where the earthquake had wrecked native houses killing a large number of people. Buildings at the aerodrome were not really damaged but aircraft in hangars had moved, damaging wing tips."[109]

In January 1929 Crowe transferred to Staff College Andover for Staff Course training. Another Irishman (and a future Air Vice-Marshal), William Munro Yool, was also sent on that course. On 07 January 1930 Crowe's promotion from Flight Lieutenant to Squadron Leader with effect from 08 January 1930 was gazetted.[110]

---

109 Cross & Cockade (International)', Volume 19, Issue Number 2, 1988, (p.63), Stuart Leslie.
110 London Gazette, Issue 33568, p.137.

He married Alicia Nora Jarratt in Knaresborough 1931.

Squadron Leader Crowe commanded the 'Demon' fighters of No.23(Fighter) Squadron from Biggin Hill for "Northland" in the annual air exercises in July 1933 and again in 1935. In the Abyssinian crisis of 1935 Crowe was posted to command No.74(F) Squadron at Malta, flying Hawker Demons. Crowe was promoted from Squadron Leader to Wing Commander.[111]

Wing Commander Crowe was assigned to Director of Operations, Department of Air Member for Supply and Organization (AMSO), with effect from 10 September 1936.[112] An Air Ministry announcement that Crowe was given temporary promotion from Wing Commander to Group Captain with effect from 01 January 1940 was gazetted on 02 January 1940.[113]

Crowe served in command of No.1 (Indian) Wing at Kohat, but returned to the Air Ministry by June 1940. On 10 June 1941 the Air Ministry announced that Crowe was promoted from (Temporary) Group Captain to (Temporary) Air Commodore with effect from 01 June 1941.[114] Crowe was stationed in RAF HQ in India from 27 October 1942, initially at AHQ Delhi.

Crowe was made a Commander of the Military Division of the Most Excellent Order of the British Empire, i.e. his was a military CBE, which was gazetted on 08 June 1944.[115] Another Irishman, Air Vice-Marshal William Tyrell, was made Knight Commander (KBE) on this date. Tyrrell's brother, like Crowe, had been an ace in World War I.

On 05 October 1944 Crowe was appointed commanding officer of No.223 (Composite) Group at Peshawar, India. He was decorated by the Chinese in respect of his wartime service in the Far East, being awarded the Order of the Cloud and Banner with Special Cravat. This was gazetted on 25 June 1946:

---

111 Flight magazine, 09 July 1936 (p.56).
112 Flight magazine of 24 September 1936 (p.320).
113 London Gazette, Issue 34765, p.24.
114 Flight magazine of 26 June 1941 (p.436).
115 London Gazette, Issue 36544, p.2582.

"Air Ministry, 25th June 1946.

The KING has granted unrestricted permission for the wearing of the undermentioned decorations conferred upon the personnel indicated in recognition of valuable services rendered in connection with the war: —

CONFERRED BY THE PRESIDENT OF THE NATIONAL GOVERNMENT OF THE REPUBLIC OF CHINA.

Order of the Cloud and Banner.

Special Cravat.

Air Commodore Henry George CROWE, C.B.E., M.C., R.A.F. (Ret'd.)".[116]

Crowe served as a Justice of the Peace following his retirement in 1946. For a man who had on several occasions been able to walk away from aircraft in which he had been shot down, it was always likely that he would engage with services for less fortunate airmen and for servicemen's welfare generally. Crowe was involved with the RAF Association and Benevolent Fund. Crowe died on 26 April 1983 at Thornton-le-Dale, North Yorkshire.

❖ ❖ ❖

---

116 London Gazette Supplement, Issue 37625, p.3219.

CRUESS-CALLAGHAN, JOSEPH

(**5 aerial victories**)

Born: 04 March 1893, Co Dublin
Died: 02 July 1918
Awards: Military Cross
Commemorated: Contay British Cemetery, France
Religion: Roman Catholic

Major Joseph Cruess-Callaghan was one of three brothers killed whilst serving with the Royal Flying Corps and Royal Air Force. "Ireland's Memorial Records" actually records four Cruess-Callaghan brothers as casualties, this arising from an erroneous duplication of Eugene. The youngest of the three brothers who died in the war, Owen, appears as 'Eugene Owen' on the War Memorial, Belvedere College, Dublin and as 'Owen' in the 1937 Reading Room of Trinity College Dublin.

Joseph was born in 1893, the eldest of six children to Joseph and Croasdella Callaghan. The Irish Census 1911 records the family as being resident at Newtown Castlebyrne, Stillorgan, Co Dublin, together with a governess and two servants. Joseph Senior was from Co Roscommon (b.1850) whilst Croasdella was from Dublin (b.1868). The Irish Census 1901 had also recorded the family as being resident at the same address. The actual name of the house was Ferndene, which was on the Deansgrange Road, Stradbrook, Blackrock, Co Dublin.

Of the six children there were five boys, three of whom joined the Royal Flying Corps or the Royal Air Force. Joseph, Stanislaus and Eugene Owen are recorded variously as Cruess Callaghan and Creuss Callaghan in the London Gazette and on their service records.

Joseph educated at Belvedere College in Dublin and later at Stonyhurst. He was known to be quite a gambler, which stayed in the family: a couple of generations later Frank and Jenny Cruess Callaghan featured on the Irish national broadcaster RTÉ, in a "Late Night Stars of Poker" television programme. However, the Cruess-Callaghan family in Ireland are most closely associated with industry: Frank Cruess-Callaghan became reasonably well known as the owner of a number of cast iron and metalwork companies, e.g. the farm machinery suppliers, Pierces, engineering company Springs and the Waterford Iron-foundries. Under his ownership, Waterford Stanley became a successful brand of cast-iron cooker manufacturers in the 1970s and 1980s. One other occupation of the Cruess Callaghan descendants is politics and public affairs: Carmencita Hederman was a Lord Mayor of Dublin and a senator in the Irish Houses of the Oireachtas (parliament), while Consuela O'Connor was a prominent environmentalist and conservationist, being a founder member of the heritage body An Taisce.

Joseph was living in Texas at the outbreak of the war, returning home to enlist with the Royal Munster Fusiliers. He subsequently joined the Royal Flying Corps from the 7th Battalion of the Royal Munster Fusiliers. He was initially posted to Norwich on 01 September 1915. On 25 January 1916 he transferred to the Central Flying School, with the rank of 2nd Lieutenant (Flying Officer). On 01 February 1916 he joined No.18 Squadron. At this time the squadron was a bomber squadron that was persevering with the Vickers FB.5 'Gunbus' before re-equipping with the FE.2b. The FE2b was a 'pusher', with the engine in the rear, propelling the aircraft forwards; the pilot sat closest to the engine with the observer in front. Although Cruess-Callaghan did not become an ace with the squadron he was not the only Irish ace to have served with this bomber squadron: Belfast man Victor Huston became an ace with No.18 Squadron, as did Galway man Albert Gregory Waller, whilst Giles Blennerhasset from Sligo scored many of his victories with the squadron.

Cruess Callaghan's first aerial victory was claimed on 26 April 1916, a Fokker E.III Eindekker, although the Germans do not have a corresponding loss on that date. According to No.18 Squadron's "Combats in the Air" submissions to the claims board[117] Cruess-Callaghan was flying F.E.2b (5232) with a Sergeant (actually 2nd Lieutenant) Mitchell as his observer when they encountered four Fokkers. Cruess-Callaghan describes the action as follows:

"Just as two of them were circling to drive at us from the rear I turned sharply towards them. The Observer got off half a drum at the first. The rest of the drum he fired at the second Fokker. Some of these last shots hit the front of the machine.

I then turned towards our lines to allow the Observer to load. Just then the third Fokker, firing at us from the rear, put the engine out of action. I put her nose down towards our lines. The other two Fokker had turned and were again firing at us from the rear. I told the Observer to crouch down. Their shooting was most accurate: bullets kept tearing past me on both sides. Some of the shots took away my elevator controls and left me without any fore and aft control. Over the lines the firing stopped. I looked into the front seat and saw the Observer lying over to the right of the nacelle with a ragged bullet hole through his skull. In crouching down he had evidently put his head on the right side of the nacelle and it was one of the shots that passed beside my right arm that killed him".

He crash-landed near Chateau de la Haie on account of the damaged controls. Cruess-Callaghan's squadron commander, G.I. Carmichael, would appear to have written in pencil "1 Fokker brought down, fight broken off", which would be a kind interpretation of the events that had transpired, although this does not preclude some third party validation of the encounter, e.g. observers on the ground may have seen one of the Germans go down on foot of the second

---

117 AIR/1/1219/204/5/2634, UK National Archives.

Fokker being hit with half a drum. Generally speaking an aircraft will not be in better flying shape having taken a half drum of Lewis gun ammunition than beforehand. The Fokker E.III Eindecker frame had steel-chrome alloy tubing instead of wood, i.e. it would have been more akin to a bicycle than the flying wood/fabric baskets that opposed it. However, the Eindecker had no ailerons on its wings, instead relying upon wing warping to control roll. Consequently any damage to control wires could have catastrophic consequences. It's entirely possible that one of the Germans suffered battle damage and limped home from the fray in a controlled descent. (The Germans do not record a fatality but this does not preclude a damaged aircraft made serviceable). Cruess-Callaghan's observer was an Irishman, 2nd Lieutenant James Mitchell, who was the son of James and Ellen Mitchell, of Cappa, Kilrush, Co Clare. He was thirty-four and had previously served with the 5th Canadian Infantry Brigade. He is commemorated at Bruay Communal Cemetery Extension, Pas de Calais, France.

On 05 June 1916 Cruess Callaghan was promoted to Captain (Flight Commander). He flew both night and day. Cruess Callaghan was wounded on 31 July 1916.[118] Three weeks later, on 27 August 1916 his brother Eugene Owen Cruess Callaghan was killed in action, serving with No.19 Squadron.

It should be remembered that—despite all the aerial victories of the aces—the vast majority of activity for those in units like No.18 Squadron was in support of army operations. Frequently the loss of enemy life inflicted from accurate artillery fire based upon photographic reconnaissance or fire direction from aircraft was more important than preventing an enemy reconnaissance patrol. It may also be borne in mind that in this context the quality of an aerial victory did not matter too much to the overall picture: whether the enemy aircraft went down out of control or was destroyed was quite secondary to the fact that it was no longer in its intended location to

---

118 *Flight* magazine of 10 August 1916 (p.666) carried the relevant notice from the War Office in which Cruess Callaghan is referenced as among the wounded.

assist German artillery. In Communiqué No.57 of October 1916, for example, Cruess Callaghan is credited with attacking searchlights with machine gun fire, extinguishing one. No.18 Squadron were bombing railways, billets and artillery batteries at this time.

Joseph Cruess Callaghan was gazetted on 03 November 1916 with the rank of Temporary Captain, with seniority to 04 October 1916. On the night of 09/10 November 1916 Callaghan—with a Sergeant Ankers as his observer—led a bombing mission on the German aerodrome at Villers, inflicting some damage and driving off an enemy aircraft that attempted to intercept them. The following night Cruess Callaghan, with Sgt Ankers, bombed Valencinnes train station, causing fires to break out there. They machine-gunned enemy searchlights on their way home, extinguishing one of the lights in the process.

He was posted to Home Establishment on 16 November 1916. A medical board examination of 20 November 1916 reported him as unfit for general service for 2 months, this assessment being reconfirmed on 29 December 1916. Cruess Callaghan was declared fit in an assessment of 06 February 1917.[119]

On 13 February 1917 Cruess-Callaghan's Military Cross citation was gazetted:

"2nd Lt. (temp. Capt.) Joseph Cruess Callaghan, R. Muns. Fus. and R.F.C.

For conspicuous gallantry in action. He displayed marked courage and skill on several occasions in carrying out night bombing operations. On one occasion he extinguished a hostile searchlight."[120]

On 22 February 1917 Cruess-Callaghan was posted to the No.2 School of Aerial Gunnery, subsequently transferring on 25 October 1917 to the No.1 School. His nickname "the Mad Major" dates from the hair-raising aerial stunts when serving as the aerial gunnery instructor there. His brother Stanislaus was killed on 27 June 1917 in a flying accident when training in Canada, and is buried at Barrie (St Mary's) Roman Catholic Cemetery, Ontario, Canada.

---
119 AIR 76/73 UK National Archives, J.C. Callaghan.
120 Supplement to the London Gazette, 13 February 1917 (29940/1540).

On 04 January 1918 Joseph Cruess-Callaghan was gazetted as Temporary Major (Squadron Commander), dated to 21 October 1917. On 01 February 1918 he was briefly assigned to No.54 Training Squadron, before being allocated to No.87 Squadron on 27 February 1918.

It was with No.87 Squadron he excelled as the "Mad Major", flying with a combination of recklessness and bravery. On 12 March 1918 he was gazetted for the rank of Squadron Commander with effect from 01 February 1918. The squadron flew the Sopwith Dolphin. Cruess Callaghan scored 4 victories in May and June in the same aircraft (serial no. D3671). Commanding officers were not supposed to engage in patrol duties, and to some extent Cruess-Callaghan would remind one of Victor Beamish in World War II.

Norman Franks' *Dolphin and Snipe Aces of World War I* (London: Osprey, 2002), p.51, contains a wonderful photo of Cruess Callaghan's Sopwith Dolphin (C4168), which is decorated with a shamrock logo on the fuselage that's over one foot in height.

On 02 July 1918 Cruess Callaghan's luck ran out, being caught within the killing range of a formation of as many as 25 German aircraft when attached to a patrol of No.60 Squadron. His gambling mindset kicked in: Cruess Callaghan attacked the formation single-handedly, presumably in an effort to scatter and cause confusion. He was shot down in flames by the great German ace Leutnant Franz Buchner of Jasta 13, the latter's 7th of 40 victories he would achieve in the war.

A member of No.87 Squadron described the fight:

"Captain Maxwell in 56 Squadron saw one machine fighting about twenty-five Germans, but the machine was hit before he could arrive close enough. I am afraid there is no doubt as to who was the pilot of that machine. He was so absurdly gallant and so absolutely without any idea of fear, that he would cheerfully take on any kind of odds. We had all implored him not to go about by himself and run such risks, but I don't think he realized that he could ever find a Hun or any number of Huns that he wasn't a match for.

We have lost in him one of the finest squadron commanders, and one of the finest fighting pilots on the Western Front today, and as such he cannot be replaced. But to us his loss is even more irreplaceable. We feel that we have lost a great stout-hearted friend, always ready to help anybody out of trouble, a gallant companion in a fight, and a sportsman to the backbone".[121]

Cruess Callaghan is commemorated at Contay Cemetery, without any corresponding Irish memorial, but his brothers Owen and Stanislaus are commemorated at the War Memorial at Belvedere College and in the 1937 Reading Room of Trinity College Dublin.

Ferndene remained in the family's hands for many decades until one of the Cruess-Callaghan sons, Frank, obtained permission to build 40 apartments on the lands of the house during the Irish property development mania of the 2000s. A lengthy battle in the planning appeals process saw the permission overturned. Unoccupied during this time—and changing hands between different developers—vandals eventually burned down Ferndene.

❖ ❖ ❖

---

[121] Mike O'Connor, *Airfields and Airmen: Somme*, pp.103-104 [Pen & Sword, 2002]

GREGORY, WILLIAM ROBERT

(8 aerial victories)

Born: 20 May 1881, Co Galway
Died: 23 January 1918, Padua, Italy
Awards: Military Cross, Chevallier of the Legion of Honour
Commemorated: Padua Main Cemetery, Italy
Religion: Church of Ireland

Major Robert Gregory is the subject of numerous myths and legends. He was the subject of four poems by William Butler Yeats, the most famous of which—'An Irish Airman Foresees his Death'—involves a person wholly unrelated to the character or beliefs of Gregory. The actual manner of Gregory's death has been the subject of so much repeated misinformation it is often difficult to re-assert the facts without making at least a passing reference to the myths.

One problem with Gregory is that the family received much information second-hand from a range of military sources, of varying quality, which was then related on to others who in turn recounted these tales as having veracity on the basis of having been told to them by the family. Gregory scored no more than 8 aerial victories yet the family often quoted a figure 3 times higher, and Yeats' poem 'Reprisals' claims 19 German planes. Similarly the claim that he was shot down in a "friendly fire" incident by an Italian pilot has taken on the air of Gospel-like certainty because members of the Gregory family had repeated it regularly. His family published a slim 40-page volume entitled *Robert Gregory 1881-1918: a centenary tribute with a foreword by his children*.[122] However, it is riven with inaccuracies regarding his military career, and evades many unpalatable issues regarding his personal life (e.g. extra-marital affairs etc) but is an excellent reference for Robert's paintings, theatre sets and other artistic and cultural engagements, e.g. book illustration, bookplate designs, woodplate and stonework.

It is perhaps best to start chronologically with Gregory. He was born on 20 May 1881 to Lady Augusta Gregory and—according to most sources—to Sir William Gregory. However, the historian R.F. Foster, in his biography of W.B. Yeats, repeats the tale that the father was actually a young local blacksmith named Seanín Farrell, who had been approached to sire the child and was then helped to emigrate to the USA. Gregory was christened William Robert (at St George's Church, Hanover Square, Mayfair, London) though he was generally known as Robert Gregory to distinguish him from Sir William.

Robert's mother was the playwright, Isabella Gregory (later styled Lady Augusta Gregory). The Gregory family was in many respects quite typical of the Anglo-Irish landlord class, and Unionist politically. Although they regarded themselves as good landlords they had opposed Gladstone's initial attempts at land reform in Ireland. For example they were hostile to the land courts system, which—when established—found almost invariably that tenants were being subjected to excessively high rents. Further, the Gregory family did not use the mechanisms of the Ashbourne Land Act 1885 to sell untenanted land to their tenants for raising additional livestock, a mechanism which was availed of by many of the more progressive landlords to enable their larger tenant farmers to build a stake and to whom subsequent ownership rights could be negotiated. Contrast this with Lord Ardilaun or Lord Kilmaine elsewhere in Co Galway, or indeed Lady Gregory's cousin, Burton Walter Persse of Moyode Castle, who made at least the token effort of allowing the purchase of 46 acres by a tenant. This may also be contrasted with the Mullaniffe O'Beirne family of Co Longford, who took the opportunity to

---

122 *Robert Gregory 1881-1918* [Colin Smythe Ltd, 1981].

sell 135 acres under the Act. (The two sons of that Anglo-Irish family were born in Warwickshire and were killed in action with the Royal Flying Corps).

Gregory's formative years would therefore have been characterized by a turbulent decade in Irish history, in which self-imagined "good" landlords became increasingly exasperated at Land Courts' findings and railed against the perceived ingratitude of their tenants for seeking to enforce their rights. It was also a decade that saw Lady Gregory move to a more sympathetic position towards tenants' rights, the Irish language and to some measure of political autonomy for Ireland. (However, some of the softening of her position regarding the right to political expression and of peaceful assembly for Irish people arose from the jailing of her English friend—later her lover—Wilfrid Scawen Blunt, who had taken a principled stand in favour of 'Home Rule' for Ireland and had been jailed in 1887 under Balfour's draconian Crimes Act, on the charge of addressing a public meeting at the Clanricarde estate in Galway).

The UK Census 1891 records Robert and his parents being resident at 3 St George's Place, St George Hanover Square, London, together with two housemaids, a cook, a butler and a "lady's maid". Robert was sent to Park Hill boarding school at Lyndhurst, Sussex in April 1891. It was here he developed a passion for cricket.

On 06 March 1892 Sir William died after a long period of bronchial and pulmonary difficulties. His will was something of a shock to Lady Gregory, with various mortgages, bequests to potential former mistresses and so forth. Robert, however, was to inherit the estate at Coole, with his mother being granted the right to reside there for the rest of her lifetime.

Robert's first rabbit-shoot took place at Coole in the Easter of 1893 but perhaps the most significant event for the family was his mother's pamphlet "A Phantom's Pilgrimage; or, Home Ruin", which was written in opposition to the second Home Rule Bill. Ultimately the Bill passed the Commons on 21 April 1893 but was defeated in the House of Lords. Robert's own political views were still unformed.

He started in Elstree School in North London in the autumn of 1893. Robert won a classical scholarship to Harrow on the strength of his Latin and started there in May 1895 at the age of 14. By the summer of 1896 Robert had established a cricket team at Coole, captained by him and composed of tenants and employees of the estate.

Robert could not remain unaffected, however, by his mother's cultural hyperactivity in the fields of playwriting, in the foundation of the Abbey Theatre and so forth. In the summer of 1897 Robert began to learn Irish. His first partridge shoot in the August when home at Coole seemed to have taken precedence over learning the Connacht Irish pronunciation, but he continued to learn Irish when in England. Better still, Lady Augusta's acquaintance with Douglas Hyde, of similar Anglo-Irish Protestant stock, provided Robert with a unique opportunity to discuss language and culture with the foremost expert of the Irish language movement. Robert and Douglas thus developed a combination of bagging pheasant and woodcock in the winter shooting whilst also helping Robert learn about the Irish language and folklore. Later Robert was to produce stage sets for Hyde's *Nativity Play*. One dark cloud for Robert was that his mother had taken upon herself the role of subsidizing the poet W.B. Yeats.

Robert's tutor at Harrow, Mr Bowen, wrote to Lady Gregory in March 1898 to indicate that Robert was bottom of his class, due to 'idleness'. His mother had just published a volume[123] on the correspondence of Robert's great-grandfather, the Under-Secretary to Ireland, 1813-1835. Typically, Robert's mother wrote in her diary "I would rather my book had failed and my boy done well".

If Lady Augusta had by 1898 become a key figure in supporting the Irish literary and cultural revival, Robert was moving towards the more orthodox political views of the Anglo-Irish ascendancy class. In 1899 he expressed his support for the Conservatives and Unionists over the Liberals in the forthcoming elections. However, despite his mother's great fear of losing Robert's affection, they travelled to Rome together in Easter 1900, in which Robert was subjected to

---

123 Mr Gregory's Letter-Box [March 1898].

a combination of high society events and lectures on Irish history, e.g. being required to accompany his mother to the graves of the exiled Irish leaders Tyrconnell and Hugh O'Neill. Robert's orthodox Unionism was perhaps a case of trying on for size the standard-issue political clothes of his father, or could also perhaps be seen as taking on a type of political camouflage for an Anglo-Irishman in England in order to allow the focus or remarkableness to be on his cricket, which seemed to arouse far more passion in him than politics.

Robert had been introduced to William Peel, grandson of Sir Robert Peel, who put Robert's mother in touch with Archibald Milman, but Robert was too young for a clerkship of the House of Commons (or perhaps just too unsuitable) and Milman refused to nominate him.[124] Robert went to Oxford instead in the autumn on 1899 to read Classics.

During the breaks in college terms Robert sketched with Jack Yeats at Coole, but although Jack enjoyed cricket it was through Lady Gregory rather than through any artistic or sporting connection that the two became acquainted. Consider also that within this circle, W.B. Yeats once had designs on the cousin of Arnold Harvey (cricketer and later Church of Ireland Bishop of Cashel & Waterford) but was warned off by Lady Gregory, who had Geraldine in mind for Robert. However, both Robert and W.B. Yeats happily sailed on the lake at Coole. In the literary circle Lady Gregory had gathered around herself Robert must nevertheless have been somewhat alienated at being a minor extra in the glittering cast. It was of course some years later that Robert allegedly capsized a boat in which he and Yeats were aboard, although Donald Thornhill Torchiana ("Yeats and Georgian Ireland"), and Torchiana and Glenn O'Malley's "Some New Letters from W.B. Yeats to Lady Gregory" [1963,1969] detail several accounts (some quite embellished tales) of mutual animosity between Yeats and Robert.

If his mother was winning respect as a writer rather than just a benefactor of others, Robert's academic trajectory was still on a

---

124 Judith Hill "Lady Gregory, An Irish Life", p.136 [Sutton Publishing, 2005]

downward spiral, a far cry from the early promise of school scholarships. After his 2nd year exams he travelled to Venice with Lady Augusta in 1900, but it was events closer to home that would affect the lives of the Gregory family to a far greater extent: in the winter of 1900 and spring of 1901 many tenants had exercised rights under the Land Acts to arbitration on the rents and the option of purchase. The Gregory family had forced many tenants through the rigors of the entire process, damaging much local goodwill needed for Lady Gregory's projects in Hiberno-English, legends and folklore, whilst also leaving Robert with a dubious legacy to inherit. In June 1902 Robert turned 21 and thus came of age for inheriting Coole. An elaborate forelock-tugging affair saw the tenants arrange bonfires and flags on the road from Gort to Coole, whilst Lady Gregory hosted a banquet for 200 more important people. However, Robert had still to finish his studies at Oxford, and it did not mark any significant change in his everyday life, although the "Wyndham" Land Act of 1903 was to prove decisive in terms of enabling tenants to buy their land through providing the necessary legal and financial mechanisms.

In the spring of 1903 Robert was given an opportunity through W.B. Yeats to produce some designs for the set and costumes of 'The Hour Glass', but it would be misleading to describe Robert as embarking on a career as an artist at that stage. By 1904 Robert was labouring under the fearsome Henry Tonks at the Slade School of Art in London. Unsurprisingly, when Augusta had a portrait commissioned of Robert-as-an-artist the portrait painter Charles Haslewood Shannon created a picture in which Robert's eyes are shut, his brushes are clean and paint tubes unopened.[125] Although W.B. Yeats alludes to this painting in his poem "The Municipal Gallery Revisited",[126] he does not comment upon the image itself. Robert contracted chicken pox in 1904, which allowed for some cover in terms of his appar-

---

125 "Robert Gregory" (oil on canvas, HLN430392) is displayed in the Dublin City Gallery, i.e. the Hugh Lane Gallery, Parnell Square, Dublin. A black and white image of the painting is reproduced in this volume.
126 David A. Ross "Critical Companion to William Butler Yeats: A Literary Reference to his Life", pp.478-479 [Infobase Publishing, 2009]

ent modest progress. In 1905 Robert was given the opportunity to design the set for 'Kincora' at the Abbey theatre. Although slow, W.B. Yeats deemed his work commendable, and it provided an entry to the life of the theatre with something to his own name rather than being seen purely in terms of his mother's financing of the theatre. A watercolour sketch by Jack Yeats of a picnic scene by the lake at Coole depicts Robert with Arnold Harvey and Lady Margaret Sackville, but there would not appear to have been any similar work of note by Robert. However, in 1905 Robert created the set for Lady Gregory's "The White Cockade", giving rise to a rare occasion in which his artistic efforts were deemed more praiseworthy than hers.

Robert graduated from the Slade School of Art in the summer of 1906. On 26 September 1906 Robert married a young-ish Welsh woman, Lily Margaret Graham Parry, at St Mary Magdalene's, Paddington. Margaret had been a fellow art student of Robert, though 3 years younger. Robert's cousin, Hugh Lane (the noted collector of Impressionist art and future donor of a priceless collection of art works to Ireland) supplied the engagement ring, and Augusta provided various gifts to the couple. Robert's best man was Augustus John, who was to become one of the foremost portrait painters of his generation. In transferring some stocks, shares and bonds to the couple, Augusta secured informally the right to continue to reside in and manage Coole, as Robert and Margaret spent time between Chelsea and Paris. Despite (or because of) Lady Gregory's Anglo-Irish background, she was delighted that Margaret was Welsh and not English.

Robert produced a unicorn image for the Dun Emer Press (later the Cuala Press), which was first used for Yeats' *Discoveries* in 1907. In March 1908 Margaret became pregnant with Richard, the first of their three children. Robert was at the studio of Jacques-Émile Blanche in Paris, whilst Margaret stencilled designs for curtains, but they also toured Italy briefly. However, their artistic activities were not self-supporting, and they were a constant drain on resources available to Coole. Robert's landscapes of Ireland were reasonable, and his stage set for 'Scapin' was well regarded, but he was slow to produce adequate material for J.M. Synge's 'The Well of Saints' and Yeats considered replacing him. Leaving aside the delicate balance between Lady Gregory and Yeats it may also be noted that Robert and Margaret sub-let their Paris apartment and returned to Coole in the summer of 1908 for the remainder of the pregnancy. As may be expected, Robert and Margaret accepted Lady Gregory's role as de facto manager of the estate, but had difficulty with the reality of Yeats' arrival for several months of the year during the summer and autumn. Yeats behaved like the head of the household when at Coole, but it must be conceded that Lady Gregory had indulged him for a decade in summers at Coole since Sir William's death and it would be a difficult transition for a difficult set of people. It was not until the summer of 1910, when Robert and Margaret's family was expanding (and Yeats was proving to be a greater drain on resources than even Lady Gregory could indulge), that Margaret had Yeats removed from the master bedroom of Coole to more modest quarters. (By 1913 Yeats was spending his summers in England with Ezra Pound).

Throughout 1909 and 1910 Robert and Margaret continued with the pretence of being Parisian artists. However, Robert also continued to design sets for the Abbey Theatre, e.g. for Yeats' "Deirdre of the Sorrows" in November 1908, for "The Image" in 1909 and for J.M Synge's "Deirdre" in January 1910. However, the Abbey was at this stage a roaring success and there was a consequent obligation to maintain the highest standards. Robert's work was good but not good enough for a theatre of such increasing stature.

The Land Courts were having an effect on the earning potential of Coole: in July 1909 several tenants had secured a 20% reduction in rents. The Land Act 1909 had also changed the landlord-tenant relationship irrevocably. The introduction of a compulsory purchase option to the operations of the Congested Districts Board had resulted in Robert making the decision to sell Coole under the terms of the legislation. However, the CDB was still only a recently established entity, with a degree of anxiety not to overstep its remit. By

GREGORY, WILLIAM ROBERT

October 1910 the CDB had still not been convinced that Coole came within the terms of the legislation. Yeats' "Upon a House Shaken by the Land Agitation" is generally accepted to have been inspired by the endgame at Coole, although the "sweet laughing eagle thoughts that grow" and the place "where passion and precision have been one" is less of a physical entity and more of the metaphorical state of transcending their present circumstances. Yeats' "Ancestral Houses", however, is a little more critical of Robert, with the great house "sinking away through courteous incompetence". A journal entry of Yeats in 1909 seems to mirror the terminology:

"I thought of this house [Coole], slowly perfecting itself and the life within it in ever-increasing intensity of labour, and then of its probably sinking away through courteous incompetence, or rather sheer weakness of will, for ability has not failed in young Gregory".[127]

At least Yeats used the phrase "courteous incompetence" rather than "weakness of will" in his poem! The Gregorys eventually began to sell the land piecemeal to tenants rather than sell the estate in its entirety to the Congested Districts Board. This satisfied some tenants but Coole was an estate in which there was tenanted and untenanted land, and also land upon which the Gregorys employed hired labour to harvest crops and tend to livestock. Lady Gregory mediated between various parties and offered a shilling in the pound towards a shortfall to Robert in a rent reduction in favour of the tenants rather than let her brother, Frank Persse, seize the tenants' cattle.[128] Robert and Margaret's second child, Augusta Anne, was born on 13 September 1911.

Robert produced a ram and goat design for the cover of his mother's play, *The Full Moon*, in 1911. This simple image, of two animals squaring off under the moon and stars, was used on the covers of all the Putnam editions of her plays. In June 1912 Robert finally had an exhibition, at the Baillie Gallery in London, which

---

127 David A. Ross "Critical Companion to William Butler Yeats: A Literary Reference to His Life", p.479 [Infobase Publishing, 2009]
128 Judith Hill, *Lady Gregory, An Irish Life* [Sutton Publishing, 2005], p.155-156.

mainly entailed paintings of Galway landscapes. In 1912 Robert's abilities in cricket saw him capped for Ireland. In a first-class match against Scotland on 29 August 1912 at Rathmines in Dublin he took 8/80, and overall his bowling average ranks well among Irish bowlers in first-class cricket (albeit his average being based only upon that match against Scotland).

The Congested Districts Board made an offer to Robert for Coole in December 1912. The combination of cash and Government stock was worth approximately £43,000 but this would amount to only £14,000 or so after all deductions and charges. Robert declined the offer.

In 1913 Margaret was expecting their third child, and Lady Gregory "bought" her a house near Newquay on the Finvarra peninsula in Galway Bay, which was named 'Mount Vernon' after George Washington's summerhouse. It was actually a house owned by the Persse family and so it was not exactly a case of Lady Gregory's money leaving her family. William Perrse and George Washington had corresponded with each other. (Some of the letters still survive in Boston. Apparently William Perrse sent a gooseberry bush to George Washington and received a stuffed turkey in return). On 21 August 1913 Robert and Margaret's 3rd child, Catherine, was born. As mentioned previously, Yeats was not made welcome that summer, and upon his offer to visit in October 1913 Robert asked Yeats to bring his own wine. Robert and Margaret asked George Bernard Shaw to be Catherine's godmother but his memorable reply of 06 September 1913 firmly but playfully rejected the offer:

"How do you know she will not abhor my opinions, or that I may be hanged yet? ... Besides, if I undertook at the font to see to her religious education, I should do it; and then where would she be?"[129]

---

129 Shaw recycled similar phrases when declining nominations for honours and tributes. When his local binman for the Synge St area of Dublin, Patrick O'Reilly, collected enough for a plaque he wrote to Shaw to approve of the inscription, who replied "Dear Pat: Your inscription is a blazing lie. I left Dublin before I was twenty and I have devoted the remainder of my life to Labour and International Socialism and for all you know I may be hanged yet".

In June 1914 Robert had a further successful exhibition, at the Chenil Gallery in London. Several paintings were sold, although it should perhaps be noted that Hugh Lane indulged the Gregorys a little through the purchase of 'Coole Lake' for the Municipal Gallery.[130]

Robert was unable to enlist at the outbreak of the war, as the protracted negotiations for the sale of Coole were still ongoing. He eventually accepted an offer from the CDB for the tenanted and untenanted lands—approximately 5,000 acres in all—whilst retaining the 1,300-acre house and demesne lands, i.e. they would attempt the transition from landlords to farmers.

In January 1915 Robert succeeded in having "The Island" exhibited at the New English Art Club, but his artistic career was over. Hugh Lane, the Gregory's family friend died in the sinking of the Lusitania on 07 May 1915. This was to give Lady Gregory several years of legal difficulties in trying to give effect to Hugh's signed-but-unwitnessed will that donated 39 pictures to the National Gallery in Dublin: the collection had been held at the London National Gallery, who had come to regard it as their own. For Robert the situation gave rise to an unexpected opportunity, albeit one about which he was not enthusiastic, as Yeats had made an attempt in June 1915 to have Robert replace Hugh Lane as Director of the National Gallery.

It is generally stated that Robert had an affair with the artist Nora Summers from late 1914 onwards. Nora Munro had also been a student of the Slade Art School and had also suffered/studied under Henry Tonks. She had married fellow student Gerald Summers in September 1912. Nora and Gerald had spent time in Italy in 1912 and 1913 working on paintings, sketches and etchings. Nora is known to have travelled around the English West Country in 1914 in a caravan, and it is suggested that Robert and Nora became reacquainted in 1915. However, it is difficult to ascertain whether Robert and Nora had any deep connection from their student years, or whether it was

---

130 There is a similarly named "Coole Lake" oil painting (1914) by Robert Gregory in the Mrs. M. Kennedy collection, as is his "Orpheus" (1901).

just some short-lived extension of artistic expression. The marriage of Nora and Gerald was none the worse for the allegations, and they went on to have five children. Their second youngest child Caitlin married Dylan Thomas, but there was a large overlapping circle of friends and acquaintances between the Gregory and Summers families, e.g. August John, Henry Lamb, Alick Schepeler, Francis MacNamara and so forth. In later years Nora was to have a relationship with Yvonne MacNamara (née Majolier). Francis was Robert's best man in 1907. Overall, there is insufficient information to make any definitive statement on Robert's relationship with Nora. However, in recent years Margaret's diaries for that period have come to light, which suggests that although a devastated Margaret had tolerated some aspects of the affair, a visit of Nora and Gerald Summers to Coole in June and July 1915 had resulted in a scandalous scene involving Nora and Robert, which left Margaret humiliated. When Lady Gregory became aware of the situation she was disgusted and furious. Augusta refused to allow Robert escort her to the station to see her off when departing for a tour of the USA. Although Augusta had an affair with Blunt, as mentioned previously, she would never have tolerated the humiliation of a partner in the manner to which Robert had subjected Margaret.[131] It is known that Margaret had a miscarriage in 1915 and although her diaries make reference to chloroform it would appear that this is nothing more than a desire to escape the marital situation, not her pregnancy.

What is certain is that Robert joined the 4th Battalion of the Connaught Rangers in September 1915. According to some accounts Robert told Yeats "I joined out of friendship".[132] In 1916 he transferred to the Royal Flying Corps. In April 1916 Robert was serving at Swingate Down near Dover, patrolling the coast on home defence duties. The Easter Rising of 1916 accelerated the exodus of Anglo-

---

131 In the *Dublin Review*, (Issue No.35 Summer 2009), there is a very well researched article by James Pethica on the matter: *Yeats' 'Perfect Man'*.
132 Gordon, Donal James *W.B. Yeats: Images of a Poet; My Permanent or Impermanent Images*, p.30. [Manchester University Press, 1970]

Irish landlords from Connacht, although the fear of agrarian violence rather than actual instances of political or agrarian violence was the driving force. This did not affect the Gregorys personally. (Of Robert's erstwhile colleagues in the Connaught Rangers the Easter Rising caused no immediate difficulty, but ultimately in June 1920 a mutiny occurred in India, partially as a consequence of British military/paramilitary policies in Ireland).

In 1981 Robert's children – Richard Gregory, Anne de Winton, Catherine Kennedy – stated that his training was difficult, e.g. his logbook records several incidents in a fortnight period in May 1916:

"May 17   Machine Smashed

May 18   Broke front strut

May 23   Buckled wheel taxi-ing

May 27   Broke vertical struts

May 30   Wheel broken".[133]

In June 1916 Robert was appointed Flying Officer. His commanding officer, Robert Loraine, was a close friend of G.B. Shaw, and thus a steady stream of praise for Robert's abilities was to reach Lady Gregory via Shaw and Yeats. Obviously, polite praise to family friends must be taken with a pinch of salt, but there would appear to have been some genuine appreciation of Robert. However, the promotion is apparently attributed to an Irishman, Major Mullholland of the Connaught Rangers and Royal Flying Corps. (This is somewhat typical of a certain Irish mentality that presumes because decisions on promotions are made by people they are therefore open to positive or negative influence, and therefore

---

133 Smythe, Colin *Robert Gregory, 1881-1918* (Colin Smythe, 1981), p.5.

likely to have been the subject of some intercession rather than just being the product of a person's ability or of being there at the right time in the war).

In July 1916 No.40 Squadron was formed, to fly the F.E.8, a "pusher" type aircraft. It was a 'scout' squadron, designed to engage with the enemy in the skies over the forthcoming Battle of the Somme. By August 1916 Robert was stationed at Bruay, with No.40 Squadron being within striking distance of both Ypres and the Somme battlefields. On 09 November 1916 he scored his first victory, a Roland whilst flying a F.E.8. By January 1917 Robert had been promoted to Flight Commander. On 09 February 1917 Robert obtained a further aerial victory, over an Albatros C, whilst flying a F.E.8 (7606). He followed the German down from about 9,000 feet to 4,000 feet, firing a full drum at 100 yards range. The Albatros dived steeply and was last seen at 500 feet, a height from which it would be reasonable to conclude the survival prospects were slim.

Due to the bad weather in Belgium Robert had managed to stage a version of Shaw's "O'Flaherty VC" on 17 February 1917 in which Mulholland starred as O'Flaherty and Robert as Tessie the maid. In March 1917 Robert scored two further victories, on 06 March 1917 and 30 March 1917, both being obtained with the first being with an F.E.8 (6384) and the second being with a Nieuport (A6680), both against Halberstadts. The 06 March 1917 aerial victory entailed Gregory firing a short burst at about 30 yards, then closing to 15 yards and firing 25 rounds into the German aircraft's fuselage. The victory on 30 March 1917 was probably over the German ace Leutnant Hans-Georg Eduard Lubbert, of Jasta 11. "Eddy" Lubbert was killed flying an Albatros DIII, so it is not certain that Gregory was the victor, but many Allied pilots mistook the wing shape of the Albatros DIII for the Halberstadt and I would imagine it to be Gregory's victory. Lubbert went down over Bailleul, not far from Arras, which is where Robert claimed his victory. The No.40 Squadron "Combats in the Air" submission to the claims board[134] states that Gregory was

---

134 AIR/1/1222/204/5/2634, UK National Archives.

GREGORY, WILLIAM ROBERT

a 12,000 feet on line patrol when he saw two Halberstadts flying among clouds south of Vimy. Gregory got on the tail of one German and fired a full drum at close range: he started firing at 40 yards and finished at 15 yards. The German turned over and was last seen side-slipping into a cloud near Bailleul. The engagement concluded at 5,000 feet.

'Cross & Cockade' [Great Britain][135] in 1973 and 1974 covered in detail the aerial victories of No.40 Squadron. Gregory is credited with having forced down an Albatros C type when flying a Nieuport. (There is passing reference to his previous 4 victories). On 06 May 1917 Robert may have forced an Albatros D scout to land. The German aircraft was not seen to crash. However, Gregory had attacked the aircraft from underneath, a tactic made popular by the great British ace Albert Ball. (It was a safe early war tactic, when there were few or no other opposing aircraft on the scene. It was also the principle behind the German night-fighter tactics of World War II, with the *Schräge Musik* "Jazz Music" upward-firing guns being used to attack the vulnerable underbelly of the British bombers). Gregory had to swerve to avoid the Albatros as it spun downwards and to clear a stoppage in his gun. He lost sight of the Albatros in this manoeuvre but other Nieuports on the patrol saw the German spin downwards. Owing to heavy anti-aircraft fire they could not follow the Albatros down but it was not seen to crash.

On 10 May 1917 he drove down another enemy aircraft. On 26 May 1917 he claimed his last victory with No.40 Squadron. According to No.40 Squadrons "Combats in the Air", Gregory was flying a Nieuport (B1548) at 19,000 feet when he observed 3 Albatros scouts at 15,000 feet, with a fourth aircraft flying above at 17,000 feet. He dived on the first aircraft, getting to within 20 yards before firing half a drum. The Albatros stalled, nose-dived, entered a spin, and then stalled again. It fell through the formation of other German aircraft, and was last seen spinning downwards. In June 1917 Gregory got to return to the UK.

---

135 Vol.4 No.4, (1973) and Vol.5 No.1, (1974).

It may also be noted that another great Irish ace, Edward 'Mick' Mannock, had encountered Robert in No.40 Squadron. Contrary to some accounts there would appear to have been no hostility between the two men, and it is possible that Robert had signed one of the facing pages of Mick's diary with the cryptic "don't let your wives sing" on 27 May 1917, perhaps a tribute to the singing, dancing and stage acting "abilities" of Mannock and the other members of the squadron.

Robert served with the Central Flying School at Upavon, Wiltshire for three months, although this was a temporary instructor role. In June 1917 Robert was awarded the Legion d'Honncur by the French Republic. In July 1917 he was awarded the Military Cross:

"On many occasions he has, at various altitudes, attacked and destroyed or driven down hostile machines, and has invariably displayed the highest courage and skill".[136]

On 16 October 1917 Robert was ordered to France, in command of No.66 Squadron. He had been promoted to Major by this stage. On 22 November 1917 No.66 Squadron were sent to Italy. By 04 December 1917 Robert was stationed at Grossa. A major Austrian offensive in December had led to a corresponding Allied counter-attack. Although Robert was not involved in offensive operations he was still in a frontline role. There was tragedy in the family, as Margaret had a miscarriage in December 1917.

On 23 January 1918 Robert was killed in an aircraft crash. One legend held that Robert had been shot down by mistake by an Italian pilot. This may appear to have been a misguided effort to console the family that Robert had not fallen in combat to the enemy. The family repeated this story for many years. (Italian records prove that there were no aircraft active in the area that day). However, WO339/42377 at the UK National Archives indicates that Robert was killed in an aviation accident, whilst the No. 66 squadron record book for the day records that Major R Gregory was flying a Sopwith Camel (B2475) on an air test exercise at 11.45 when reported killed,

---

136 *Flight* magazine of 26 July 1917 (p.753)

the machine wrecked at Monastiero. There is one story that claims Robert had been inoculated shortly before his final flight and may have suffered an adverse reaction. The RAF Museum has provided me with a copy of the casualty card for Robert, which states that he was "last seen at 2,000 feet near Monastiero. Went into spin and crashed to ground with engine full on. Investigation fails to discover cause of accident".

Lady Gregory received the news by telegram on 01 February 1918 when returning from a holiday in Galway with Margaret and the children. Lady Gregory had to return to Galway to inform Margaret of the news. Within days Lady Gregory had requested Yeats to write something by which the family could remember him.

Flight magazine of 07 February 1918 (p.160) carried a short obituary on Robert, followed by a lengthy obituary on 21 February 1918, in which his career as an artist was somewhat exaggerated:

"He was educated at Harrow, where he took the first classical scholarship of the year, and went on to New College, Oxford. Afterwards he studied painting in Paris under Blance, who declared that his work "had reached the highest level of artistic and intellectual merit". He exhibited at the New English and other galleries paintings of West Irish landscape. The Abbey Theatre in its earlier days owed much to the beautiful scenes painted and designed by him".[137]

Yeats wrote an obituary/eulogy for the *Observer* Sunday newspaper on 17 February 1918. Yeats' note of appreciation was not untruthful but did overegg the pudding a little: "I have known no man accomplished in so many ways as Major Robert Gregory ... His very accomplishment hid from many his genius. He had so many sides: painter, classical scholar, scholar in painting and in modern literature, boxer, horseman, airman ... that some among his friends were not sure what his work would be. To me he will always remain a great painter in the immaturity of his youth". Apart from aviation magazines such as *Flight* there were numerous other artist and sports publications that carried appreciations of Gregory, e.g. the *Illustrated*

---

137 *Flight* Magazine, 21 February 1918, p.209.

Sporting and Dramatic News of 23 February 1918 published the following:

"After leaving college he studied at the Slade and under Blanche in Paris, and as an artist attracted considerable attention. He was also an all-round sportsman. A good shot, a fine boxer, and excellent slow-breaker bowler [cricket], and a fearless horseman and point-to-point rider. He belonged to the Authentic Co. Galway and Phoenix Cricket Clubs, and got eight of the wickets for the Gentlemen of Ireland v Scotland match the last time he played in Dublin. At Oxford he was chosen as light-weight boxer against Cambridge, and in Paris as a candidate for the amateur championship of France. One of the leading members of the 'Galway Blazers' writes: 'A gallant fellow, one of the very best, I don't suppose he knew what fear was, for a more fearless horseman never rode over this country'. Major Gregory evidently carried these qualities from the hunting field to the fighting line, whence his Colonel wrote: 'his skill and courage were superlative', and one of his Flight Commanders adds 'A really fine airman, and a dead game man'."[138]

The references to colonel and flight commander were quoted from the *Harrow Memorials of the Great War*, which also stated that "he always did more than was asked of him" and he was "always out to do as much work as anyone else, and a little more, and, though officially not supposed to go over the lines, he came with us nearly every day".[139]

G.B. Shaw reassured Lady Gregory that, when he visited Robert in February 1917

"… in abominably cold weather, with a frostbite on his face hardly healed, he told me that the six months he had been there [with No.40 Squadron] had been the happiest of his life. An amazing thing to say considering his exceptionally fortunate and happy circumstances at

---

138 Gordon, Donal James *W.B. Yeats: Images of a Poet; My Permanent or Impermanent Images*, p.31. [Manchester University Press, 1970]
139 Philip Lee Warner, *Harrow War Memorials of the Great War, Volume V* [Publisher: the Medici Society Ltd, 1920]

home, but evidently he meant it. To a man with his power of standing up to danger—which must mean enjoying it—war must have intensified his life as nothing else could; he got a grip of it that he could not through art or love. I suppose that is what makes the soldier".[140]

However, Yeats' knowledge of Robert—combined with Lady Gregory's determination that her son have a greater legacy than the unrealized potential exhibited fleetingly in some stage props or paintings—resulted in Yeats writing 4 poems to deal with the Gregory family. (Ostensibly they were written about Robert, but in many respects were about Lady Gregory's grief and Yeats' coming to terms with the loss suffered by a family he knew so well).

"Shepherd and Goatherd" deals primarily with Lady Gregory's grief, but the question of Robert's legacy is one which remains elusive:

> i{Shepherd.} You cannot but have seen
> That he alone had gathered up no gear,
> Set carpenters to work on no wide table,
> On no long bench nor lofty milking-shed
> As others will, when first they take possession,
> But left the house as in his father's time
> As though he knew himself, as it were, a cuckoo,
> No settled man. And now that he is gone
> There's nothing of him left but half a score
> Of sorrowful, austere, sweet, lofty pipe tunes.

However, the poem most associated with Robert—"An Irish Airman foresees his Death'—is one in which Yeats ignores Robert's Unionist perspective and places him closer to his mother's views on the Irish in the service of British Empire, whilst also attempting to bestow an individuality in terms of personal accountability and motivation for Robert's decision to become an aviator:

---

140 Judith Hill "Lady Gregory—An Irish Life", p.295, quoting a letter of Lady Gregory to John Quinn. Also referenced in Yeats' appreciation of 17 February 1918 in the *Observer*.

> "Those that I fight I do not hate
> Those that I guard I do not love
> ….
> Nor law, nor duty bade me fight,
> Nor public men, nor cheering crowds,
> A lonely impulse of delight
> Drove to this tumult in the clouds;"

Yeats apparently had quite some difficulty in composing "In Memory of Major Robert Gregory", as there were numerous interventions by Lady Gregory regarding the content of many of the stanzas. Yeats had started composing the poem in April 1918 when visiting Coole, but the poem has the feel of a compromise or of being collaboration by committee. It attempts to present Robert as a renaissance man, with a regular refrain "soldier, scholar, horseman, he" but the overall effect of the poem is closer to portraying Robert as the everything-to-everyone in the manner of the German phrase "eierlegene Wollmilchsau" the wool-bearing, egg-laying, dairy-producing pig.

"Reprisals" makes reference to 19 aerial victories by Robert, but the poem is largely concerned with using Robert as a stick with which to beat the British authorities over the lawlessness of their campaign of subjugation in Ireland at the time. Locally the Troubles of this period had affected the Gregorys' part of Galway badly: Robert's cousin Frank Shawe-Taylor, had been murdered on 03 March 1920. As in so many of these cases, it is unclear as to whether the motivation was an ill-conceived combination of local agrarian agitation and political violence. However, it would appear that local republican agitators had engineered a situation in which various demands were made for rights of way to be established through lands that Shawe-Taylor didn't own but was the local land agent. Typically demands were being made that were not in his power to grant, but they served nicely to render him a target. Ironically, Shawe-Taylor had been instrumental in tenants' rights and the redistribution of land:

his proposals to George Wyndham for a Land Conference resulted in the 1902 conference chaired by Lord Dunraven that eventually gave rise to the Wyndham Land Act 1903. Lady Gregory's brother, Frank Persse, was forced to abandon Ashfield: the death sentence pronounced upon him by some republican splinter group seemed to arise from a bizarre interpretation of military or naval correspondence. Frank's godson Rodolph Algernon Persse had been killed whilst serving with the King's Royal Rifle Corps. (Algernon Persse, of Lough Cultra Castle, had died some years previously). The initial missing in action notifications would have borne the inscription "On His Majesty's Service" on the envelopes. For some reason this led the maverick group to conjure a deliberate misunderstanding, as they sought to pretend they believed that Frank was "a spy" and publicly denounce him as such. Shots were fired through the window and doors of Ashfield. (Several of Robert's cousins had died in the war: Dudley Persse had been killed on 01 February 1915 whilst serving with the Royal Dublin Fusiliers in France). The Persses also lost Roxborough, from which they were burnt out in 1922. The Persse family has first received grants of confiscated land in counties Galway and Roscommon in the 1670s, so it was a sad and bitter end to a long association with the area. Frank Persse arranged the sale of Coole demesne in October 1920 on behalf of Lady Gregory and Margaret. He sold it to a group of former tenants for just £9,000, an unacceptably low amount but better than nothing, which in effect was all the Congested Districts Board (CDB) had to offer given the number of estates they had taken on board that year.

If the much of the British media focus was on "anarchy" Lady Gregory's journals record the other side of the story, e.g. on a journey home from the Burren on 27 September 1920 she noted the following:

"I had been told that Feeney's house in Kinvara had been burned in the night ... and we passed by the ruined walls in the town. A little farther, at the cross roads, there was another ruin, McMerney's the smith. His house had also been burned down in the night by soldiers and police. He and his family had found shelter in the cart shed. It seemed so silent, we had always heard the hammer in the smithy and seen the glow of the fire".

Also on 27 September 1920 two lorries of soldiers had driven into Gort, firing live rounds randomly, searching people and raiding houses. At least one house was burnt. (Lady Gregory sent a regular anonymous article "The Week in Ireland" to the Nation newspaper to detail local and national outrages or atrocities committed by Crown forces). On 01 November 1920 Ellen Quinn, the young, pregnant wife of one of Robert's former tenants, Malachi Quinn, was killed by random gunfire from Black and Tans. On 14 November 1920 Fr Michael Griffin was killed by the Auxiliaries and his body dumped in a bog near Barna, which was an effort to make a statement that the Catholic clergy bore guilt for the death of Protestants and would be silenced accordingly. Similarly so was the abduction and murder of two young local men—Patrick and Harry Loughnane—by the Black and Tans near Shanaglish in late November 1920. (They were abducted on 26 November 1920 and their bodies found in December 1920). One of the Loughnanes was in the IRA, sometimes attributed the rank of 2nd Lieutenant, with Beagh Company, Gort Battalion, and had participated in an ambush at Castledaly on 30 October 1920 in which an R.I.C. officer was killed and 4 others disarmed. However, much of the violence by Crown forces was against innocent civilians, with the death of an IRA activist being coincidental. Further north in Co Galway, near Tuam, a Michael Moran of Carramoneen was "shot while trying to escape". In January 1921 a Jim Kirwan of Ballinastack, Corofin was "shot while trying to escape" when working in a field with his father. However, the vast majority of incidents that occurred on a daily basis were of destruction of property and possessions, life-threatening events to small tenant farmers but not necessarily in themselves fatal. Galway was relatively quiet in comparison with other parts of Ireland, although there were dozens of incidents on almost a daily basis. Lennox Robinson's "Lady Gregory's Journals, 1916-1930" (1946) covers many of the incidents of this nature.

There is a litany of local misdeeds recorded but it is Robert who is used as a procedural device through which Yeats can give rise to Lady Gregory's exasperation and disgust at the irreparable damage done to British rule in Ireland in this period.

Yeats' poem urges Robert to "rise from your Italian tomb" and stay:

> "Till certain second thoughts have come
> Upon the cause you served, that we
> Imagined such a fine affair:
> Half-drunk or whole-mad soldiery
> Are murdering your tenants there.
> Men that revere your father yet
> Are shot at on the open plain."

However, if "Reprisals" had little to do with Robert's life, the actually existing Robert had left a bitter legacy for his family in his death. His will, apparently written on a train on the way to the front, and dated 14 September 1916, stated the following:

"I wish to leave everything I have to my wife Margaret Gregory. I wish her to have the fullest freedom in the upbringing of my children and the management of my house and estate".

The last sentence was a near-impossibility to apply to the situation as it prevailed at Coole: Lady Gregory had been the manager of the house and estate, and had spent considerable sums of her own money on Coole whilst Robert and Margaret had lived between London and Paris. From Margaret's perspective, she and Robert had generously accommodated Lady Gregory years after Robert became absolute owner and that Lady Gregory had no legal right to reside surviving William's original will. However, both women had been united in grief, and Robert's 3 children had spent several months at Coole each year being raised by their grandmother. A grudging compromise was reached, but it was no thanks to Robert's cowardice in failing to make specific provision in his will to address his family's complex circumstances and in making such an odious link between conferring responsibility with the upbringing of his children with the management of his house and estate.

However, the situation had not been helped by Yeats' family: his sister Lily regarded Margaret as "just a little suburban minx … in the suburbs they like to move every three years". It conjures up images of Alan Clark's damning of Michael Heseltine as "a man who bought his own furniture" and by extension not one to properly associate with those who inherited the stately pile. Some of Lily's bitchiness was not unfounded: Margaret had living-room curtains and other fixtures and fittings stripped from the house, even as Lady Gregory resided there in her final stages of breast cancer. However, Lady Gregory regarded Yeats' wife Georgiana with disdain, noting "his wife has money, though perhaps not so much as he was led to believe". There was little support for either Margaret or Lady Gregory in their rapidly diminishing circle in Ireland, let alone Galway.

However, Margaret was the sole survivor of an IRA ambush on 15 May 1921, in which the local District Inspector of the Royal Irish Constabulary (RIC) Captain Cecil Blake was murdered, together with his wife Eliza and two British officers – Captain Fiennes Cornwallis and Lieutenant Robert McCreery of the 17th Lancers. Captain Cornwallis was the son of Colonel Cornwallis, former Conservative MP for Maidstone in Kent. Lieutenant McCreery was a recent graduate from Cavalry School. The IRA would have regarded both as legitimate targets in the conflict of the time and both men would also have perceived themselves as combatants. Similarly, Blake had been a former officer in the Royal Horse Guards and a vet with the RSPCA before the war, and had served with the Royal Field Artillery during the war. (Artillery was horse-drawn). He would have taken death as part of the price for serving with the Auxiliary Division (which were notionally auxiliary support to the police, not the Army, but were recognized by all sides as being engaged in military/paramilitary operations). However, Eliza "Lily" Blake (née Akerman) was pregnant and defenceless when murdered: the reports cite multiple wounds, having been hit by several rounds of shotgun pellet. The murder would appear to be deliberate, although it is unlikely that either she or Margaret could have identified any of the IRA volunteers. However, at least one of the IRA volunteers claimed that she was armed. All five occupants of the car were leaving a tennis party at the Bagot house at Ballyturin near Gort. (Ballyturin House was abandoned by the Bagot family and now lies in ruins). The IRA had been hoping to decapitate the British Auxiliary leadership in south Galway, with District Inspector Biggs being among their intended targets in this ambush.[141] However, District Inspector Blake was still a high value target.

This incident helped galvanize Margaret to assert herself to sell over Lady Gregory's desire to hold onto Coole, which she had rented from Margaret. However, an attempted break-in in May 1922 brought home to Lady Gregory of the precarious nature of the situation. (For example, the Gough's residence at Lough Cutra had unofficially been requisitioned by one faction of Irish government 'Irregulars' to serve as a hostel for Catholic refugees from the Belfast pogroms, but had been restored to the family by a rival faction: these were dangerous times and an window of opportunity for every category of criminal who could place a patriotic label over any plundering). Although Coole survived being burnt out in the Irish Civil War it ultimately was sold to the Department of Agriculture for forestry in March 1927, thus severing Robert's final legacy as a hunting, fishing and shooting resort for a wide circle of British and Irish civilian and military friends, and his children's link with Ireland.

On 08 September 1928 Margaret remarried, to the Gregorys' neighbour Guy Vincent Hugh Gough, of Lough Cutra.

Overall the four poems in which Robert features are not representative of his life or death. Even Robert's grave at Padua proved to

---

141 Note: the Bureau of Military History has recently released accounts by IRA volunteers Daniel Ryan, Thomas Keely, Joseph Stanford, Patrick Glynn and Michael Reilly. The full contents of these statements are beyond the scope of this book but many of their accounts of various actions in Galway are recommended reading for those with an interest beyond aviation history.

be a source of contention. It had been marked with a wooden cross, made by members of his squadron from aeroplane parts, until it was replaced. In 1923 Lady Gregory commented that the wooden cross "made with love" had been replaced with a stone "just the same as every other stone, made by contract".[142]

✦ ✦ ✦

---

[142] Judith Hill "Lady Gregory, An Irish Life", p.300 [Sutton Publishing, 2005]

GRIBBEN, EDWARD

(5 aerial victories)

Born: 10 September 1890, Co Down
Died: UNKNOWN
Awards: Military Cross
Religion: Church of Ireland

Edward Gribben was born at "Avondale", Cultra, Hollywood, Co Down.

The Irish Census 1901 records Edward being resident at Ballycultra, Hollywood, Co Down with his widowed mother Isabella, his aunt Mary Coutes and his sister Isabella.

The Irish Census 1911 records Edward as still being resident with his mother and sister in Hollywood, along with a servant. Gribben is described in the census return as an "Engineer, Motor Works Manager". His service record[143] also confirms this, stating that his 'occupation in civil life' was at Chamber Motors Ltd, University St, Belfast, Ireland from 1906 to 1914.

He joined 5th Battalion, Royal Irish Rifles on 04 August 1914. He was appointed 2nd Lieutenant with effect from 15 August 1914.[144]

He transferred into the RFC in 1916. On 18 August 1916 Gribben was sent to the 1 School of Aeronautics, transferring to 2 School of Aeronautics on 24 August 1916. The Supplement to the London

---
143 AIR 76/196 UK National Archives, Edward Gribben.
144 London Gazette 01 September 1914, Issue 28886, p.6906. Also Supplement of 23 April 1915, in which appointment dates are revised, Issue 29141, p.4041.

Gazette of 21 August 1916 confirmed Gribben's promotion from Temporary Lieutenant with the Reserve Battalion to Temporary Lieutenant with effect from 14 July 1916. On 03 October 1916 was transferred from 5 Reserve Squadron to No.24 Squadron, subsequently moving to 34 Reserve Squadron on 10 November 1916.

On 12 January 1917 Gribben was appointed Lieutenant (Flying Officer) with effect from 24 December 1916, which was gazetted on 12 January 1917.[145] Flying Sopwith 2 seaters, Gribben joined No.46 Squadron on 15 February 1917. He was transferred on 08 March 1917, subsequently moving to No.70 Squadron on 28 March 1917. This squadron flew Sopwith Camel single-seaters. On 17 July 1917 Gribben scored his first aerial victory, over an Albatros DV south of Gheluvelt. Throughout July and August 1917 Gribben was to amass 5 victories, only one of which was against a DFW 2-seater, the all the others being over Albatros fighters. Several of Gribben's victories were in large-scale mêlées. Although the RFC communiqués are often dull, functional items in comparison to the individual combat reports, they can often give an idea of the overall scale of some of the larger engagements. RFC Communiqué No.100 of 1917, for example makes reference to Gribben in one such encounter:

"In a fight between a large EA formation and SE5s of 56 Squadron and Sopwith Camels of 70 Squadron, Lt A Maybery destroyed one EA, and then he and Lt V [Verschoyle] Cronyn, also 56 Squadron, shot down another EA which crashed. Lt E Gribben, 70 Squadron, got on the tail of one EA which spun down and crashed, while Capt C Collett of the same squadron engaged one EA which antiaircraft reported to have crashed".[146]

Gribben was transferred to Home Establishment on 03 September 1917, from which he was assigned to No.44 (Home Defence) Squadron on 06 September 1917. Gribben mainly flew night operations in the defence of London. On 26 September 1917 the award

---

145 London Gazette 12 January 1917, Issue 29900, p.498.
146 Chaz Bowyer [ed] "Royal Flying Corps Communiqués 1917-1918", p.99 [London: Grub Street, 1998]

of the Military Cross to Gribben's was gazetted, although the citation was not actually published on that date. On 30 November 1917 Gribben was transferred to Aero Experimental Station at Ipswich. On 08 February 1918 Gribben was appointed Flight Commander, with effect from 01 January 1918.

On 08 January 1918 Gribben's citation for the Military Cross was gazetted:

"Lt. Edward Gribben, R. Ir. Rif., Spec. Res.. & R.F.C.

For conspicuous gallantry and devotion to duty on offensive patrols. In every combat he has been most conspicuous, continually attacking superior numbers of the enemy, destroying some and driving others down out of control. He fights with great dash and skill, and whenever any machine of his formation is in difficulties, he is invariably at hand to render assistance".[147]

On 23 February 1918 he was appointed Temporary Captain on appointment as Flight Commander, which was gazetted on 23 February 1918, being dated to 01 January 1918. Gribben appears on the Air Force List of May 1918 as a Lieutenant (Temporary Captain) with effect from 01 April 1918.

On 23 September 1918 he was transferred from the Aero Experimental Station to the Air Ministry, from which he was assigned to No.41 Squadron on 29 September 1918. No.41 Squadron were engaged in home defence duties. Gribben was wounded on 04 October 1918, just days after returning to combat duties. According to Franks et al in "Above the Trenches", Gribben's Sopwith Camel was badly shot up by a Fokker D.VII, causing him to crash-land with a wounded arm. Gribben was initially treated at Brighton throughout the month of October 1918, subsequently being transferred to Belfast on 13 November 1918. He was not discharged until 07 December 1918.

The War Office announced on 14 February 1919 that Gribben was to be promoted to Captain with the 5th Royal Irish Rifles, with effect from 16 March 1917 but would not be entitled to pay or

---

147 London Gazette Supplement, 08 January 1918, Issue 30466, p.601.

allowances other than for the period at which he was acting at that grade. Gribben was to remain seconded to the RAF.[148]

A Medical Boards examination of 20 February 1919 declared him unfit for 12 weeks. On 24 March 1919 Gribben returned to the Aero Experimental Station but was reporting to Cambridge for temporary duty. On 09 March 1919 he was transferred out of the Mid-Area to the SW Area.

Gribben was back on experimental machines on 13 July 1919 with an Experimental Squadron. On 04 October 1919 he was assigned to 86 Wing of 186 Group, based at Farnborough. Being a guinea pig was something from which Gribben never flinched but his health must have suffered: on 15 October 1919 he was injured in an aeroplane accident, being admitted to Cambridge Military Hospital, Aldershot on that date.

Gribben was assigned to the School of Rations, then on 16 December 1919 to the "S. of 1(S)ARD", which I take to imply an aircraft repair depot assignment, but his flying career was over. The London Gazette of 13 February 1920 carried a notice that Gribben, a Captain (Flying), had been transferred to the Unemployed List with effect from 24 January 1920.[149]

On 04 May 1920 Gribben was granted a short service commission as Flight Lieutenant (A), retaining his last substantive rank. This was gazetted on the 04 May 1920. However, on 10 August 1920 a notification issued from the Air Ministry to the effect that the previous notice of May (in respect of Gribben's short service commission) had been cancelled. The Supplement to the London Gazette of 22 February 1921 confirmed that Gribben relinquished his commission in the Royal Ulster Rifles with effect from 01 April 1920. Gribben retained his rank of Captain.[150]

However, the medal index card generated in respect of Gribben indicates that he also saw service as a Lieutenant in the 1st Yorkshire

---

148 London Gazette Supplement, 14 February 1919, Issue, 31179, p.2256.
149 London Gazette, 13 February 1920, Issue 31779, p.1833, and Supplement, Issue 31179, p.2256.
150 London Gazette Supplement, Issue 32236, p.1526.

and Lancashire Regiment prior to joining the 5th Royal Irish Rifles. This record would appear to date to 1922, at which time Gribben's address had been updated from 'Avondale, Cultra, Hollywood, Co Down' to 'Berkley Hall, 31 Holland Park Avenue, London W.11'.

Gribben flew over 40 different types of machines, including numerous experimental types, over the course of his career.[151] The Royal Aircraft Establishment at Farnborough may in the modern era be associated with the Hawker Harrier or the Concorde, but in Gribben's time it was the former Balloon Factory. The 'factory' element had been dropped by 1918, when research was the establishment's focus. Designations such as "FE" (Fighting Experimental), "RE" (Reconnaissance Experimental) or "SE" (Scout Experimental) related to the roles the aircraft were intended to perform. However, Gribben had occasion to encounter numerous prototypes such as the "AE" (Armoured Experimental) and "CE" (Coastal Experimental). Gribben's legacy to aviation may well be his exceptional work as a test pilot rather than his military achievements as an ace.

On 14 March 1930 the War Office announced that Captain Edward Gribben MC, 18th London Regiment, late 5th Battalion Royal Ulster Rifles (Special Reserve), was confirmed as Captain with effect from 15 March 1930. Gribben is recorded as having being in the Supplementary Reserve of Officers.[152]

The London Gazette 13 November 1934 published a noticed that Gribben had been promoted from Captain to Lieutenant Colonel with effect from 01 November 1934.[153] At this stage he was with the 18th London Rifles.

Passenger lists would appear to suggest that Edward Gribben (b.1890) travelled on the Queen Mary from Southampton to New York. The Cunard White Star liner would have been a glamorous mode of transport. The ship departed Southampton on 22 July 1936. Gribben is recorded as being an 'executive' but was travelling 'tourist' class. His

---

151 AIR 76/196 UK National Archives, E. Gribben.
152 London Gazette, 14 March 1930, Issue 33588, p.1648.
153 London Gazette Supplement, Issue 34104, pp.7271-7272.

wife Margaretta was also recorded as travelling with him. They gave their address as 91 Cromwell Road, London and their nationality as Northern Ireland. Tracing this couple from the electoral registers for the Borough of Kensington and Chelsea reveals a Captain Edward Gribben and a Margaretta Elenor Blanche Gribben as being resident at 39 Courtfield Gardens in the Redcliffe Ward. They were resident at that address in 1927, 1928, 1929, 1930, and 1933, sharing the first and second floors of a four storey over basement house with several others.

One difficulty in tracing Gribben's military career in both world wars is the large number of Edward Gribbens with whom he can become confused, e.g. the RAF Muster Roll for 1918 records E.J. Gribben under the service number 40124. However, that individual was an Air Mechanic (3rd Class) who had joined the flying services on 01 June 1916. Similarly, in World War II a Captain Edward Gribben MC (74853) was gazetted on 20 October 1939 in respect of an appointment as Flight Lieutenant with effect from 01 September 1939, with seniority backdated to 1 November 1938. That particular Edward Gribben was also gazetted on 16 December 1941. However, there was another Edward Gribben, an Edward James Gribben (35838), who was promoted with effect from 12 October 1939 and who ultimately went on to reach the rank of Wing Commander in the RAF, an OBE being gazetted on 01 January 1945 in respect of the New Year Honours list.

Similarly, the Edward Seaton Gribben appears to have died on 18 April 1965 at the RAF Hospital Uxbridge. However, his widow was 'Bessie Gribben'.

It is likely that Gribben may have served as an army reserve in World War II rather than with the RAF. His wife, Margretta Eleanor Blanche Gribben, of "The Chateau, Cushendall, Co Antrim" died on 08 February 1965. Her estate was valued at £56,699. Probate was granted to Northern Bank, which suggests that Edward pre-deceased her.

❖ ❖ ❖

HARTIGAN, EDWARD PATRICK

(**5 aerial victories**)

Born: 28 March 1893, New York, USA

Died: 20 November 1917

Commemorated: Longuenesse (St Omer) Souvenir Cemetery, Pas de Calais, France.

Religion: Roman Catholic

Hartigan was born in Manhattan, New York, USA. His parents returned to Ireland when he was about 5 years old. Patrick and Johanna Hartigan (née Casey) lived at Clonagh House, Reens, Ardagh, Co Limerick with their children. This was a substantial farm.

The Irish Census 1901 records the family as being resident at Clonagh. Patrick K Hartigan is 33, his wife Johanna 31. They had five children and five servants (four of these were farm servants whilst one was employed as a cook/domestic servant). Of their children Sarah was the eldest, aged 12, followed by Mary (aged 10), Luke (aged 8), Edward (aged 6) and Tate (aged 4). All five children are recorded as having been born in the USA. By the time of the Irish Census 1911 the family were all still resident at Clonagh, but only one servant was present. Eddie enjoyed the country life, and was reputedly a good horseman and having an accurate shot.

Eddie and his brother Luke joined the 8th Battalion of the Royal Munster Fusiliers on 20 August 1915. Four of their cousins also signed up. A more distant relation, Captain Larry Roche, appears on their attestation papers. On 14 September 1915 Edward was promoted to Lance Corporal and on 14 December 1915 to Corporal. On 17 December 1915 the 8th Battalion sailed from Southampton to Le Harve, as part of the 16th (Irish) Division. The 8th Battalion was largely annihilated in the Battle of the Somme, being merged with the 1st Battalion of the Royal Munster Fusiliers in November 1916.

Edward had received a commission as temporary 2nd Lieutenant on 27 September 1916, which was gazetted on 17 October 1917. He applied for a transfer to the Royal Flying Corps in 1917. His brother Luke stayed with the 1st Munsters and fell in the 3rd Battle of Ypres (Passchendaele) on 15 August 1917.

Hartigan joined No.57 Squadron on 27 September 1917 following a period of training in July and August 1917.[154]

His first combat experiences came immediately upon arrival, when sent on a series of bombing missions over Flanders on 27th, 28th and 30th September 1917. Hartigan was observer with Captain David Sydney Hall piloting their DH4. Hartigan's first aerial victory came on 02 October 1917. Hartigan was the observer in a DH4 (A7568) flown by Captain Hall. They were leading a formation to bomb the German aerodrome at Abeele. On their return journey the 5 DH4s were attacked by about 15 Albatros D.V scouts from Jasta 18. In the ensuing dogfight 3 of the 5 DH4s were lost, with 5 crew killed and one taken POW. However, Hartigan and Hall claimed 4 victories. (However, notwithstanding the possibility of several enemy aircraft being damaged, the Germans only record one fatal casualty from that combat).

Hartigan had suffered frostbite in his fingers from the high altitudes and the exposed nature of the observer's position. His service record, however, does not contain a medical board examination, but given the frontline position of No.57 Squadron it would perhaps be not unexpected for treatment and certification to be dealt with at a field hospital. What is certain is that in October 1917 Hartigan wrote some letters to friends and family as his fingers recovered. He was back in action by the end of October.

---

154 AIR 76/213 UK National Archives, EP Hartigan.

On 19 October 1917 his appointment as 2nd Lieutenant, Flying Officer (Observer) with effect from 28 September 1917 and with seniority to 23 August 1917, was gazetted.[155]

On 28 October 1917 Hartigan and Hall claimed another victory. However, on 20 November 1917 Hall and Hartigan crashed whilst on a weather test flight, on the first day of the Cambrai offensive. According to one of Hartigan's friends from the Royal Munster Fusiliers, William J Borthistle (a Dubliner then serving with No.25 Squadron and later killed on 29 January 1918), it would appear that Hall and Hartigan were flying in low clouds when they crashed. Borthistle wrote "I simply feel that my best pal in the World has gone … Eddie and I applied for the RFC together, came home together, and returned out here, but unfortunately could not get to the same squadron. However, after about seven weeks separation, by jolly good luck, we got on to the same aerodrome, and we saw quite a lot of each other until his Squadron was moved … I shall never forget both Eddie and Luke".[156]

Captain Hall was posthumously awarded the Military Cross. His medal citation refers to Haritgan's role in several of Hall's aerial victories "He himself shot down one in flames and another out of control, while his observer shot down two in flames".

Hall and Hartigan were buried side-by-side at Longuenesse (St Omer) Souvenir Cemetery. Hartigan's sister, Catherine Johnson, died in 1992. In St Mary's Cemetery, Rathkeale, Co Limerick her headstone has a small inscription to commemorate her brothers Luke and Edward Hartigan.

✦ ✦ ✦

---

155 London Gazette Supplement, 19 October 1917, Issue 30342, p.10742.
156 Old Limerick Journal, Vol.42, Winter 2006, article by Alan Johnson.

HAZELL, TOM FALCON

(43 aerial victories)

Born: 07 August 1892, Co Galway
Died: 04 September 1946
Awards: Military Cross, Distinguished Service Order, Distinguished Flying Cross and Bar
Religion: Church of Ireland

Tom Falcon "Bill" Hazell was one of Ireland's foremost aces. His aerial exploits against enemy aircraft and kite balloons have given him a special place in British military aviation history: Hazell was not only one of the premier 'balloon-busters', a skill which required considerable skill and courage against such well defended targets, but he also achieved remarkable success against enemy aircraft, having flown a variety of types in a number of different squadrons. Hazell served as a highly successful ace with No.1 Squadron before qualifying as an instructor at the Central Flying School and subsequently returning to action in 1918, becoming the highest-scoring pilot with No.24 Squadron.

Hazell's pre-war career has a number of gaps but it is generally accepted that he enlisted at the outbreak of the war in the South Irish Horse, being commissioned as an officer in the Royal Inniskilling Fusiliers. For example, in *British and Empire Aces of World War I* (Osprey 2001) by Christopher Shores and Mark Rolfe, Hazell is described as having attended the University of London until 1910 prior to joining the South Irish Horse in September 1914.

This would mostly accord with the details of the Irish Census of 1901 and 1911, and the UK Census 1911. The Irish Census 1901 records Hazell as being resident at Cashel (in the District Electoral Division of Moyrus), Co Galway. Tom is recorded under his birth name, "Falcon". His father Thomas was from Co Galway but his mother Cecil was from England. Thomas Senior is described in the census return as being a "land agent and magistrate". Hazell had two sisters (Frances, April) and two brothers (Cecil, Arthur). The family lived with a governess and four other servants. Tom Falcon is not present with the family in the Irish Census 1911, but another sister, Phyllis, had since been born. Their complement of servants stood at four, consisting of a chauffeur, a parlour maid, a housemaid and a cook/domestic servant. In the Irish Census 1911 Tom's mother is described as having been from Somerset.

Tom is recorded in the UK Census 1911 as being resident at Manor House, Tonbridge, Kent. His name is "Tom Falcon" in these records, with his place of birth being recorded as Clifden, Co Galway. Cecil Henry Hazell, his brother, was also a boarder there. Tonbridge was a reasonably prestigious public school, with close links to the Worshipful Company of Skinners, one of London's oldest livery companies. Manor House was one of 12 houses at Tonbridge, it being one of the boarding houses.

Hazell enlisted with the South Irish Horse as a private at the outbreak of the war. However, Hazell's medal card[157] records him as having been a Lieutenant in the Royal Inniskilling Fusiliers and a Captain in the Royal Air Force, with no mention of his service with the South Irish Horse. He was commissioned as an officer with the 7th Battalion of the Royal Iniskilling Fusiliers by late 1914.

Because of the sheer number of aerial victories it would be wholly impractical to detail all 43 here without losing any semblance of biographical structure. In Appendix I to this biography several of Hazell's aerial victories are listed, e.g. all his aerial victories when flying the Nieuport, including the type of enemy aircraft defeated on

---

157 UK National Archives reference WO 372/9.

each occasion. However, as Hazell's aviation career has been covered extensively in so many sources it would be remiss of me to not mention several which would be of interest to those with a curiosity in aerial combat.

Norman Franks' *Nieuport Aces of World War I* (Osprey, 2000) (pp.14-16) refers to Captain Hazell's 20 victories when flying Nieuport Scouts with No.1 Squadron, whilst his *SE 5/5a Aces of World War I* (Osprey) (p.38) covers Hazell's victories with No.24 Squadron.

In Mike O'Connor's excellent *Airfields and Airmen: Somme* (Pen & Sword) there is a detailed account of Hazell's near-deadly escape from the German ace Ernest Udet after destroying a balloon Udet's flight was guarding. Similarly, in Jon Guttman's *Balloon-Busting Aces of World War I* (Osprey, 2005) Hazell's encounter with Udet is also described, (pp.27-28).

Leaving aside the considerable body of aviation literature, Hazell's military career has plenty of interesting turns over the years. Starting chronologically, it would appear that Hazell served with 5 Reserve Squadron in Warwickshire from 12 April 1916 to 28 April 1916 whilst undergoing flight training. It is known that Hazell survived a bad crash in June 1916. On 28 June 1916 Temporary Lieutenant Hazell, Royal Inniskilling Fusiliers, was to be transferred to the General List, as a Flying Officer in the RFC.[158]

On 04 March 1917 Hazell achieved his first aerial victory, sending down a German out of control near Westhoek when flying a Nieuport with No.1 Squadron. He scored a further victory in both April and May 1917, but in June 1917 Hazell really made an impact, obtaining 6 victories in that month alone.

On 08 June 1917 Hazell was in a dogfight in which Herman Goring led the formation of German aircraft. Had Hazell gotten Goring's Albatros instead of the one he actually destroyed then the course of 20th century history could have been very different:

"A patrol from 1 Squadron were in the air by 5.25am. The Nieuports, led by Hazell, were attacked by five Albatri from Jasta 27, led

---

158 London Gazette Supplement, Issue 29643, p.6414.

by Herman Goring, the jasta Fuhrer. Hazell attacked an Albatros with a broad white band painted around its black fuselage behind the cockpit and his fire hit the enemy scout, which turned over before going down in a vertical dive. At some time during the fighting, Jasta 27 were joined by elements of Jasta 8 and two Nieuports were shot down behind the German lines: Second Lt R S l Boote was taken POW by Oblt Voigt of Jasta 8 and an Australian, 2Lt F D Slee, was also taken prisoner. 2Lt E G Nuding's machine was badly shot about, he crashed behind the British lines and the Nieuport was wrecked.

In the 1930s, Goring, who claimed Slee, wrote a highly colourful account of the fight, describing Slee as a brilliant, dashing flyer, with five victories to his credit, who put up a tremendous fight before being shot down. In actual fact, Slee had been with 1 Squadron for only four days, posted straight from flying school".[159]

The London Gazette Supplement of 12 June 1917 (Gazette Issue 30127) reports Hazell's promotion from Flying Officer to temporary Captain, with effect from 25 May 1917, this latter date for seniority purposes is confirmed on p.192e of the Army List of 1917.

On 26 July 1917 Hazell's Military Cross citation was gazetted: "Temp. Lt Thomas Falcon Hazell, Gen. List and R.F.C.

For conspicuous gallantry and devotion to duty. On several occasions he displayed marked courage and determination in attacking and destroying hostile aircraft".[160]

Hazell became an instructor with the Central Flying School with effect from 26 June 1918. He was described as Lieutenant (temporary Captain) Hazell, being graded as Major (Flying) upon appointment was Instructor. This was gazetted on 16 August 1918.[161] However, by this stage, on 04 July 1918 Hazell—having returned to action with No.24 Squadron—scored a victory over a Fokker D.VII, sending it down out of control near Cerisy. Over the course of July 1918 he

---

159 Alex Revell "British Single Seater Fighter Squadrons on the Western Front in World War 1", [Schiffer Publishing, 2006].
160 London Gazette Supplement, Issue 30204, p.7630.
161 London Gazette, Issue 30846, p.9581.

was to obtain 5 further aerial victories when flying the SE.5a (E1388), with 4 of these against well-defended balloon targets.

On 08 August 1918, according to RAF Communiqué No.19 of 1918, Hazell engaged in ground attack against some targets of opportunity, firing at guns and limbers which were on the road to Rosieres. Several units broke away into the fields and got bogged down. The S.E.5A was not armoured for ground attack operations and any successful attacks on ground targets usually brought it into the effective range of small arms fire from ground forces. However, August 1918 was proving to be a remarkable month, in which Hazell was to achieve an outstanding 11 aerial victories in that month alone. He also had a spectacular escape. In *A History of 24 Squadron Royal Air Force* by Captain A.E. Illingworth (1920) Hazell's survival is recorded in an incident against Jasta 4:

"August 22nd—We are pushing up north of the Somme today. Hazell again put up a marvelous show when sent out to keep balloons down, and deliberately shot one down under the very noses of its escort of seven Fokkers, which afterwards came down and riddled his machine with holes—petrol tank first shot—then his propeller and two longerons, in spite of which he fought his way back with eyes full of petrol, and landed in the aerodrome within thirty minutes of starting off".

The great German ace, Leutnant Ernst Udet, in his autobiography "Mein Fliegerleben" (published in English as "Ace of the Iron Cross"), describes the encounter, with Udet claiming Hazell as his 60th victory:

"An excited voice on the telephone: "Two balloons have just been shot down here. The enemy squadron is still circling over our position".

We take off at once, the entire fourth Staffel with all available machines. We head towards Braie at three thousand metres altitude. Below us the chain of German balloons, obliquely above us the British squadron, five SE5's. We stay below them and wait for their attack. But they hang on and seem to be avoiding a fight.

Suddenly, one of them darts past me down towards the balloons. I push down and go after him. It is their leader. The narrow streamer flaps in front of me. I push down, down, down. The air screams at the windshield. I must catch him, stop him from getting to the balloons.

Too late! The shadow of his aircraft flits across the taut skin of the balloon like a fish through shallow water. A small blue flame licks out and creeps slowly across its back. At the next moment a fountain of fire shoots up where, just a moment ago, the golden yellow bag had floated with a silken glow.

A German Fokker comes at the Englishman; a second, smaller fireball lights up alongside the larger one, and the German aircraft hits the ground wrapped in smoke and flame.

In a very tight turn, the Englishman goes almost straight down. The troops at the balloon cable winch scatter, but the S.E.5 has already flattened out and sweeps westward, hugging the ground. He is down so low that the machine and its shadow merge into one. But now I am one his tail and a wild chase begins, hardly three metres above ground. We hop telegraph poles and dodge trees. A mighty jump, the church steeple of Marécourt, but I hang on to him. I'm not about to let go.

The main highway to Arras. Flanked by high trees, it winds through the landscape like a green wall. He flies to the right of the trees, I to the left. Every time there is a gap in the trees I fire. Alongside the road, on a meadow, German infantry is camped. Although I am on his neck, he fires at them. This is his undoing.

At that moment I jump the treetops—hardly ten metres separate us—and fire. A tremor runs through his machine; it wavers, tumbles into a spin, hits the ground, bounces up again like a stone rebounding from the water, and disappears in a mighty hop behind a small birch grove. A dust cloud rises".[162]

---

[162] Mike O'Connor "Airfields and Airmen: Somme" [Pen & Sword, 2001]. Also quoted in Jon Guttman "Balloon-Busting Aces of World War I", pp.27-28, [London: Osprey, 2005].

Udet then describes an indecisive encounter with the other three S.E.5s intent on vengeance. However, despite what Udet thought he had seen—or perhaps despite the dramatic ending Udet would have liked to see—Hazell managed to nurse home his crippled aircraft (B8422). It was struck off the squadron strength as being beyond repair.

Hazell finished the war with a remarkable 43 aerial victories to his name. Although the victory standards vary between the different air forces, Hazell's score would be the joint 21st highest score of the war if one were to regard all victory claims equally. Of the famous aces ahead of him nearly every one is a household name, e.g. from Albert Ball (44 victories), to Werner Voss (48 victories), James McCudden (57 victories), Ernst Udet (62 victories), Billy Bishop (72 victories), René Fonck (75 victories) and Manfred von Richthofen (80 victories). Hazell, Mannock (61) and McElroy (47) are the three Irishmen in this illustrious company.

The citation for Hazell's Bar to the Distinguished Flying Cross (DFC) was gazetted on 02 November 1918:

"Lieut. (T./Capt.) Thomas Falcon Hazell, M.C., D.F.C.

This officer has accounted for twenty- seven enemy machines and four kite balloons.

On the 8th August he shot down two machines out of control, and destroyed a third in the air. In these combats he was so heavily engaged that all his instruments were wrecked, and only one strand of his elevator control cable was intact. Relentless in attack, Capt. Hazell displays disregard of personal danger in a marked degree.

(The award of the D.F.C. to this officer is also announced in this Gazette. M.C. gazetted 26th July 1918)."[163]

As may be noted, Hazell's achievements were outstripping the rate at which military honours were being awarded. Confusingly, his DFC citation was also gazetted in the same issue:

"Lieut. (T./Capt.) Tom Falcon Hazell, M.C.

---

163 London Gazette Supplement, Issue 30989, p.12960.

This officer is conspicuous for his bravery and skill, having destroyed twenty enemy machines and four kite balloons. On one occasion, while attacking troops on the ground, he observed seven enemy scouts above him; he at once engaged them, shooting down one out of control. Some days later he, with another pilot, attacked a kite balloon, driving it down in flames; they then attacked a second balloon, driving it down in a deflated condition.

(The award of a Bar to the D.F.C. is also announced in this Gazette; M.C. gazetted 26th July 1918)".[164]

On 05 November 1918 the Air Ministry announced that Hazell had been promoted to acting Major with effect from 22 October 1918. However, the military honours were still only catching up with his astonishing kill rate. The award of the Distinguished Service Order (DSO) was gazetted on 09 February 1919:

"Capt. (A./Maj.) Tom Falcon Hazell, M.C., .D.F.C1. (FRANCE)

A brilliant fighter, distinguished for his bold determination and rare courage, he has accounted for twenty-nine enemy machines, twenty being destroyed and nine driven down out of control; he has also destroyed ten balloons. On 4th September he rendered exceptionally valuable service in leading his flight to attack hostile balloons that were making a certain road impassable.

Within an hour three of these balloons were destroyed, Major Hazell accounting for two.

(M.C. gazetted 26th July, 1917; D.F.C. gazetted 2nd November 1918, Bar to D.F.C. same date)".[165]

Hazell's brother Cecil resigned his commission as Captain in the Royal Marines on 25 April 1919. Hazell's career at this stage was also on a slight downward trajectory as he lost rank in the post-war era, e.g. the London Gazette of 13 May 1919 (Gazette Issue 31336) reported that Hazell had relinquished the rank of Acting Major with effect from 02 April 1919 but the London Gazette of 01 August 1919

---

164 London Gazette Supplement, Issue 30989, p.12966.
165 London Gazette Supplement, Gazette Issue 31170, p.2032.

(Gazette Issue 31486) reports Hazell's promotion to Captain (Aeroplane).

Flight magazine of 08 July 1920 (p.708) carries an excellent photo of Hazell engaging in the destruction of a balloon during an RAF pageant. It was his wartime party piece. Page 710 of the same edition also carries a brief description of Hazell when describing a simulated combat.

On 30 June 1922 Hazell was among those promoted from Flight Lieutenant to Squadron Leader in the Air Ministry's half-yearly promotion list.[166]

Flight magazine of 28 December 1922 (p.791) contains details of an Air Ministry notice that Squadron Leader Hazell was transferred from No.55 (Iraq Command) to command No.45 Squadron (Iraq Command) and back again over the course of November 1922. There was some difference between the squadrons: No.55 Squadron were involved in what could euphemistically be described as "air policing" operations, although most of the tribes subjected to military aerial bombardment from D.H.9As would beg to differ with any definition that bore even the slightest resemblance to policing or patrolling. No.45 Squadron ("the Flying Camels") were engaged in troop transportation, mail services but also some ground support operations in Iraq and Palestine.

Flight magazine of 15 March 1923 (p.150) contained a notice that Major Hazell's arranged marriage to a Miss Riddick would not be taking place. It's unclear as to whether Hazell was left with a spare ring at the altar or whether he called it off. However, in other respects Hazell was becoming "non-effective", as he was transferred to RAF Depot on 22 July 1923. From one depot to another, Squadron Leader Hazell was transferred to No.III Squadron, Duxford, to command, with effect from 01 December 1923.[167] This was an old airfield that had been used by No.8 Squadron during the war and

---

166 London Gazette, Issue 32725, p.4942.
167 *Flight* magazine of 29 November 1923 (p.731).

No.2 Flying Training School until April 1923, when No.19 Squadron was re-formed there.

Hazell continued his migration around the airfields and depots. On 11 June 1927 he was posted to RAF Depot, Uxbridge. This was the HQ for the Air Defence of Great Britain (ADGB) due to its proximity to London, but Hazell was not involved in this aspect of Uxbridge. Hazell was placed on the retired list at his own request, which was gazetted on 19 July 1927.[168]

It's unclear as to whether Hazell continued to reside in the UK for any appreciable length of time. There are claims that in World War II Hazell served from February 1944 onwards as Company Commander of "D" Company, Pattingham Home Guard, which formed part of the 24th Staffordshire (Tettenhall) Battalion. However, in an Irish Times obituary of 07 September 1946 Hazell is described as being generally known as "Bill" and that his name was Falcon. He died at Newport, Co Mayo on 04 September 1946, and had supposedly been "a director of the aluminium factory at Nenagh" and a member of the United Services Club, Dublin. The Irish Times article may well be correct but it should be remembered that by this stage "Bertie" Smyllie was not as sharp as he'd been previously, and so although he could well recount some unprintable tale regarding Hazell or some other airman it was often the case that he had mistaken the person for a brother or even a completely different person of vaguely the same name. Accordingly, if there is an Irish Times article of the "Irishman's Diary" nature, there is often the potential for error in comparison to those written by the paper's reporters and journalists.

❖ ❖ ❖

---

168 London Gazette of 19 July 1927, Gazette Issue 33295, p.4649.

HEGARTY, HERBERT GEORGE

(8 aerial victories)

Born: 31 October 1887, Co Galway
Died: UNKNOWN
Awards: Military Cross
Religion: Church of Ireland

Captain Herbert George Hegarty is something of an enigma. There are several competing claims as to his origins. The UK Census 1881 records a Herbert Hegarty being born in Stockton-on-Tees, Co Durham to an Irish couple, Edward and Ellen Hegarty. However, a different Irish couple—Alexander (an Inland Revenue Official) and Margretta—appear in the UK Census 1891 in Scotland and the UK 1901 Census in England, with 5 sons born in England, Ireland and Scotland. Their Herbert Hegarty son is Scottish-born in 1887. On the other hand, the Irish Civil Registration Indexes record a Herbert George Hegarty being born in the 4th quarter (Oct-Dec) 1885 in Oughterard, Co Galway. Similarly there was an interview between a RFC veteran H.G. Hegarty with Anglia Television in 1977, but that particular individual was shot down and taken POW on Easter Sunday 1917.

The actual Irish Herbert George Hegarty was of No.60 Squadron, an ace and hailed from Co Galway. The Irish Census 1901 records Herbert's parents—John and Blanche—and one of his sisters (Pauline Ruth) as being resident in Clonbur, Co Galway, with three servants. The Irish Census 1911 records his parents, Dr John

Hegarty and Blanche du M Hegarty, resident in Clonbur, Co Galway with two servants. It is recorded that the Hegartys had four children and that Dr Hegarty was from Co Galway but that Mrs Hegarty was originally from Dublin.

Following the genealogical trail via the excellent Irish Genealogy website[169] it would appear that Dr John Adam Hegarty of Clonbur, Go Galway married Blanche du Moulin Dockeray of 10 South Frederick St, Dublin on 01 May 1882 in St Ann's Church, Dublin. Blanche's father was John William Dockeray, a clerk in holy orders.

John William Dockeray was a prominent Church of Ireland clergyman, and had served as Rector of Cong in the Diocese of Tuam, Co Galway at one stage. His son, Cecil Eustace Dockeray, (Blanche's brother and Herbert George Hegarty's uncle), was killed on 29 April 1916 in the Easter Uprising. British soldiers shot Dockeray and Mr William John Rice, who were both night clerks at Arthur Guinness. They were killed in separate incidents, together with two Canadian officers, a Lieutenant Worswick and a Lieutenant Lucas of 2nd King Edward's Horse. The Guinness Brewery had made great efforts to encourage its staff to enlist in support of the British war effort and—following the usual token court martial hearing and exoneration of the British soldiers in question who'd done the shooting—Guinness made the point of issuing a statement to refute any suggestion that the murdered men had been in any way associated with Sinn Féin.

Herbert George Hegarty's family were to become reasonably well known in the horticultural world. A pink variety of the Kaffir Lily (Schizostylis coccinea), called "Mrs Hegarty", is named after his mother Blanche. Her stock of *Schizostylis* at Poleska, Clonbur came from Lord Mountmorres of Ebor Hall, Clonbur, Co Galway. (This chap was assassinated on 25 September 1880 near Rusheen, probably not for evicting tenants—which he did—but for his role as a magistrate. Herbert's father Dr John Hegarty had to attend the scene, finding 6 gunshot wounds on the body). Blanche Hegarty's lily was exhibited in London and won an Award of Merit in 1921. The

---

169 See http://churchrecords.irishgenealogy.ie/reels/d-344-3-6-092.pdf

HEGARTY, HERBERT GEORGE

Hegartys are believed to have made a not-insignificant sum from the lily.

As may be noted, the Irish Census returns for 1901 and 1911 made no reference to Herbert and two of his other three siblings. This is perhaps the point at which so much confusion creeps in, although the matter is relatively straightforward. Firstly, Canadian records[170] list a Lance-Corporal Cecil John Hegarty (regimental number 24259) of the 13th Battalion, 3rd Infantry Brigade. His service records indicate that he was from "Poliska, Clonbre, Galway". However, looking at an actual scan of the Attestation Paper for Cecil John Hegarty it shows his DOB as 18 May 1890 and his next of kin as Mrs B du M Hegarty of Poliska, Clonbur, Galway. This is Herbert's brother Cecil, who later rose to the rank of Captain. The other sister of Herbert and Cecil was Mary Emily Catherine Moira Hegarty, who married Edward Pellew Quinan—the brother of Barrington "Punch" Quinan, a Calcutta-born Irishman who was killed in World War I serving with the Royal Flying Corps. Mary ultimately became Lady Quinan, as her husband General Sir Edward Quinan added a lengthy sequence of initials after his surname.

Herbert, however, did not emigrate to Canada with his brother. He was actually based in Hong Kong at the outbreak of the war. Hegarty is mentioned in the London and China Telegraph of 17 July 1916, on page 4, which states that Mr Herbert George Hegarty was to be a second lieutenant in the Scouts Company of the Hong Kong Volunteer Corps.

Further, there is a U.S./Canada Border Crossing record for Herbert G Hegarty on 03 April 1917 and 04 April 1917. He arrived at Victoria, British Columbia from Hong Kong on the "Empress of Russia". His birthplace was recorded as "Clonbud", Ireland, and being born in 1882. Presumably this is a mis-transcription and it was intended to make reference to Clonbur, Co Galway. The 1882

---

[170] 'List of Officers and Men Serving in the First Canadian Contingent of the British Expeditionary Force, 1914'. Compiled by the Pay and Record Office, Canadian Contingent, 36 Victoria St, London, SW.

date may well be 1887: it is uncommon for a horizontal bar to be placed on the number 7, thus allowing for potential confusion with the number 2 if followed with a full stop. It would appear that Hegarty had travelled from Hong Kong to Canada to enlist. However, I cannot locate a file in respect of Hegarty on the database of Attestation Papers and Enlistment Forms of the Canadian Expeditionary Force.

This is further confirmed by the passenger lists of the 'St Paul', which travelled from New York to Liverpool in April 1917, arriving in Liverpool on 30 April 1917. Hegarty travels First Class. His occupation is described as "banker's assistant" with his 'country of last permanent residence' being China although his address is given as "Poliska, Clonbur, Co Galway". In all likelihood Hegarty, now thirty years of age, may have had the intention of enlisting in Canada with his brother but continued to the UK to do so instead.

Hegarty's service record[171] states that his date of birth was 31 October 1887 and that his permanent home address was Poliska, Clonbur, Co Galway. (Poliska House is still in existence). Hegarty's next-of-kin is recorded as Mrs E.J. Hegarty of "Lampeter, Mount Hermon, Woking, Surrey". (Apparently Lampeter Close is just off Mount Hermon Road in Woking).

Solving the mysteries of Hegarty's Hong Kong journey, his records state that in civilian life Hegarty was a banker with the Hong Kong & Shanghai Banking Corporation (HSBC) from 1909 to 1917. (Confusingly his work address is given as 9 Gracechurch St, which was the bank's HQ address in the City of London). Quite why he returned to Europe from Hong Kong via Canada is a matter for speculation.

Regardless of whether Herbert George Hegarty reached the Royal Flying Corps via a combination of Galway, Hong Kong, Canada and Woking it is clear that Hegarty was promoted to Temporary 2nd Lieutenant with effect from 08 June 1917.[172]

---

171 AIR 76/220 Herbert George Hegarty, UK National Archives.
172 Supplement to the London Gazette of 30 June 1917 (Gazette Issue 30158).

Hegarty began his training with 5 Training Squadron on 14 July 1917. He transferred to 28 Training Squadron on 13 September 1917, being appointed Flying Officer with effect from 08 September 1917. (On 03 October 1917 he was confirmed in the rank of 2nd Lieutenant). On 15 September 1917 Hegarty was transferred to the 2 Aerial School of Aeronautics, subsequently being posted to the Central Flying School's "A" Squadron on 16 October 1917.

On 28 November 1917 Hegarty finally got to a frontline squadron, joining No.60 Squadron, flying S.E.5s. However, his impact was not immediate: that winter Hegarty did not achieve his first victory until 28 January 1918, when he sent an Albatros D.V down out of control near Kortemarck.

Hegarty was to steadily increase his score over the following months, with two aerial victories in February, one in March and two in May. One of his victims went down in flames. Royal Flying Corps Communiqué No.133 of 1918—one of its final communiqués prior to amalgamation into the Royal Air Force—records Hegarty's victory of 30 March 1918:

"2nd Lt HG Hegarty, 60 Squadron, dived on one EA scout flying at 1,200 feet and drove it down to 500 feet. The EA went over in a vertical bank, then crashed in the village of Theux".[173]

Hegarty had no qualms over getting in close with the S.E.5A, something which was considered tactically hazardous and not the best use of the aircraft's superior climb and dive performance relative to the maneuverability of the German aircraft. Royal Air Force Communiqué No.7 of 1918 record's Hegarty's victory of 14 May 1918:

"2 Lt HG Hegarty, 60 Sqn, observed an EA two-seater flying west at a low height. Lt Hegarty attacked the EA and fired 300 rounds at a range of 100 yards, closing until he almost collided with the EA. The EA side-slipped to the ground and attempted to land on a small

---

173 Chaz Bowyer [ed] "RFC Communiqués 1917-1918", p.248 [London: Grub Street, 1998].

hill with trenches on the crest, ran into the trenches and half turned over".[174]

Hegarty's final victories are generally recorded as having occurred on 30 June 1918 and 01 July 1918. On these 2 consecutive days he flew an S.E.5a with the serial number D5992, destroying an Albatros D.V near Rainecourt and a Halberstadt C near Bray.

However, Hegarty's service record claims that he was transferred to No.99 Squadron on 20 June 1918 to be temporary Captain. The London Gazette of 05 July 1918 refers to Hegarty's appointment as Temporary Captain with effect from 13 June 1918. It would therefore appear that Hegarty remained with and fought for No.60 Squadron regardless of any notional appointment date elsewhere when promoted. Hegarty was transferred from No.60 Squadron to Home Establishment on 16 July 1918, subsequently being posted to Mid-Area HQ on 07 August 1918.

Hegarty was awarded the Military Cross; its citation was gazetted on 18 September 1918:

"T./2nd Lt. Herbert George Hegarty, R.A.F.

For conspicuous gallantry and devotion to duty on offensive patrols. During recent operations he destroyed four enemy machines and drove down two. He is a bold and fear- less pilot, and has done splendid work".[175]

Hegarty's service record also makes reference to "Major General J.M. Salmond, R.A.F. Communiqué No.9" in respect of the Military Cross. This suggests that the award may have been based upon combat report submitted to the Air Ministry prior to this communiqué, which covers the period 27 May 1918 to 02 June 1918.

Hegarty was assigned to 4 Flight School, serving there from 08 August 1918 to 06 February 1919 when he was released to Oswestry in Shropshire for dispersal.[176] On 28 March 1919 the London

---
174 Christopher Cole [ed], *RAF Communiqués 1918* (Tom Donovan Publishing, 1990), pp.76-78.
175 Supplement to the Edinburgh Gazette of 18 September 1918, Issue 13322, p.3399
176 AIR 76/220 UK National Archives, Herbert George Hegarty.

HEGARTY, HERBERT GEORGE

Gazette stated that Hegarty had been placed on the Unemployed List with effect from 06 February 1919.

Hegarty is mentioned in *Sixty Squadron R.A.F.—A History of the Squadron from its Formation* by Group Captain A.J.L. Scott, CB, MC, AFC (William Heinemann/George H. Doran Company, 1920), e.g. see pages 89,106, 111 and 130; however, this book only attributes one specific victory to Hegarty (p.106). The real star of that particular book is the Irish ace William E Molesworth: several of his letters are included, plus some pencil sketches and watercolours. Hegarty remains under-represented in the "Hell in the Heavens" genre of aviator memoirs. In modern, more rigorous history publications, e.g. Alex Revell's informative *No.60 Squadron RFC/RAF* (London: Osprey, 2011), Hegarty does not feature at all.

Of the 26 aces who served with No.60 Squadron there were 4 Irish aces: Hegarty, Molesworth, Sydney Pope and Alfred William Saunders. Further, it would appear that Pope and Molesworth had some considerable overlap in service, e.g. Pope used Nieuport (B1652) for an aerial victory on 08 June 1917 and Molesworth used the same aircraft on 29 June 1917 and 11 July 1917 for 2 aerial victories. However, there was little overlap between the years of service between the 4 Irishmen, with Molesworth and Pope being very much the 1917 Irish team and with Hegarty and Saunders being the 1918 team. (Irish early war representation in No.60 Squadron would include people like Major Francis Fitzgerald Waldron, killed on 03 July 1916). Nothing should be read into the presence or absence of a reference to Hegarty relative to any other of the Irish aces in the various memoirs of No.60 Squadron veterans.

An examination of passenger records indicates that on 01 April 1919 Hegarty travelled on the 'Tamba Maru' from Birkenhead, destined for Yokohama, Japan. He travelled 1st Class, with his 'country of intended future permanent residence' being recorded as 'China'. Hegarty travelled alone.

The Singapore Free Press and Mercantile Advertiser of 26 June 1920 (page 3, advertisements column 2) contains reference to a Herbert

George Hegarty, which would suggest that Hegarty at the very least had a continuing financial interest in the Far East.

On 14 September 1923 Hegarty travelled on the 'Caledonia' from London to Hong Kong. On this occasion he took his wife Eleanor and their two children – Eleanor (aged 3) and Patrick (aged 1) – to China. The family travelled 1st Class. His occupation was still a 'banker' and their former address in the UK was 'Lampeter, Mount Hermon, Woking, Surrey' as previously described. It would appear that a nurse, Ms Lily Lunn accompanied them.

It is not known as to what became of them: as mentioned previously there are just too many Herbert George Hegartys to reliably trace the Irish ace among the endless trail of paperwork.

❖ ❖ ❖

HERON, OSCAR ALOYSIUS PATRICK

(13 aerial victories)

Born: 17 September 1896, Co Armagh

Died: 05 August 1933, Dublin

Awards: Distinguished Flying Cross, Croix de Guerre (Belgium)

Commemorated: Glasnevin Cemetery, Dublin.

Religion: Roman Catholic

Oscar was the eldest son of Charles and Annie Heron (née McKenna).

The Irish Census 1901 records the family as being resident at English Street Lower in Armagh Town. Oscar was the eldest of 3 sons. His parents were both National School teachers, i.e. primary school teachers. The family also had a domestic servant, which would suggest that Charles and Annie might have had some residential facility to their schoolhouse or some allowance in respect of same. The Irish Census 1911 records the family as being resident at Banbrook Hill in Armagh City. Oscar's grandfather, Jeremiah McKenna, was resident with them at the time, being described as a widower. He was a pensioner, formerly with the prison service and originally from Limerick city. Oscar's father Charles was originally from Co Tyrone whilst his mother Annie was from Co Kildare. The family had 3 domestic servants present. However, given that one of these (Anne Doody) was aged 60 and from Co Kildare it would suggest that she may have been formerly on the staff of Jeremiah McKenna and/or have been known to Annie Heron. Oscar's father, Charles, was the Principal of St Patrick's National School, Banbrook Hill.

There are contradictory accounts of Heron's service prior to transferring to the Royal Flying Corps. On the one hand Heron is claimed by the Inns of Court OTC whilst other accounts cite the Connaught Rangers. However, it is generally reported that Heron— a Cadet—had been appointed temporary 2nd Lieutenant (on probation) on 13 December 1917 by a War Office announcement of 20 December 1917.[177]

Heron is mentioned in Norman Franks' *Sopwith Camel Aces of World War I* (London: Osprey, 2003) on p.64, and in *Above the Trenches*. However, there is little reference to him in the various accounts of No.70 Squadron. Of their 19 aces, 2 were Irish: Edward Gribben and Oscar Heron. Shortly after the formation of the Royal Air Force (01 April 1918) Heron was assigned to No.70 Squadron, in May 1918.

On 30 June 1918 Heron scored his first aerial victories, when flying a Sopwith Camel (D6492), sending down an Albatros D.V out of control and destroying another in flames. In August and September 1918 he obtained further aerial victories, both over the excellent Fokker D.VII. However, in October 1918 Heron managed a spectacular "killing spree", scoring 9 aerial victories, 3 of these being Fokker D.VIIs sent down in flames. He also shared the capture of a Fokker D.VII on 09 October 1918. RAF Communiqué No.28 of 1918 gives an idea of the odds he faced and the aggression shown:

"Lt O.A. Heron, 70 Sqn, dived on one of 15 Fokker biplanes, which broke up in the air after 100 rounds had been fired at it. He then attacked another which was on the tail of a Camel and shot it down in flames".[178]

---

177 Third Supplement to the London Gazette of 20 December 1917 (Gazette Issue 30438, pp.13325-13326).
178 Christopher Cole [ed] "Royal Air Force Communiqués 1918", p.213 [Tom Donovan Publishing, 1990].

RAF Communiqué No.29 of 1918 (14th to 20 October 1918) records Heron as being awarded the DFC, although this was not announced generally at the time. However, on 29 October 1918 the Air Ministry announced that 2nd Lieutenant O.A.P. Heron, with effect from 23 October 1918, was promoted to Temporary Captain whilst employed in an acting capacity as Captain (Aeroplane).

Heron's Distinguished Flying Cross (DFC) citation was gazetted on 08 February 1919:

"2nd Lt (Acting Capt) Oscar Alois Patrick Heron (France)

An officer conspicuous for his skill and daring in aerial combats. He has accounted for eight enemy aeroplanes. On 28 September he attacked, single-handed, three Fokkers; one of these he shot down. On another occasion he, in company with five other machines, engaged six Fokkers, all six being destroyed, 2nd Lieutenant Heron accounting for two".[179]

Flight magazine of 31 July 1919 (p.1017), citing the London Gazette of 15 July 1919, stated that Heron had been awarded the Belgian Croix de Guerre, although I cannot locate a corresponding Belgian reference. *Flight* magazine of 28 August 1919 (p.1169) cited an Air Ministry notice of 19 August 1919 in which it announced that 2nd Lieutenant Heron had been graded as Captain for purposes of pay and allowances from 01 May 1919 whilst employed as Captain (Aeroplane). I cannot reconcile these statements, as the London Gazette of 05 September 1919 states that Heron was transferred to the Unemployed List with effect from 10 August 1919.[180] However, a subsequent notice in October 1919 indicates that he was appointed Flying Officer from Pilot Officer.[181]

On 21 June 1921 Heron arrived at Liverpool on the *City of Poona*, an Ellerman Line steamship, returning from Bombay via Karachi. Adjacent names to Heron in the passenger list were Lieutenant BR Godley and Lieutenant PJ Gaynor of the Indian Army, and Captain ERN Herbert of the British Army. However, it is unlikely that they were travelling together, more likely to have gathered together as men in uniform.

---

179 London Gazette Supplement, Issue 31170, p.2041.
180 London Gazette, Issue 31539, p.11247.
181 London Gazette, Issue 31616, p.13034.

Heron gives his nationality as "Irish", with his permanent residence being described as India. Ireland's civil registration marriage index indicates that in the fourth quarter of 1921 Heron got married in Bangalore.

Curiously, Heron's service record[182] is largely empty. It contains a reference to the London Gazette in which there was a notice to the effect that Flying Officer Heron had been transferred to Reserve Class "C" on 07 November 1922. This matches up with various public announcements, e.g. *Flight* magazine of 16 November 1922 (p.679), quoting the London Gazette of 07 November 1922, also reported that Heron had been transferred to Reserve Class C.

In Heron's largely empty service record there is a further reference to a London Gazette notice, this one dated 09 November 1926, stating that Heron had relinquished his commission on completion of service, with effect from 07 November 1926. This is also reported in *Flight* magazine of 18 November 1926 (p.755).

By this stage, however, it is possible that Oscar Heron may have joined the Irish Air Corps. It is unclear as to when he joined: the media reports at the time of his death suggested that Heron was an officer of the Air Corps at the time of its formation in 1922. However, the Irish Military Archives have released the Irish Army Census of 1922 in electronically searchable format. Heron is not among the officers present at Baldonnel. Looking at the other available information to hand does not corroborate any claim to Heron being with the Irish Air Corps; the Irish equivalent of the Army List was a memo from C Hogan to CIC, dated 18 October 1922 (Irish Military Archive A/07279). This states that the *Cabhlach Eitileacht Éireann* (Aviation Department of the Army) had the following officers:

Comdt-General W.J. McSweeney (Commanding Officer)
Comdt E Broy (Adjutant)
Captain J Arnott (Acting 2nd in command of flying)
Captain T Donnelly (Quartermaster)

---

182 AIR 76/223 Oscar Heron, UK National Archives.

The remaining 12 officers were mainly ex-RAF pilots and observers, including Lt W Delamere (later head of the Irish Air Corps), J.C. Fitzmaurice (later to be famous as a crew member on the 'Bremen' for the inaugural East-to-West trans-Atlantic crossing in 1927).

However, it is not inconceivable that Heron joined shortly after the *Cabhlach Eitileacht Éireann* was reconstituted as the Irish Air Corps. Heron's rank of Captain would not have required long either, as it was a fluid situation: allegedly Captain John Arnott (Acting 2nd in command of flying) was frog-marched to the dock at gunpoint when it was discovered that he had been a member of the 'Black and Tans'.

It may be noted that, by this stage, Heron's native County Armagh had—through the provisions of the Government of Ireland Act 1920 of December that year—become part of the entity known as Northern Ireland. No partition of Ireland was ever going to be completely successful, but this one had been based on a decision of the Ulster Unionist Council of the Ulster Unionist party as to which counties should be included in the Government of Ireland Act 1920. Churchill's reference to the "dreary steeples" of Fermanagh and Tyrone underplay the deadly nature of British political misjudgment in refusing to allow for some adequate mechanism for a political settlement. The Local Government Elections of January 1920 and 12 June 1920 had seen Nationalist majorities elected in 3 of the 8 principal local authorities (Counties Fermanagh and Tyrone, and Londonderry Corporation) of what were to be later included in the entity known as Northern Ireland, and many nationalists had hoped the local elections would have given rise to the realization of the right to self-determination. (In any event these councils were suspended for seeking allegiance with the entity known the Republic of Ireland, which claimed jurisdiction on all 32 counties of Ireland). However, large Unionist minorities existed in Co Fermanagh and Co Tyrone. Similarly, Nationalist majorities existed in southern areas of Co Armagh and Co Down. In this context several sub-county local authorities, e.g. urban and rural district councils, declared allegiance to Dáil Éireann, including Newry and Downpatrick in Co

Down. By the time the Anglo-Irish Treaty came into effect in 1922 this soon gave rise to a further peculiarity, as there continued to exist a 32-county entity known as Poblacht na hÉireann (the Republic of Ireland) with the allegiance of elected representatives from areas of what were now within the entities known as Northern Ireland and the Treaty-created *Saor Stat Éireann* (the Irish Free State), which was to supersede the Southern Ireland entity that was supposed to have been created under the partition-based Government of Ireland Act 1920. Further, the transfer of a number of functions previously unintended for Northern Ireland now became a necessity due to the repeal of the application of the provisions of the Government of Ireland Act 1920 for the area that had now become the Saor Stat Éireann, e.g. old Dublin Castle powers in respect of matters as mundane as the Potatoes Importation (Ireland) Order 1920 were delegated to the new Northern Ireland parliament at Stormont, whilst a whole host of Government of Ireland (Adaptation of Enactments) Orders were required for matters as diverse as the Weights and Measures Acts 1878-1919, the Tramways (Ireland) Acts 1860-1900, although of course many of the former Dublin Castle powers now fell to the UK's Home Secretary, notwithstanding the presence of an Under-Secretary in Belfast who had reported to Dublin in the immediate post-war years. One other matter of note in the emerging situation was that the Irish White Cross facilitated tens of thousands of Catholics who had been burned out of Northern Ireland. Although the numbers were not large in terms of the overall population or in the context of other comparable European conflicts of the 1920s, many Northern nationalists saw it as a political admission that Northern Ireland was unwilling or unable to protect its Catholic minority.

The collapse of the Royal Irish Constabulary (RIC) in many parts of what was to become Northern Ireland had seen the formation of an Ulster Special Constabulary, which had been intended by some British and Unionist politicians as a means of re-arming the Ulster Volunteer Force (UVF) with more up to date army weaponry, whilst for others it was essential means of guaranteeing the safety of

Protestants in Counties Fermanagh and Tyrone, as the RIC confined itself to barracks at night and/or it restricted itself to policing operations rather than the quasi-military role required to combat IRA operations from those large swathes of territory in which there were nationalist majorities. The "Specials", however, may have attracted many anxious and dedicated Unionists but it also attracted every category of sectarian thug from among that community. Unsurprisingly, the arming of that element ensured that hundreds of Catholics were the subjects of extra-judicial killings by the Ulster Special Constabulary, often the distinction between official and unofficial operations being maintained only by the holding of an inquest for those killed until this process too was suspended by the Northern Ireland government. However, it was not the regularity with which assassinations and killings took place that further alienated the Nationalist and Republican community from the new Northern Ireland statelet but also the stark fact that the "Specials" were intended to be a sectarian force: their role was not to police as such but to police Catholics, e.g. from Heron's native Armagh city there were numerous incidents exemplifying the harassment experienced by even quite prominent Catholics. On 24 May 1922 and on 06 June 1922 Cardinal Logue was stopped just outside Armagh city by Lisnadill "Specials". The eighty-one year old Cardinal was subjected to a through search on both occasions, with Church papers being rifled through by the Specials and the anointing oil (oil of "Chrism" as it used to be called) used for confirmation ceremonies being tampered with by the "Specials". On one of the occasions, when the Cardinal objected to being searched, the officer had an excuse to give an order to "cover that man with a rifle" and for weapons to be aimed at the Cardinal from point-blank range. A similar incident occurred on 15 June 1922, in which the elderly Cardinal was forced to stand at the roadside in view of the passing traffic and made empty his pockets. (Of course local Unionist thugs in uniform take guidance from the dog whistle of those in leadership positions. In Christmas 1922 Cardinal Logue was prevented from celebrating midnight mass in Armagh Cathedral by the Unionist minister for Home Affairs, Dawson Bates, who imposed a curfew and instructed the Cardinal that he would place a cordon at the cathedral gate and arrest any attempted mass-goers).

Heron was one of a small minority of northern Catholics who relocated to the Irish Free State, rather than return to Northern Ireland after World War I. His brother Charles was to become a Superintendent in An Garda Síochána, the police force of the Irish Free State. It was nevertheless emphatically one of choice rather than a forced migration.

Heron joined the Irish Air Corps at an important juncture: the 'Army Mutiny' of 1924 would appear to have been used as a pretext to purge the Irish Air Corps of some of its ex-RAF personnel (e.g. McSweeney, J.J. Flynn, W.D. Hardy and so forth). However, Heron would not appear to have suffered any particular difficulties when serving with the Irish Air Corps. By the time of his death in August 1933 would appear to have held an important instructorial role in the Irish Air Corps.

In Lieutenant Colonel Michael C. O'Malley's outstanding *Military Aviation in Ireland, 1921-1945* (Dublin: UCD Press, 2010) it is suggested that Army GHQ had intended to send Captain Heron and a Lt A. Russell on an RAF flying instructors' course at the Central Flying School, RAF Wittering in February 1932. However, within days Russell was replaced by a Lt D.J. McKeown. Then, in early January 1932, it was decided to only send one officer instead of the others. A Lt W. Keane was selected for the course, which lasted from 02 February 1932 to 16 April 1932. O'Malley did not get to the bottom of the matter but any number of reasons could have applied, e.g. Heron was ex-RAF and the Irish Army were making a point of stamping out that culture in favour of an army-support mindset for the Irish Air Corps. Similarly, Russell and McKeown were graduates of the 1922/1923 wings' course and thus not adequately qualified to take on instructional training duties. In any event Keane, a cadet from the 1926-1928 class—who therefore had neither an RAF nor an IRA background—was to perform well at RAF Wittering and became a highly respected instructor in the Irish Air Corps.

Regarding Heron's death, on 05 August 1933 he was flying a 2-seater Vickers Vespa, with Private Robert Tobin as his crew. They were engaged in a mock dogfight with 3 Avro Cadet aeroplanes as part of the inaugural Dublin Air Pageant. Heron failed to pull the aircraft out of a spin. Captain Heron was killed in the crash whilst Private Robert Tobin died of wounds the following day. They crashed in view of Heron's wife and a crowd of 12,000 at the Phoenix Park. Three days previously Lieutenant J.P. Twohig was killed in a crash whilst rehearsing for the air pageant.

Heron left a wife but no family.

✦ ✦ ✦

HUSTON, VICTOR HENRY

(**6 aerial victories**)

Born: 13 October 1890, Belfast
Died: 10 April 1941
Awards: Military Cross, Order of Merit (Chile)
Commemorated: St George's Chapel, Westminster Abbey, London
Religion: Church of Ireland

Major Victor Huston is one of only a handful of pilots to become an ace with a bomber/reconnaissance squadron, and in his case only Blennerhasset, Huston and Waller (all fellow Irishmen) were to achieve this with No.18 Squadron.

Huston was the son of William Wentworth Huston and Elizabeth Victoria Huston (née Simpson). He was one of 9 children, and had 5 sisters and 3 brothers. The Irish Census 1901 records the family as being resident at Waterloo Gardens in the Duncairn Ward of Belfast. Huston's father was a "box manufacturer", originally from Armagh. His mother was from Kildare. The family would appear to have moved around quite a lot: his sisters Eileen and Dorothy, and his brother Claud, were born in South Africa[183], whilst Victor and the others were born in Belfast. However, Huston does not appear in the Irish Census 1911—only seven of the children are still resident at Waterloo Gardens.

---

183 The Irish Census 1911 reports that Eileen was born in the Cape Colony, whilst Dorothy was born in Cape Town.

There was a Victor H Huston who sailed on the 'Lake Manitoba' from Belfast to St John's, Newfoundland, Canada on 31 March 1910, although it would appear his age was misrecorded as 24 instead of 20. He travelled as a 2nd class passenger. The British Columbia marriage registrations record Huston as having married Sarah Ballie on 11 November 1912[184]. Her parents were Robert Baillie and Sarah Brown, originally from Scotland.

Victor Huston joined the Canadian Expeditionary Force (Canadian Army Service Corps) in Vancouver. Canadian records[185] indicate that Victor Henry Huston was a Corporal (regimental service number 36122) and serving with the Divisional Supply Column (Motorized Transport). In Huston's Attestation Paper his occupation is described as "motor engineer" and his previous military service is recorded as having been with the 11th Hussars. His next-of-kin address was 522 Richards St, Vancouver, British Columbia. Huston signed his papers on 18 September 1914, which were certified on 28 September 1914. It would appear that Huston arrived in France in 1915.

I cannot find a passenger list in which Sarah Florence Huston is recorded. However, on Huston's service record the next-of-kin address for Mrs. S.F. Huston is recorded as "90 Castellain Road, Maida Vale", which suggests a wartime move to London.

Huston was appointed a temporary 2nd Lieutenant in the Canadian Army Service Corps with effect from 13 September 1915, which was gazetted on 01 October 1915.[186] Victor's brother, Corporal Gerald Marcus Huston, was killed on 07 December 1915 when serving with the Royal Engineers.

---

184 "British Columbia Marriage Registrations, 1859-1932," index, FamilySearch (https://familysearch.org/pal:/MM9.1.1/JD8Z-B7H : accessed 11 Aug 2012), Victor Henry Huston and Sarah Baillie, 11 Nov 1912.
185 "List of Officers and Men serving in the First Canadian Contingent of the British Expeditionary Force, 1914". [Pay & Record Office, Canadian Contingent, 36 Victoria Street, London SW].
186 London Gazette, Issue 29312, p.9651.

HUSTON, VICTOR HENRY

Huston transferred to the Royal Flying Corps, being assigned to the No.2 School of Aeronautics on 22 July 1916.[187] He transferred from Bournemouth to No.27 Reserve Squadron, and was then posted to Gosport, on 06 September 1916. Huston was appointed a Flying Officer, which was gazetted on 28 December 1916.[188] He was initially posted to No.28 Squadron on 08 December 1916, and then served with No.18 Squadron from 17 December 1916 onwards.

Huston scored his first aerial victory on 15 February 1917, when flying a F.E.2b (A5445), destroying a German two-seater over Grevillers. On 05 April 1917, when flying a F.E.2b (4969), with the Irish ace Giles Blennerhasset as his observer, they sent down 2 German Albatros D.II fighters over Inchy.

Of the "Combats in the Air" reports for the squadron, a report on 24 April 1917 indicates that a F.E.2b (4998), piloted by Huston with a Lt E.A. Ford as his observer, was on photographic duties at 10,000 feet between Baralle and Bourlon when they encountered a number of German aircraft of various types. Huston reported the following:

"Fired one double drum at an Albatros scout at about 250 yards while he was circling from our left front towards our rear. The tracers appeared to strike the machine, which went down in a vertical nose-dive over Dury.

Fired about 60 rounds with back gun at another Albatros scout who was diving on the formation from the side. Range about 300 yards. He dived between Baralle and Villers Gagnicourt. A few minutes later a machine was seen on the ground near this point, and a plate was exposed of the place".[189]

Despite the foregoing only one aerial victory was attributed to Huston and Ford for the engagement. In February, April and May 1917 Huston was to achieve six aerial victories in all. This was an

---

187 AIR 76/246, Victor Henry Huston, UK National Archives.
188 Supplement to the London Gazette of 28 December 1916 (Gazette Issue 29882, pp.12644-12645).
189 Air/1/121920452634, ref.363. UK National Archives.

excellent outcome considering that No.18 Squadron was not a 'scout' squadron and that at the outset of Huston's time with the squadron the adverse weather conditions in January 1917 would have limited the opportunities for photographic reconnaissance.

Huston was awarded the Military Cross, which was gazetted on 18 June 1917:

"Lt. Victor Henry Huston, A.S.C. and R.F.C.

For conspicuous gallantry and devotion to duty He has rendered valuable service when on photographic reconnaissance. He has always shown the greatest skill and courage in leading attacks on hostile machines, and thus enabling valuable photographs to be secured behind the lines".[190]

Huston was returned to Home Establishment on 07 July 1917, being assigned to Hendon AA Park on 15 August 1917. Huston was injured on 15 September 1917. There are a number of Medical Boards examinations recorded on his service record, which—on 17 October 1917—initially certified him as "unfit general service 2 months. Home service 7 weeks, fit light duty. Received 3 weeks leave". A further examination of 17 November 1917 stated that Huston was unfit for service for 2 months, being permitted light duty but no flying.

Huston was then posted to Norwich AA Park on 07 December 1917 for home service, but no flying duties were permitted. A medical board examination of 10 January 1918 continued to prohibit flying.

However, this did not prevent Huston from being promoted to the office of temporary Captain, which was gazetted on 07 January 1918, with the appointment dated to 05 August 1917.[191] Despite being prohibited from flying duties, Huston was not idle however, and on 21 February 1918 he was ordered to "report to Room 12 Covent Garden Hotel". However, on 07 March 1918 an assessment permitted limited dual flying duties but a subsequent assessment

---

190 London Gazette Supplement, Issue 30135, p.6006.
191 London Gazette Supplement, Issue 30461, p.423.

stated "no flying until ordered by next MB". On 20 March 1918 Huston was appointed Captain, graded as 'Flight Commander', which was gazetted on 07 May 1918.[192] This was described as a "special appointment'. However, a medical board assessment of 04 May 1918 stated that Huston was "unfit general service, 4 weeks" but was fit for Home service flying duties.

Huston was loaned to the Chilean government on 20 August 1918 on "special duties" for 1 year. His role was to instruct and assist the Chilean Air Force: Britain had supplied 14 seaplanes and 50 aeroplanes to Chile. Obviously, there was still no trans-Atlantic aerial service at the time. The Passenger Arrival Lists (Ellis Island), 1892-1924 record Victor Henry Huston as having arrived on 30 September 1918 from Liverpool on the 'Adriatic'. Presumably in deference to his Armagh and Kildare parentage his ethnicity is described as 'British, Irish'.[193]

It would appear that he reported for duty with the Chilean authorities on 19 October 1918. *Flight* magazine of 19 December 1918 (p.1431) reported that the Chilean Minister of War at Santiago de Chile had announced on 12 December 1918 that on that date a Lieutenant Godoy, of the Military School of Aviation, had flown from Santiago to Mendoza in Argentina using a Bristol. It took one and a half hours to fly over the Cordilleras of the Andes, establishing a height record. The announcement stated that "the Minister of War takes this opportunity of congratulating the British Government upon the excellence of this British aeroplane, and feels that the result of the flight does the greatest honour to the instruction given to Chilean airmen by the British Major Huston".

Huston's instruction duties had indeed borne early fruit: a further telegram stated that Lieutenant Godoy flew from Espejo to

---

192 Third Supplement to the London Gazette, Issue 30761, p.5457.
193 "New York, Passenger Arrival Lists (Ellis Island), 1892-1924," index, FamilySearch (https://familysearch.org/pal:/MM9.1.1/JJZK-S3L : accessed 11 Aug 2012), Victor Henry Huston, 30 Sep 1918; citing Adriatic, United States National Archives, Washington, D.C.

Mendoza, a distance of 247 miles, in 1 hour 28 minutes, maintaining an average height of 20,000 feet.

Flight magazine of 09 January 1919 (p.55) reported that the first batch of aircraft had reached Valparaiso. These were to form the nucleus of the Chilean air service. Huston—once again described as 'Major Huston'—was to act a chief instructor of the new force. An Engineer-Lieutenant Solano was to be in charge of the technical side for the Naval section. (The combination of seaplanes and aeroplanes must have given rise to quite a number of logistical headaches).

Huston received the Chilean Order of Merit. However, I have been unable to identify any record of the award being conferred on Huston or any permission granted by the King to facilitate him accepting the honour. (Usually permission to accept foreign military decoration would be published in the London Gazette).

Huston ceased secondment to the Royal Air Force with effect from 30 September 1919. This was gazetted on 21 November 1919.[194] Huston returned to Army duty and relinquished his temporary RAF commission with effect from 30 September 1919, which was gazetted on 23 January 1920. However, Huston suffered the indignity of his name being spelt incorrectly, as "Houston", but a corrected notice issued in the London Gazette of 20 February 1920.[195] However, these official movements to his Army-versus-RAF home grade designations did not affect Huston's service in Chile, where he set a South American altitude record of 7,076 metres on 26 November 1919. From the material available from Chile, however, Huston would appear in some photographs to have an officer's staff but in other photographs a walking stick. It is possible that Huston never fully recovered from his wartime injuries.

On 14 December 1920 Huston departed from Valparaiso, Chile to Liverpool on the 'Oropesa'. In the passenger lists his profession is still recorded as 'adviser to Chile Govt' and his address as being the Chilean Legation in London.

---

194 London Gazette Supplement, Issue 31652, p.14266.
195 London Gazette, Issue 31788, p.2074.

Huston's relationship with South America does not end at this stage: on 01 April 1921 there is a Victor Huston recorded as being one of the 178 passengers on the 'Andes', which sailed from Southampton to Buenos Aires. His address is recorded as 32 Westbourne Terrace, London and his intended final destination as being Chile. (Could this have been a journey to collect his Order of Merit?)

Huston was killed in an air raid on Coventry on 10 April 1941. The Commonwealth War Graves Commission records his address as 66 Dorset House, Gloucester Place, London NW1. Huston died at Gulson Road Hospital in Warwickshire. Huston's Military Cross and Chilean Order of Merit are recorded but his age is misdescribed as being 45 instead of 51. This may have arisen from the manner in which the number 0 was written in his date of birth, e.g. in his Canadian attestation papers the 1890 looks a little like 1898, so it would be unsurprising if it could also look like 1896 in other documentation penned by him, such as a driving licence or other identification papers found on his person.

In the British Columbia Death Registrations 1948, at Ruskin, B.C., Canada, the death of Sarah Florence Huston is recorded as having occurred on 02 February 1948. Sarah died aged 55, her DOB being given as 07 August 1892. Sarah's marital status is described as "widow", which confirms that Victor pre-deceased her[196].

Further research or reading:

The Chilean National Museum of Aeronautics have several publications in which Huston is mentioned, including photographs of him with Godoy and Cortinez:

- Museo Nacional Aeronáutico y del Espacio Boletín N°8: Una Publicación de la Sección de Historia (July 2009);[197] and

---

196 "British Columbia Death Registrations, 1872-1986," index, FamilySearch (https://familysearch.org/pal:/MM9.1.1/FLP8-NY3 : accessed 11 Aug 2012), Victor Henry Huston in entry for Sarah Florence Huston, 02 Feb 1948.
197 Page30: http://www.museoaeronautico.gob.cl/espanol/publicaciones/boletin-8.pdf

- Efemérides de la Aviación: una Publicación del Museo Nacional Aeronáutico Y del Espacio Dirección General de Aeronáutica Civil (November 2010).[198]

The Chilean Air Force also feature Huston in several of their journals, e.g. in the 80th anniversary of the Fuerza Aérea de Chile, "PUBLICACIÓN DE LA FUERZA AÉREA DE CHILE - VOL. LXIX - N° 251 – 2010".[199]

✦ ✦ ✦

---

[198] Pages 27,60, 85 88, 90, 91. http://www.museoaeronautico.gob.cl/espanol/publicaciones/efemerides.pdf
[199] ISSN 0716-4866, Edición Aniversario, pp.12-14.

KELLY, EDWARD CAULFIELD

(5 aerial victories)

Born: 1896, Galway

Died: 01 July 1942, New Guinea

Commemorated: St George's Chapel, Westminster Abbey, London

Religion: Roman Catholic

Edward Caulfied Kelly is sometimes recorded as Caulfield-Kelly in RFC and RAF communiqués.

He was born in Ballinasloe, Co Galway to Edward J and Margaret Kelly. Edward was the eldest of 3 sons, according to the Irish Census 1901 and 1911. Kelly's parents ran a hotel on Dunlo St in Ballinasloe, Co Galway with his grandmother. Although Kelly's father and grandmother were from Co Roscommon his mother was not a West of Ireland lady, hailing from Co Wicklow. Edward was 15 at the time of the 1911 census and is described as a scholar.

According to his service record[200] Kelly had been a student at Trinity College Dublin from June 1913 to December 1914. However, he does not appear on the University of Dublin Roll of Honour. Kelly joined the Leinster Regiment, obtaining a commission as a 2nd Lieutenant, attached to the Royal Dublin Fusiliers. He subsequently transferred to the Royal Flying Corps in 1917, reporting to Reading on 12 March 1917. By 05 April 1917 Kelly was with No.45 Squadron. On 09 May 1917 he scored his first aerial victory, flying as the

---

200 AIR 76/270 Edward Caulfield Kelly, UK National Archives.

observer in a Sopwith 1 ½ Strutter (A8225) piloted by 2nd Lt William Wright. They destroyed an Albatros D.III north-west of Seclin. This was a shared victory with another aircraft from No.45 Squadron.

Throughout the month of May 1917 Kelly was to achieve 5 aerial victories, 4 of which were with Wright with one other being with a Lt Geoffrey Cock. Two of his victims went down in flames. Kelly's last victory came on 28 May 1917, destroying an Albatros D.V in flames over Comines. Kelly was wounded in the engagements that day.

Kelly was hospitalized on 29 May 1917 and was transferred back to Home Establishment on 30 May 1917. It had been an extremely short career at the European frontline but quite a distinguished one. Official developments were slow to catch up with Kelly's situation. On 11 June 1917 the London Gazette reported Kelly's promotion to Flying Officer (Observer) with effect from 21 May 1917 and seniority backdated to 07 April 1917.

On 07 August 1917 a medical board examination held that Kelly was unfit for general service for a 3 month period. However, there must have been some secondary complications with pneumonia or influenza, as a further medical board examination of 21 November 1917 recommended service in a warm climate.

On 11 October 1917 Kelly was assigned to HQ ETB, from which they assigned him to No.3 Training Squadron on 15 October 1917. There is a gap in Kelly's service record but it would appear that at one stage he was transferred to No.21 Squadron. (To the best of my knowledge, 3 TS formed the basis of No.86 Squadron).

On 27 July 1918 Kelly was assigned to 38 Training Wing, 58 Training Squadron, which was based in Egypt. He was assigned to No.144 Squadron on 04 August 1918. This squadron had been formed on 20 March 1918 and had only been assigned to the RAF's Palestine Brigade on 14 August 1918. The squadron had DH9 bombers. The aerial bombardment of the Turkish forces throughout September 1918 was decisive in the success of the Arab Northern Army under Sherif Feisal and Colonel TE Lawrence. No.144 Squadron largely annihilated sections of the Turkish Eighth and Seventh

Armies, with the capture of the Turkish forces east of the Jordan (the entire Fourth Army) also being facilitated. However, Kelly ended up in hospital again and on 20 September 1918 was returned to Base Depot, Mid East.

On 02 August 1918 Kelly's promotion to Temporary 2nd Lieutenant, Leinster Regiment, was gazetted.[201] The promotion was with effect from 29 May 1918. On 31 October 1918 Kelly was assigned to HQ Training Brigade. It would appear that over the course of the winter Kelly worked at a succession of training facilities. On 17 January 1919 Kelly's promotion was amended to state that he had been promoted from Lieutenant (Observer) to Lieutenant (Aeroplane) with effect from 29 May 1918.[202]

On 06 February 1919 he was assigned to 60 TDS, from which he ended up with 30 TS on 01 July 1919. At this stage 30 TS was training in the DH9. Eventually, on 14 August 1919, 30 TS returned to RAF Northolt, Uxbridge. Kelly was granted a short-service commission, as Flying Officer, which was gazetted on 12 September 1919.[203] The effective date was stated as 12 September 1919, which suggests that the return of the training squadron had entailed some category of decommissioning of its officers and other ranks. However, there is another notice in respect of Kelly, in the London Gazette Supplement of 11 September 1919 (Issue 31546, p.11446). This states that Lt E.C. Kelly was to be acting Captain (with pay and allowances as Lieutenant), 13 September 1917, with seniority from 11 April 1917. (Kelly is also described as being with the 3rd Norfolk Regiment, which may indicate a typographical error).

Regardless of what exactly transpired in September 1919, Kelly's days with the RAF were nearing an end. On 17 February 1920 the London Gazette reported that Kelly had resigned his commission on the grounds of ill health.[204]

---

201 London Gazette, Issue 30825, p.9118.
202 London Gazette, Issue 31131, p.906.
203 London Gazette, Issue 31548, p.11468.
204 London Gazette, Issue 31784, p.1948.

On 19 March 1920 Kelly travelled on the 'Nankin', a Peninsular & Oriental Steam Co ('P&O') ship, from London to Bombay. He travelled First Class, with his occupation being described as a 'Broker's Assistant'. His ultimate destination was recorded as the Federated Malay States.

However, there is a competing claim that Kelly had a very brief spell in the Merchant Navy. (His discharge number reads as 1102814). His discharge papers are stamped at Merchant Marine Office, Tilbury, on 28 April 1924. The card reads "1st voyage". However, there is a further discharge card (816480) for an "E.C. Kelly" dated 10 December 1930, stamped at the Merchant Marine Office, Poplar East. The ship is referenced as '129078'.

It is therefore not clear as to how Kelly came to live in Papua New Guinea but he was taken prisoner by the Japanese forces in 1942. Kelly was killed in the sinking of the *S.S. Montevideo Maru* on 01 July 1942. Kelly was recorded as having been an agricultural inspector based as Kavieng, New Ireland, and was 46 at the time of his death. The sinking of the *S.S. Montevideo Maru* in the South China Sea off the Philippines claimed the lives of 1,053 Australian troops and civilian internees. It remains Australia's worst maritime disaster. Also killed were an Alfred Ernest Dickenson Banks from Dublin and a Walter James Ryan from Tullow, Co Carlow. On 22 June 1942 an American submarine, the *USS Sturgeon*, tracked the vessel, believing it to be carrying cargo. The submarine launched 4 torpedoes, sinking the Montevideo Maru on 01 July 1942. Among the notable casualties was the Rev Syd Beazley, uncle of the Australian Labour Party leader Kim Beazley. Tom Vernon Garrett, the grandfather of Peter Garrett, the lead singer in Midnight Oil, was also killed. (This was to be referenced by Garrett in the song "In the Valley").

Kelly's death is sometimes the subject of confusion, as there was a Private E.C. Kelly who was taken prisoner in World War II, but that particular E.C. Kelly was a Private in the Hampshire Regiment (No.5504719, POW No.6119) who was detained at Wolfsberg in Germany and survived the war. Further there was an Edward Kelly, serving with the Merchant Navy, who was the son of an Edward and Margaret Ellen Kelly, who was killed on the *S.S. Akeld* on 09 March 1940. However, although matching Kelly's parental details and matching the story of a World War II death for the Irish ace, this particular Edward Kelly was married to a Maria Kelly of Windynook, Gateshead, Co Durham.

✦ ✦ ✦

LEATHLEY, FORDE

(8 aerial victories)

Born: 17 February 1896, Co Tyrone
Died: 25 August 1982, Cannes, France
Awards: Military Cross
Religion: Church of Ireland

Forde Leathley was born on 17 February 1896 at Trillick, Co Tyrone. In many publications he is recorded as having been born at Dunboyne, Co Meath—for example see the magnificent *Above the Trenches*—but this is an understandable error, as Leathley was raised in Co Meath from an early age and it was his correspondence address on his Royal Aero Club aviator's certificate.

The Irish Census 1901 records Leathley as being resident with his parents at Waterloo Place in Dublin. His father was the Reverend James F Forde Leathley. His mother was Elizabeth HS Forde Leathley. Forde's sister, Kathleen, was also present. The Rev James Forde Leathley was originally from Dublin. Forde's mother Kathleen was from Co Wexford. Both Forde and his sister Kathleen were born in Co Tyrone. The family's two servants—Margaret Jane Crean and Alice Crean—were both from Co Tyrone, which suggests they may have accompanied the family to Dublin. The Irish Census 1911 records the family as being resident at Dunboyne, Co Meath. His sister Kathleen is not present, though the census does record that both children in the family were still alive. The Rev James Forde Leathley is described as "Rector" by this stage.

Some confusion can arise in relation to Leathley's service records: there was a Desmond Forde Leathley who served with the Australian infantry forces. However, it is clear from the registers of the Royal Military College at Sandhurst that Leathley was admitted on 18 February 1915. His date of birth was recorded as 17 February 1896, with his father's profession being recorded as Clergyman. Leathley left Sandhurst on 16 June 1915, which was gazetted on 15 June 1915. He joined the Royal Inniskilling Fusiliers as a 2nd Lieutenant.[205] Leathley is the subject of two medal index cards, as "Forde Leathley" and "Forde Leathly" but it's clear that it is the same officer. He served with the 1st Battalion of the Royal Inniskilling Fusiliers. He fought in Gallipoli in August 1915.

Leathley was promoted to Flying Officer (Observer) with seniority to 06 March 1917, on secondment from the Royal Inniskilling Fusiliers. This gazetted on 27 June 1917.[206] One of his medal cards indicates that Leathley served with 29 Training Squadron. When transferred into frontline service Leathley was posted to No.57 Squadron. This was not a scout/fighter squadron but had a long-range bombing and reconnaissance operational role. However, the squadron was to produce half a dozen aces during the war, with Leathley and Eddie Hartigan being the Irish ones.

Leathley scored his first victory on 30 April 1917, as observer in an F.E.2d (A1966) piloted by Lt CS Morice. They sent an Albatros D.III down out of control over Buissy. However, they did not have things their own way. In *Pusher Aces of World War I* (London: Osprey, 2009), by Jon Guttman and Harry Dempsey (p.77), it's stated that a F.E.2d crewed by Lt CS Morice and Forde Leathley was hunted by Ltn Heinz Geiseler of Jasta 33 and was forced to land near Roclincourt, its engine having seized from a holed radiator. However, Leathley had survived "Bloody April".

No.57 Squadron were re-equipped with the Airco D.H.4 in May 1917. Over the course of July and August 1917 Leathley was to score

---

205 London Gazette, Issue 29193, pp.5759-5760.
206 London Gazette Supplement, Issue 30152, p.6362.

7 victories with American-born, Canadian-raised Major Ernest Graham Joy as pilot (various D.H.4s), all against Albatros D.V fighters. RFC Communiqué No.102 reports several actions in which Leathley was involved on 17 August 1917:

"When on a reconnaissance, Major EG Joy and Lt F Leathley, 57 Squadron, shot down an Albatros scout out of control... When returning from a bomb raid, Major EG Joy and Lt F Leathley, 57 Squadron, were attacked by four EA who dived on them from behind. Lt Leathley shot down three of these in turn out of control".[207]

Leathley was awarded the Military Cross. This was reported on 26 September 1917, but the citation was not gazetted until 09 January 1918:

"Lieut. Leathley, R. Inns. Fus. and R.F.C. –

For conspicuous gallantry and devotion to duty in making photographic reconnaissances and in fighting enemy aircraft. Since April he has taken part in numerous combats, during which seven hostile machines have been driven down and destroyed either by him or his pilot, and although attacked by superior numbers of the enemy, his skill and offensive spirit have enabled him to carry out photographic reconnaissances".[208]

In this edition the Military Cross citation of another Irish ace, Edward Gribben, was also published.

Leathley was promoted from Temporary Lieutenant (Observer Officer) to Temporary Lieutenant (Aeroplane and Seaplane) with effect from 11 May 1918. He continued to serve with the RAF in the post-war era. In August 1919 it was reported that Leathley had retained the rank of Lieutenant (Aeroplane).

Flight magazine of 08 January 1920 (p.54) reported an announcement that Forde Leathley was to marry Ida, daughter of the later Mr George Edward Foster of 7 Bickenhall Mansions, London. This was

---

207 Chaz Bowyer [ed] "RFC Communiqués 1917-1918", p.110 [London: Grub Street, 1998]
208 Supplement to the London Gazette, Issue 30466, p.622 for citation; London Gazette Issue 30308, p.9977 for original award announcement.

followed up with a further announcement in *Flight* magazine of 13 May 1920 (p.532) that Leathley and Ida Foster had married on 27 April 1920 at St George's Church, Hanover Square, London.

Leathley's main medal card[209] indicates that this Victory medal was to be issued by the Air Ministry and that his 15 Star would issue in respect of the Royal Inniskilling Fusiliers. The latter card is dated 04 April 1921. His address at the time is given as "Central Flying School, R.A.F., Upavon" but with 'Bickenhall Mansions, W.1' being inscribed alongside this. Bickenhall Mansions are in the Marylebone area of London. Nowadays the apartments are worth several millions each but back in Leathley's time the address would not have been quite so prestigious, notwithstanding their proximity to Baker Street and so forth. It is also the address of his in-laws, the Fosters. On the other version of Leathley's medal card the address is simply given as "South Eastern Area, Royal Air Force, Covent Garden Hotel, Strand".

Flying Officer Leathley was promoted to Flight Lieutenant with effect from 30 June 1922.[210] Leathley would appear to have transferred between Iraq, British Trans-Jordan, Palestine and Egypt. However, *Flight* magazine of 17 July 1924 (p.457) reported that Leathley had been assigned to the Aircraft Depot, Egypt with effect from 21 June 1924. On 04 November 1924 the Air Ministry announced that Leathley had been placed on the half-pay, scale B, with effect from 04 November 1924.[211] Subsequently, Leathley was placed on the retired list with effect from 27 January 1925.[212]

The births, deaths and marriage registration details for Gloucestershire indicate that a Forde Leathley married a Beryl K Price in the fourth quarter of 1926 whilst the British Telephone Directory from 1927 to 1932 records a Forde Leathley as being resident at Old Mill House Chalford, Gloucestershire.

---

209 WO 372/12, UK National Archives.
210 London Gazette, Issue 32725, p.4942.
211 The London Gazette of 04 November 1924, Gazette Issue 32988.
212 London Gazette of 27 January 1925 (Gazette Issue 33015), p.595.

It would appear that Leathley enlisted in World War II with the King's Royal Rifle Corps. The London Gazette Supplement of 15 November 1940 records Leathley as being promoted to Lieutenant with effect from 05 October 1940. Leathley's new service number is reported as 152043.[213]

I can find no details of his post-RAF occupation but the British phone book of 1946 records a Major Forde Leathley MC as being resident at 67C Holland Road, West Kensington, London. However, the records of the now-defunct Norwood College in Yorkshire state that a Major Leathley was a physics teacher for evening classes, from 1947 onwards. It is likely that Leathley retired to Cannes. He died on 25 August 1982, at 21 rue Felix Faure, Cannes, Alpes-Maritimes, France.[214]

❖ ❖ ❖

---

213 London Gazette, Issue 34992, p.6555.
214 London Gazette of 02 October 1986, Issue 50672, p.12793.

Airco D.H.2 'pusher' (Crown Copyright, Imperial War Museum, Q 67534)

Sidney E Cowan   Patrick A.L. Byrne   David M. Tidmarsh

Images 2, 3, and 4 courtesy Royal Aero Club Trust.

Captions:
1. F.E.2d 'Pusher'. An officer demonstrates the precarious position an observer should take to operate the rearward firing Lewis gun.
2. Victor Henry Huston (taken when serving in Chile)
3. Giles Noble Blennerhasset
4. Joseph Cruess-Callaghan (note the non-regulation shamrock cap badge).

Captions:
1. Nieuport 17 C1. This excellent French-built fighter, like the SPAD, was hugely important to the RFC and RNAS. (The Germans produced a replica of a captured Nieuport, called the Siemens-Schuckert D.I)
2 E.D. Atkinson (Royal Aero Club Trust)
3. W.E. Molesworth as a student at the Royal Military Academy, Sandhurst, 1913.

Captions:
1. S.E.5A fighter of Mick Mannock's 85 Squadron. (Crown Copyright, Imperial War Museum, Q 12051)
2. Edward 'Mick' Mannock (Imperial War Museum, Q 60800)
3. George Edward Henry McElroy (Royal Military Academy, Sandhurst)

Captions:
1. Sopwith F1 Camel (Crown Copyright, Imperial War Museum, Q 67556)
2. Maurice Lea Cooper, in RNAS uniform (Royal Aero Club Trust)
3. Guy William Price, in RNAS uniform (Royal Aero Club Trust)
4. Oscar Aloysius Patrick Heron, seated in centre with Irish Air Corps squadron

Captions:
1. Airco D.H.4 bomber (Crown Copyright, Imperial War Museum, Q 80861)
2. Forde Leathley (Royal Military Academy, Sandhurst)
3. Albert Gregory Waller. Note the observer's "Flying O" on his uniform. (Royal Aero Club Trust).

Captions:
1. Portrait of Robert Gregory by Charles Haslewood Shannon (Collection: Dublin City Gallery The Hugh Lane)
2. Robert Gregory's RAF casualty card (The RAF Museum)

Captions:
1. Douglas Hugh Moffat Carbery (Royal Aero Club Trust)
2. Henry George Crowe (Royal Aero Club Trust)
3. Edward 'Mick' Mannock (Royal Aero Club Trust)
4. Alfred William Saunders (Royal Aero Club Trust)

MANNOCK, EDWARD 'MICK'

(61 aerial victories)

Born: 20 May 1887 or 24 May 1887, 21 May 1888 or 21 May 1889 in Aldershot, Hampshire; Brighton, Sussex; Ballincollig, Co Cork.

Died: 26 July 1918

Awards: Victoria Cross, Military Cross and Bar, Distinguished Service Order with 2 Bars.

Commemorated: Arras Flying Services Memorial, France; Wellingborough War Memorial, Northamptonshire; War Memorial, St Mary the Virgin, Wellingborough, Northamptonshire; Mannock Memorial Plaque, Canterbury Cathedral, Kent.

Religion: Roman Catholic

Edward Corringham Mannock has been the subject of dozens of books and hundreds of articles, yet many aspects of his life remain the subject of controversy. It is not even agreed as to where he was born, neither is his date of birth, nor is the location of his death.

Mannock has been claimed by various imperialists as the ideal to which the military should aspire. He is held in special regard by socialists. To those in favour of Home Rule for Ireland and for Unionists he also holds great appeal.

His father was an English soldier, Corporal Edward Corringham aka Mannock. Edward served with the Royal Scots Greys as a cavalryman. Edward was not Scottish, though his mother Margaret (née Riley) was from Edinburgh. Mick's mother, Julia Sullivan, was from Ballincollig, Co Cork. Mick's father converted to Catholicism to marry Julia. Mannock's parents were married at Saints Mary and John's Church, Ballincollig, Co Cork on 04 February 1883.

In 1884 Mick's older sister, Jessie, was born in Scotland, where Mannock's regiment was stationed. On 13 June 1886 Mick's older brother, Patrick Corringham, was born at Aldershot, Hampshire; once again, another garrison town.

Mick could potentially have been born at Preston Cavalry Barracks in Brighton, Sussex, where Sergeant Mannock was stationed between 1887 and 1888 with the 2nd Dragoons, the Royal Scots Greys. However, the noted aviation historian Norman Franks categorically searched the English General Register Office for a birth record relating to Mannock but there is no corresponding entry for an Edward Mannock in England and Wales during the 1880s. An Irish birth is therefore a possibility. However, there's also an Edward Moore Mannoch who is regularly mistaken for Mick, but this chap, although a close match (born in 1883/1884), managed to return from Calcutta to London on 19 June 1921 aboard the *City of Marseilles*. Another red herring sometimes bandied about online forums is the birth certificate relating to Edward John Mannoch. He was born in Clerkenwell on 27 April 1888 and was baptized at Clerkenwell St Peter. However, that child died in July 1888 and was buried at Holborn.

In the UK Census 1891 the Mannock family were living at 76 Spencer Road, St Pancras, London. Mick's father, Edward Senior, falsely claims to have been born at St Pancras, London. Previous UK Census returns (e.g. 1871) indicate that Edward was born in Surrey in 1857 to a Margaret Mannock (b.1823, Edinburgh, Scotland). Edward Senior's brothers Michael (b.1850) and Thomas (b.1853) were both born in Ireland; his sister Christina was born in Middlesex.

Curiously, Edward Senior's other brother, John Patrick "Jack" Mannock (b.1859), the professional billiards player, claims in the UK Census 1901, (whilst resident at The Grove, Hammersmith), to have been born in London but in the UK Census 1911 (whilst resident at Leppoc Road, Clapham), claims to have been born in Dublin. Clearly several of the Mannocks liked to adjust their birthplaces between Ireland and England as the circumstances suited.

In the UK Census 1891 Mick's mother is recorded as being from Ireland. His sister Jessie is recorded as aged 7 and having been born in Scotland. His brother Patrick is recorded as being aged 5 and born at Aldershot, Sussex. Mick is recorded as being aged 3 and born at Brighton, Sussex. His younger sister Ann ('Nora') was 7 months old, and had been born in Ireland.

However, it is not completely unlikely that Mannock was born in Ireland. His mother Julia had a number of small children, variously born in Scotland and England, and may have wished to return to Ireland for family support at this time. Julia certainly did so for the birth of Mick's younger sister, Ann. Throughout his adult life, e.g. in his aviator's certificate and in his military service papers, Mick recorded his birthplace as Ballincollig, Co Cork. Julia Sullivan Corringham/Mannock, of course, had been born and raised in Ballincollig, Co Cork.

Some of Mick's detractors would point out that the apple hadn't fallen too far from the tree, e.g. his father re-invented himself several times, using the surname Corringham(e) for several years; listing his birthplace as St. Pancras in the 1891 Census; listing, again in 1891, that he was "of independent means" when he was merely living on the £40 lump sum he received upon being discharged from the cavalry. Further, Edward's brother John P Mannock was a billiards shark, making money in a notoriously betting-friendly occupation, although it would appear that the Mannock family were an ordinary middle class, middle of the road sort with just a few wild ones.

Mick's early youth was spent in Highgate, at which point his father had resumed using the surname Mannock following his discharge from the 2nd Dragoons. The general narrative from many of Mick's biographers is that Edward Senior was a violent drunk. This usually arises in the context of Mick being seen to overcome adversity in his childhood years. However, it would appear that Mick's father re-enlisted, joining the 5th Dragoon Guards at a Liverpool depot in 1893.

The 5th (Princess Charlotte of Wales') Dragoon Guards were posted to India, and the family moved there. They lived at Meerut, north of Delhi, and Mick in effect grew up in and around the area where his father was stationed. Some of Mick's detractors referred to his cod-Irish accent, but in reality he lived with his Irish mother whilst his father was stationed at various overseas postings; his sisters and brother had been born in England, Ireland and Scotland; he was reared in India. Overall his accent would have been a product of all these influences. It should also be mentioned that, in September 1899, Mick's father was posted to South Africa during the Second Boer War, and opted to stay there—transferring into the 7th Royal Dragoon Guards for the remainder of the war rather than return to India with his regiment. Mick in effect grew up with his Irish mother in India, having spent nearly a decade of his life there.

Mick was educated by the Jesuits in India. However, it is not his education that is generally commented upon but another event at this stage of his life: Mick contracted a seriously debilitating amoebic infection there. In Ira Jones' biography and in MacLanachan's "Fighter Pilot" this was dramatized into the myth of "the ace with one eye", i.e. a congenital defect from which he never recovered. Later biographers, such as James Dudgeon, and Frederick Oughton and Vernon Smyth, also entertain the myth to greater or lesser extents. Given that they were writing in the post-World War II era of living legends such as Douglas Bader—who flew with no legs—the pre-war melodramatics of Jones or MacLanachan would no longer hold such remarkability. Adrian Smyth dispenses with the myth altogether, giving a detailed analysis of the contradictions and inconsistencies in the tale.

One other aspect of Mick's early life in India would be the appalling disparity of wealth and power he would have experienced there and his disgust at same. This is often given as being the basis upon which his socialist beliefs were formed. However, this is just a little too convenient: there were many other influences on his belief system, not least the return to the UK in his mid-teens, at an age when he would have been quite conscious at the extent to which a former soldiers' family would have experienced the reality of poverty in England. The family returned to England in 1902, living at the Cavalry Depot in Canterbury. Mick's father deserted his family shortly after his return from the Boer War.

The family moved to Jones Cottages in September 1906. Mick's youngest sister, Ann 'Nora', was allowed attend the local St Thomas' RC school, but the older children had to work to support the family. Mick worked in a greengrocers and a barber's shop but physically he was not suited, having recurring bouts of malaria, not to mention the stark fact that he was getting too old to be kept on boy wages and was easily replaceable. Mick's brother Pat had gotten a job as a clerk in the National Telephone Company, and Mick joined him there in 1908.

Mick had trained with the [Anglican] Church Lads' Brigade, mainly due to the influence of Cuthbert Gardner, a local solicitor. From Christ's soldier to the Territorial Force was not a big leap for Mick, as it entailed the outdoor life, showing initiative, teamwork and making good use of his organizational skills. A family friend, Fred Rawson, had encouraged his participation but Mick would not have been unfamiliar with horses from his father's time in the cavalry and so was promoted several times. However, his friendship with Gardner kept Mick engaged in debating societies and other activities that contrasted sharply with the weekend soldiering.

In 1911 Mick transferred from the ledger clerk position to become a linesman for the National Telephone Company. He had not been suited to the office life but had done his duty to keep the family income stable for those initial years back in England. (He still sent remittances to his mother after he moved from Canterbury). The National Telephone Company posted him to Wellingborough, Northamptonshire. In the UK Census 1911 Mick was living at 64 Melton Road, Wellingborough, which was the house of Albert Walter Joyce. Both

Mick and Joyce were recorded as being telephone inspectors. Mick is once again recorded as being born at Brighton, Sussex, just as he had been in 1891, although it must be conceded that Joyce completed the census forms, not Mick, and it was Joyce who signed the relevant declaration on the census form.

Mick worked with the British Post Office Engineering Department. It is known at this stage that Mick was regarded as a socialist.[215] He was also known as 'Pat' or 'Paddy', which could probably be attributed to his unusual accent, with its mix of Cork, India and Canterbury. Smith also points out that Mannock played cricket and football in Wellingborough with the local Wesleyan congregations, which undermines the "ace with one eye" myth. Mannock continued to worship as a Catholic, and is recorded on the 1914-1918 'Roll of Honour' on St Mary the Virgin church on Knox Rd, Wellingborough. There was a locally active Labour organization, which had contested the December 1910 election against the sitting Liberal MP in East Northamptonshire. Mick became good friends with the local ILP organizer in Wellingborough, A.E. "Jim" Eyles. He moved in to the spare room of the Eyles family home at 183 Mill Road, Wellingborough. All of Mannock's many biographers agree on the significance of 'Jim' Eyles' family to Mick, it being a family environment to him and a political soundboard through which he developed his beliefs. Mick participated in the local YMCA mock parliament. Mannock sat as MP for Waterford, in honour of John Redmond, the leader of the Irish Parliamentary ('Home Rule') Party. Mannock's organizational efforts and political activism as the party secretary in the local Labour movement is attributed as being a key factor in Walter R Smith's breakthrough for Labour in Wellingborough in the General Election of 1918.

In February 1914 Mick moved to Turkey, to exploit the opportunities for an experienced rigger in the cable-laying operations at the 'Société Anonyme Ottoman des Téléphones'. Although Anglo-German relations were not particularly bad in the region, e.g. the

---

215 Adrian Smith, *Mick Mannock, Fighter Pilot*, pp.25-38. (Palgrave, 2001)

Berlin-Baghdad railway project was one of mutual interest, there was nevertheless a degree of local hostility to the British, as it was an erstwhile ally who had conspired to engineer a puppet regime in Egypt, had done nothing to aid the Young Turks in the Italo-Turkish War of 1911-1912 and had wavered in supporting its former Ottoman ally when Russia backed Bulgaria, Greece, Montenegro and Serbia against the Turks in the Balkan Wars of 1912 and 1913. Mannock had not picked the most opportune time to seek work in Constantinople. However, he secured work as a supervisor of linesmen and was subsequently promoted to an administration role. With the outbreak of war in August 1914 Mannock was unlucky in the general 'keep calm and carry on' position of the Foreign Office, who expected a short war and wanted to keep Turkey neutral for as long as possible, a position which was contradicted by the hawkish military elements in the Admiralty, which had sought to seize two new battleships awaiting delivery to the Ottoman navy. However, the net result was that British citizens were not evacuated upon the outbreak of war. Subsequently, when two German warships sought and were granted refuge in the Dardenelles, a British ultimatum to the Ottoman Empire resulted in events overtaking one another in a series of retaliatory actions, with the eventual outcome being a British declaration of war on 05 November 1914.

Mannock was interned with a large number of British and French nationals, in effect taken hostage to discourage any further British naval shelling of unfortified coastal towns and villages. The British reaction was to seize Ottoman consular staff, which provided some high-profile hostages as bargaining chips but the Royal Navy's shelling of Gallipoli in May 1915 nearly resulted in the Ottoman Empire deploying its internees/hostages as human shields. During the months of Turkish custody the internees suffered appalling conditions. Mannock's release was secured on 01 April 1915, and although he was of military age he was suffering from dysentery and malaria. However, Mannock was able to pass an army medical less than two months later, which tends to suggest that the various lurid accounts of Mick's POW experiences at the hands of a non-European enemy may have been formed in the post-World War II era in the light of a very different non-European enemy, Japan.

However, regardless of the degree of maltreatment at the hands of the Turks, Mannock had developed a hatred of the enemy. The degree and intensity of it has been the subject of some speculation over the years but it would appear to be genuine and not some device invented by biographers to explain the determination and drive that Mannock later exhibited in his prosecution of the war as a fighter pilot. The Irish historian Peter Berresford Ellis made the point "even with an understanding of his personal experiences as the source of Mannock's hatred of his enemies, one does wonder how he reconciled his previous pre-war socialist international proletarian solidarity with that later ruthlessness. Probably it was simply war that changed him". However, Mannock's initial service was with the Home Counties Field Ambulance, hardly the most bloodthirsty outfit. At Halton Park Mannock managed to arrange a mock parliament at the sergeant's mess. He represented Newmarket, appropriate for someone with his equine experience but unusual for a staunch socialist. Various accounts seem to indicate that he was quite pro-war and still quite a socialist orator. However, the RAMC was not the place for Mannock, as he was in effect 'back from the front' and in a combatant's state of mind whereas his colleagues were still untrained and untested civilians for whom the war would still probably have seemed quite remote; Mick sought appointment as an officer cadet in the Royal Engineers.

His transfer to the Royal Engineers Signal Section took Mick to Bedfordshire in March 1916. He was promoted to temporary Second Lieutenant by June 1916 but his time with the Royal Engineers was not a happy one: he was nearly 29 or 30, quite a contrast to the intake of young cadets; he was still politically quite vocal, in an atmosphere that would have been quite elitist and not at all tolerant at what they would have perceived their servant-class speaking ill of what they imagined to be social superiors. Mannock was not popular. There is no evidence that Mannock had any arguments over Irish politics, although the Easter Rising in 1916 would have occurred at the time he was in Bedfordshire. Although none of Mannock's biographers have identified any correspondence between Mick and Jim Eyles on the Irish situation from this period it is not unlikely that he would have faced some unease over the use of British field artillery in the narrow civilian-populated inner city streets of Dublin. Perhaps he would have been aware of the reaction of many Irish nationalists serving with the British army, e.g. the former Irish Nationalist MP for East Tyrone, Tom Kettle, had spent decades in the effort to secure the British promise of Home Rule for Ireland and felt this work had now been undone but that the rebels "will go down to history as heroes and martyrs, and I will go down—if I go down at all—as a bloody British officer." Mannock opposed violent insurrection but would probably have still been the subject of much anti-Irish prejudice that the events would have unleashed.

Mannock applied for a transfer to the Royal Flying Corps in June 1916. The "ace with one eye" proponents invent various schemes through which he could have passed the medical, and indeed the succession of medicals he had taken in the previous 18 months. It would appear that Mannock had been motivated to transfer as a consequence of a chance encounter with an old workmate from Northampton, Eric Tompkins, who was based at the Central Flying School at Netheravon in Wiltshire.

Mick was posted to 10 Training Squadron, which was based at Joyce Green at Dartford Creek. It was here Mick first encountered James McCudden, who had been sent there to instruct students on how to survive a spin. Mannock took on board what was said but upon putting a D.H.2 into a spin at well below the danger level of 2,000 feet and recovering, he was lucky to survive, landing just inches from a shed containing explosives. Despite being severely reprimanded Mick nevertheless completed training and passed as a pilot. In Joyce Green he began to keep a diary. One of the earliest inscriptions on its facing pages is by the Irish poet Paul Charles Stacpoole O'Longan, who on 14 March 1917 wrote the typically gloomy psuedoprofoundic teenage material "Let the world got to pot for we will be there ourselves soon". In March Mick was posted to Clarmarais.

There is not much in the diary of this period in terms of deep personal thought. In April there is reference to him leaving a show early in disgust, which probably reflects the puritanical streak in Mannock, which in civilian life often manifested itself in his seriousness and his hard work ethic. There is also passing reference to a Jeannette, a local French teenager who worked in the mess, but the relationship would appear to have been platonic. Mannock was posted to No.40 Squadron on 06 April 1917 and by 08 April 1917 had broken an axle on landing, having lost his leader in the foggy conditions. Already this may have started whispers of cowardice and that Mannock had deserted from his formation. He was certainly quite unpopular in the early weeks of his time with No.40 Squadron. Partially it was down to his outspokenness: Mannock had a lot of life experiences, some very good technical and mechanical knowledge, and a strong desire to get involved. This would not have sat well with a culture of deference, in which new pilots would have been expected to hold their tongue. Also a factor may have been that someone from Mannock's socio-economic and socio-cultural background should have been expected to "know one's place" when in the company of gentlemen officers. However, the assault on Vimy Ridge was underway and Mannock wanted to get stuck in. This was "Bloody April", during which the Royal Flying Corps was being slaughtered in the effort to ensure the offensive at Arras could be maintained. The British lost 245 aircraft, 211 pilots and observers killed and 108 taken POW. The German Luftstreitkrafte lost only 66 aircraft, and Manfred von Richthofen's Jasta 11 scored 89 victories alone. However, the RFC succeeded in continuing to direct artillery shellfire, to conduct aerial photography reconnaissance of German positions and disposition, and to engage in bombing raids. Their actions probably saved thousands of infantry lives but it was at enormous relative cost: the average life of a RFC pilot in April was just 18 hours of flying time.

Trenchard's insistence on "no empty chairs at breakfast" ensured a conveyor-belt mentality, in contrast to the hope that it would raise morale to have pilots and observers refrain from dwelling upon those who were lost in combat each day. Mannock's outspokenness would have been deeply unpopular at a time when the culture was still one of understatement and "stiff upper lip" as everyone tried to fathom just what was expected of them and what the prospects of survival for a new recruit actually were.

In Mick's diary of 20 April 1917 it is recorded that on the previous day Mannock had survived a serious mechanical failure when up on gun practice. This seemed to prompt him to undertake his own gunsighting, which may have been taken as a lack of confidence in the riggers and armourers and/or a need to reassure himself of the flightworthiness of an aircraft before he took to the air. It of course fed into the rumours that Mick had lost his nerve, was a coward, an idle boaster who avoided fights through endless flying hours of gun practice.

Mannock struck up an unusual friendship, with Desmond Herlouin de Burgh. He was a Unionist from Co Monaghan, a member of the Anglo-Irish gentry. de Burgh was the son of Colonel Ulick George Campbell de Burgh and Anna Blance Constance Paget, of Scarva House, Clones, Co Monaghan; grandson of Thomas de Burgh of Oldtown, Naas, Co Kildare and grandson of Baroness of Donoughmore of Knocklofty, Co Tipperary. de Burgh later rose to the rank of Air Commodore and was killed in a military flying accident during World War II.

Typically, both men argued passionately on every subject, ranging from politics to the conduct of the war. de Burgh had played Mrs O'Flaherty[216] in the debut performance of G.B. Shaw's "O'Flaherty VC", alongside two other Irishmen—Robert Gregory (as Tessie the Maid) and Captain Denis Osmund Mulholland (as O'Flaherty)—and so he would have been a central enough character in the life of the squadron. In April 1917 de Burgh had accounted for at least two

---

216 Gale K Larson, *Shaw and History* (Penn State Press, 1999), p.91.

German aircraft. The friendship with de Burgh seemed to have at least helped Mannock into some social engagement with the other members of the squadron, although the Mannock-de Burgh arguments were regularly finished off with a round of boxing. de Burgh is quoted as saying:

"We had two things in common, he and I, so that I came to know him well (although I doubt if any man saw much beneath the surface of him)—we were both Irishmen, and we both dearly loved an argument. He was the only man in the mess who would talk beneath the surface. Many was the time when we would argue fiercely on some highly controversial subject such as politics, socialism or religion—he usually won the argument, though heavens knows what his views really were. As a curious contrast to the warfare of the tongue, Mannock was very keen on boxing, and as I had done a good deal, we often used to blow off steam by having a 'set to' in the mess … I think, on the whole, that I used to give more than I gave, as he had the height on me, and a slightly longer reach; but I had him at footwork".[217]

The sight of two Irishmen arguing and then brawling may not have been the most dignified way to become known in the squadron. However, de Burgh had at least touched upon a point that, for all Mannock's public views on politics, religion and so forth he was still quite enigmatic on a personal level and that few would get to know the real man.

Another observation of de Burgh was:

"As far as I know, there were only two things which would rattle him, and he would always "rise" to them, if drawn: the first was his very bitter hatred of the Germans, and the second was "Society" women. The former has been amply confirmed by others. The latter caused us all no small amount of amusement—it was only necessary to leave a copy of one of the weekly papers open showing "The

---

217 Frederick Oughton (ed) "The Personal Diary of 'Mick' Mannock VC, DSO (2 Bars, MC (1 Bar)", pp.153-154 [Spearman, 1966].

beautiful Lady ... who is organising a charity concert in aid of ... etc" for Mannock to go off the deep end for about half an hour".[218]

This should not be taken that Mannock had any particular dislike of women. Rather it was more a manifestation of his dislike of the realities of *noblesse oblige* in which the peasants were expected to be grateful for what their lords and masters were doing. It was also an expression of his disgust at high society social occasions in which a vacuous hostess would regard a pilot as a social prop to decorate a function or event, perhaps much in the way a previous generation could have relied upon the occasional cavalry officer or naval captain as human wallpaper background material to fill out an important event. Mannock's experiences as a child among the families of military and diplomats in India did not endear him to the ruling class, and his time with the expatriate community in Constantinople led him to wearing a cygnet ring at social functions, which seems to suggest some social unease with engaging with the consular class generally. However, Mannock was quite socially awkward in many respects, and perhaps his outbursts at Lady such-and-such were an effort at giving expression to his anger at inequality and injustice.

On 22 April 1917 Mannock wrote "Now I can understand what a tremendous strain to the nervous system active service flying is... When it is considered that seven out of ten forced landings are practically 'write offs', and 50% are cases where the pilot is injured, one can quite understand the strain of the whole business".

Mannock's early experiences with No.40 Squadron seem to be one of increasing anxiety. Externally there was the pressure arising from the common perception that he had lost his nerve. There was the overwhelming weight of expectation he had placed on himself to succeed. Each incident in which he failed to properly close on an enemy or a further day that passed with another squadron casualty would have compounded his anxiety. He was badly shot up on

---

[218] Frederick Oughton (ed) "The Personal Diary of 'Mick' Mannock VC, DSO (2 Bars, MC (1 Bar)", p.154 [Spearman, 1966].

07 May 1917, with Captain Keen reporting on his return that he believed Mannock had been shot down. Mick was badly shaken upon his return. Later that day, in an attack on German observation balloons, of the 6 aircraft they lost Captain Nixon and of the survivors Lts Hall and Scudamore crashed on the aerodrome, while Lts Parry and Redler crashed behind British lines. Only Mannock made it home, but he was again badly shot up. He had, however, scored his first aerial victory, destroying a balloon.

On 09 May 1917 Mannock was part of a 3-man patrol when they engaged a German aircraft. In the encounter Mannock was bounced by three other enemy aircraft and suffered engine failure.

"I thought it was all up. We were 16,000 feet up at the time. I turned almost vertically on my tail—nose-dived and spun down towards our own lines, zig-zagging for all I was worth with machine-guns crackling away behind me like mad. The engine picked up when I was about 3,000 feet over Arras and the Huns for some reason or other had left me. I immediately ran into another Hun (after I had climbed up to 12,000 feet again) but hadn't the pluck to face him. I turned away and landed here with my knees shaking and my nerves all torn to bits. I fell a bit better now, but all my courage seems to have gone after that experience this morning".[219]

Mannock was probably also suffering from oxygen-deprivation-induced fatigue as a consequence of high-altitude flying, with ocular strain and earache also being likely side-effects. He told the Eyles family that "I always feel tired and sleepy, and I can lie down and sleep anywhere or at any time".[220]

Days later, after further squadron losses, Mannock missed out on several combats due to being sent on various other duties such as retrieving aircraft from Omer. It was clear that Major Tilney was aware of the extent to which Mannock was under strain but also was

---

219 Frederick Oughton (ed), *The Personal Diary of 'Mick' Mannock VC, DSO (2 Bars, MC (1 Bar)*, pp.74-75 (Spearman, 1966).
220 Adrian Smith, *Mick Mannock Fighter Pilot—Myth, Life and Politics* (Palgrave, 2001), p.74.

not in a position to rotate frontline staff from the squadron to Home Establishment unless they were at breaking point. Mannock notes in his diary that MacKenzie was sent on 14 days leave. Mannock's excessive caution in arming and checking his own machine, and in engaging in endless gunnery practice, would have given the impression of fussy perfectionism, control-freakery and a whiff of combat-avoiding cowardice. However, the hostility to Mannock was lessening as the month passed and he was earning respect as he continued to stay alive. On 16 May 1917 he went to Omer for rest and recuperation with Captains Gregory and Keen, and Lieutenants Bond, Jake, Thompson and Redler. It was a short respite, as on 19 May 1917 he had a forced landing.

At least Mannock's No.40 Squadron had upgraded from the F.E.8 to the Nieuport: his friend, the gloomy teenage Irish poet Paul Charles Stacpole O'Longan, ended up in No.41 Squadron, which was still attempting to persevere with the obsolete F.E.8, a venerable 'pusher' that was no longer fit for frontline service. On 23 May 1917 O'Longan was part of a patrol in an F.E.8 (A4915) when he managed to help drive off several Albatros scouts that had attacked a formation of F.E.2ds. The Germans must have been amused as the obsolete F.E.8s helped combine with the 'Fokker fodder' F.E.2d to help the latter escape. O'Longan didn't last for long however, being killed on 01 June 1917 by the German ace Oblt Hans Bethge of Jasta 30. O'Longan's rudder (A4887) became part of the 'trophy wall' decorating the roof of the hangar that housed Bethge's Pfalz scout.

On 02 June 1917 Mannock wrote "our Captain Gregory—just gone back to H.E. [Home Establishment]—has been awarded the 'Legion de Honneur' for specially good service. He deserved it!" This tends to confirm the absence of any hostility between the two, which is sometimes implied in accounts of No.40 Squadron. Indeed the facing pages of Mannock's diary bear inscriptions from various pilots. However, the entry in which a quotation from Gregory is recorded "Don't let your wives sing!" is dated 27 May 1917 and may actually be in Mannock's hand-writing, as the subsequent note below records that he was killed in an air accident in February 1918; this latter note definitely being Mannock's handwriting. On balance it would appear that Mannock bore no malice or hostility to Gregory, and as Gregory was quite similar in profile to de Burgh and other Anglo-Irish landlords in No.40 Squadron with whom Mannock got on well for some reason.

On 07 June 1917 Mannock wrote "I brought my first dead certain Hun down this morning". (He had scored at least two victories in May and June that had not been awarded). Mannock's description of the kill does not accord with the bloodthirsty monster he is generally imagined to be. He writes:

"I was only ten yards away from him—on top so I couldn't miss! A beautifully coloured insect he was—red, blue, green and yellow. I gave him 60 rounds at that range, so there wasn't much left of him. I saw him go spinning and slipping down from 14,000 [feet]. Rough luck but it's war and they're Huns".[221]

His victim was probably Vzfw Eberlein of Jasta 33, who was wounded but survived.

The 'Combats in the Air' reports for No.40 Squadron record that on 09 June 1917 Mannock shot up two German aircraft, expending a whole drum of ammunition. He reported "hits were observed with no apparent effect". Mannock nevertheless stated that a third German went down after being attacked by Lt Bond. However, Bond gave no reciprocal verification to Mannock's efforts. Sometimes the effect of an attack isn't immediate, e.g. a leaking petrol tank can still ignite, a damaged elevator control can seriously malfunction or a wounded pilot can lose consciousness. Mannock was still isolated even if his improving aerial skills were gaining increasing respect.

Mick was to swing between exultation and despair, e.g. on 14 June 1917 Mannock shot down two Germans and claims that "I felt like the victor in a cock-fight!" but within days had received an eye injury and writes "Feeling nervy and ill during the last week. Afraid I am

---

221 Frederick Oughton (ed) "The Personal Diary of 'Mick' Mannock VC, DSO (2 Bars, MC (1 Bar)", p.105 [Spearman, 1966].

breaking up". His demeanour would change accordingly. One kill described by Mannock does show that he still had plenty of empathy for humanity:

"Had the good fortune to bring a Hun two-seater down in our lines a few days ago. Luckily my first few shots killed the pilot and wounded the observer (a Captain) besides breaking his gun. The bus crashed south of Avion. I hurried out at the first opportunity and found the observer being tended by the local M.O. and I gathered a few souvenirs, although the infantry had first pick. The machine was completely smashed, and rather interesting also was the little black and tan terrier—dead—in the observer's seat. I felt exactly like a murderer. The journey to the trenches was rather nauseating—dead men's legs sticking through the sides with putties and boots still on—bits of bones and skulls with the hair peeling off, and tons of equipment and clothing lying about. This sort of thing, together with the graveyard stench and the dead and mangled body of the pilot (a NCO) combined to upset me for a few days".[222]

The dead NCO was Vzfw Reubelt. The "Captain" was actually Lt H Bottcher. Their DFW aircraft was from Schlasta 12.

Mannock got to take leave in June 1917. Visiting his family was a difficult experience: his mother was drinking more heavily and was back in England, having briefly lived in Belfast with Mick's sister Jessie, who's marriage was disintegrating. Mannock gave his mother money but went on to stay with the Eyles family. As Smith records:

"[t]he Eyles family had never seen him so totally immersed in any one subject, nor so enthusiastic. Pat [Mick, not his brother Patrick] could be found standing on the table, playing out untried methods of attack, with Jim putting on a brave face—or keeping a straight face—as he pottered around the kitchen waiting to be shot down. Mannock acknowledged that age was not on his side, but felt sure he could compensate for 'the weakness of the flesh' by spending long periods of time in concentrated thought, working out fresh tactics in his

---

[222] Frederick Oughton (ed) "The Personal Diary of 'Mick' Mannock VC, DSO (2 Bars), MC (1 Bar)", pp.118-119 [Spearman, 1966].

head—hard thinking would reap its reward once he came to put theory into practice ('You watch me bowl them over when I return!)".[223]

Mannock also visited his cousin Patrick, son of the billiards shark J.P. Mannock. This tends to dismantle the myth that the Mannock family had disowned Julia and her children.

If Mannock was still facing bouts of nausea before he flew he was becoming increasingly confident when in the air. Some have equated this as being akin to an actor before going on stage or an artist before a performance but Mannock was not some drama queen: he killed people. There was real life and death gravity to his actions. The killing did not dehumanize him at this stage; if anything his increasing proficiency and confidence led him to being more magnanimous with the enemy. On 20 July 1917 Mannock was to write:

"This morning we went out north as far as Armentieres, Keen leading a six patrol. Ran into three of the finest Hun pilots I ever wish to meet. Had quite an exciting and enjoyable ten minutes scrap. Those Huns were artists. Do what I could I couldn't get a line on them, and it was six against three. Eventually they flew off, apparently none the worse for the encounter. I shall always maintain an unsullied admiration for those Huns. The aircraft battery people reported the battle as one of the most splendid exhibitions of tactics they had ever seen. We did nothing but swear".[224]

One small consolation from the theft of material from the UK National Archives was that the thieves/vandals were most likely stealing to order for collectors whose interest in 'wartime celebrities' did not stretch to all aerial encounters, just the aerial victories. Consequently there are several accounts of indecisive combat engagements in which Mannock was not awarded a kill, e.g. the squadron's 'Combats in the Air' report for 27 July 1917 states that Mannock was part of an offensive patrol that attacked 7 Albatros scouts near Lens. Mick, flying a Nieuport (B3554), stated the following:

---

223 Adrian Smith "Mick Mannock, Fighter Pilot", p.79 [Palgrave, 2001].
224 Frederick Oughton (ed) "The Personal Diary of 'Mick' Mannock VC, DSO (2 Bars), MC (1 Bar)", pp.124-125 [Spearman, 1966].

"Attacked one Albatros scout, coloured purple, with white crosses on fuselage, and fired approximately 50 rounds at close range, hits were observed, but owing to Aldis Sight fogging up completely and broken stay-bolt on Aldis Fixing, aim was inaccurate.

The EA swung off East and was then attacked by another Nieuport. The EA formation drew off east, Nieuports following to re-engage. Eventually EA went very low so Nieuports returned".

Mannock had probably crippled the Albatros, but neither Mick nor Lt H.A. Kennedy (a Canadian) nor 2nd Lt John Henry Tudhope (a South African) were awarded an aerial victory for that encounter, for which they had also submitted claims. However, the situation does bring to light the problem with Mick's self-maintenance regime on the gunsight and mounting: it was not good enough, notwithstanding whatever previous reassurance it had afforded him.

On 19 August 1917 Mannock wrote in his diary:

"Had a splendid fight with a single-seater Albatross Scout last week on our side of the lines and got him down. This proved to be Lieutenant von Bartrap, Iron Cross, and had been flying for 18 months. He came over for one of our balloons—near Neuville-St Vaast—and I cut him off going back. He didn't get the balloon either. The scrap took place at 2,000 feet up, well within view of the whole front. And the cheers! It took me five minutes to get him to go down, and I had to shoot him before he would land. I was very pleased that I did not kill him. Right arm broken by a bullet, left arm and left leg deep flesh wounds … had a great ovation from everyone. Even Generals congratulated me. He didn't hit me once".[225]

His diary of this time also makes reference to the elusive "purple man", which most aviation historians would identify as the great German ace Werner Voss. Mannock records "he's a marvel … he manoeuvred so cleverly". Once again it must be taken that, for all the outward Hun-hating bluster, Mannock was still capable of respecting his enemies. His comments echo those of his friend McCudden,

---

[225] Frederick Oughton (ed) "The Personal Diary of 'Mick' Mannock VC, DSO (2 Bars), MC (1 Bar)", pp.128-129 [Spearman, 1966].

who—in the course of the engagement that resulted in the death of Voss—praised his skill and bravery.

On 05 September 1917 Mannock wrote in his diary of several encounters the previous day, during which he had sent down a German aircraft in flames. "I got in about 50 rounds in short bursts whilst on the turn, and he went down in flames, pieces of wing and tail etc dropping away from the wreck. It was a horrible sight and made me feel sick.... Prior to that—at 9.40 a.m. I had a beautiful running fight with another two-seater at 17,000 feet from Bruay to east of Lens. This one got away notwithstanding the fact that I fired nearly 300 rounds at close range. I saw the observer's head and arm lying over the side of the machine—he was dead apparently—but the pilot seemed to be alright. He deserved to get away really as he must have been a brave Hun".[226]

The foregoing would suggest that although Mannock publicly bragged of getting a "flamerino" and was full of outward Hun-hating bravado, privately he considered it to be a sickening sight. He also seemed to have some respect for his surviving victims. Of the potential matching candidates for these 2 German losses the second may have been from FAA 240, Vzfw Eddelbuttel (wounded) and Lt Kuhn, whilst the first was most likely from FA 235: Vzfw G Frischkorn survived, Lt F Frech was killed. However, the "who got who" game is quite unreliable, as aircraft crash in a different area from where the original engagement took place, and pilots often see what they want to see instead of what actually happened. An aircraft in a spin towards the ground may well look like it is disintegrating; it is often impossible for an RFC pilot to follow down an enemy aircraft, as they majority of engagements take place over German-held territory. Mannock sent several down in flames, but in this particular instance it would appear to have been an ordinary destruction.

As it transpires, a balloon observer, Lt G. Pilgrim, saw a German Halberstadt drop a container near British lines a few days later. The

---

[226] Frederick Oughton (ed) "The Personal Diary of 'Mick' Mannock VC, DSO (2 Bars), MC (1 Bar)", pp.141-145 [Spearman, 1966].

message said "To the British Flying Corps. The 4th Sept I lost my friend Fritz Frech. He fell between Vimy and Lieven. His respectable and unlucky parents beg you to give any news of his fate. Is he dead? At what place found he his last rest? Please throw several letters that we may find one. Thank before, His friend, K.L. PS: If it is possible, please send a letter to the parents, Mr Frech, Konisberg, i, Pr. Vord Vordstadt 48/52". It took several months for this to reach Mannock, but he did write to the parents. The Germans regularly dropped canisters to notify the RFC of the fate of British casualties over German lines, and there was a corresponding obligation to let the Germans know of the fate of casualties if requested.

Mannock was awarded the Military Cross, which was gazetted on 17 September 1917:

"T./2nd Lt. Edward Mannock, R.E. and R.F.C.

For conspicuous gallantry and devotion to duty. In the course of many combats he has driven off a large number of enemy machines, and has forced down three balloons, showing a very fine offensive spirit and great fearlessness in attacking the enemy at close range and low altitudes under heavy fire from the ground".[227]

He ceased keeping the diary in September 1917. Most likely it was due to the sheer pressure of operations: he could not record every thought on the dozens of men he was sending to their deaths. Mannock had scored 6 victories in September 1917 alone. Interestingly, although Mannock's medal citation mentioned three balloons, he was actually only awarded one aerial victory against balloons for the period in question. However, the practice varied so much in terms of how these were awarded and it's therefore no surprise that Mannock's final tally of aerial victories remains the subject of so much debate.

On 27 September 1917 Mannock intervened to save the life of the German ace Leutnant Waldhausen (the "Eagle of Lens"), who had been shot down by the South African Lieutenant Tudhope of No.40 Squadron, and/or Major Charles Booker and Herbert Thompson

---

227 London Gazette Supplement, 30287, p.9577.

of No.8 (Naval) Squadron. Waldhausen had shot at a kite balloon observer before being shot down, and the troops on the ground wanted to execute Waldhausen. In an interview with the Imperial War Museum on 12 March 1973, Herbert Thompson recounts the tale of a dispute between various squadrons over claiming Waldhausen's Albatros DV, as Mannock forcefully claimed it for Tudhope and No.40 Squadron. (The tone is somewhat Mannock-as-Irish-savage-barbarian in the context of their dispute over the claim, rather than about Mannock keeping Waldhausen alive). Thompson also recalled that many years later he met Waldhausen, who claimed that his aircraft had only been hit 3 times: once in the engine, which did the damage, but was also hit in the fuselage and that Thompson's shots had resulted in a hit on Waldhausen himself in the encounter.

Mannock was awarded a Bar to his Military Cross, which was gazetted on 18 October 1917.

Mannock was unhappy with the transition of No.40 Squadron from Nieuports to the S.E.5A. Apparently General "Boom" Trenchard was visiting the squadron when Mannock was returning from a combat flight in which the gun had jammed. Apparently not recognizing Trenchard's rank he launched into a lengthy tirade when asked about the performance of the squadron's new mounts, whilst Major Tilney tried to made placatory noises and interjections to shut up Mannock. The S.E.5A had an interrupter gear to allow a machine-gun fire through the arc of the propeller in the same way German aircraft had for years, but consequently this synchronized Vickers gun on the S.E.5A had a much slower rate of fire than the traditional Lewis gun on a sliding-rail ("Foster") mounting on the top of the Nieuport's wings. The Vickers gun was also more prone to jamming. However, despite Mannock's rant, a few days later Trenchard sent a gunnery officer from HQ over to the squadron for further feedback on the specific difficulties being encountered.

In August 1917 George McElroy joined the squadron, crashing several aircraft in the opening months. He eventually got his first victory in December 1917. He dived into a German formation and scattered them when MacLanachan's flight could have manoeuvred into a position from which they could have taken out several more than the single aircraft victory McElroy had achieved. Instead of praise from Mannock he got a dressing-down, being called a spailpín, but Mannock wasn't overly disappointed with "McIrish" and it was left to MacLenachan ("McScotch") to congratulate McElroy on doing so well with his first victory. Mannock and McElroy were to become good friends, but the incident also brings up another point: Mannock was becoming a leader in strategic formation flying and tactics.

Mannock was given extended leave on 06 January 1918, being returned to Home Establishment with effect from 02 January 1918: although the RFC hadn't fully comprehended the need to rotate pilots and to ascertain the optimal levels of frontline service relative to other roles such as training duties there was nevertheless an awareness of the impact it was having in individual cases and circumstances. Mannock was reassigned from HQ Training Brigade to No.74 Squadron on 11 February 1918. The squadron was still not fully developed, and did not reach France until 30 March 1918. Mannock drew heavily on his own personal experiences when teaching pupils at the squadron whilst it was based at Hertfordshire. He would not necessarily have been a good instructor but his mantra "always above; seldom on the same level; never underneath" was drummed in to pupil's minds. Mannock also emphasised the use of height advantage was essential for the S.E.5A in encounters with the Fokker Dr.I triplane, as the S.E.5A could climb and dive, while the Fokker's advantage lay with its manoeuvrability, and so the emphasis was on avoiding dog-fight situations.

It was with No.74 Squadron that Mannock made friends with Henry Eric Dolan. As mentioned in Appendix II, I do not include Dolan as Irish on account of him being of Irish ancestry, which is beyond the scope of this book. Dolan was born in England, but his brother was born in South Africa. Mannock took Dolan under his wing and several of Dolan's "shared" victories have in effect been attributed to Mannock. (However, I do not support this view that

Mannock had dozens of unattributed victories: they are mostly there, albeit in a "shared" category on many occasions). Also at No.74 Squadron was Irish ace William Jameson Cairnes. He was commander of "C" Flight whilst Mannock commanded "A" Flight of the squadron. (The other Flight Commander was Major Wilfred Ernest Young, who had served with No.19 Squadron and became an ace with No.74 Squadron).

Ira "Taffy" Jones served with No.74 Squadron, and it is his biography of Mannock that also helps build the legend of this unit as "Tiger Squadron", with over 200 victories in the few months of the war it was mobilized (April-Nov 1918). However, this is not to say that it was not a formidable squadron—e.g. apart from Jones and Mannock there was the brilliant New Zealander Keith Caldwell and the Mannock-aged "old man" Benjamin Roxburgh-Smith—but overall the squadron's 17 aces would stand as broadly comparable to other squadrons with a like-for-like combat role. One remarkable aspect of No.74 Squadron, however, was their excellent kill: loss ratio, as they were to lose less than 40 pilots and observers in the corresponding period. (Of course, several of these were high-profile casualties, such as Cairnes and Dolan).

However, Mannock's mental deterioration was continuing. Previously, his fears of being shot down in flames had been recounted to many, and it was known that Mannock claimed he would shoot himself if his aircraft caught fire, but it soon became clear that it was an morbid obsession. It did not affect his ability to kill, as on 12 April 1918 he scored two victories, and a sent a German down in flames on both 23 April 1918 and 29 April 1918. The following day he crashed a German 2-seater on the British side of the lines, killing both its crew. However, the magnanimity with which he treated opponents was diminishing with his increasing fear of being shot down in flames. After Manfred von Richthofen's death on 21 April 1918 a member of the squadron proposed a toast to the Red Baron but Mannock walked out in disgust. A quote sometimes attributed to Mannock is " I hope the bastard went down in flames" but this is probably more likely to have been uttered by Jones, who embraced the concept of total warfare and was known for shooting at German pilots who had parachuted from their aircraft[228]. However, von Richthofen was not held in high esteem by British pilots either, a criticism being that he was always protected by the large "Flying Circus" behind him and that he would break off an attack if he encountered any significant fire from a pilot/observer.

However, the contrast between Mannock's respect for his victims when at No.40 Squadron and the increasingly morose Hun-hating human wreck that was emerging at No.74 Squadron is quite stark. In one incident he strafed a German 2-seater they had forced down, killing the pilot and observer (most likely Flgr Zimmermann and Vzfw Speer of Sch 10). This would not be particularly exceptional, as many similar incidents appear in other squadrons' accounts at various stages of the war. What is generally noted is the vehemence of Mannock in his defence of his actions afterwards when back at the mess. The death of his protégé Henry Dolan on 12 May 1918 sent Mannock into a vengeful rage, but this should not be misunderstood as merely some dramatic pretext to allow a warrior's killing ability be contextualized, e.g. it was not Achilles avenging the death of Patroclus when slaying Hector and then mistreating the body of his fallen enemy. Mannock was very much a professional pilot, and the discipline and controlled aggression would be closer to that shown in his days when boxing with de Burgh in the mess room. Although Mannock would appear to have taken additional "vengeance" flights he still retained a sense of responsibility and loyalty to this other charges. Nevertheless it may be noted that prior to Dolan's death on 12 May 1918 Young's "B" Flight had also lost Stuart-Smith, Bright and Skeddon whilst "C" Flight had lost Begbie. Mannock had trained the majority of these men at London Colney in Hertfordshire, so it would have weighed heavily upon him.

Mannock achieved 20 victories in May 1918, of which at least 6 went down in flames. In one fight on 21 May 1918 he scored a

---

228 McScotch "Fighter Pilot", pp.84-85 indicates Mannock's concern was with honouring Lt Begbie, who went down in flames and as to whom the toast should have been made.

triple-victory, destroying all three opponents near Hollebeke. Mannock had perfected the "deflection shot" in which one estimates the angle and speed of both aircraft and hits the opponent as it passes through the intended position. It had the advantage of avoiding lengthy manoeuvring to get on the tail, or at the blind spot in the case of a 2-seater, but flying like this required steady nerves and so it must be assumed that Mannock was still mentally stable. Much is made of one incident in which he prances around the mess, celebrating some "flamerinoes" with a 'sizzle, sizzle, wonk' dance, but this should be understood in the context of trying to raise morale among new recruits, including a nervous 17 year old South African pilot, 'Swazi' Howe, who Mannock was to assist with his first kill later that week. Mannock wasn't quite psychopathic Hun-hater he is often portrayed as being, but he was certainly on the way to a mental breakdown.

Mannock also harboured a deep resentment with high command for not supplying parachutes to the RAF pilots. The artillery observation balloon crews were permitted parachutes, and the Germans had devised several techniques for pilots and observers to have them stored on board or worn on the person, but the RAF was still suspicious that it may tempt pilots to abandon an aircraft before it was completely necessary. Ludendorff's northern offensive in the spring of 1918 had put the RAF under tremendous pressure, losing 1,000 aircraft in 5 weeks. Mannock would have been acutely aware of the attrition rate, and the expendability of the men at his disposal, but he and 'Grid' Caldwell are lavished with praise for keeping squadron morale high. The Canadian ace, 'Clem' Clements recalled:

"We developed into a family really, Grid and Mick saw to that, an efficient, happy team ... On the rare occasions that gloom did settle in the mess, Mick was just the man to handle it. He didn't give a hoot how he did it, as long as the men ended up happy and morale was maintained. He was always the life and soul of the party, although this never interfered with our respect for his authority".[229]

---

229 James Dudgeon "Mick", p.125. Quoted in Smith "Mick Mannock, Fighter Pilot", p.107.

In a letter dated 16 June 1918 Mick wrote to his sister Jess he admitted that:

"Things are getting a bit intense just lately and I don't quite know how long my nerves will last out … These times are so horrible that occasionally I feel that life is not worth hanging on to myself".[230]

In June 1918 Mannock was to obtain a further 11 victories—including another triple victory—before being promoted to take command of No.85 Squadron. Mannock was in no fit mental state to be placed in a greater position of responsibility than he already had as Flight Commander in No.74 Squadron. His sense of duty and loyalty to the men and his excellent formation flying tactics and teamwork development were being misdirected into a post of even greater responsibility, at a time when he needed to be taken off frontline duties. When Mannock returned to the Eyles family, on leave prior to the appointment, he was unable to control the shaking and twitching in his hands. In the kitchen at Mill Rd he broke down completely:

"His face, when he lifted it, was a terrible sight. Saliva and tears were running down his face; he couldn't stop it. His collar and shirtfront were soaked through. He smiled weakly at me when he saw me watching and tried to make light of it; he would not talk about it at all. I felt helpless not being able to do anything. He was ashamed to let me see him in this condition but could not help it, however hard he tried".[231]

Mannock apparently got to succeed the great Canadian ace "Billy" Bishop as head of No.85 Squadron on the grounds that the pilots thought James McCudden, Bishop's originally intended successor, as being too common. They must have been unaware that Mannock was of similar Irish Catholic working-class background. Whatever the reasons behind Mannock getting the nod it was certainly an experienced squadron, and for whom Mannock's efforts at

---

230 Ira "Taffy" Jones, "King of Air Fighters", p.235.
231 James Dudgeon "Mick", p.154, quoting Jim Eyles. See also Adrian Smith "Mick Mannock, Fighter Pilot", pp.119-120, which also contains reference to similar impressions from his sister-in-law Dorothy Mannock on Mick's state and survival prospects.

perfecting formation flying combat tactics would be greater rewarded than with just keeping inexperienced pilots alive in No.74 Squadron.

Of course "Taffy" Jones' biography of Mannock adds plenty of real and imagined conversations with Mannock that can neither be confirmed nor refuted. One story is that Mannock claimed to Jones that he had reached Bishop's score of 72. This is a recurring problem with the Mannock legend: among his many, many admirers there's a tendency for them to denigrate the achievements of others. Bishop was disliked by many British pilots, but it was not his fault to have been a success relatively early in the war, in the days when the 'lone wolf' was supreme. His era naturally gave way to that of the team players like McCudden and Mannock. It is unlikely that Mannock reached that score, but even if he did it is not to anyone's credit to put down Bishop rather than just celebrate Mannock's proven successes. Jones almost reaches parody when he dresses up Mannock in grand imperial rhetoric, e.g. Mannock is supposed to have said "Don't forget, Taffy, when you see that tiny spark come out of my SE, it will kindle a torch to guide the future air defenders of the Empire along the path of duty". Having reassured the young male readers of the 1930s that they were to be the burning torches of a future war, Jones then went on to tick another box in the requirements for a humanizing element: Mannock had a sweetheart, an Irish nurse called Sister Flanagan, to whom he intended to propose once the war was over.

However, one well recounted incident, and so probably authentic, is that of 20 July 1918. At a farewell luncheon for his friend Gwilym Hugh "Noisy" Lewis (author of "Wings over the Somme"), Mannock and McElroy remonstrated with one another over flying too low and following victims too far down to verify their victories. Lewis, many decades later, in 1990 at the age of 93, gave an interview to the Imperial War Museum, recorded by Brad King. Lewis repeats a version of the account first-hand. Lewis also gives a very positive account of his experiences with Mannock, describing him as the finest patrol leader they ever had.

MANNOCK, EDWARD 'MICK'

What is certain is that on 26 July 1918, in his 3rd week in charge of No.85 Squadron, and with a 7 further kills to his name, Mannock took a rookie New Zealand pilot, Donald Inglis, out on a mission to get his first kill. Mannock riddled a Junkers CL1, a relatively new type of German 2-seater, killing the observer/gunner and allowing Inglis finish it off. However, they had followed the aircraft too far down, and were within range of machine-gun and rifle fire from the German trenches. Both Mannock and Inglis were hit by ground fire. Inglis managed to crash land on the Allied side of the lines but saw Mannock go down in flames.

There has been much speculation as to the exact location Mannock was buried and whether he did shoot or jump before the crippled aircraft caught fire. It is possible that he was killed by ground fire and/or that his body fell or was thrown clear from the wreckage. The personal effects returned by the Germans after the war indicate that the body may have been singed but was not burned. The aviation historian Norman Franks has undertaken painstaking research to establish the location of Mannock's crash site, while Mike O'Connor, another prominent military historian—in his "Airfields & Airmen" series—revises his estimation of the location of Mannock's remains over the course of his excellent series of works on RFC, RNAS and RAF cemeteries.

What is reasonably certain is that Mannock scored a minimum of 61 aerial victories. Mannock had scored a dozen victories subsequent to the award of the Bar to his DSO. However, a Second Bar to his DSO had been in the course of approval, and was gazetted on 03 August 1918:

"*Air Ministry, 3rd August, 1918.*

His Majesty the KING has been graciously pleased to confer the undermentioned rewards on Officers of the Royal Air Force, in recognition of gallantry in flying operations against the enemy:—

Awarded a Second Bar to The Distinguished Service Order.

Lt. (T./Capt.) Edward Mannock, D.S.O., M.C. (formerly Royal Engineers).

205

This officer has now accounted for 48 enemy machines. His success is due to wonderful shooting and a determination to get to close quarters; to attain this he displays most skilful leadership and unfailing courage. These characteristics were markedly shown on a recent occasion when he attacked six hostile scouts, three of which he brought down. Later on the same day he attacked a two-seater, which crashed into a tree.

(The announcement of award of Distinguished Service Order, and First Bar thereto, will be published in a later Gazette)".[232]

On 16 September 1918 the citation for Mannock's DSO and for the First Bar were both gazetted:

"T./2nd Lt. (T./Capt.) Edward Mannock, M.C., R.E., attd. R.A.F. For conspicuous gallantry and devotion to duty during recent operations. In seven days, while leading patrols and in general engagements, he destroyed seven enemy machines, bringing his total in all to thirty. His leadership, dash and courage were of the highest order". (p.10869)

"T./2nd Lt. (T./Capt.) Edward Mannock, D.S.O., R.E., and R.A.F.

For conspicuous gallantry and devotion to duty. In company with one other scout this officer attacked eight enemy aeroplanes, shooting down one in flames. The next day, when leading his flight, he engaged eight enemy aeroplanes, destroying three himself. The same week he led his patrol against six enemy aeroplanes, shooting down the rear machine, which broke in pieces in the air. The following day he shot down an Albatross two-seater in flames, but later, meeting five scouts, had great difficulty in getting back, his machine being much shot about, but he destroyed one. Two days later, he shot down another two-seater in flames. Eight machines in five days—a fine feat of marksmanship and determination to get to close quarters. As a patrol leader he is unequalled.

(D.S.O. gazetted in this Gazette)".[233] (p.10858)

---

232 London Gazette Supplement, 30827, p.9197
233 London Gazette Supplement, 30901, p.10858 and p.10869.

However, it was imperative that some recognition would be given for Mannock's sustained efforts at going beyond the call of duty over a prolonged period of time. A campaign began to have Mannock awarded a posthumous Victoria Cross. Ronald McNeill, who was later elevated to the peerage as Baron Cushendun, was the local MP for Canterbury, and was strongly supportive of the campaign; ironically, he was a staunch Ulster Unionist who would have bitterly opposed Mannock's views on 'Home Rule' for Ireland. (Canterbury had been represented by Irish unionists previously: Major Francis Bennett-Goldney represented the constituency until killed in France when serving with the RASC. Bennett-Goldney was a suspect in the theft of the Irish Crown Jewels in 1907). In July 1919 the Air Minister, Winston Churchill, obtained Royal Assent for the award of the VC to Mannock. The award is what is termed a 'periodic' award, i.e. it is not for a specific instance of bravery but for outstanding courage over a particular period.

On 18 July 1919 Mannock's Victoria Cross was gazetted. The citation reads as follows:

"*Air Ministry*
Hotel Cecil, Strand, W.C.2.,
18th July, 1919.

His Majesty the KING has been graciously pleased to approve of the award of the Victoria Cross to the late Captain (acting Major) Edward Mannock, D.S.O., M.C., 85th Squadron Royal Air Force, in recognition of bravery of the first order in Aerial Combat: —

On the 17th June 1918, he attacked a Halberstadt machine near Armentieres and destroyed it from a height of 8,000 feet.

On the 7th July 1918, near Doulieu, he attacked and destroyed one Fokker (red-bodied) machine, which went vertically into the ground from a height of 1,500 feet. Shortly afterwards he ascended 1,000 feet and attacked another Fokker biplane, firing 60 rounds into it, which produced an immediate spin, resulting, it is believed, in a crash.

On the 14th July 1918, near Merville, he attacked and crashed a Fokker from 7,000 feet, and brought a two-seater down damaged.

On the 19th July 1918, near Merville, he fired 80 rounds into an Albatross two-seater, which went to the ground in flames.

On the 20th July 1918, East of La Bassee, he attacked and crashed an enemy two-seater from a height of 10,000 feet.

About an hour afterwards he attacked at 8,000 feet a Fokker biplane near Steenwercke and drove it down out of control, emitting smoke.

On the 22nd July 1918, near Armentieres, he destroyed an enemy triplane from a height of 10,000 feet.

Major Mannock was awarded the undermentioned distinctions for his previous combats in the air in France and Flanders: —

Military Cross. Gazetted 17th September 1917.

Bar to Military Cross. Gazetted 18th October 1917.

Distinguished Service Order. Gazetted 16th September 1918.

Bar to Distinguished Service Order (1st). Gazetted 16th September 1918.

Bar to Distinguished Service Order (2nd). Gazetted 3rd August 1918.

This highly distinguished officer, during the whole of his career in the Royal Air Force, was an outstanding example of fearless courage, remarkable skill, devotion to duty and self- sacrifice, which has never been surpassed.

The total number of machines definitely accounted for by Major Mannock up to the date of his death in France (26th July, 1918) is fifty —the total specified in the Gazette of 3rd August 1918, was incorrectly given as 48, instead of 41".[234]

It's unclear why they revised downwards Mannock's tally to 41 from 48, as the higher figure accurately matches squadron records. Overall Mannock accounted for at least 61 enemy aircraft and remains one of the RAF's highest-ever scoring aces. He is Ireland's greatest fighter pilot ever.

---

234 London Gazette Supplement, 31463, p.9136.

In all likelihood Mannock was the greatest RAF pilot of all time: it is not just through the narrow metric of kills that he should be judged (although he does remain one of the highest-scoring Allied pilots of all time), rather his combat career must be taken as a whole—no-one inspired such devotion as a Flight Commander, and when given command of a squadron he brought an unprecedented level of success. Mannock was the master tactician, who enhanced the capability of those with whom he flew. For a socially awkward and introverted man he excelled at motivating and keeping up morale among his colleagues. He put himself beyond any considerations of personal health and wellbeing, and went far beyond even the highest call of duty in prosecuting the war.

Mannock's legend would not be complete without another appearance by his pantomime villain father. Some accounts claim that Edward Senior turned up for the medal ceremony, made off with the VC and that it had to be retrieved from a pawnbrokers by the other family members. This is probably a by-product of the various film scripts that abounded, which built upon the violent drunken ogre that had emerged in the account of Mannock's early childhood by Jones, Oughton, Dudgeon and others. In reality the VC remained in the family for many years.

Mannock remains one of the most successful yet enigmatic and misunderstood fighter aces of the war. Although many pilots' memoirs are full of praise for Mannock it is uncertain as to what his post-war legacy would have been had he survived. A Carmarthenshire lad like Jones could imagine Mannock to be a future Prime Minister but in reality Mannock would not have survived in the shark pool of parliamentary politics, not least the catastrophic Ramsay MacDonald coalitions of the 1920s and 1930s. A more likely scenario would be Mannock joining the mass ranks of unemployed demobilized soldiers, perhaps returning to fight the Germans over Spain in the 1930s. Indeed, quite how he would fare in a Polikarpov I-16 against a Messerschmitt Bf-109 would be open to speculation: Mannock wouldn't have survived for long, nor would he have prevented the slaughter at Guernica or slowed the march of fascism in the late 1930s, but he would have made an impact and perhaps inspired people in a way unimagined by Jones in his apotheotic worship of the "King of the Airfighters".

✦ ✦ ✦

MCCLINTOCK, RONALD ST CLAIR

(**5 aerial victories**)

Born: *13 July 1892, Co Carlow*
Died: *22 June 1922*
Awards: *Military Cross*
Religion: *Church of Ireland*

McClintock was born at Rathvinden, Leighlinbridge, Co. Carlow. He was the youngest son of Susan Heywood McClintock (née Heywood-Collins) and Arthur George Florence McClintock, J.P. for Carlow, Down, Kildare, King's County (Offaly) and Wicklow.

The Irish Census 1901 records Ronald as being resident with his brother Stanley and their parents Arthur and Susan at Leighlinbridge, Co Carlow, together with four servants. Arthur is described as being a "land agent", and was born in Dublin. Susan was from Glasgow, Scotland. The Irish Census 1911 records Ronald as being present at his brother's house at Mahonstown, Co Meath. (In the 1911 Census his parents at still resident at Leighlinbridge, together with Ronald's brothers Robin La Poer and Edward Stanley McClintock and his sister Jane Catherine McClintock.

According to 'Amorial families: a directory of gentlemen of coat-armour' (Volume 2) by Arthur Charles Fox-Davies [Edinburgh, TC & EC Jack], several of the brothers of Ronald also served in the British Army, e.g. John Heywood Jocelyn McClintock was a Lieutenant in the 18th Hussars, and Edward Stanley McClintock was a Captain in the Royal Artillery; another brother served in the Great War, e.g.

Lt-Colonel Arthur George McClintock of the 8th Hussars won the DSO.

One problem with tracing McClintock's own service history arises from the fact that there was a Major Robert Singleton McClintock of the Royal Engineers (a Boer War veteran) who keeps turning up in records as "R.S. McClintock". From Ronald's war medals records[235] it is stated that he enlisted as a Private in the Ceylon Planters' Rifle Corps (No.2167) before obtaining a commission as a 2nd Lieutenant in the West Lancashire Brigade of the Royal Field Artillery. It would appear that McClintock enlisted on 17 November 1914 and served in Egypt before transferring to the Royal Flying Corps. McClintock was promoted from 2nd Lieutenant to Temporary Lieutenant with effect from 05 July 1915.[236]

In December 1915 McClintock joined No.2 Squadron as an observer. He later became a pilot. On 28 March 1916 McClintock had a close encounter, according to Royal Flying Corps Communiqué No.32, of March 1916:

"2nd Lt Williams and Lt McClintock, 2 Sqn, took some photographs urgently required by the 1st Corps. They had to fly at 3,000 feet owing to the gale. One of the elevator controls was shot away and the machine was riddled with bullets". [237]

McClintock was promoted from Flying Officer (Observer) to Temporary Lieutenant with effect from 04 April 1916.

On 26 October 1916 his engagement to Mary Gordon (Milly) Laird was announced in *Flight* magazine (p.942). *Flight* magazine of 14 December 1916 (p.1100) confirmed the wedding date as 20 December 1916 to Molly at the Church of the Holy Trinity, Kensington Gore. They were to have 2 children.

The Army List of 1917 records McClintock as a temporary Captain in the Army with effect from 17 January 1917, 3 West Lan-

---

235 WO 372/12, UK National Archives.
236 London Gazette Supplement, Issue 29285, p.8835.
237 Christopher Cole (ed) "Royal Flying Corps Communiqués 1915-1916", p.130. [Tom Donovan, 1990]

cashire Brigade, Royal Field Artillery. On 06 February 1917 it was announced that 2nd Lieutenant (Temporary Lieutenant) McClintock had been promoted from Flying Officer to Flight Commander with effect from 01 January 1917. On 28 June 1917 the War Office announced that McClintock, a 2nd Lieutenant (temporary Lieutenant)(temporary Captain, RFC) would retain the temporary rank of Captain, RFC, and to remain seconded.[238] This was always something of an administrative balancing act, of allowing an officer act to several ranks above his home grade whilst not losing the tenuous relationship between responsibility and promotion. In July 1917 he was promoted to No.64 Squadron as Flight Commander. In March 1918 No.64 Squadron was re-organised, having been re-equipped with the SE.5a, and flew ground attack operations in addition to the scout/fighter squadron duties. McClintock scored his first aerial victory on 18 March 1918. Over the course of March he achieved 3 further aerial victories. His final victory with the squadron came on 02 April 1918, the destruction of an Albatros D.V over Fricourt. RAF Communiqué No.1 of 1918 reports the encounter:

"Capt R.S.C. McClintock, while leading a patrol of 64 Sqn, observed seven EA scouts against which he led his patrol; he engaged one EA, diving at it and firing about 100 rounds at 40 yards range. The EA went into a flat spin and fell completely out of control and was observed to crash".[239]

However, McClintock was not the only Irish ace to serve with No.64 Squadron: Edward Dawson Atkinson also scored most of his victories with the squadron. (Additionally, there were two other aces of Irish parentage who served with No.64 Squadron: James Anderson Slater and Edmund Tempest).

In late April 1918 McClintock became Flight Commander of No.3 Squadron. There were 9 aces who achieved this status with this squadron during the war, but many others had served in its ranks,

---

238 London Gazette Supplement, Issue 30155, p.6398.
239 Christopher Cole [ed] "Royal Air Force Communiqués 1918", p.20. [Tom Donovan, 1990]

e.g. the great ace James McCudden served with the squadron as a mechanic. (McCudden had originally served with the Royal Engineers and No.3 Squadron had its origins in the Air Battalion of the Royal Engineers).

Flight magazine of 16 May 1918 (p.546) quoted the London Gazette Supplement of 07 May 1918, which reported McClintock's promotion to Temporary Major while employed as Major (Flying), with effect from 20 April 1918.

McClintock was awarded the Military Cross, which was gazetted on 22 June 1918:

"Lt. (T./Capt.) Ronald Sinclair McClintock, R.F.A. and R.F.C.

For conspicuous gallantry and devotion to duty. On one occasion he shot down two enemy machines, and on the following day he attacked and shot down a hostile two-seater machine at a height of 100 feet. He has led upwards of forty patrols and has performed much valuable work on low-flying reconnaissance and bombing patrols. As a flight commander he has been untiring in his care of personnel and machines, and as a patrol leader he has displayed the greatest courage and resource".[240]

As one may note, he was misrecorded as 'Sinclair McClintock' instead of 'St Clair McClintock'.

McClintock continued to serve in the RAF following the armistice. *Flight* magazine of 07 August 1919 (p.1066) reported McClintock's promotion to Captain (Aeroplane). I do not have a reference to cite as to when McClintock's period as Acting Major and acting Captain came to an end but *Flight* magazine of 10 March 1921 (p.179) reported that Flight Lieutenant McClintock was in attendance at the King's Levee of 07 March 1921 at St James' Palace:

According to 'Twenty Four—the magazine of XXIV Squadron Association' (Issue 15, Summer 2008, p.8) McClintock was killed when his Sopwith Snipe collapsed. *Flight* magazine of 06 July 1922 (p.390) also carried an article on his death. On 22 June 1922, while serving as a Flight Lieutenant with No. 1 School of Technical Train-

---

240 Supplement to the London Gazette, 22 June 1918 (30761/7418).

ing, in Middlesex, McClintock was killed in a crash involving a Sopwith Snipe (F2409). The aircraft, which had been used previously by No. 24 Squadron's award-winning relay team, collapsed and McClintock fell from a considerable height to his death, less than 4 months after the birth of his daughter, Pamela Mary McClintock. His older child, John Arthur Peter McClintock, born 30 April 1920. John became a Flight Lieutenant with the RAF and was killed in action on 09 November 1940.

✦ ✦ ✦

MCCORMACK, GEORGE

(5 aerial victories)

Born: 1896, Belfast
Died: 28 March 1928, Amman, British Trans-Jordan
Commemorated: Ramleh War Cemetery, Israel
Religion: Methodist

George McCormack was born in Belfast in 1896. It is most likely that he was the son of a Belfast postman, Noble McCormack, and Elizabeth McCormack (née Hawkes), who had married on 04 December 1897 at University Road Church, Belfast. The McCormacks had 8 children. The Irish Census 1901 records the family as being resident at Donard St, in the Ormeau Ward of Belfast, Co Down. George's father was from Co Monaghan and his mother was English, from Canterbury in Kent, but George and his sister Philippa Mabel, were Belfast-born. The Irish Census 1911 records the family as being resident at Naples St, in the St Anne's Ward of Belfast, Co Antrim. All of George's sisters and brothers were Belfast-born.

Looking at the Ulster Covenant there are 2 George McCormack covenanters but neither would appear to be George, as one was from Larne, Co Antrim whilst the other was from Co Tyrone.

George's father enlisted in the Pioneer Division, Royal Irish Rifles (123127) and served with the Labour Section of the Royal Engineers. Noble died on 18 May 1918, several months after being discharged on ill-health grounds.

George joined the Royal Irish Rifles as a cadet at eighteen years of age in 1915, and received a commission of second lieutenant in the same year, and was later transferred to the 10th Reserve Regiment of Cavalry at Curragh Camp. According to an Irish Times obituary in 1928, George was on duty in Dublin during the 1916 Rebellion and was wounded. Subsequently he took part in the heavy fighting at Messines, and was severely wounded[241].

On 04 December 1916 the War Office announced McCormack's promotion "from a Reserve Cavalry Regiment" to temporary 2nd Lieutenant dated to 22 November 1916 but with seniority from 04 October 1915.[242]

McCormack flew F.2bs with No.22 Squadron as an observer. It was a reconnaissance unit. McCormack scored his first aerial victory on 03 September 1918, destroying a Pfalz D.XII in a Bristol F.2b (F5820) piloted by an American, Lt Chester Thompson. McCormack and Thompson were to achieve ace status together: over the course of a 3 week period in September 1918 they accounted for 5 enemy aircraft. Their 5th victory came on 24 September 1918 over Cambrai, with McCormack being wounded.

Thompson was not to fare too well afterwards: although he scored further victories in September—including one with Irishman Lt William Tyrrell—he was shot down east of Cambrai on 29 September 1918 and was taken prisoner of war.

McCormack survived his wounds and continued to serve with the RAF after the war. There is a suggestion that he was wounded again in October or November 1918 but I cannot find a matching record. Given his unfortunate record of being wounded on land and in the air it is no surprise that McCormack had no luck in his post-war RAF career either: when serving on the North-West Frontier in 1919 he was forced to land with a bullet in his fuel tank. He was taken

---

241 There was a medal index card for him—WO 372/12—but there is not much information on it, i.e. he didn't receive the 1914 or 1915 star, which confirms his late entry to the war.
242 London Gazette Supplement, 29847, p.11833.

prisoner and ransomed. According to the Irish Times "his safe return excited such interest that he was specially presented to the Viceroy, and, on his return to England, was presented to the King". Flight magazine of 16 February 1922 (p.113) reported that McCormack had attended the King's Levee on 10 February 1922, so there is probably some truth to the story.

The London Gazette of 04 March 1922 reported McCormack's promotion from 2nd Lieutenant (Honorary Lieutenant) to Lieutenant with effect from 23 August 1918. This may appear to be quite a backdating of a promotion but in reality was just updating the actual situation in terms of McCormack's status. Flight magazine of 13 December 1923 (p.757) reported an Air Ministry announcement that Flying Officer McCormack had been transferred to No.111 Squadron, Duxford with effect from 12 December 1923. McCormack remained a Flying Officer for many years. On 01 January 1927 the Air Ministry announced McCormack's promotion to Flight Lieutenant.

Flight magazine of 29 December 1927 (p.885) reported that McCormack had transferred to No.14 Squadron, Middle East. Another Irish ace, Henry George Crowe, was one of the Flight Commanders of that squadron. The Squadron Leader was Edward Garden Hopcraft, which is quite an uncommon surname in the flying services. Robert George Hopcraft, an English-born architect with an Irish mother was to fight with the RNAS, and after the war become a well respected architect in Ireland, with many prominent public buildings in both the Irish Free State and Northern Ireland to his name. However, I cannot confirm the connection to the "Irish" Hopcraft.

On 28 March 1928 McCormack was severely injured whilst flying a D.H.9A of No.14 Squadron near Amman. Leading Aircraftman J Kimberly was killed flying with McCormack, with the latter succumbing to his injuries in the immediate aftermath of the crash. Both men are buried in Ramleh War Cemetery.

The Squadron Operations Record Book of No.14 Squadron[243] records the D.H.9A as having crashed while on the mail flight to Ramleh. It barely receives a mention and is one of a litany of crashes that year. The next most significant entry in the operations record book relates to His Majesty the Emir Abdullah presenting the prizes at the Squadron Sports on 21 April 1928 but that the occasion was somewhat interfered with by low-flying clouds of locusts.

The *Irish Times* of 31 March 1928 and *Weekly Irish Times* of Saturday, 07 April 1918 reported his death, with a brief obituary. McCormack was undecorated for his wartime service, and remains one of Ireland's forgotten aces.

❖ ❖ ❖

---

[243] AIR 27/191, UK National Archives.

MCELROY, GEORGE EDWARD HENRY

(**47 aerial victories**)

Born: 14 May 1893, Co Dublin

Died: 31 July 1918

Awards: Military Cross and 2 Bars, Distinguished Flying Cross and Bar

Commemorated:

Laventie Military Cemetery, La Gorgue, France

War Memorial Cross, St Mary's Church, Donnybrook, Dublin.

Religion: Church of Ireland

Captain George McElroy was one of the Allies' highest-scoring aces of the war.

He was born at Donnybrook, Co Dublin to Samuel and Ellen McElroy (née Synnott). In the Irish Census 1901 the family are recorded as being resident in Beaver Row, Donnybrook. George was the eldest of the children. At this stage he had one brother (Robert) and 3 sisters (Eileen, Louisa and Elizabeth). For such a large household they only had one servant. Both of George's parents were from the Irish midlands. George's father, Samuel, was a primary school teacher, originally from Co Roscommon. George's mother, Ellen McElroy (née Synnott) was from Co Westmeath, and is described as being a "work-mistress", which roughly equated to teaching assistant. According to George's parents' marriage registration details, Ellen was living at 38 Glengarriffe Parade at the time of their marriage, which would suggest that they met in Dublin and not in Roscommon or Westmeath. They married on 18 July 1892. McElroy's father Samuel used to enter a school choir to the Feis Ceoileanna Irish cultural festivals, which was quite unusual for a Church of Ireland school, but he used also teach French and other non-curriculum subjects to the children. His interest in choral matters extended to his participation in the choir of St Mary's Church, Donnybrook for many decades.

They and another family shared the house, according to the census return recorded by James Savage. The other family is recorded as being one headed by a Robert Frater Luke, a sexton. He and his wife Mary Ann had 4 daughters between the ages of 3 and 12 living with them. If this seems surprisingly overcrowded then it may be noted that the next adjacent building on Beaver Row was the local National School (i.e. the primary school). The Luke and McElroy families were the only Protestants living on the street. Although a large public transport depot takes up much of modern-day Beaver Row, and the numbering on the address has changed over the decades, it would appear that McElroy lived on the banks of the river Dodder in Donnybrook.

By the Irish Census 1911 McElroy was a boarder at the Mountjoy School, on Mountjoy Square in Dublin. (This school was in later decades to merge with the Hibernian Marine and the Bertrand & Rutland School to form Mount Temple Comprehensive—a school with a great reputation for developing original talent, e.g. Irish musicians such as Cactus World News, Damien Dempsey and U2 were to study there). McElroy was one of only a handful of Dublin students at Mountjoy, which seemed to cater for Protestants from rural areas that would not have had the population threshold to support a Protestant school. The school was also the headquarters for the Incorporated Society for Promoting Protestant Schools in Ireland.

George's parents were still living beside the school on Beaver Row, with 5 children in 1911. Although George and Eileen had moved out—Eileen was a boarder at the Collegiate School run by the Incorporated Society (for Promoting Protestant Schools in Ireland) near Celbridge in Co Kildare—Louisa Margaret, Mary Elizabeth and Robert Samuel were still there, since joined by Olivia Frances, William Alfred and John Richard McElroy. As may be noted, George was from a family of modest means, with the eldest children receiving their post-primary education from a special Protestant-funded resource that largely relied upon rental income from estates bequeathed to it. Several of George's uncles emigrated from Ireland to the USA, as did those on his mother's side, which gives rise to a substantial number of American descendants of the McElroy and Synnott families.

It is nevertheless suggested that McElroy was a student at Trinity College Dublin from 1913 to 1914. However, this notion is dispelled somewhat by the fact that the University of Dublin does not include George on the rolls of honour in the 1937 Reading Room of Trinity College, which commemorates the 3,529 members of TCD, the Dublin University OTC and employees who served in the war. However, Edward Caulfield Kelly is similarly excluded, so perhaps nothing too much should be read into the matter, e.g. they could have been first year undergraduate drop-outs or temporary tutorial staff who were the servants or agents of particular lecturers.

McElroy enlisted with the Royal Irish Regiment at the outbreak of the war, serving as a motorcycle courier. (His RAF service record details his eligibility for the 'Mons Star' arising from his army service). It is often suggested that in May 1915 he sought a commission in the Royal Irish Regiment, but he served on the Western Front and suffered badly from a mustard gas attack in the battles for Ypres.[244]

---

244 One problem with tracing McElroy's army service history (i.e. pre-Royal Flying Corps) is that there was a Private G.H. McElroy from the Coldstream Guards who was given a commission as a Temporary 2nd Lieutenant in the King's Own Scottish Borderers in October 1915. Similarly this G.H. McElroy was transferred from the Training Reserve to serve with the King's African Rifles later in the war.

Allegedly McElroy was recuperating at home in Dublin at the outbreak of the Easter Rising in 1916 but refused to fire on his countrymen and was sent to a southern garrison for the duration of the summer as punishment. Numerous sources make reference to this claim, e.g. this is referenced in Neil Richardson's informative *A Coward if I Return, A Hero if I Fall: Stories of Irish soldiers in World War I* (O'Brien Press, 2010), which features extensive material on several of the Irish aces (pp.126-142). However, I have not had sight of the various regimental records that would confirm the various details of McElroy's service in the British Army. On the other hand the records of the Bureau of Military History include an account by Provisional Government Minister and Treaty signatory Robert Barton (WS0979) in which he stated that he was permitted to go home on the dubious pretext of having no uniform. (It was at a tailors' shop in Dame St, which was under siege). Barton, serving with the 10th Battalion of the Royal Dublin Fusiliers, returned a week later from the family estate in Co Wicklow to help manage the ownership of prisoners' effects, prevent further looting by British troops and to engage in routine duties to bring back to normal the civilian life in the city (e.g. he located and returned the keys to a Fitzpatrick's boot-making shop in Duke Street). It is therefore quite possible that McElroy was given some pretext for not having to fire on fellow Irishmen and was then assigned non-combat military duties.

The records of the Royal Military Academy at Woolwich do indicate that George Edward Henry McElroy was enrolled as Cadet No.10089 in 1916. He was aged 23, his DOB was recorded as 14 May 1893, but his religion was misrecorded as "RC". His alma mater was recorded as Mountjoy and his father's occupation as being the schoolmaster of Donnybrook School. McElroy came 55th in the order of merit on joining. He was 41st in the order of merit on leaving, graduating on 26 February 1917. His commission in the Royal Garrison Artillery is recorded as 28 February 1917. This information would suggest that he entered Woolwich in late May 1916. However,

McElroy's service record[245] suggests that he was a Gentleman Cadet at the Royal Military Academy, Woolwich, from 1915 to 1916, but the RAF may have based these dates on McElroy's various applications to obtain a commission.

The Royal Regiment of Artillery had evolved from a series of mergers but it retained 4 sub-branches. The Royal Garrison Artillery, as the name would imply, had their origins in manning the guns of coastal artillery batteries, and those of the forts and fortresses of the Empire. The Royal Horse Artillery and Royal Field Artillery had the mounted and unmounted artillery corps. The RHA had its origins in providing artillery support for cavalry operations in the field of battle whilst the RFA managed the medium calibre artillery pieces close to the front line. There also existed a Royal Artillery designation for those tasked with managing the storage of munitions and supply to units in the field.

On 12 March 1917 McElroy was posted to 1 SMA, which presumably relates to Stow Maries Aerodrome. Training Squadrons were initially called Reserve Aeroplane squadrons, but from January 1916 were known as Reserve Squadrons (RS) and from May 1917 as Training Squadrons (TS). Following McElroy's service record at this time therefore suggests movements from RS to TS units but in actual fact only indicates his service with the same training squadron.

On 31 March 1917 he was transferred to 14 Reserve Squadron, thereafter to 6 Reserve Squadron (later re-designated 6 Training Squadron). On 28 June 1917 McElroy was appointed Flying Officer whilst at 6 Training Squadron. He was briefly posted to 54 Training Squadron from 02 July 1917 to 15 July 1917. On 20 July 1917 2nd Lieutenant G.E.H. McElroy was confirmed in his rank whilst seconded to the Royal Flying Corps, with effect from 28 June 1917.[246] On 27 July 1917 the War Office announced that G.E.H. McElroy,

---

245 AIR 76/317 George Edward Henry McElroy, UK National Archives.
246 London Gazette Supplement, Issue 30193, p.7407.

Royal Artillery (Royal Garrison Artillery) was promoted to 2nd Lieutenant with effect from 09 February 1916.[247]

McElroy entered France on 16 August 1917, being posted to No.40 squadron. On 23 August 1917 McElroy was assigned to Mannock's 'A' Flight of No.40 Squadron. He crashed 2 Nieuports and was almost sent home for further training, but Mannock persuaded Major Tilney to retain McElroy, who he had nicknamed "McIrish" to differentiate him from William MacLanachan "McScotch". McElroy would not be considered a competent pilot on the Nieuport 17—the American Bill Lambert recounts some spectacular crashes by McElroy—but he was to prove a major success with the S.E.5a, scoring some spectacular victories and becoming the highest-scoring pilot on that type.

Royal Flying Corps Communiqué No.108 of 1917 reports on one of McElroy's early unconfirmed claims:

"Lt GEH McElroy, 40 Squadron, attacked a hostile balloon south-east of Lens and saw it smoking, but owing to anti-aircraft fire could not see further result. Anti-aircraft observers report that at this time a hostile balloon was seen to break loose".[248]

This claim, of 07 October 1917, was not awarded.

On 28 December 1917 McElroy obtained his first aerial victory, though many accounts attribute this to Mannock riddling the LVG aircraft and setting up the crippled 2-seater for McElroy to administer the coup-de-grace. A word of caution, however, should be noted when these sort of claims are made, as they usually were part of a larger agenda to talk up Mannock's victories to over 100. No pilot in his memoirs ever seems to have attributed one of their own victories to Mannock, it is always someone else's first victory that was de facto an unclaimed Mannock victory and, as in the case of McElroy or Dolan, it is almost invariably that of a dead pilot. From the "Combats in the Air" report it would appear that the German 2-seater was

---

247 London Gazette Supplement, Issue 30206, p.7740.
248 Chaz Bowyer [ed] "RFC Communiqués 1917-1918", p.148 [London: Grub Street, 1998].

"very dark coloured, light coloured underneath" and that McElroy didn't spare the ammo, firing 100 rounds at just 50 yards. However, McElroy actually overshot the falling LVG such was the angle of his dive, but upon turning he could see the German crash. MacLanachan "McScotch" witnesses the encounter and is recorded in the combat report as the confirming source for McElroy's victory. (Actually McElroy's dive had scattered a formation of German aircraft, losing the other No.40 Squadron S.E.5a the opportunity to use their positional and height advantage to inflict greater losses: Mannock is reported to have criticized rather than praise McElroy for his first victory).

For such a spectacularly inept pilot there has been occasional skepticism as to how McElroy could ever have reached 47 aerial victories over a seven-month period. However, if anything McElroy's tally is understated: there was a tendency towards caution by Major Tilney and Captain Napier with McElroy's early claims of January 1918. For example, No.40 Squadron's "Combats in the Air" files[249] for 13 January 1918 reports on McElroy's victory over a 2-seater Rumpler when flying SE5A (B598). McElroy follows the British A.A. to locate the target. (The British used white smoke in their antiaircraft whilst the Germans used black, which made for easy cooperation between A.A. batteries and their air support). McElroy got underneath the enemy aircraft, firing two long bursts of 100 rounds each at 100-150 yards distance. McElroy suffered broken landing wires in the encounter and so was unable to follow his victim down. However, there is a note on the record to the effect that "C" Battery A.A. had seen the fight but were also unable to see the final result due to haze. This suggests that McElroy's claims were being the subject of external validation in any submissions to the claims board. Similarly a report of 19 January 1918 records McElroy, in SE5a (B598), attacking a blue-and-white camouflaged DFW over Vitry. McElroy fired 60 rounds from just 10 yards' distance, which is practically point-blank range. The German was followed down to 2,000

---

249 AIR/1/1222/204/5/2634, UK National Archives.

feet, McElroy firing as the opportunity arose. However, the note to the claim states "this E.A. confirmed as crashed by observers of "D" Battery A.A.", which once again suggests that McElroy's claim required external validation before being declared as 'destroyed'. Similarly, the same "Combats in the Air" file papers for 24 January 1918 describe two separate encounters in which McElroy engages enemy aircraft at close range, flying an SE5A (B598). He is credited with one of the aircraft, a green DFW 2-seater, between Oppy and Henin-Lietard but is not given credit for the second aircraft, which he actually hit from above and below at very close range. In fact it would appear that McElroy was only granted the first claim on the basis that "E Battery" had observed the encounter. It is therefore unfair on McElroy for his 47 aerial victories to be seen as an inflated figure: if anything this is an understatement, given the amount of aircraft McElroy engaged in aerial combat and damaged.

Throughout the month of January and mid-February 1918 McElroy was to score victories over several German 2-seaters, with double victories on 05 February 1918 and 17 February 1918. RFC Communiqué No.126 of February 1918 reports on McElroy's double-victory of 05 February 1918:

"Lt G McElroy, 40 Squadron, singled out a DFW and when within 100 yards range fired 100 rounds. Pieces were seen to fall from the EA's tail and fuselage and it went down in a slow spin and crashed. He then observed a DFW which was pointed out to him by anti-aircraft fire; he dived, fired about 200 rounds, and the EA burst into flames".[250]

That particular communiqué also disclosed that McElroy had been awarded the Military Cross, although it was not gazetted at the time. On 31 January 1918 it was reported that G.E.H. McElroy had been promoted from temporary 2nd Lieutenant to temporary Lieutenant with effect from 09 August 1917 and was to remain seconded

---

[250] Chaz Bowyer [ed] "RFC Communiqués 1917-1918", p.212 [London: Grub Street, 1998].

to the Royal Flying Corps.[251] McElroy was to finish his first spell with No.40 Squadron with 11 victories. On 18 February 1918 he transferred to No.24 Squadron, being promoted to Flight Commander.

No.24 Squadron also flew the S.E.5a. McElroy was quickly into his stride, sending down an Albatros D V out of control south of Honnecourt on 21 February 1918, then destroying a Fokker DR I in flames east of Laon on 26 February 1918. RFC Communiqué No.128 of 1918 records McElroy as being awarded a Bar to his Military Cross, although this was not gazetted.

In March and April 1918 McElroy was in the thick of the action, scoring 8 victories in March, including double victories on 08 March 1918 and 29 March 1918. RFC Communiqué No.133 of 1918 records the following sequence of victories on 29 March 1918:

"Capt GEH McElroy, 24 Squadron, saw five EA scouts behind their lines west of Foucaucourt. He climbed above the clouds and approached the EA through a gap, apparently unobserved, then dived on one Albatros scout, firing 100 rounds into it at a range of from 100 to 20 yards. Pieces were seen to fall off the EA's fuselage and it went down completely out of control, crashing between Foucaucourt and the River Somme. Capt McElroy also shot down one EA out of control".[252]

On 25 March 1918 Lieutenant (Flying Officer) G.E.H. McElroy's promotion to temporary Captain whilst serving as a Flight Commander, with effect from 16 February 1918 was gazetted.[253] Interestingly it describes his army regiment as being the Royal Regiment of Artillery.

On 22 March 1918 the London Gazette (Issue 30597, p.3745) reported that McElroy had been awarded the Military Cross but did not publish the citation. This award related to his achievements with No.40 Squadron, not No.24 Squadron.

---

251 London Gazette Supplement, Issue 30503, p.1509.
252 Chaz Bowyer [ed] "RFC Communiqués 1917-1918", p.247 [London: Grub Street, 1998].
253 London Gazette Supplement, Issue 30594, p.3710.

On 01 April 1918, the very first day of the RAF, its Communiqué No.1 of 1918 reported on McElroy's exploits:

"Capt GEH McElroy, 24 Sqn, dived on three EA scouts; he reserved his fire until within 100 yards range and then fired a burst of 100 rounds from both guns into one EA which immediately went down in a slow spin and crashed north of Ignaucourt".[254]

The same communiqué was to record that on 04 April 1918 McElroy was to account for another enemy aircraft in a similar ridiculously against-the-odds encounter:

"Capt GEH McElroy, 24 Sqn, engaged one of a formation of about eight EA scouts flying east over the lines; he attacked one of the EA, firing a burst into it from 50 yards range. The EA went down in a spin and crashed north of Warfusee".

According to the same RAF communiqué McElroy was, on 07 April 1918, to account for several more German aircraft:

"Capt GEH McElroy, 24 Sqn, dived on three EA two-seaters and reserved his fire until under the tail of the nearest, into which he fired 70 rounds at 50 yards range. The EA fell in a nose-dive and crashed three miles east of Marcelcave. Shortly afterwards, while flying through the clouds at 3,000 feet, he saw three SE's being attacked by five enemy triplanes. Capt McElroy got on the tail of one of the triplanes and fired 20 rounds at point blank range into it. The EA went down in a spin and crashed north of Moreuil Wood".

McElroy was to record 6 aerial victories in April. McElroy's MC citation was actually gazetted on 24 August 1918, somewhat out of sequence, but this volume is concerned with the order of precedence rather than the bureaucratic proceduralism that led to this being gazetted well after a host of subsequent awards:

"2nd Lt. George Edward Henry McElroy, R.G.A. and R.F.C.

For conspicuous gallantry and devotion to duty. He has shown a splendid offensive spirit in dealing with enemy aircraft. He has

---

254 Christopher Cole [ed] "RAF Communiqués 1918", p.17 [Tom Donovan 1990].

destroyed at least two enemy machines, and has always set a magnificent example of courage and initiative".[255]

On 22 April 1918 the award of a Bar to the Military Cross was gazetted:

"2nd Lt. George Edward Henry McElroy, M.C., R.G.A., and R.F.C.

For conspicuous gallantry and devotion to duty. When on an offensive patrol, observing a hostile scout diving on one of our aeroplanes, he opened fire, and sent down the enemy machine in an irregular spin out of control, when it finally crashed completely.

Later in the same day, he sent down another enemy machine in flames. On another occasion, when on offensive patrol, he singled one out of four enemy machines, and sent it down crashing to earth. On the same day he attacked another enemy machine, and, after firing 200 rounds, it burst into flames.

On a later occasion, he opened fire on an enemy scout at 400 yards range, and finally sent it down in a slow spin out of control.

In addition, this officer has brought down two other enemy machines completely out of control, his skill and determination being most praiseworthy.

(M.C. gazetted 26th March 1918)".[256]

On 12 April 1918 McElroy was hospitalized and was invalided to England. A medical board examination reported that he was unfit for 4 weeks. McElroy returned to service via 28 Training Squadron and No.90 Squadron in May and June 1918. No.90 Squadron was to have been a fighter squadron but never saw active service in the war and was disbanded before the war ended.

McElroy returned to No.40 Squadron on 14 June 1918, being reunited with a much-changed Mick Mannock, who was at this stage nearing the end of his service with No.74 Squadron. McElroy at this stage had 26 victories to his name, and was one of the highest-scoring Allied aces.

---

255 London Gazette Supplement, Issue 30862, p.9914.
256 London Gazette Supplement, Issue 30643, p.4822.

McElroy was awarded the Second Bar to his Military Cross, i.e. in effect he had won the Military Cross three times over. On 26 June 1918 the citation was gazetted:

"Lt. (T./Capt.) George Edward Henry McElroy, M.C., R.G.A., and R.F.C.

For conspicuous gallantry and devotion to duty. While flying at a height of 2,000 feet, he observed a patrol of five enemy aircraft patrolling behind the lines. After climbing into the clouds, he dived to the attack, shot down and crashed one of them. Later, observing a two-seater, he engaged and shot it down out of control. On another occasion he shot down an enemy scout which was attacking our positions with machine-gun fire. He has carried out most enterprising work in attacking enemy troops and transport and in the course of a month has shot down six enemy aircraft, which were seen to crash, and five others out of control.

(M.C. gazetted 26th March 1918).

(1st Bar gazetted 22nd April 1918)".[257]

On 26 June 1918 McElroy also re-opened his account with No.40 Squadron, destroying a DFW 2-seater just south-east of Annay. McElroy then managed to destroy three balloons in less than a week. Balloons were well defended targets but the RAF had been tasked with this difficult role at a time when the situation on the ground was so chaotic.

McElroy scored double victories on 02 July, 08 July, 13 July, 15 July and 25 July 1918. Several of his victories were shared with Lt Gilbert Strange and Lt Indra Roy. Indeed, McElroy seemed to have built quite a friendship with Indra Lal "Laddie" Roy, the only Indian pilot to reach ace status in the war. Many decades later Irish newspapers and historians would receive letters from various Indian student biographers of Roy inquiring of his Irish friend McElroy. Roy went down in flames on 22 July 1918 in a dogfight between No.40 squadron and the Fokker D VIIs of Jasta 29.

Wing Commander Gwilym Lewis, in an interview for the Imperial War Museum in 1990, recalls Mannock's admonishment of

---

257 London Gazette Supplement, Issue 30813, p.8753.

McElroy on 20 July 1918 for following down a kill too low when attempting to confirm the victory. Mannock was killed on 25 July 1918 doing just that, and McElroy just days later.

On 31 July 1918 McElroy was shot down and killed; some sources claim by Vzfw Gullmann of Jasta 26, although the majority of sources claim he was shot down by ground fire.

In Norman Franks' *Who Downed the Aces in World War I?* [London: Grub Street, 1996] there is good detail on the competing accounts of what potentially transpired:

"McElroy had taken off alone on the morning of the 31st [July] in his S.E.5 E1310, a virtually new machine with just 11 hours' flying time in its log book. It was hard for the Squadron to comprehend when he simply failed to fly home. Some time later the Germans dropped a note to say that he had been shot down by AA fire after shooting down a two-seater—probably a Hannover CL of Schlasta 19 lost this day. He came down and was buried at Laventie. However, Unteroffizier Gullmann of Jasta 56, claims to have shot down a S.E.5 south-west of Armentieres at 10.15, and Laventie is south-west of this town. It was the German's first and only victory and it seems inconceivable that someone of McElroy's ability should be brought down by such a novice, although it must be said that Gullmann had been with the unit since early February, had survived thus far, and continued to survive until October. Also, this appears to be the only S.E.5 lost this day. One might be uncharitable and suggest Gullmann saw McElroy fall and made a claim, for it seems equally inconceivable that the Germans would go to the trouble of dropping a note saying how McElroy had died if he had truly been shot down in combat. Wouldn't they too make some mileage out of bringing down someone so distinguished? Another WW1 mystery."

For such a distinguished pilot it is difficult to understand how he was not awarded the Distinguished Service Order, the royal warrant in respect of which had been amended in July 1918 to include officers of the Royal Air Force as being eligible for the award.

However, neither the DSO nor the DFC can be awarded posthumously, but fortunately previous recommendations in relation to McElroy's achievements were acted upon. On 03 August 1918 McElroy's Distinguished Flying Cross citation was gazetted:
"Lt. (T./Capt.) George Edward Henry McElroy, M.C.

A brilliant fighting pilot who has destroyed thirty-five machines and three kite balloons to date. He has led many offensive patrols with marked success, never hesitating to engage the enemy regardless of their being, on many occasions, in superior numbers. Under his dashing and skilful leadership his flight has largely contributed to the excellent record obtained by the squadron".[258]

In this same edition Edward Dawson Atkinson and Samuel Marcus Kinkead, (a South African with a father from Ballykelly, Co Derry), were similarly honoured with the DFC.

On 21 September 1918 McElroy's Bar to the Distinguished Flying Cross was gazetted:
"Lieut. (T./Capt.) George Edward Henry McElroy, M.C., D.F.C. (Royal G. Artillery).

In the recent battles on various army fronts this officer has carried out numerous patrols, and flying at low altitudes, has inflicted heavy casualties on massed enemy troops, transport, artillery teams, etc., both with machine-gun fire and bombs. He has destroyed three enemy kite balloons and forty-three machines, accounting for eight of the latter in eight consecutive days. His brilliant achievements, keenness and dash have at all times set a fine example, and inspired all who came in contact with him.

(M.C. gazetted 26th March 1918,
1st Bar 22nd April 1918,
2nd Bar 26th July 1918,
D.F.C. gazetted 3rd August 1918)".[259]

In this same edition Captain Edgar James McClaughry, (an Australian with a father from Larne, Co Antrim), also received a bar to

---

258 London Gazette Supplement, Issue 30827, p.9201.
259 London Gazette Supplement, Issue 30913, p.11248.

the DFC. Mannock's old friend Ira "Taffy" Jones was similarly honoured on that date.

George is commemorated on the War Memorial Cross at St Mary's Church, Donnybrook, Dublin. Other Irish aviators commemorated on the memorial are the aces Maurice Lea Cooper and Sydney Edward Cowan, together with Sydney's brother Philip Chalmers Cowan, Gerald Lovell Backhouse and Richard Patrick Hemphill.

George's mother, Ellen McElroy, died in 1922. George's brother, William Alfred McElroy, is commemorated on the War Memorial Cross in St Mary's Church, Donnybrook. He was killed in action in World War II, a Lieutenant in the Royal Naval Volunteer Reserve. He died in the HMS "Kongoni" on 23 February 1945 and is buried at Dar Es Salaam War Cemetery in Tanzania. The Royal Navy's Fleet Air Arm Station at Durban, South Africa is usually attributed with the "HMS Kongoni" designation but there was also a South African Air Force base there. It would appear that McElroy died of illness on the island of Zanzibar. He had served as pilot with No.753 Squadron at Arbroath, Scotland in the early stages of the war, before being transferred to No.796 Squadron at Tanga, Tanganyika. It was only in the late stages of the war he was assigned to No.726 Squadron, which were based at Durban, South Africa.

George's other two brothers were qualified doctors, one serving in East Africa, the other being made a Fellow of the Royal College of Surgeons.

Samuel McElroy died in 1948, according to Irish Times of 17 January 1948.

✦ ✦ ✦

MCLAUGHLIN, ROBERT

(**6 aerial victories**)

Born: 23 July 1896, Belfast
Died: UNKNOWN
Awards: Distinguished Flying Cross
Religion: Presbyterian

Captain Robert McLaughlin was born in Belfast on 23 July 1896. However, Ireland's Civil Registration Indexes indicate two Robert McLaughlins being born at Belfast in the Jul-Sept quarter of 1896. Further, the Irish Censuses of 1901 and 1911 contain quite a number of Robert McLaughlins, whilst the Medal Record Index cards contain dozens of Robert McLaughlins who served with numerous Irish regiments, mainly the Royal Inniskilling Fusiliers. However, Robert's next-of-kin in his service record is stated as "Mrs A McLaughlin", which would suggest that Robert was the son of Agnes McLaughlin (Presbyterian) of Fitzroy Avenue in the Cromac ward of Belfast. Agnes was born in Scotland but her four children—John, Hugh, Bessie and Robert—were all Belfast-born. Tracing this family back to the Irish Census 1901 it would appear that they were resident at Ballyholme Road, Bangor, Co Down. Robert's father Hugh was still alive, and the two older siblings—William and Agnes—were also present, as was a domestic servant. Robert was a lead manufacturer, originally from Co Antrim.

There were 30 Robert McLaughlins who signed the Ulster Covenant in 1912, none of whom match Robert in terms of geographical location.

Robert's service record[260] indicates a next-of-kin address for his mother as '61 South Parade, Belfast, Ireland'. This address seems to be validated to 04 October 1923. By late 1925 the address recorded is '10 Sandford Avenue, Bloomfield, Belfast'. (Much later in his postwar career his address is recorded as 'c/o Shanghai Municipal Electrical Dept Power Station, Shanghai, China').

McLaughlin joined the air services, as a cadet without previous service in an army regiment. His service record states that McLaughlin had been an engineering student at the municipal technical institute whilst working at Combe Barbour Engineers in Belfast from 1912 to 1917. He had graduated with a BSc in Mechanical Engineering. (McLaughlin's former employer was to go out of business in the inter-war years but his son Bill Barbour was to become a codebreaker in World War II and in later life a prominent member of the non-sectarian unionist Alliance Party of Northern Ireland).

On 18 May 1917 McLaughlin was appointed to No.2 Officer Cadet Wing, Hursley, Winchester, subsequently training at No.2 School of Aeronautics at Oxford, from 29 June 1917 to 03 August 1917. McLaughlin was then assigned to No.8 Training Squadron, from 04 August 1917 to 14 September 1917, after which he served with the Central Flying School. On 24 August 1917 McLaughlin's promotion to 2nd Lieutenant, General List (on probation), was gazetted, with effect from 02 August 1917.

McLaughlin's service with the Central Flying School entailed a transfer to B Squadron on 15 November 1917. On 04 December 1917 the London Gazette carried a notice that McLaughlin had been appointed as a Flying Officer—confirmed in rank of 2nd Lieutenant—with effect from 05 November 1917. Throughout the winter of 1917/1918 McLaughlin continued to serve with the Central Fly-

---

260 AIR 76/324 Robert McLaughlin.

ing School. He subsequently transferred to No.2 ASA on 06 March 1918.

On 27 March 1918, just days before the amalgamation of the Royal Naval Service and the Royal Flying Corps into the Royal Air Force, McLaughlin was appointed to No.1 (Naval) Squadron, which were flying Sopwith Camels from Ste Marie Cappel aerodrome at the time.

On 01 April 1918, with the formation of the RAF, the No.1 (Naval) Squadron of the RNAS became No.201 Squadron of the RAF. On 01 April 1918 McLaughlin's promotion to Lieutenant was published in the Air Force List. No.201 Squadron was unusual for a former RNAS squadron insofar as it had a long history of co-operation with the RFC over the Western Front, having been posted there in January 1917. It was a highly diverse body of men: only 8 of their 18 aces were British. Their highest-scoring ace, Samuel Marcus Kinkead, was a South African born to an Irish father and Scottish mother; Stanley Rosevear, Anthony Spence, James Forman and Hazel Wallace were Canadian; Richard Minifle and Roderic Dallas were Australian; Thomas Culling and Foster Maynard were from New Zealand and Robert McLaughlin was Irish.

McLaughlin fought with No.201 Squadron over France. On 09 May 1918 he scored his first aerial victory, destroying an Albatros D.V over Bapaume. Later in May he chalked up two further victories, one of which was a shared victory with—among others—Captain Kinkead. RAF Communiqué No.6 of 1998 reported his victory of 09 May 1998:

"Lt R McLaughlin, 201 Sqn, singled out one EA and fired a burst of about 50 rounds into it at close range. The EA immediately went down in a slow spin and finally broke up in the air. The wreckage of this EA was seen by another pilot to crash".[261]

On 19 June 1918 McLaughlin's No.201 Squadron were deployed in a ground attack role, supported by No.60 Squadron. In a bombing

---

261 Christopher Cole [ed] "RAF Communiqués 1918", pp.68-69 [Tom Donovan Publishing, 1990].

raid on Bancourt aerodrome twenty-four 25-lb bombs were dropped from 500 feet, bursts being observed among the hangars, after which the machines descended lower and over 3,000 rounds were fired into the hangars and huts believed to be officers' quarters. At least one enemy aircraft on the ground was set aflame. Most of the raiders suffered battle damage. McLaughlin's Sopwith Camel (D9587) crash-landed near Acheux—the aircraft was a write-off.

On 08 August 1918 McLaughlin was shot down in flames in the Battle of Amiens. He survived and was back in the cockpit later that afternoon. Just days later, on 12 August 1918, McLaughlin shared in the destruction of 2 Fokker D.VII fighters over St Christ. In September 1918 McLaughlin's promotion to Captain (Aeroplane) was gazetted, which was dated to 27 August 1918.

On 02 November 1918 McLaughlin's DFC citation was gazetted: "Lt. Robert McLaughlin.

On the morning of 8th August this officer successfully bombed enemy transport and engaged three machine-gun sections, killing and scattering these detachments. Later on, while bombing a dump, he was attacked by eight Fokkers, who shot him down in flames. Except for slight burns he escaped injury, and, returning to his squadron, he was once more flying in the afternoon, having specially requested to be allowed to do so. A splendid example of courage and determination".[262]

On 28 December 1918 McLaughlin was transferred to the No.3 Flying School, where he served until 10 March 1919 when sent to Oswestry dispersal centre. A notice in the London Gazette of 25 March 1919 stated that McLaughlin had been transferred to the unemployed list, but this was rescinded, with a correcting notice in the London Gazette of 04 April 1919, which stated that McLaughlin had been transferred to the unemployed list with effect from 14 March 1919.

A medical board assessment deemed McLaughlin fit for Special Reserve. On 01 December 1925 McLaughlin was appointed to

---

262 Supplement to the London Gazette, 2 November 1918 (30989/12969).

No.502 Ulster Bombing Squadron Special Reserve at the rank of Flying Officer. (This was gazetted on 01 December 1925). McLaughlin's role was in the General Duties Branch. On 06 April 1927 McLaughlin was transferred to 'Class C' from the Special Reserve. This was gazetted on 12 April 1927. According to his service record it would appear that this was an appointment of 5 years.

However, the reference to McLaughlin's next-of-kin address as being "c/o Shanghai Municipal Electrical Dept, Power Station, Shanghai, China" may well date to 1927: on 07 April 1927 a Robert McLaughlin sailed on the 'Kashmir', a Peninsular & Oriental ('P&O') ship from London, destined for Shanghai, China. He travelled 2nd Class, his occupation being described as 'engineer'. Robert's last place of permanent residence was recorded as 'Northern Ireland' and his address as "34 Ebrington Gardens, Bloomfield, Belfast". It would appear that he travelled alone.

On 06 April 1932 McLaughlin relinquished his commission upon the completion of his 5 years' service a 'Class C' reservist. This was gazetted on 05 April 1932.

On 07 July 1932 Robert McLaughlin arrived on the 'Highland Brigade' from Argentina. His occupation was given as 'engineer' and the proposed address in the UK was given as 'Chartered Bank, 38 Bishopsgate'. Robert's previous country of residence was listed as 'China'. However, on this journey home he had travelled First Class, which suggests some improvement in fortune.

McLaughlin didn't stay in England for long. Perhaps the interwar years were not conducive to resettlement in the UK or Ireland. On 15 October 1932 the 'Laconia', a Cunard Line ship, sailed from Liverpool to New York. A 36-year old engineer called Robert McLaughlin was a passenger, with his initial destination port being 'New York' but his final destination being 'China'.

On 25 November 1960 a Robert Frank McLaughlin arrived as a visitor to the UK. His country of last permanent residence was given as 'Singapore' and his stated intention was to visit the UK for 7 to 8 weeks. The 'Anchises', an Ocean Steamship liner, had departed from

Hong Kong and arrived in Liverpool. It is quite possible that this is the same Robert McLaughlin but in the absence of any corroborating evidence I cannot definitively link this particular record to the Irish ace.

On 22 September 2000 McLaughlin's medals were auctioned by Dix Noonan Webb. His DFC, British War and Victory Medals reached a hammer price of £3,100—far higher than the £1,500-£1,800 estimate. Their auction catalogue borrows heavily from McLaughlin's service record, but this would not preclude the possibility of it being an estate sale.

I have been unable to find a matching record for either the death or burial of Robert McLaughlin: it is quite a common name.

❖ ❖ ❖

MILLS, ALFRED STANLEY

(15 aerial victories)

Born: 26 June 1897, Belfast
Died: UNKNOWN
Awards: Distinguished Flying Cross
Religion: Presbyterian

Lieutenant Alfred Mills was born on 26 June 1897 in Belfast, the youngest of 11 surviving children to James and Ana Maria Mills. Alfred's father was a foreman carpenter. The Irish Census 1901 records the family as being resident at Woodvale Road, Belfast. Alfred's parents are recorded as both having been born in Co Down but all ten of the children present were Belfast-born. Alfred's father is a foreman joiner; two of his older brothers are joiners and another brother is an iron moulder. In the Irish Census 1911 the family are still resident at Woodvale Road, Belfast. By this stage only seven of Alfred's brothers and sisters are still resident at the family home.

An Alfred Mills of 50 Woodvale Road, Belfast at Belfast City Hall, signed the Ulster Covenant. He was the only Irish ace to have done so but certainly not the only Ulster covenanter to have served in the RFC, RNAS or RAF. Thus far I've identified approximately 50, but this is most likely a gross underestimate.

Mills studied a Campbell College Belfast, from 1908 to 1914. He enlisted with the 11th Battalion of the Argyll & Sutherland Highlanders. He transferred to the Royal Flying Corps in November 1917. On 22 November 1917 he was posted to Reading, then to the 3 School of

IRISH AVIATORS OF WORLD WAR I

Aerial Gunnery at New Romney, and subsequently to the 1 School of Aerial Gunnery at Hythe on 07 January 1918.

In 'Above the War Fronts' it is stated that on 24 March 1918 Mills was an observer in a BF2b (B1122) piloted by 2nd Lieutenant Campbell when they were brought down by machine gun fire.

On 07 April 1918 Mills was posted to No.20 Squadron on appointment as 2nd Lieutenant (Flying Observer). The squadron had a number of famous aces with Irish heritage, e.g. Denis Latimer's father was from Co Louth, whilst JJ Cowell was from Co Limerick.

Mills' first victory came on 09 May 1918, in a BF2b flown by Lieutenant L.M. Price, when they destroyed a Fokker Dr.I triplane in flames near Lille. RAF Communiqué No.6 of 1918 describes Mills' observer/gunnery skills:

"Lts M Price and A Mills, 20 Sqn, whilst on offensive patrol with nine other Bristol fighters, engaged a formation of EA triplanes. One of the EA got on to the tail of their machine and two drums were fired into it, whereupon the EA burst into flames and fell burning".[263]

Communiqué No.9 of 1918 later in May 1918 reports Mills' observer/gunner actions against considerable odds:

"Capt TP Middleton and Lt A Mills, 20 Sqn, while leading a patrol, attacked nine EA. Capt Middleton fired at one Albatros scout at close range, which fell into the Canal at Lille. He then side-slipped on to one of seven Pfalz Scouts at which Lt Mills fired. This machine broke up in the air".[264]

He was to obtain 6 further victories in May 1918, as observer gunning for Captain Thomas Percy Middleton and Lt William McKenzine Thompson (a Canadian sometimes confused with Chester William McKinley Thompson of No.22 Squadron).

On 02 August 1918 Mills' Distinguished Flying Cross citation was gazetted:

"2nd Lt, (Hon. Lt.) Alfred Mills.

---

[263] Christopher Cole [ed] "RAF Communiqués 1918", p.67 [Tom Donovan 1990].
[264] Christopher Cole [ed] "RAF Communiqués 1918", p.102 [Tom Donovan 1990].

MILLS, ALFRED STANLEY

A capable and gallant observer who has been very successful in destroying enemy machines by reason of excellent marksmanship.

He has accounted for many enemy aircraft in a short period of time, and has generally fought against larger formations than his own. When on reconnaissance 8,000 yards behind the enemy lines he saw a hostile balloon on the ground; descending to 1,700 feet, he and his observer engaged and destroyed it. He then completed his reconnaissance.

On another occasion, when on photography work, he was attacked by nine hostile scouts".[265]

On 06 September 1918 Mills was once again in a BF2b (E2470) when shot up badly but he was unharmed. On that morning he scored 2 further aerial victories, both of which came against the excellent Fokker D.VII. RAF Communiqué No.23 of 1918 reports Mills shooting down in flames one of their attackers on 06 September 1918. Over the course of the month of September 1918 Mills achieved 6 aerial victories.

Mills was hospitalized on 03 October 1918, being transferred to the Prince of Wales Hospital. The description on his service record is "invalided" but that does not imply permanent disability and disfigurement. Mills was notionally assigned to the Armaments School at Uxbridge on 06 November 1918 for general duties until a further medical board examination. On 10 February 1919 Mills was sent to Crystal Palace for dispersal. The London Gazette of 01 April 1919 included a notice to the effect that Mills had been transferred to the Unemployed List with effect from 12 February 1919 but a further notice issued on 30 September 1919 to state that the previous notice had been cancelled.

On 23 January 1920 the London Gazette announced that 2nd Lieutenant (Honorary Lieutenant) Mills had relinquished his commission with effect from 12 February 1919 but again a notice issued to state that the notification of 01 April 1919 has been cancelled.

---

265 London Gazette Supplement, Issue 30827, p.9202.

Mills had come from a large family of hard-working people. However, somewhere in the post-war unemployment crisis the war-wounded veteran went astray: in October 1924 Mills was remanded at Marylebone on bail for 2 months on a charge of theft. He was convicted and sentenced to several months' imprisonment.

Mills service record[266] does not have any formal record of proceedings other than a reference to an extract from the Daily Express of 10 October 1924. However, it is clear that he was deprived of his Distinguished Flying Cross.

✦ ✦ ✦

---

266 AIR 76/348 UK National Archives, Alfred Mills.

MOLESWORTH, WILLIAM EARLE 'MOLEY'

(**18 aerial victories**)

Born: 14 March 1894, Andaman Islands

Died: 22 October 1955

Awards: Military Cross with Bar, Medaglia d'oro al Valore Militare (Italy)

Religion: Anglican

Lieutenant Colonel William Earle Molesworth is one of four Indian-born Irish aces of World War I. He was born on the Andaman Islands in the Indian Ocean, the son of Winifred Anne Weekes and Colonel Molesworth, C.I.E., C.B.E., of the Indian Army Medical Service. William's grandfather was Lieutenant Colonel Anthony Oliver Molesworth. William was a descendant of Viscount Molesworth of Swords, Co Dublin. (Molesworth Street in Dublin is named after Richard Molesworth, 3rd Viscount Molesworth). William's mother's family, the Weekes of Hazeldeane, Monkstown, Co Cork, were a prominent Anglo-Irish family. William's grandfather, Thomas Earle Weekes, was a Justice of the Peace for Co Cork. However, unlike the Molesworths, the family did not have a long-standing connection to Ireland, having only arrived in the previous century. In another link to Irish aviation, William's sister, Kathleen Winifred Molesworth, married Alfred Alyson Fennell Minchin, who was related to the Anglo-Irish aviator Frederick Frank Reilly Minchin—a notorious character, who died in an attempt at the West-East crossing of the Atlantic.

Molesworth was educated at Marlborough College from 1908 to 1911. The UK Census 1911 records him as being present at Preshute House of the college in Wiltshire, a boarder, or—in their parlance—'in static pupillari'. Molesworth spent two years at the Royal Military College at Sandhurst, 1912-1914. Cadet Molesworth's promotion to 2nd Lieutenant upon graduation from Sandhurst was gazetted on 07 August 1914.[267]

Molesworth served on the Western Front from October 1914 to March 1916. He had been wounded in December 1914 but had returned to frontline service with the Royal Munster Fusiliers. On 08 December 1914 his promotion from 2nd Lieutenant to Lieutenant in the Royal Munster Fusiliers was gazetted.[268]

In August 1916 Molesworth transferred to the Royal Flying Corps.[269] He was posted to Oxford on 28 October 1916, then transferred to the Central Flying School on 06 October 1916, from where he was assigned to 8 Reserve Squadron. Upon appointment as Flying Officer on 26 December 1916 Molesworth was returned to the Central Flying School. His promotion was gazetted on 12 January 1917.

On 21 February 1917 Molesworth was posted to No.60 Squadron. This was a famous and highly decorated fighting unit by this stage of the war. Unsurprisingly, this part of Molesworth's military career has been well documented, with numerous excellent sources to put his achievements in context, e.g. Norman Franks' *Nieuport Aces of World War I* (London: Osprey, 2000); Alex Revell's *No.60 Squadron RFC/RAF* (London: Osprey, 2011) contains some wonderful quotes from Molesworth.

However, Group-Captain A.J.L. Scott's *Sixty Squadron R.A.F.—A History of the Squadron from its Formation* (London: William Heinemann; New York: George H Doran Company,1920) remains one of the best

---

267 London Gazette, Issue 28864, p.6206.
268 London Gazette Supplement, Issue 29001, p.10560.
269 AIR 76/352, UK National Archives, William Earle Molesworth.

sources of original accounts of Molesworth's military service as an aviator.

One letter, which is dated March 1917, describes Molesworth's early experiences after joining the squadron:

"I don't think I told you about a Boche we brought down last week. We got him quite near the aerodrome—apparently he had lost his way in the clouds. He appeared out of them at about 3,000 feet over our heads. Of course, every available machine dashed off in pursuit, and caught him up in a few minutes, as he was forced to turn from the lines by some old F.E. Birds. [F.E.8 "pushers"]. They all went for him and he had to land in a ploughed field near-by. He put the machine down quite well, without crashing anything, but one of his pursuers, who belonged to the squadron next to us, turned upside down in his excitement when landing. However, he did not hurt himself, and managed to prevent the Hun from setting his machine on fire, by holding a Very pistol at his head… Afterwards I had a chat with the prisoner in French, and found out that he was a star pilot, having a number of our machines to his credit and the inevitable Iron Cross".[270]

Royal Flying Corps Communiqué No.81 of 1917, which covers the period 25 March 1917 to 31 March 1917, actually credits Lt A Binnie and Lt Molesworth with a "forced to land" victory each, but they were not granted these claims. The capture of aircraft was still granted in some circumstances but by and large 'forced to land' aerial victories were not being included in pilots' tallies although they would often be mentioned in medal citations.

In another letter dated March 1917 Molesworth writes:

"No luck for me in the Hun line yet, although the beggars seem to be running on the ground all right.

Three of us went out the other day, and had the most hectic time. The clouds were about 3,000 feet and very dense, with gaps here and there. We crossed the lines and expected to get it pretty hot from

---

[270] A.J.L.Scott "Sixty Squadron R.A.F.—A History of the Squadron from its Formation", pp.25-28 (London: William Heinemann; New York: George H Doran Company,1920)

Archie [anti-aircraft fire], but strangely enough, nothing happened. Heading towards Croisille, we came out of a thick cloud and saw a most extraordinary sight. For miles around every village was a blazing mass with smoke columns, like great water-spouts, ascending upwards to the clouds. Along the roads one could see lines of retreating men making for the Hindenburg defences, which we could plainly distinguish owing to the amount of barbed wire entanglements round them. Suddenly we were met by a perfect tornado of bursting 'archies', and so were forced to turn into a cloud. This cloud was so thick that we all promptly proceeded to lose ourselves. I looked at my compass and saw that it was pointing west, so carried on. At last, after about half an hour's flying, I found myself alone in an opening in the clouds. Below me were dozens of shell-holes filled with water; round about, black clouds and sheets of driving rain. I knew I was somewhere near the lines, and yet could not decide in which direction to turn. Trusting to the compass I still pushed on west, and at last the shell-holes disappeared. Just as my petrol was giving out I spotted some hangars. There was nothing for it, so I decided to land. Coming down to about 200 feet I did a half-circle to get into the wind, and to my utter disgust saw a large party of Germans on the ground. I therefore made up my mind that it must be a Hun aerodrome. No machines were out, owing to the 'dud' weather, so I landed, jumped out of the machine, seized the Very pistol, and was just going to fire it into the grid when I saw, to my amazement, two mechanics in khaki before. Evidently the party I had seen were German prisoners. When the old kite had been filled up I pushed off again, and got home after about an hour's run. On arrival I heard that the other two had lost themselves as well, but had managed to get back. In future I shall take jolly good care to get to know the country better before playing about in the clouds".[271]

On 22 April 1917 Molesworth, flying a Nieuport (B1569) scored his first aerial victory, driving down an Albatros D.III out of control near Vitry. RFC Communiqué No.85 also credits him with damag-

---

271 Group-Captain A.J.L.Scott "Sixty Squadron R.A.F.—A History of the Squadron from its Formation", pp.33-35. (London: William Heinemann; New York: George H Doran Company,1920).

ing a balloon on this day. However, neither Molesworth nor 2nd Lts Penny and Lloyd were awarded victories for these claims. However, the Irishman Desmond de Burgh blew a hole in a balloon with a Le Prieur rocket that day, but the rocket passed through the balloon without causing it to explode. (The Germans dragged it down, the fabric emitting smoke, but de Burgh was awarded the victory, highlighting the inconsistency in the scoring system).

Two days later Molesworth destroyed a balloon at Boiry Notre Dame. Here is Molesworth's account of the event as described in his own words:

"Still more excitement! I tackled my first balloon yesterday, and consider it even more difficult than going for a Hun; at least, I think one gets a hotter time. We had received orders a week ago that all balloons *had* to be driven down or destroyed, as they were worrying our infantry and gunners during the advance.

We had been practising firing the Le Prieur rockets for some time … We did not think these were much of a success, owing to the difficulty of hitting anything, so decided to use tracer and Buckingham bullets instead. These are filled with a compound of phosphorous and leave a long trail of smoke behind them… We all went off individually to the various balloons which had been allotted us. I am glad to say most of us managed to do them down. I personally crossed the trenches at about 10,000 feet, dropping all the time towards my sausage, which was five or six miles away. It was floating in company with another at about 3,000 feet, and reminded me of that little song 'Two Little Sausages'.

I started a straight dive towards them, and then the fun began. Archie [flak] got quite annoyed, following me down to about 5,000 feet, where I was met by two or three strings of flaming onions, luckily too far off to do any damage.

Then came thousands of machine-gun bullets from the ground— evidently I was not going to get them without some trouble. I zigzagged about a bit, still heading for the balloons, and when within two hundred yards opened fire. The old Huns in the basket got wind up and jumped out in their parachute. Not bothering about them, I kept my sight on one of the balloons and saw the tracer going right into it and causing it to smoke.

As our armament consists of a Lewis gun, I had to now change drums. This is a pretty ticklish job when you have about ten machine guns loosing off at you, not to mention all the other small trifles! However, I managed to do it without getting more than half a dozen or so bullet-holes in my grid [aircraft].

By this time the second balloon was almost on the floor. I gave it a burst, which I don't think did any damage. The first sausage was in flames, so I buzzed off home without meeting any Huns. On the way back a good shot from Archie exploded very near my tail, and carried away part of the elevator. Don't you think this is the limit for anyone who wants excitement? I must say

I prefer it to the infantry, as one gets decent food and a comfortable bed every night, if you are lucky enough to get back".[272]

Molesworth was promoted to Temporary Captain (Flight Commander) in May 1917, which was dated to 26 April 1917, and was gazetted on 14 May 1917. On 02 June 1917 his secondment as Captain to the Royal Flying Corps was also gazetted. Molesworth had an eventful May and June, destroying an Albatos D.III on 29 June 1917, but getting himself into a number of near-fatal encounters. In a letter dated June 1917 Molesworth wrote:

"Yesterday I had the narrowest shave I've ever had since I first started Boche-strafing. I was properly caught out this time, and really thought things were all up.

We were just over the Drocourt Switch, near Vitry, when a dozen Huns got what you might call 'uppish'. We tumbled into a proper mix-up and, as there were only five of us, the Huns managed to break up our formation. We arranged that, should this happen, we were to return to the line independently and re-form, so I started towards Arras, following the Scarpe.

---

[272] Group-Captain A.J.L.Scott "Sixty Squadron R.A.F.—A History of the Squadron from its Formation", pp.50-53 (London: William Heinemann; New York: George H Doran Company,1920)

Just as I was passing over Gavrelle I espied three fat Hun two-seaters making south-east.

'Here we are, my son', say I to myself. 'We'll just hop down and put the gust up one of these Huns'.

No sooner said than done. I pushed my nose down and, when within range, opened fire. The next thing I knew was a perfect hail of bullets pouring round me. Here is a rough description of my thoughts during the few minutes followed:

"Crackle! Crackle! Crackle!

'My cheery aunt! There's a Hun on my tail'.

'By jove! The blighter is making my grid into a sieve. Confound him!'

'Let's pull her up in a good climbing turn and have a look at him'.

'Heavens! It's "The Circus". [The Red Baron's Flying Circus].

'I wonder if old Richthof is the leader. The dirty dog nearly caught me out this time. Silly ass! Didn't hold his fire long enough, or he'd have made me into cold meat my now'.

'Let's give him a dose and see how he likes it'.

'Here he comes straight at me, loosing off with both guns'.

'I hope we aren't going to collide'.

'Missed! Bon! Everything's A1. Wish I'd hit him, though!'

'I must pull her round quick on he will be on my tail'.

'Hang! I can't shoot for toffee, but he's pretty "dud" too, thank heavens!'

'Once again, boys, round with her. Let him have it hot'.

'No good. Try again'.

'Confound it! There's my beastly drum empty. I must spin and change it'.

'Good enough! Now where's the blighter?'

'My Harry! He has got me stiff this time; here he comes down on me from the right.'

'Crack! Crack! Crack! Bang! Zip! Zip!'

'There goes my petrol tank; now for the flames.'

'Cheerio! No luck this time, you old swine. Wait till I get you next show.'

'Here goes for the ground.'

Luckily for me, my friend and his pals, who had been watching the scrap, thought I was done for. They therefore chucked up the sponge and departed.

I managed to pull the machine out, just scraping over the trenches. The engine was still running, although the petrol was pouring out all over my legs. A few minutes afterwards the engine conked out altogether, and I had to land in a field. I was immediately surrounded by a crowd of men, who had seen the fight. Amongst them were some artillery officers, who took me off to their mess and offered me a 'tot', which was very thankfully received, while they sent off a message to the squadron. The following is the official list of damage done to my machine:

Six bullet holes in propeller.

Cowling shot away.

Large holes in bottom of petrol tank and sides.

Main spar right-hand top plane broken.

Rear right-hand under-carriage strut badly damaged.

Twenty-eight holes in fuselage and ten in the planes—two or three missing the pilot's seat by less than an inch".[273]

However, it was not just enemy aircraft that were a danger—in June 1917 Molesworth survived a forced landing that would have killed many a less experienced pilot: at 12,000 feet, the engine malfunctioned and part of the cowling broke away, hitting the wings and fuselage. He managed to keep control until the aircraft reached 2,000 feet then took it down via a side-slip and making a landing into the wind. The No.60 Squadron literature generally credits Molesworth with driving down out of control an Albatros D.III on 11 July 1917 when flying a Nieuport (B1652). However, in his own recollec-

---

[273] Group-Captain A.J.L.Scott "Sixty Squadron R.A.F.—A History of the Squadron from its Formation", pp.66-69 (London: William Heinemann; New York: George H Doran Company,1920)

tions, a damaged German aircraft escaped him after Molesworth's gun jammed. Although the Royal Flying Corps discouraged media attempts to lionize individual pilots it is clear that propaganda had to make some concession to public demand for heroes. In this regard No.60 Squadron was ideal material for newsreel. In July 1917 Molesworth was filmed for cinema:

"Charlie Chaplin isn't in it now with us! We were cinematographed the other day. Some of us stood in a row and tried to look pleasant and unconcerned, but this was rather difficult, as everyone was making rude remarks about us. We then bundled into our new grids [the S.E.5], which we had just got, and started off on a stunt formation, nearly running down the old cinema man to put the wind up him. After we had done a circuit, my radiator began to boil, and I was forced to come down. Thank heavens it was a good landing, as the old man was still at it turning the handle. My part of the show was to be known as 'Pilot landing for more ammunition after fierce fight'."[274]

The new S.E.5a was to prove an excellent machine in the context of the endless swapping of aerial superiority between the Allies and Central Powers. In August 1917 Molesworth was to achieve 2 victories with the S.E.5a. Molesworth describes his victory on 05 August 1917, piloting S.E.5a (A4851) over Hendecourt when he sent an Albatros D.III down in flames:

"The new grids [S.E.5s] are a great success, and we have been hard at work training and doing line patrols.

Three of us, led by our famous 'Hun-strafer' [Bishop], used them over the lines for the first time on the 5th. As a rule we only fight in flights, but on certain occasions we volunteer for a 'circus', that is a mixed formation generally composed of the best pilots in the squadron.

Our numbers were not overwhelming this time, but we know that the Huns had got pukka wind-up by the way they disappeared when

---

[274] Group-Captain A.J.L.Scott "Sixty Squadron R.A.F.—A History of the Squadron from its Formation", p.101 (London: William Heinemann; New York: George H Doran Company,1920)

we arrived on the line, so we felt quite confident in taking on twice as many as ourselves. Of course we were all out for trouble, as we wanted to show what the new machines could do. As soon as our leader spotted a formation of Huns, he was after them like a flash. I think there were seven of them, but we were all much too excited to count. Suddenly they saw us coming, and tried desperately to escape, but our leader got into his favourite position, and the rear Hun hadn't a ghost of a chance. The next instant he was a flaming mass.

We had simply had it all over the Boche for speed and, as we had the height, they could not possibly get away. I picked my man out as he was coming towards me, and dived straight at him, opening fire with both guns at close range. He suffered the same fate as his companion.

A burning machine is a glorious but terrible sight to see—a tiny red stream of flame trickles from the petrol tank, then long tongues of blazing petrol lick the sides of the fuselage, and, finally, a sheet of white fire envelops the whole machine, and it glides steeply towards the ground in a zigzag course, leaving a long trail of black smoke behind it, until it eventually breaks up. There is no doubt that your first Hun in flames gives you a wonderful feeling of satisfaction. I can well imagine what the big-game hunter must think when he sees the dead lion in front of him. Somehow, you do not realize that you are sending a man to an awful doom, but rather your thoughts are all turned on the hateful machine which you are destroying, so fascinating to look at and yet so deadly in its attack".[275]

His other victory that month came on 09 August 1917, when he destroyed an Albatros D.V when flying S.E.5a (A8392), but his aircraft was badly shot-up in the encounter, losing a large chunk of this tail plane. Molesworth had performed magnificently with No.60 Squadron and had achieved 6 aerial victories—usually sufficient for the awarding of the Military Cross—so it was no surprise that in

---

275 Group-Captain A.J.L.Scott's "Sixty Squadron R.A.F.—A History of the Squadron from its Formation", pp.101-103 (London: William Heinemann; New York: George H Doran Company,1920)

August 1917 Molesworth was told of his immanent decoration in the context of being rotated to Home Establishment duties. Molesworth's service record indicates that the Military Cross was awarded on 26 September 1917 and was ultimately gazetted on 09 January 1918.

Molesworth had survived "Bloody April" and had taken on the best of Manfred von Richthofen's "Flying Circus" that summer. For any Army officer on secondment to the Royal Flying Corps it would be a fine record to have in the context of one's overall military career. However, Molesworth's career as an aviator was not finished yet. In the winter of 1917 he was posted to 62 Training Squadron.

On 20 October 1917 Molesworth returned to the frontline, joining No.29 Squadron, which were still equipped with Nieuports. Molesworth did not take long to add to his tally. On 08 November 1917 he destroyed 2 enemy aircraft in flames. (According to RFC Communiqué No.113 of 1917 he took on 15 German aircraft when securing the first of those victories). Later that month he sent down an Albatros D.V out of control near the Houlthoulst forest area.

No.29 Squadron was commanded by Major James McCudden, son of a Co Carlow man, and one of three brothers to die serving with the RFC and RAF. Although McCudden is almost invariably associated with No.56 Squadron he had spent time in command of No.29 Squadron. Of the 25 or so aces who had served with No.29 Squadron there were not many with Irish connections, e.g. apart from Molesworth there was Captain Sydney Edward Cowan, and of Irish parentage or Irish ancestry there were only McCudden and the Canadian Henry Coyle Rath. However, there had been several other prominent Irish pilots who had served with the squadron, e.g. there was also Captain Ernest William Barrett, who had returned from Singapore to serve in the war and had been killed in the squadron's early days. The son of a famous Galway family, William Arthur Grattan-Bellew, had been killed in March 1917 with No.29 Squadron. Similarly, William Kerr Magill Britton had been wounded in action in December 1916 before being killed in May 1917 with the squadron.

The winter of 1917/1918 proved to be a particularly bad one for flying operational purposes. However, Molesworth achieved 5 aerial victories in January 1918. Molesworth's Military Cross citation was gazetted on 09 January 1918:

"Capt. William Earle Molesworth, R. Muns. Fus. and R.F.C.

For conspicuous gallantry and devotion to duty on offensive patrol. He has frequently led his patrol against superior numbers of the enemy, destroying some and dispersing others. He has also brought down two balloons and has proved himself to be a dashing and fearless pilot of great skill and determination".[276]

RFC Communiqué No.124 of 1918 records a double-victory by Molesworth on 24 January 1918:

"Capt W Molesworth, 29 Squadron, while leading a patrol, attacked a two-seater EA from behind and fired a drum at 150 yards range. The EA fell completely out of control. He then attacked another EA at about 100 yards range. A burst of smoke appeared and the EA dived east out of control and crashed".[277]

Molesworth scored 3 victories in February 1918 and one final victory in March 1918, but was transferred back to Home Establishment on 17 March 1918, St Patrick's Day. It would appear that Molesworth returned to the Central Flying School on 27 May 1918. The Supplement to the London Gazette of 26 March 1918 records Molesworth's award of a Bar to the Military Cross—Gazette Issue 30597, p.3744—but the actual citation was not gazetted until 24 August 1918:

"Capt. William Earle Molesworth, M.C., R. Muns. Fus. and R.F.C.

For conspicuous gallantry and devotion to duty. He has done excellent work as patrol leader, handling his formations with great skill and courage. He has destroyed four enemy machines and driven several down out of control".[278]

In June 1918 Molesworth married Dorothy Loftus Steele, daughter of Colonel St George Loftus Steele. The next-of-kin address on

---

276 Supplement to the London Gazette 09 January 1918, Issue 30466, p.631.
277 Chaz Bowyer [ed] "RFC Communiqués 1917-1918", p.204 [Grub Street 1998]
278 London Gazette Supplement, Issue 30862, p.9904.

his service record reads as "Kelston, Hythe, Kent" and "Edgemont, Reigate, Surrey".

On 16 August 1918 Molesworth was gazetted as an Instructor, graded for pay purposes as a Major (Flying). This was dated to 26 June 1918.

On 04 September 1918 Molesworth transferred to No.158 Squadron. This squadron had been formed in May 1918, originally envisaged as a fighter squadron but was subsequently converted to a ground attack role by the time it became operational. It was equipped with the Sopwith T.F.2 Salamander ground attack aircraft but did not see active service in World War I, and was disbanded on 20 November 1918. (Production of the Salamander had proven troublesome, as the armour plating had become increasingly problematic in the tempering process. The "TF" designation was to denote "trench fighter" but it had no specialized ground attack equipment, merely additional armour to reduce vulnerability to ground fire. By the end of the war less than 50 Salamanders had been supplied, from an initial order of 500 aircraft).

The supplement to the London Gazette of 12 September 1918 records the King's permission for Molesworth to wear the Silver Medal for Military Valour conferred by the King of Italy.[279]

On 16 October 1918 Molesworth was hospitalized, not returning to No.158 Squadron until 26 October 1918, after which he was transferred to 45 Training Depot Station (TDS). On 31 January 1919 Molesworth's status as an Instructor—graded for purposes of pay as Major (Flying) and dated to 04 September 1918—with the Central Flying School had been gazetted.[280] On 18 April 1919 it was further reported that Molesworth had been promoted from Captain to Acting Major, with effect from 03 September 1918, i.e. from the time of his transfer to No.158 Squadron following his service as an Instructor at the Central Flying School.[281]

On 09 April 1919 it would appear that Molesworth had been scheduled for dispersal but that this was subsequently cancelled. In

---

279 London Gazette Supplement, Issue 30895, p.10743.
280 London Gazette, Issue 31157, p.1537.
281 London Gazette, Issue 31302, p.5045.

the end Molesworth transferred from 45 TDS to No.108 Squadron on 21 May 1919. No.108 Squadron had been a bomber squadron during the war but was in the process of being stood down by the time Molesworth had transferred there. It was disbanded in July 1919, by which stage Molesworth had been redeployed to 8 Aircraft Acceptance Park at Lympne. It would appear that No.120 Squadron had been given the role of providing airmail services between Lympne and Cologne but that this ended in September 1919 after which No.120 Squadron moved from Lympne to Hawkinge. With No.108 Squadron disbanded Lympne was transferred to the civil authorities.

On 15 October 1919 Molesworth returned to the Royal Munsters. The London Gazette of 07 November 1919 reported that Molesworth had relinquished his commission with effect from 15 October 1919. This was also confirmed via the Supplement to the London Gazette of 02 December 1919, which reported that Captain W.E. Molesworth, Royal Munster Fusiliers, had been restored to the establishment with effect from 15 October 1919.[282]

In the medal card index Molesworth's address is given as "1st Bn, Royal Munster Fusiliers, Crownhill Barracks, Plymouth, Devon on 21 June 1921". It is unclear as to how long Molesworth served with the Royal Munsters prior to their disbandment but the *London Gazette* of 12 September 1922 lists Captain W.E. Molesworth's transfer from the Royal Munster Regiment to the Royal Sussex Regiment with effect from 13 September 1922 and with seniority from 07 April 1917. Similarly, the *London Gazette* of 20 October 1922 records a Captain W.E. Molesworth, Royal Sussex Regiment, being granted a temporary appointment with the Royal Traffic Officers from 01 September 1922 to 28 September 1922.[283]

On 13 February 1924 the *London Gazette* carried a War Office notice to the effect that Molesworth was to be a Captain with the Royal Tank Corps (as it was then known) with effect from 13 February 1924. The Peninsular & Orient Steam Navigation Company ('P&O') ship 'Khy-

---

282 London Gazette Supplement, Issue 31670, p.15008.
283 London Gazette, Issue 32757, p.7371.

ber' arrived in London on 11 May 1924, having travelled from Kobe, Japan via Shanghai, China. On board was Captain W.E. Molesworth, his wife Mrs D. Molesworth and child Miss P Molesworth. Undoubtedly this is William, Dorothy their child Pamela. Interestingly he is still described as being an 'Army Officer' in the passenger list details, which suggests more than just a series of peacetime temporary appointments. On 27 February 1931 the War Office announced that Captain W.E. Molesworth M.C. was promoted to Major in the Royal Tank Corps (as it was still then known) with effect from 28 February 1931.[284]

Molesworth served in World War II. However, I do not have a service record in respect of this but it is known that ultimately he rose to the rank of Lieutenant Colonel in the Royal Tank Regiment. However, Molesworth served with the 1st Battalion. It's known that the 1st and 6th Battalions were part of the Heavy Armoured Brigade in Egypt. From a quick examination of passenger lists it's clear that on 17 March 1941 (St Patrick's Day) the 'Dominion Monarch' arrived in Liverpool from New Zealand via Cape Town, Mombasa and the Middle East. In the category of First Class "Service" (as opposed to "Civilian") Passengers there was a Colonel W.E. Molesworth, his wife Dorothy and their twenty-one year old daugher Pamela. Their intended address in the UK was given as Cruicksfield, Duns, Berwick, Scotland. Their previous place of residence was listed as being Egypt. It's believed that Molesworth served out part of the war in charge of supplies for the Royal Armoured Corps. Tracing the basic sequence of promotions it would appear that Major Molesworth was promoted to Lieutenant-Colonel with effect from 01 April 1940.[285] On 30 September 1941 the War Office announced that Lieutenant-Colonel Molesworth (under the service reference number 8675) had been placed on retired pay with effect from 13 September 1941.[286] On 15 March 1949 the War Office announced that Molesworth had

---

284 London Gazette, Issue 33693, p.1355.
285 London Gazette Supplement, Issue 34821, p.1895, 02 April 1940.
286 London Gazette Supplement, Issue 35290, p.5642, of 30 September 1941.

ceased to belong to the Reserve of Officers for the Royal Tank Regiment due to having reached the age limit of liability to being recalled.

Molesworth's address is given as 242 Tilehurst Road, Reading in his later years. Probate was granted to his widow, Dorothy Loftus Molesworth, and to Pamela Langham (wife of Robert Anthony Langham). His effects were worth £3,032 5s.9d. in March 1956.

In 'Above the Trenches' it is stated that a number of Molesworth's letters were published in 'Flypast' magazine in 1979. These are most likely a selection of those published from Molesworth's time with No.60 Squadron.

✦ ✦ ✦

O'GRADY, CONN STANDISH

(**9 aerial victories**)

Born: 04 October 1888, Dublin
Died: 07 May 1968
Awards: Military Cross, Air Force Cross
Religion: Church of Ireland

Squadron Leader Conn Standish O'Grady served in both World War I and World War II. A highly regarded glider pilot, O'Grady was to continue flying until late in life.

O'Grady was born in Dublin on 04 October 1888 to Standish O'Grady and Margaret O'Grady. Conn's parents were both from Co Cork. The Irish Census 1901 records the family as being resident at Highfield Road, Rathmines, Dublin. Conn and his older brother Carew are both present, as are their parents and two servants. Conn's other older brother, Hugh Art O'Grady, editor of the *Cork Free Press*, was not present. (Hugh was later to write a biography of their father in 1929, and was ultimately to become a Professor of the Transvaal University College, Pretoria, South Africa). The Irish Census 1911 records Conn as still being resident with his parents. The family are resident at Milltown Road, Dublin. Conn's father describes himself as an 'author' and a 'historian'. Standish James O'Grady was a writer and a friend of W.B. Yeats. In the 1890's he achieved a measure of success with translating various Celtic myths and legends into English and publishing them in modern prose, e.g. as romantic tales shorn of their pre-Christian mythology. However, of his histories, "The Story of Ireland" was disliked by even his Victorian contemporaries as being too intellectually dishonest in its treatment of the Cromwellian conquest of Ireland. Standish James O'Grady is sometimes mistaken for his cousin Standish Hayes O'Grady, another figure in Celtic literature. (Neither man should be confused with Standish O'Grady, 1st Viscount Guillamore). In the Irish Census 1911 Conn is described as an engineer. He had by this stage recently graduated from Trinity College Dublin, with the degrees of BA and BAI in 1910.

Conn initially worked with the Congested Districts Board on various engineering works before emigrating to Canada. O'Grady found work with the Canadian Department of the Interior, being deployed to conduct surveys in rough country for the water, power and reclamation service. However, O'Grady's service record[287] states that his occupation in civil life was as an engineer with the Dominion Government, Ottawa, Canada from 1911 to 1918, and also as being an engineer with Farrall & O'Grady of Edinburgh, Scotland. (Presumably this latter appointment relates to his occupational status in the inter-war years).

O'Grady joined the Royal Flying Corps in July 1916, being gazetted on 07 August 1916 in respect of his appointment on probation as temporary 2nd Lieutenant with effect from 25 July 1916.[288] O'Grady initially was sent to Reading, being posted with 7 Reserve Squadron until 12 September 1916, after which he trained with 'C' Squadron, Central Flying School. On 17 November 1916 his position as 2nd Lieutenant was confirmed, and on 18 November 1916 O'Grady was gazetted on appointment as 2nd Lieutenant (Flying Officer) with effect from 31 October 1916. By this stage O'Grady had been posted to 8 Reserve Squadron, serving there from November 1916 to March 1917.

Following a short spell at the Central Flying School O'Grady was sent to No.23 Squadron on 04 April 1917. Of the 19 aces who served with this squadron, quite a number had Irish connections, e.g.

---

287 AIR 76/379 Conn Standish O'Grady, 13 pages.
288 London Gazette Supplement, Issue 29697, p.7762.

their highest-scoring ace was the Scot, William Kennedy-Cochran-Patrick, who had Irish ancestry on both sides of his family; James FitzMorris was another Scot of Irish ancestry; the American-born, English-raised Lovell Dickens Baker had an Irish-American father and had enlisted with the Royal Dublin Fusiliers prior to joining the Royal Flying Corps.

However, it was a hugely diverse squadron: in addition to Baker the aces James Pearson and Clive Warman were American; Harry Compton, Arthur Fairclough, Douglas McGregor, Alfred Eddie McKay, George Marks and John MacRae were all Canadian; Herbert Drewitt was a New Zealander. Only 8 of the squadron's 19 aces were British, and even then Harold White had emigrated from England to Canada as a child and was raised and died in Canada. If anything it was surprising that O'Grady was the only Irish-born ace with the squadron. (On a related point, sometimes No.23 Squadron is mistaken for 23 T.D.S., which was based at Baldonnell, near Dublin. The regular squadrons and the TS training squadrons—later arranged into TDS—were distinct entities).

On 30 April 1917 O'Grady scored his first victory, flying a SPAD S.VII (A262), and sending down out of control an Albatros D.III over Inchy-en-Artois.

Over the following months—to August 1917—O'Grady went on to score 8 further victories with No.23 Squadron, most of which were achieved in a SPAD with the serial number B3556. Some were shared victories but the majority were against the Albatros D.III and D.V fighters, several sent down in flames. For example, RFC Communiqué No.102 describes O'Grady's victory on 20 August 1917:

"2nd Lt SC O'Grady, 23 Squadron, saw a fight taking place between Allied and German aircraft so joined in and drove one EA off a Nieuport's tail. He then saw a black and white EA firing into a Spad from behind. He drove it away from the Spad and finally shot it down out of control, and it crashed and burned on the ground".[289]

---

289 Chaz Bowyer [ed] "RFC Communiqués 1917-1918", p.114 [London: Grub Street, 1998].

O'Grady is mentioned in Jon Guttman's *SPAD VII Aces of World War I* [London: Osprey, 2001] and in *SPAD VII –vs– Albatros DIII: 1917-1918* [London: Osprey, 2011], as he was one of the SPAD's premier DIII-killers.

The gazetting of O'Grady's promotions seem to be somewhat out of sequence. On 14 September 1917 his promotion from Lieutenant to Temporary Captain with effect from 01 August 1917 is reported. However, on 23 August 1917 his promotion from Temporary Captain to Flight Commander with effect from 11 August 1917 had already been reported. Regardless of the foregoing, O'Grady had been appointed Flight Commander, and returned to Home Establishment on 15 September 1917. His leave was extended to 15 October 1917 after which O'Grady was sent to the Northern Training Brigade and assigned to No.81 Squadron.

O'Grady's service record indicates that he was awarded the Military Cross on 26 September 1917, which was gazetted on that date—Supplement, Issue 30308, p.9978—and that the citation was gazetted in on 09 January 1918:

"2nd Lt. Conn Standish O'Grady, R.F.C., Spec. Res.

For conspicuous gallantly and devotion to duty in leading fighting patrols against superior numbers of enemy aircraft. He has himself brought down three enemy machines completely out of control, and others were seen to be destroyed, and his dash and determination when outnumbered by the enemy have continually won the highest praise".[290]

No.81 Squadron had originally been formed in January 1917 as a training unit but was not mobilized for active service. It was disbanded on 04 July 1918, well before the end of the war. O'Grady was subsequently transferred to 23 Wing, and in November 1918 was serving with 34 TDS. On 07 November 1918 O'Grady's promotion to Captain was gazetted. O'Grady's next-of-kin address for his wife was amended in 1918 from '107 Anglesea Road, Donnybrook, Dublin' to 'c/o Hill Rowan Esq, 32 Belsize Road, South Hampstead,

---

290 London Gazette Supplement, Issue 30466, p.633.

NW'. Subsequently it was amended to '27 Belsize Square, NW3'. On 13 March 1919 O'Grady transferred from 34 TDS to 23 Wing.

On 06 June 1919 the London Gazette reported that O'Grady had been transferred to the Unemployed List with effect from 24 May 1919. However, there is a note to the effect that on 29 August 1919 O'Grady was "mentioned for valuable services" on the Army List. O'Grady did not return to Canada, despite the post being kept open for him by the Canadian authorities. Initially he worked with Boving & Co, Engineers, then striking out as a consulting engineer on his own account. He became a corporate member of the Institute of Civil Engineers in 1919.

When joining the reserve his name was also recorded as "Standish Conn O'Grady". A medical board examination of 30 January 1925 deemed him fit for Class "A" Reserve. He was gazetted on 10 February 1925 on probation in the General Duties Branch, Reserve of Air Force Officers, Class A, with the humble rank of Flying Officer.[291]

O'Grady was required to undergo the embarrassment of a refresher course, which he attended in Renfrew from 16 March 1925 to 37 March 1925. Typically the resulting assessment found that O'Grady was a "very capable pilot, suited to SSF [single-seat fighter] aeroplanes—Category 1". O'Grady's address is recorded as 'Craighleith, Edinburgh', Scotland, with his wife's permanent address recorded as '13 Royal Terrace West, Kingstown, Ireland'. This would explain Renfrew as an assessment location. On 11 August 1925 O'Grady was confirmed in rank as a Flying Officer.[292]

On his second refresher course in February and March 1926, O'Grady was described as a "very capable pilot whose general flying and landings are excellent. Suited to SSF aeroplanes—Category 1". This regular refresher course assessment became a regular opportunity to pay homage to O'Grady, e.g. in June 1926 O'Grady was "a very capable pilot whose general flying and landings are very

---

291 London Gazette, Issue 33019, p.995.
292 London Gazette, Issue 33074, p.5366.

good. Suited to all types—Category 1". The following month he was described as "an officer of good type and a very good pilot".

On 31 January 1928 his promotion to Flight Lieutenant was gazetted,[293] and later that year had occasion to impress whilst flying the Armstrong Whitworth at his refresher course. However, although granted a further 5 years in the Class A Reserve from 10 February 1928 O'Grady's advancing years were counting against him. On 10 February 1933 he was granted a further 5 years but in the Class C reserve and this was gazetted on 02 May 1933.[294]

During this time, in 1931, O'Grady was appointed Lecturer in Civil Engineering at Armstrong College, University of Durham. O'Grady joined the Newcastle Gliding Club in 1936, becoming their chief flying instructor, but although his chief passion was gliding he also enjoyed hill walking and mountaineering. In the University of Durham he was a leading instructor in the University Fencing Club. At the Los Angeles Olympics 1932 a fellow Dubliner, Judy Guinness, represented Great Britain and Northern Ireland, winning a silver medal, but it would appear that O'Grady chose to represent Ireland at International level despite the infrequency of their participation in international competition.

O'Grady served as a flying instructor in World War II, mainly in South Africa. Initially he flew Avro Ansons and Fairey Battles with No. 5 Air Observers Navigation School, RAF Weston-Super-Mare, Somerset from May to August 1940. Subsequently, at No. 45 Air School, Oustshoorn, South Africa, he trained pilots from October 1941 to October 1943. O'Grady was awarded the Air Force Cross, which was gazetted on 01 January 1944.[295] O'Grady resigned his commission with effect from 24 March 1944, leaving the RAF with the rank of Squadron Leader.[296] In 1944 O'Grady returned to the

---

293 London Gazette, Issue 33352, p.689.
294 London Gazette, Issue 33936, p.2941.
295 London Gazette Supplement, Issue 36309, p.44.
296 London Gazette Supplement, Issue 36462, p.1665.

University of Durham, being promoted to Senior Lecturer. He retired in 1954.

O'Grady died in on 07 May 1968. Warm tributes were paid to him in many obituaries, notably in the Institution of Civil Engineers.[297]

Further reading, further research material:

O'Grady's private papers are available for perusal at the Imperial War Museum, which includes his flying log books from his service with the RFC and RAF, along with other documentation relating to his period as an instructor in World War II and also when the subject of refresher training with the RAF Reserve in the inter-war years. I had hoped to include two images from the collection in this volume but unfortunately the time-frame for tracing the copyright holder(s) could not be reconciled to the demands of the publication process.

✦ ✦ ✦

---

297 ICE Proceedings, Volume 42, Issue 2, 01 February 1969, pp.323-324.

POPE, SYDNEY LEO GREGORY "POPPY"

(6 aerial victories)

Born: 27 March 1898, Co Dublin

Died: 05 November 1980

Awards (chronologically):

Military Cross (1917); Distinguished Flying Cross (28 May 1926); Air Force Cross (01 March 1929); Knight Commander, Order of Orange and Nassau (Netherlands)—20 October 1942; Mentioned in Despatches (08 June 1944); Commander of the British Empire (01 January 1946).

Religion: Roman Catholic

Air Commodore Sydney Pope was born in Dublin to William and Elizabeth Pope, and one of seven children, most of whom were born in Co Waterford. In the Irish Census 1901 the family were resident in Co Kilkenny. Sydney's father describes their religion as being "Roman Catholic, or idolater according to HM Edward VII".

Now it is universally accepted that Edward VII made many peculiar announcements in the many decades waiting to take the throne but I cannot find any particular anti-Catholic phrase of this nature being attributed to him.

The family had a governess and two domestic servants. Sydney's father was a wine and spirit merchant, originally from Iowa, USA. Sydney's mother was from Melbourne, Australia. It's unclear as to why he was named Sydney but the 'Leo' and 'Gregory' elements of the name may well have arisen in the context of Leo XIII and Gregory XVI.

In the Irish Census 1911 Sydney and his younger brother Philip are resident with their aunt and uncle, Patrick and Mary Forde, in the subdivision of a house in Lower Baggot Street, Dublin. Sydney was a student of Marist College, Dublin. The Fordes were running a private hospital from the house. The rest of Sydney's family would appear to have left Ireland by this stage. In the UK Census 1911 Sydney's older sister Ethel is a boarder and elementary school pupil teacher at a convent school near East India Dock in Poplar. I have been unable to find a matching immigration record for the USA or Australia in respect of the other members of their family. However, it is known that Sydney was also educated at St Joseph's College, London.

Sydney enlisted as Private with the Inns of Court O.T.C. on 23 August 1915. He was later promoted to Lance Corporal. Flight magazine of 22 June 1916 (p.520) reports Pope's promotion to Temporary 2nd Lieutenant, from the Inns of Court OTC. Pope was awarded RAeC Certificate No. 2074 in August 1916. Pope's promotion to temporary 2nd Lieutenant was gazetted on 23 September 1916.

Pope joined No.60 Squadron in April 1917, 'Bloody April'. His first aerial victories did not come until June 1917. Flying a Nieuport (B1652) he sent an Albatros down out of control near Vitry on 08 June 1917. On 20 June 1917 he scored again with the Nieuport (B1679), this time against an Albatros D.V over Equerchin.

When No.60 Squadron converted from Nieuports to the S.E.5 (and the S.E.5a shortly thereafter) Pope's kill-rate improved considerably. He achieved 4 further aerial victories by mid-November 1917, all of these being confirmed destructions rather than out-of-control victories.

RFC Communiqué No.113 of 1917, which covers the period 06 November 1917 to 12 November 1917, reports three of Pope's victories, including a double-victory on 08 November 1917:

POPE, SYDNEY LEO GREGORY "POPPY"

"A second patrol of this squadron [No.60 Sqdn] engaged a two-seater near Houthem which was destroyed by 2nd Lt SLG Pope, who shortly after destroyed a two seater".[298]

In Scott's history of No.60 Squadron, Pope is mentioned:

"On November 8, Pope, an old member of the squadron, who had come through the Arras battle with us, destroyed two hostile two-seaters in one day. This was a good pilot and a popular officer, who for some reason was a long time before he began to get Huns, but, having once found his form, became a very useful and formidable fighter. He went home soon after this, and showed himself to be an exceptionally gifted trainer of pilots, both in flying and fighting".[299]

Pope was wounded in action, being forced down near St Julien on 18 November 1917. He was transferred to the Home Establishment later that month, being re-assigned to the Central Flying School. *Flight magazine* of 21 February 1918 (p.212) reported on Pope's promotion from Temporary 2nd Lieutenant to Temporary Lieutenant. Subsequently, Pope was promoted from Lieutenant to Temporary Captain, with the rank of Captain (Aeroplane), which was gazetted on 16 August 1918.

It would appear that Pope served with one of the former RNAS squadrons, flying Sopwith Snipes. (I have examined the 'Squadron Operations Record Book' for 203, 205 and 217 Squadrons—AIR 27/1197, AIR 27/1217 and AIR 27/1338—but have found no reference to Pope. It has been suggested that he served with No.208 Squadron but I see no reference on the Air Force Lists). However, by mid-1919 Pope had transferred to the army of occupation.

Flight magazine of 28 August 1919 (p.1171) reports a notice in the London Gazette of 19 August 1919, which reports that Pope had been re-graded to the rank of Captain (Aeroplane) for the purposes of pay and allowances whilst serving at the grade. However the London Gazette

---

298 Chaz Bowyer [ed] "RFC Communiqués 1917-1918", p.167 [London: Grub Street, 1998].
299 Group-Captain A.J.L.Scott's "Sixty Squadron R.A.F.—A History of the Squadron from its Formation", p.79 (London: William Heinemann; New York: George H Doran Company,1920)

of 22 August 1922 stated that Pope had relinquished the rank of Captain (A) for pay and allowance purposes, with effect from 04 August 1919. From all the grading/re-grading of the immediate post-war years it would appear that Pope had served with the army of occupation and subsequently relinquished that commission.

Pope's appointment as Flying Officer (Aeroplane & Seaplane) was gazetted on 24 October 1919.[300] It would appear that Pope was awarded a Short Service Commission at the rank of Flying Officer (Aeroplane & Seaplane) and was appointed Qualified Flying Instructor (QFI) at the RAF (Cadet) College, Cranwell. *Flight magazine* of 11 May 1922 (p.275) quotes from the London Gazette of 28 April 1922, which states that Pope has been granted a permanent commission in the RAF, retaining rank and seniority at the level of Flying Officer, the short service commission of 24 October 1919 being cancelled.

Pope flew with No.8 Squadron from April 1922 onwards. It had served in an Army Co-operation role for much of the war, but in the early 1920s spent time in Egypt and Mesopotamia (Iraq). In the RAF Half-Yearly Promotion List issued by the Air Ministry on 30 June 1923, Pope was promoted from Flying Officer to Flight Lieutenant. *Flight magazine* of 25 October 1923 (p.663) reported that Flight Lieutenant Pope had been posted to No.55 Squadron, Iraq with effect from 24 September 1923. *Flight magazine* of 12 February 1925 (p.89) reported that Pope had been transferred to RAF HQ Egypt on 24 December 1924. However, nothing much can be read into the rotation of RAF personnel at this time.

Pope was best man in the wedding of Robert Darley Whelan, eldest son of Rev. P.S. Whelan of Brenchley Vicarage and Miss Barbara Marion Celia Wrey, younger daughter of Sir Bourchier and Lady Wrey, of Tawsden, Brenchley, Kent. The wedding took place on 12 August 1925.[301]

Pope was awarded the DFC for his service in Iraq. No.55 Squadron had been a Bomber Squadron in World War I, forming part of

---
300 London Gazette, Issue 31616, p.13034.
301 Flight magazine of 03 September 1925 (p.569).

the Independent Force (the forerunner of RAF Bomber Command) from July 1918 onwards. In the post-war years it had been disbanded and re-formed in 1920.

Popular culture suggests that the RAF operations in Iraq in the 1920s consisted of nothing more than gassing Kurdish rebels. However, although No.55 Squadron flew from Mosul in the early 1920s by May 1924 it was based at RAF Hinaidi (Hinaida) near Baghdad. A dispute had broken out between Assyrian recruits and the local population in Kirkuk in Sulaimaniya province in May 1924, which resulted in Air Vice Marshall Higgins ordering 2 platoons of the Royal Inniskilling Fusiliers from Baghdad to Kirkuk to quell disturbances. This further exacerbated the situation and Sheikh Mahmud declared a full-scale Jihad against the British forces. Aircraft from several squadrons (Nos. 6,8,30,40,45,55 and 70) were involved in the bombing of Sulaimaniya in May 1924.

Although the province had been carved from the dismembered remnants of the Ottoman Empire under the Treaty of Sèvres (10 August 1920)—and had been granted to the British to administer as part of the League of Nations mandate—the Turks had not relinquished territorial claims to Mosul and the surrounding areas. Following the overthrow of the Sultan and the Turkish War of Independence led by Mustafa Kemal Ataturk, the Treaty of Lausanne—which came into force on 06 August 1924—had superseded the Treaty of Sèvres, but the fate of Mosul had been left to the League of Nations to resolve and this had not been concluded by the time the various revolts and uprisings were taking place. There had already been a series of incidents in the early 1920s between British and Turkish forces. Although British troops re-occupied Sulaimaniya by late July 1924 there were still minor clashes between the British and Sheikh Mahmud's forces, and also a series of skirmishes between the British and Turkish forces over the late summer and early autumn months of 1924.

Pope was awarded the Distinguished Flying Cross (DFC). There is no actual citation in the London Gazette of 28 May 1926 but it carried the following general citation for a number of officers and other ranks:

"The King has been graciously pleased to approve of the undermentioned awards in recognition of gallant and distinguished service in connection with the operations in Iraq during the period September to November 1924".[302]

Air Ministry records note the following:

'Flight Lieutenant Pope constantly led patrols with great fearlessness and determination, often at low altitudes through mountain passes infested with the enemy, and frequently under severe fire. He carried out over 90 hours' operational flying in one month and at all times set a splendid example of courage and zeal.'

By February 1927 Pope had transferred to No.22 Squadron. No.22 Squadron was in effect an integral part of the Aeroplane Experimental Establishment at Martlesham Heath, Suffolk. The purpose of the squadron was to test new aircraft prior to their acceptance into service with the RAF.

Flight magazine of 24 February 1927 (p.94) reports the award of the DFC to Pope, with the Investiture being held by the King at Buckingham Palace on 15 February 1927. Pope participated in a handicap race on Good Friday, 15 April 1927. Pope was flying a De Havilland Moth (G-EBPG) in a 20 mile race, part of the Bournemouth Easter Meeting race series. Pope came 2nd in his race.[303]

Pope would appear to have become an air race regular, flying in the Bournemouth Whitsun Meeting at Ensbury Park Racecourse on that bank holiday weekend of 04 June 1927 to 06 June 1927.[304] Pope was flying a blue De Havilland Moth in a number of races. *Flight* magazine of 09 June 1927 (p.369) features a photograph of Pope leading another aircraft in one of the races.

At the Royal Aero Club committee meeting of 14 September 1927 Pope was elected to the committee. In February 1928 Pope

---

302 London Gazette, Issue 33166, p.3458.
303 Flight magazine of 14 April 1927 (p.215).
304 *Flight* magazine of 02 June 1927 (pp.358-359).

got engaged to a Miss Pamela Young, youngest daughter of Dr A Cameron Young, Ipswich. *Flight* magazine of 15 March 1928 (p.171) reports that Pope was one of those in attendance at a levée held by the King at St James' Palace on 06 March 1928.

Pope's career was to take on hair-raising turn on 24 February 1929, when he survived a crash via parachute. According to Francis K Mason's *British Fighters since 1912* (Naval Institute Press, 1992) Pope survived the disintegration of a prototype Parnall Pipit single-seater, bailing out at less than 1,000 feet and successfully parachuting down. However, some decades later, in the auction catalogue of his medals, a short biography of Pope states that the incident occurred some time after his arrival at Martlesham in 1927:

"In February 1927, Pope joined 22 Squadron at the Aeroplane and Armament Experimental Establishment, based at Martlesham Heath, where he became the first R.A.F. test pilot to save his life by parachute. Whilst at the Parnall factory at Yate, testing a Parnall Pippit, a single-seater fighter undergoing acceptance trials, Pope felt a twitch when at 800 feet. He glanced over his shoulder and was just in time to see the rudder and fin floating away in mid-air behind him. Deciding that the time had come for him and the Pippet to part company, pope jerked the throttle shut, pulled the nose up and reached down to undo the straps of his Sutton harness".

It is suggested that Pope spent precious seconds tugging at the string of his pencil that he had been using to record test data! Apparently after this struggle with his harness Pope only managed to bail out at 300 feet. There was more drama to come:

"After a struggle he managed to force his bulky frame through the cockpit opening and free of the aircraft only to find that the ripcord handle was not where it was meant to have been. He had somersaulted and was falling feet-first; below him he could see a row Africa Star tall oaks coming up fast. In that same split second he saw the ripcord ring hanging by his leg—it had slipped from its sheath. He reached down, gave it a despairing tug and his chute blossomed out above him with a bump. As he reached up to grasp the lift webs his feet slashed through the top branches on to the ground.

"The people over at the aerodrome hadn't seen me get out," Pope said. "When they came running over they expected to find me in the wreckage. Instead I was running round the field like a madman, making sure that my back, which had received a severe jar, was in working order. The only visible injuries were two scratches on my ankle."

It is not difficult to resolve the discrepancy between the dates as it would appear that only two prototypes of the Parnall Pipit were built. One crashed in October 1928, when the tailplane spar fractured. The pilot survived, but with a broken neck. Pope flew the second prototype, with a strengthened tailplane featuring support struts. This crashed in February 1929, with Pope surviving via parachute and treetops. However, the melodramatic story of surviving a bail-out at 300 feet is not supported in other contemporary reports.

On 01 March 1929 Pope was awarded the Air Force Cross, which was gazetted on that date. Air Ministry records detail the following:

"Flight Lieutenant Pope commands a flight in No. 22 Squadron, which is under the technical administration of the Aeroplane and Armament Experimental Establishment. For nearly two years he has been engaged in the daily work of testing high speed single-seater machines, and although the work is often of a hazardous nature, he always shows unflagging zeal and energy, thereby setting a splendid example to all".

The Edinburgh Gazette of 05 March 1929[305] also reports Pope being awarded the AFC. *Flight* magazine of 04 April 1929 (p.268) reports Flight Lieutenant Pope being awarded the Air Force Cross at an Investiture held by the King at Buckingham Palace on 28 March 1929.

Flight magazine of 06 June 1929 (p.469) carried a lengthy article on the parachute. In a reference to the incident involving Pope it stated that he got free at 1,000 feet and landed using the Irvin parachute. (Pope is described as being over 6 feet tall and weighing

---

305 Edinburgh Gazette, Issue 14527, p.239.

POPE, SYDNEY LEO GREGORY "POPPY"

15 stone). Pope had therefore become a member of the 'Caterpillar Club', i.e. those which had survived a successful descent via parachute. Pope would have received a gold tie-pin of caterpillar design from the Irvin Air Chute Company of Buffalo, New York.

On 01 August 1929 Pope's transferred to the Air Ministry with the Department of the Air Member for Supply and Research (AMSR) with effect from 13 July 1929. This was a research and technical development service branch but there would not appear to have been any prohibition of Pope flying in a private capacity. In the King's Cup Air Race to Hamworth on 05 July 1930 Pope flew an Avro V but had to retire at the Manchester leg of the race.

Flight magazine of 29 August 1930 (p.981) refers to Pope as being one of just 47 British-based parachute survivors, members of the 'Caterpillar Club' of which there were 300 worldwide.

On 02 February 1932 Pope's promotion from Flight Lieutenant to Squadron Leader with effect from 01 February 1932 was gazetted.[306] Pope was subsequently transferred to No.54 Squadron, Hornchurch, with effect from 07 March 1932.

On 01 July 1932 Flight magazine (pp.598-599) reported Pope's participation in mock-fighting, with Pope leading No.54 (Fighter) Squadron in the event, an attack on an aerodrome. In the air exercises that took place between 18 July 1932 and 22 July 1932, Pope led No.54 Squadron in the "Northlands" -v- "Southlands" exercises. Pope's squadron were flying Bristol Bulldogs from Upavon. Pope did not stay long with No.54 Squadron. In September 1933 Pope transferred to command No.801 (FF) Squadron. This was a Naval Air Squadron. (In the post-war years the Royal Navy had been granted a successor to the Royal Naval Air Service, but only in respect of seaborne duties not assigned to RAF Coastal Command, i.e. the Fleet Air Arm did not re-gain the former RNAS squadrons numbered in the 200s, e.g. seaplane or coastal and maritime patrol aircraft). The Fleet Air Arm was founded on 01 April 1924. No.801 Squadron was formed in April 1933, flying Hawker Nimrod biplanes from HMS Hermes.

---

306 London Gazette, Issue 33795, p.709.

Flight magazine of 18 June 1936 (p.660) reported that Squadron Leader Pope had been transferred to the School of Naval Co-operation, Lee-on-the-Solent, for duty as Adjutant, with effect from 27 May 1936. On 02 April 1937 Pope's promotion from Squadron Leader to Wing Commander with effect from 01 April 1937 was gazetted.[307] Subsequently, Wing Commander Pope was appointed to RAF Station Debden to command with effect from 21 April 1937. RAF Debden had been opened in April 1937. Pope's command was of two grass landing strips. However, it was subjected to continuous improvement and by the outbreak of World War II the grass airstrips had been replaced with concrete.

However, *Flight* magazine of 14 July 1938 (p.36) reported that Wing Commander Pope led a formation of 11 Hawker Hurricanes of No.111 (Fighter) Squadron and 4 Gloster Gladiators of No.87 (Fighter) Squadron in escorting a Vickers Valentia bomber transport and 2 Avro Ansons from RAF Northolt in an attempt at crossing to Paris. They made the journey in 66 minutes, being escorted by French Amiot bombers and Dewoitine fighters. The exercises by the Hurricanes and Gladiators were well received in Paris.

In March 1939 Pope transferred to No.226 Squadron. This squadron had only been reformed in March 1937, flying the Fairey Battle light bomber. In the Battle of France the squadron suffered grievous losses, being evacuated in May and June 1940. However, Pope was not in command of the attack on the Albert Canal that resulted in Wicklow-born Donald Garland winning a posthumous VC—Garland flew with No.12 Squadron, which also used the Fairey Battle. Pope's son is currently writing his biography, which will cover Pope's World War II career in detail. Given that Pope served as a Wing Commander and was promoted several times during the course of the war, it is therefore likely that he would have been party to a number of decisions regarding operational deployments. However,

---

307 London Gazette, Issue 34385, p.2126.

it would appear that Pope was relieved of his command at No.226 Squadron. This may relate to the failure of No.226 Squadron in reaching objectives with the Fairey Battle, but could equally relate to Pope's exasperation at the waste of human life in attempting to deploy the slow, heavy single-engined bomber against well-defended targets. Losses were exceeding 50% per mission even before the fall of France. Pope's career did not suffer however, as he was promoted to acting Group Captain.

In June 1940 Pope was appointed in command of RAF Leuchars, which was the base from which No.224 Squadron attempted to engage German flying boats and Condors in the North Sea. *Flight* magazine of 13 June 1940 (p.535) reported that Pope had been promoted from Wing Commander to Group Captain with effect from 01 June 1940. It would appear that over the course of 1941 and 1942 Group Captain Pope commanded various training resources, most notably the transfer of RAF No.32 Operational Training Unit (OTU) from England to Patricia Bay, Victoria, British Columbia, Canada. The unit used Bristol Beaufort torpedo bombers to train Australian, British, Canadian and New Zealand crews, subsequently upgrading to the Handley Page Hampden heavy bomber.

Pope went in the opposite direction of the Handley Page Hampden crews, as he was posted to command RAF Syerston in Nottinghamshire. This base had originally seen Polish-crewed Wellington bombers being replaced by Royal Canadian Air Force (RCAF) crewed Hampdens, and subsequently Lancaster heavy bombers. Pope's command of the base coincided with its transition to a station for bomber crew training. It was to become known at the Lancaster Finishing School, but there was also a Bombing and Gunnery Defence Training Flight based there in 1942 and 1943.

On 20 October 1942 Pope's permission to wear the Commander of the Order of Orange-Nassau with Swords, which had been conferred by the Queen of the Netherlands (Royal Decree no.12 of 15

January 1942, Commandeur in de Orde van Oranje-Nassau met de zwaarden), was gazetted.[308]

It would appear that by 1944 Pope had returned to command RAF Leuchars and its maritime patrol squadrons. His command is described as No.53 Base. However, No.53 (Operational) Base was formed in January 1943 and was composed of RAF Waddington, RAF Skellingthorpe and RAF Bardney. This was part of No.5 Group, which was based in Lincolnshire throughout World War II. Pope was mentioned in despatches in June 1944.

Flight magazine of 04 January 1945 (p.22) reports Acting Air Commodore Pope to be appointed to command of a base in Bomber Command. However, I cannot find a reference to the actual appointment in the Air Force Lists to another base.

On 01 January 1946 Pope became a Commander of the Military Division of the Most Excellent Order of the British Empire, i.e. his was a military CBE in the New Year Honours List.[309]

According to information contained in the auction of Pope's medals many years later, the Air Ministry recommendation is recorded as follows:

"Acting Air Commodore S. L. G. Pope, D.F.C., A.F.C., No. 53 Base.

This officer was appointed to command an operational station in October 1943, and in February 1944 took over command of No. 53 (Operational) Base. He has a strong personality and has proved to be a most capable and efficient base commander who has successfully organised the squadrons under his command to a high standard. His efforts and ability have contributed much towards the success of Bomber Command's operations."

Pope retired on 02 March 1946, having had an interesting and varied career. It's quite ironic that Pope survived being brought down without a parachute and was nearly killed when relying upon one in his test flight years.

---

308 London Gazette Supplement, Issue 35750, p.4542.
309 London Gazette, Issue 37407, p.33.

POPE, SYDNEY LEO GREGORY "POPPY"

Pope died in November 1980 in Worthing, West Sussex. Pope's medals—both his service medals and gallantry awards, amounting to 10 medals and awards in all—were auctioned by Dix Noonan Webb on 18 June 1997 for £2,400, which was less than the estimate of £2,500 to £3,000.

❖ ❖ ❖

PRICE, GUY WILLIAM

(12 aerial victories)

Born: 06 July 1895, Co Down
Died: 18 February 1918
Awards: Distinguished Service Cross and Bar
Commemorated:
Arras Flying Services Memorial, Pas de Calais, France
1914-1918 Memorial Plaque, St Columba's College, Dublin
Religion: Church of Ireland

Flight Commander Guy William Price was one of 4 Irish aces to have served with the Royal Naval Air Service.

Price was born on 06 July 1895 in Rostrevor, Co Down to Frederic Walter Price and Francesca d'Orange Price.

It is unclear what connection the family had with Co Down: the marriage of Frederick Walter Price of Lower Gabwell House, Stoke in Teiguhead, Devon and Francesca d'Orange Rambaut, of 27 Mespil Road, Dublin, took place in St Stephen's Church, Dublin on 25 January 1893. Francesca's father, William Hantenville Rambaut, was a clerk in holy orders. However, the address of Francesca's sister, Charlotte Louise Rambaut, who married in Cork on 12 December 1900, was given as 6 Church Avenue, Rathmines, Dublin, which suggests that Guy and Francesca's family were not well settled in Dublin either.

The Irish Census 1901 records Guy's family as residing near the village of Delgany, Co Wicklow. Guy's father is described as a "landed proprietor" from Devonshire. Guy's mother was from Co Dublin. Guy's older sister—Aileen d'Orange—and his younger sister (Norah) were also born in Co Down. Their younger brother, Rambaut, was born in Co Wicklow. The family was living with a governess, a nurse, a cook and a parlour maid.

The Irish Census 1911 records Guy as being a boarder at St Columba's College, Taylor's Grange, Dublin. (Consequently, Price appears on the St Columba's College 1914-1918 Memorial Plaque).

Price's service record[310] indicates that he joined the RNAS on 05 October 1914. He was initially stationed at Calshot, although Flight magazine of 25 December 1914 (p.1232) reported Price being awarded RAeC Certificate No.987 on 09 December 1914, whilst flying a Grahame-White biplane at the Grahame-White School, Hendon.

Price was appointed Flight Lieutenant on 25 June 1915. Price was posted to the seaplane station at Felixstowe on 05 July 1915. It would appear from his service record that Price forfeited 6 months' seniority at the grade of Flight Lieutenant as a result of a court martial hearing in October 1916 (more of which will be explained later), i.e. his appointment date of 25 July 1915 reading as 25 December 1915 for promotion purposes. This often gives rise to confusion regarding Price's appointment date. Price transferred from Felixstowe to Chingford, and was subsequently posted to Dover where he was trained on Morse Semaphore.

Price was appointed to Dunkirk in December 1915, and was posted to HMS Riviera, a seaplane carrier ship. On 31 March 1916 a review on Riviera of Price's progress was a case of being damned with faint praise, as he was described as being "a zealous officer with moderate ability to command, but is improving". A further review on 30 June 1916 noted "very great improvement in every respect, both as Pilot and Officer". Subsequently, on 01 October 1916 Price was

---

310 UK National Archives, ADM 273/4, p.77, Guy William Price.

described as being a "good plucky pilot. Lacking in powers of command and sense of responsibility as an officer".

Price had by this stage flown over 100 hours on aeroplanes and seaplanes. Unfortunately for Price he was discharged from Riviera as a result of a court martial. He was tried on two counts:

"(1) made mention in a private letter the position of one of HM Ships,

(2) was guilty of an act to the prejudice of good order and naval discipline in that he did in a private letter criticize an operation carried out by HMS Riviera."[311]

The sentence, as mentioned previously, was the forfeiture of 6 months seniority at his rank. He was dismissed from the ship and was severely reprimanded. This led to Price being posted to South Shields to serve as an Instructor at Windermere in October/November 1916. However, things did not go well at his new posting, a review on 01 December 1916 stated "this officer is of no use, either for instructional or executive work. His presence is detrimental to the carrying out of instructions and the general work of the station. I submit he may be drafted to another Station".

A week later Price was sent to Calshot, with a note on his personnel file to the effect that he was to be reported on within a month regarding his fitness for remaining with the RNAS.

The Commanding Officer at Calshot reported on 12 January 1917 "fairly good seaplane pilot and his general behaviour has been v.g. Appears slow in his actions, not very quick-witted and does not seem energetic. I do not consider him suitable as Instructor, or very capable of executive duties, but am of opinion he would make efficient officer if he tried, and I certainly think C.O. Windermere's report on him is very exaggerated. He is very desirous of being given another chance and is most anxious to rejoin an Aeroplane Wing in France. I suggest he is very likely to make good".

This whole sequence of events has the feel of Milan Kundera's novel *The Joke*, in which a young man is sentenced to working in the

---

311 UK National Archives, ADM 273/4, p.77, Guy William Price.

mines for a letter to a friend in which he is insufficiently grave in his sentiments. Giving away the location of a ship is a serious matter but being critical of poor operational decisions regarding the use of seaplanes should be tolerable criticism in his correspondence with others. Soldiers in the trenches were given much greater latitude in expressing their frustrations with the shortcomings of military campaigns. The subsequent attempt to shoehorn the Ulster-born, Wicklow-raised, Dublin-educated pilot into an Instructorial role was a flawed one: by all accounts on the Riviera he was a good pilot but an indifferent officer. It would have been better at the outset to send Price to a naval squadron upon the completion of the court martial proceedings.

However, the review by the C.O. at Calshot led to Price being posted to Yarmouth in January 1917 and subsequently to Plymouth in February 1917. By late April 1917 Price was flying seaplanes from Dover. His review at RNAS Dover on 30 June 1916 reported a "very experienced Short [seaplane] pilot". Price transferred to RNAS Dunkirk on 1917, with a review of 01 October 1917 finding him to be "exceptionally good and plucky pilot. Good command". By November 1917 he was recommended for promotion. Price was made an acting Flight Commander.

Price initially served with 13 (Naval) Squadron before transferring to 8 (Naval) Squadron as acting Flight Commander. This squadron—later No.208 Squadron of the RAF—had been formed in France in October 1916, equipped with Sopwith 1 ½ Strutters, Sopwith Pups and Nieuport scouts. It had conducted its first offensive patrol on 03 November 1916. It had been briefly re-equipped with Sopwith Triplanes in March 1917 before being re-equipped with Sopwith Camels in July 1917.[312] It would appear that Price joined the squadron in the course of these various re-organisations.

Price did not achieve his first aerial victory until 05 December 1917, when he destroyed an Albatros DV over Cite St Auguste when flying a Sopwith Camel (B6311). Within minutes of that victory he shared in a further victory with Flight Sub-Lieutenant WH Sneath (B3821) over another Albatros DV. The next day Price scored a further shared

---

312 AIR 27/1239 No.208 Squadron, UK National Archives.

victory. By the end of December 1917 Price had achieved 5 aerial victories, 4 of which were shared. Price had become one of 26 aces with 8 (Naval) Squadron of the RNAS, later No.208 Squadron of the RAF, which claimed nearly 300 victories by the end of the war. A review of 25 December 1917 reported "good command. In the short time he has been with Squadron he has proved thoroughly reliable officer".

On 01 January 1918 Price's promotion from Flight Lieutenant to Acting Flight Commander with effect from 31 December 1917 was gazetted.[313]

On 02 January 1918 Price shot down Lt Gunther Auffahrt of Jasta 29 in flames. Auffahrt was killed. Price was to achieve 6 victories in January 1918, 2 of which were shared. I am reluctant to participate in the "who got who" game, as often the records are inconclusive. In 'Above the Trenches' the death of Uffz F Jacobs of Jasta 12 is attributed to Price. Overall 3 of Price's victories involved enemy aircraft going down in flames and 3 others were confirmed destructions.

Price's Distinguished Service Cross citation was gazetted on 22 February 1918:

"Flt.-Cdr. Guy William Price, R.N.A.S.

In recognition of the gallantry and determination displayed by him in leading offensive patrols, which have constantly engaged and driven away enemy aircraft.

On the 2nd January 1918, he observed seven Albatross scouts, and, crossing the lines in the clouds, he attacked one, which fell vertically, bursting into flames, and crashed to the ground.

He has on several other occasions driven enemy aircraft down out of control".[314]

Price's service record indicates that the "several other occasions" in his citation relate to 06 December 1917, 27 December 1917, 28 December 1917 and 02 January 1918.

The citation for the award of a Bar to the Distinguished Service Cross was gazetted on 16 March 1918:

---

313 London Gazette Supplement, Issue 30541, p.88.
314 London Gazette Supplement, Issue 30536, p.2304.

"Flt. Cdr. Guy William Price, D.S.C., R.N.A.S.

For consistency and determination in attacking enemy aircraft, often in superior numbers.

On the 22nd January 1918, when on offensive patrol, he observed seven Albatross scouts. He dived and fired into one of the enemy aircraft, which stalled, side-slipped, and eventually fell over on its back, disappearing through a thick bank of clouds, and was observed by others of our machines to fall completely out of control.

On several other occasions he has destroyed enemy machines or brought them down completely out of control".[315]

Price scored 6 aerial victories in January 1918. His final victory came on 16 February 1918, which was shared with Flight Sub-Lieutenant WH Sneath (B6356) and Flight Sub-Lieutenant HH Fowler (B3832). Price was killed on 18 February 1918 during a low ground-strafing mission against enemy positions. His Sopwith Camel was shot down by the German ace Theodor Rumpel of Jasta 23.

With Price having served in the RNAS there was always the prospect of a girl in at least one port, if not every port. Arthur Tyler & Co, Solicitors of London placed a notice in the London Gazette of 29 July 1919 on behalf of Guy's mother Francesca d'Orange Price, in the standard legal equivalent of casting lots for his robes.[316] Price's address was recorded as 23 Clarinda Park, West Kingstown, Co Dublin.

Price was described as having a "Captain Kettle" beard, in Norman Franks' *Sopwith Camel Aces of World War 1: Volume 52 of Aircraft of the Aces*, (Osprey Publishing, 2003). It is believed that C.J. Cutcliffe Hyne's Captain Kettle was based on a South Shields captain, Davey Proffit. If Price's RNAS service record were to be believed he would be closer to Blackbeard on matters of compliance with naval discipline during his time at South Shields.

✦ ✦ ✦

---

315 London Gazette, Issue 30581, p.3395.
316 London Gazette, Issue 31478, p.9633.

PROCTOR, THOMAS

(5 aerial victories)

Born: 23 August 1888, Co Armagh

Died: 27 September 1918

Commemorated: Arras Flying Services Memorial, Pas de Calais, France

Religion: Methodist

Sergeant Thomas Proctor was born on 23 August 1888 to Elizabeth Proctor. His next-of-kin address is recorded as 47 Lanark St, Belfast but he was actually born in Lurgan, Co Armagh. The Irish Census 1911 records Thomas as being resident at Wilton St, Woodvale, Belfast, Co Antrim. Thomas' mother Elizabeth, a widow, is described as being a linen weaver, as is Thomas' sister Elizabeth. Thomas was a "machine oiler in mill".

There were 7 Thomas Proctors who signed the Ulster Covenant, but none are a sufficiently close match to be identifiable as the Irish ace.

As in the case of several other Irish aces, Proctor served with the Royal Naval Air Service. However, his active service was with the Royal Flying Corps and later the Royal Air Force (212137), fighting with No.88 Squadron and scoring all his victories with this squadron. Accordingly, Proctor is not an RNAS ace.

Proctor was a sergeant, and is neither the Thomas Augustus Pugh Proctor (DOB 25 July 1898) nor the Thomas Proctor (DOB 08 January 1900) recorded in various Air Ministry officer files.[317] There

---

317 AIR 76/413, UK National Archives.

is a Thomas Proctor is recorded as an Ordinary Seaman, Able Seaman, with Service Number R/1783 in the Admiralty Records.[318] However, his date of birth is recorded as 07 August 1887. Similarly, he is recorded as Royal Naval Volunteer Reserve Division ('Palace'), under the Service Number Z/2624. His date of birth is once again recorded as 07 August 1887.[319] However, despite the proximity of age, this is not the Irish Thomas Proctor of No.88 Squadron. Similarly, there was a Thomas Ward Proctor from Belfast recorded under the service number J22083, but his date of birth was 13 July 1895.

The Irish ace Thomas Proctor served with the Royal Naval Air Service under Service Number F12137. His date of enlistment is recorded as 19 February 1916 in his RNAS service record.[320] Just 5'6" he was tattooed and had a scar on his right forearm. Although his pre-war occupation was a "town labourer" he served as an Air Mechanic 2nd Class, receiving a "very good" rating in all reviews conducted whilst serving in the RNAS. From 19 February 1916 to 09 September 1917 Proctor was assigned to President II (Dover). This was a shore establishment, not a ship. From 10 September 1917 Proctor transferred to Daedalus (Eastchurch), serving there until 31 December 1917 when he was reassigned to President II (Dover). He was transferred to President II (Dunkirk) on 15 January 1918, then subsequently to Daedalus (Dunkirk) from 01 February 1918 until the merger of the RNAS into the Royal Air Force. The references to Daedalus in conjunction with Eastchurch and Dunkirk signified that Proctor had been assigned to the shore establishment at Lee-on-Solent, "HMS Daedalus" but had not necessarily been based at the Seaplane Training School there, as Daedalus was similar to President as a notional establishment as a mechanism for assignment of personnel.

Proctor served as an observer with No.88 Squadron. His first victory came on 31 May 1918 when his Bristol F.2b (C821), which was

---

318 ADM 339/1, UK National Archives.
319 ADM 337/66, UK National Archives.
320 ADM 188/584, Thomas Proctor, UK National Archives.

piloted by Allan Hepburn, engaged an Albatros DV over Ostend. They sent it down out of control. On 02 June 1918 the same pairing in the same aircraft send an Albatros DV down in flames between Middlekerke and Ostende.

Proctor's next victories did not come until August 1918, scoring 3 victories with two different pilots. He was the only Irish ace to have served with No.88 Squadron, but it was a diverse group: the highest-scoring aces were Kenneth Conn, a Canadian, and Edgar Johnston and Allan Hepburn, both Australian. Of the squadron's claimed 147 victories Proctor was the only Irish contributor, although the mother (Elizabeth, b.1859) of Coventry-born ace William Wheeler was from Derry and the mother (Mary Jane, née Cuthbert, b.1868) of Kent-born ace Robert James Cullen was from Ballinskelligs, Co Kerry. There were Irish casualties with No.88 Squadron, e.g. 2nd Lieutenant Stephen Griffin from Ennis, Co Clare who was killed on 18 May 1918.

According to *Bristol F2 Fighters of World War I*, by Jon Guttman and Harry Dempsey, p.67, (London: Osprey, 2007), Proctor was killed in action on 27 September 1918 when his Bristol F.2b (E2153) was shot down by German ace, Vizefeldwebel Friedrich "Fritz" Classen of Jasta 26, for the latter's 9th of his 11 victories. Both Proctor and his pilot, Lt Cuthbert Foster, were killed. They had been engaged in an escort role for aircraft of No.103 Squadron who were on a bombing mission. During the flight they were attacked by a number of enemy aircraft and Cuthbert was seen to perform a double loop in an attempt at outmanoeuvring a German aircraft that was on their tail. According to the British accounts, they were seen flying low and heading for the British lines. However, in the immediate aftermath of combat it is often difficult to gauge whether an aircraft has engine trouble or has been badly shot up. In 'Above the War Fronts' it is stated that they were shot down near Abancourt.

Regardless of the exact sequence of events, Proctor has no known grave. They had met a formidable enemy: Royal Prussian Jagdstaffel ("Jasta") 26 scored 177 aerial victories for the loss of less than 30 casualties (killed, wounded or taken prisoner) in the course of the war—at least 17 aces served with Jasta 26, of whom 12 achieved that status with the unit and it is recognized as one of the elite flying units of aviation history.

A war gratuity was paid on 30 January 1920 to Proctor's next-of-kin.

✦ ✦ ✦

SAUNDERS, ALFRED WILLIAM

(**12 aerial victories**)

Born: 16 January 1888, Dublin
Died: 22 May 1930
Awards: Distinguished Flying Cross
Religion: Church of Ireland

Captain Alfred William Saunders was born in Dublin on 16 January 1888 to Amelia Adelaide Saunders (b.1859), a hospital nurse from London, and Matthew Johnston Saunders, a contractor.

The Irish Census 1901 records Saunders living at 14 Leinster St, Dublin, with his mother, his older sister Margaret Elizabeth and his brothers Arthur George and William John. All four siblings were born in Dublin. Their London-born grandmother is also resident with them. In the Irish Census 1911 Alfred William is no longer resident with his mother, who still lists herself as married—even though for the second census in a row her husband is not present. However, there is a 67-year-old Matthew Johnston Saunders recorded as being an inmate at Northbrook Road, Rathmines, Dublin. This is described as being an "old man's asylum" in the census returns. The building itself still stands, a 'Gothic revival' pile with spire, tiny cell-like windows and a peculiar asymmetrical design. Matthew Johnston Saunders recorded his occupation as that of a "contractor". Originally from Co Wicklow he had 7 children, of whom 6 were still alive in 1911.

Alfred's brother William John Saunders was to become the sketch artist Paddy Drew. (There are numerous Pathé newsreels of the 1930s and 1940s in which Drew sketches caricatures Chamberlain, Hitler and so forth for the cameras. As one may note, the surname 'Drew' is common enough but is also the past tense of 'draw', i.e. the pseudonym being a pun). According to the excellent IrishGenealogy.ie website, of Alfred's other siblings, Margaret Elizabeth Saunders was baptized on 25 February 1883. The family address was given as 14 York St, Dublin. Arthur George Saunders of the same address was baptized on 25 August 1884, and William John Saunders of the same address was baptized on 27 May 1891. (He was baptized in the Rotunda Chapel, which potentially suggests a scare regarding the likelihood of survival. His DOB was 18 May 1891). However, it would appear that Letitia Adelaide Saunders of 14 York St, Dublin was baptized on 25 February 1879, and Matthew John Saunders of 14 York St was baptized on 25 June 1880, i.e. Alfred had older sisters and brothers who had moved on by the time the family were recorded in Leinster St in the Irish Census 1901.

Saunders originally served with the Royal Field Artillery. He obtained his Royal Aero Club certificate on 20 July 1916, flying a Maurice Farman biplane at the Military School, Catterick Bridge. Saunders' address on his certificate is 9B Kelfield Gardens, North Kensington, London. In August 1916 Saunders was appointed 2nd Lieutenant in the Royal Flying Corps, which was gazetted on 20 September 1916.[321] It was also reported in Flight magazine on 28 September 1916, (p.829).

In Spring 1917 it is believed that Saunders survived a bad crash. On 04 October 1917 Saunders' promotion from 2nd Lieutenant to Temporary Lieutenant was gazetted.[322] The War Office announcement was also reported in Flight magazine on 04 October 1917 (p.1033).

Saunders' service with No.60 Squadron is only briefly mentioned in Scott's history of the squadron (pp. 111, 115) but Saunders would

---
321 London Gazette Supplement, Issue 29756, p.9175.
322 London Gazette Supplement, Issue 30322, p.10260.

have joined well after Molesworth, Pope and so forth had passed through. RAF Communiqué No.6 of 1918, which covers the period 06 May 1918 to 12 May 1918, reports Lt A.W. Saunders as having achieved at least one aerial victory at this time. The No.60 Squadron histories generally record Saunders as destroying 2 Albatros DV fighters on 10 May 1918. Alex Revell's history of No.60 Squadron also makes reference to several of Saunders' victories but, as in the case of several other writes, Saunders does not have the same impact as Molesworth in terms of personality or profile.

RAF Communiqué No.7 of 1918 reports Saunders' destruction of a German scout on 16 May 1918:

"Lt AW Saunders, 60 Sqn, drove down one EA scout in a spin. At about 3,000 feet the EA pulled out of the spin and flew east. Lt Saunders engaged the EA again and fired long bursts into it from both guns at close range, whereupon the EA dived to the ground and crashed badly near Beaulencourt".[323]

Another Irishman with No.60 Squadron, Herbert George Hegarty, also destroyed a German aircraft on that day. However, on 02 July 1918 Saunders really showed his rate of improvement, being awarded a triple-victory in respect of the following claim of destructions and collisions:

"Five machines of 60 Sqn, led by Lt A.W. Saunders, saw a formation of six Pfalz scouts 7,000 feet below flying over Villers Bretonneux. The patrol went down and attacked the EA at the tail end of the left-hand side of the formation. A drum of Lewis and a long burst of Vickers were fired at it by Lt Saunders, whereupon it went down vertically and was seen to crash by an A.A. battery. The second EA on the left of the leader suddenly turned to the right and collided into the EA leader, both machines collapsing and crashing into the Bois de Pierret. A Hannoveraner which was firing at one of our S.E.s was then attacked; it dived to within 50 feet of the ground when it flattened out, flying east. Lt Saunders then became separated from

---

323 Christopher Cole [ed] "RAF Communiqués 1918", p.82 [Tom Donovan 1990].

his patrol and saw three Pfalz scouts, which he attacked and chased east. On coming home he saw an EA attacking an S.E.5 and joined in, whereupon this EA also flew east. Lt Saunders was fighting altogether 45 minutes".[324]

Saunders was almost immediately awarded the Distinguished Flying Cross (DFC) in respect of the action, which suggests that he may have been recommended for a higher award. The DFC citation was gazetted on 03 August 1918:

"Lt. Alfred William Saunders.

A gallant and determined officer whose fighting spirit and enthusiasm has been a splendid example to his squadron. On one occasion whilst leading his formation of six machines, he attacked six enemy aeroplanes. Diving from 11,000 to 3,000 feet, he singled out a group of three, and shot down one. He then engaged the other two, which in their endeavour to get away collided and crashed".[325]

Saunders was promoted to temporary Captain (Aeroplane), which was gazetted on 09 August 1918.[326] This was also reported in Flight magazine on 15 August 1918 (p.923). RAF Communiqué No.19 of 1918 reports Saunders taking on targets of opportunity on 08 August 1918:

"Capt A.W. Saunders, 60 Sqn, dived on a Fokker biplane, which he observed to go down in a spin and crash. Soon afterwards he attacked another enemy machine, which fell through the clouds out of control, and on following it down he saw a train, into which he fired from 50 feet, circling twice round the engine. Though heavily fired at from the ground and shot in the seat of his machine, and having fired all his ammunition away, Capt Saunders returned".[327]

Saunders would appear to have done well as a Flight Commander, his patrol accounting for 4 enemy aircraft on 09 August 1918.

---

324 Christopher Cole [ed] "RAF Communiqués 1918", p.126 [Tom Donovan 1990].
325 London Gazette Supplement, Issue 30827, p.9203.
326 London Gazette, Issue 30836, p.9383.
327 Christopher Cole [ed] "RAF Communiqués 1918", p.154 [Tom Donovan 1990].

Saunders' post-war career took many twists and turns, some of which are not fully explained. It is believed that Saunders served briefly with the short-lived Lithuanian Air Force of the inter-war years. Saunders was notionally transferred to the Unemployed List on 31 October 1919, which was gazetted on 13 January 1920.[328] Apparently Saunders joined the Lithuanian Air Force on 31 October 1919 and was released on 17 January 1920. The RAF had the task of supplanting the Germans in their advisory and training roles supplied to enable Lithuania hold its ground in the conflicts between Poland and the USSR and their neighbours. Saunders was one of a number of "civilian volunteer" advisors to the Lithuanians.

Whilst farmed out to Lithuania it would appear that Saunders was promoted to Flying Officer, which was gazetted on 12 December 1919.[329] Saunders was subsequently promoted to Temporary Lieutenant in the Royal Army Service Corps from Temporary 2nd Lieutenant, with effect from 10 December 1919, which was gazetted on 30 December 1919.[330]

As one will note, the foregoing sequence of appointments are contradictory: either Saunders was a civilian or he was in military service. However, Brigadier-General Frank Percy Crozier (who later served as head of the Auxiliary Division of the RIC in Ireland) did serve as Honorary Major-General, Lithuanian Army, and it was therefore not unlikely that some fellow Irishmen would be part of the Lithuanian quasi-military, quasi-civilian set-up. Saunders was released from the Lithuanian service on 17 January 1920. He was lucky to have gotten out of the particular time.

Contemporary media reported that "Lenin's Pilot" had been arrested:

"An aircraft made a forced landing near Kovno, Lithuania. It contained Fritz Platten, his wife and two Germans. Platten had once been the leader of the Swiss Social Democrats and had negotiated

---

328 London Gazette, Issue 31730, p.562.
329 London Gazette, Issue 31685, p.15483.
330 London Gazette Supplement, Issue 31710, p.16107.

the passage of Lenin and Trotsky through Germany to Russia in 1917. Platten was arrested by the Lithuanian authorities. His luggage contained large quantities of Bolshevik propaganda".[331]

By 1921 the Polish-Lithuanian situation was further deteriorating, e.g. on 30 August 1921 it was reported from Warsaw that 3 Lithuanian aeroplanes had appeared over Vilna territory, apparently in breach of the Armistice.

Zeligowski's troops fired on the aircraft, with the Polish air force also engaging them. Consequently two Lithuanian aircraft were forced to land in the territory of Central Lithuania. The pilots were released on parole. The Lithuanian Government issued a communiqué, which stated that on 27 August 1921 that these aircraft had been flown without authorization by two air mechanics. The Lithuanian Government applied through the League of Nations Control Commission for the return of the two aircraft and the surrender of the defectors, who it claimed had been in communication with Warsaw prior to the incident.

It should of course be remembered that there was a monthly review of "revolutionary movements" to UK Cabinet throughout 1920 and 1921, in which there were numerous unreliable accounts of what was imagined to be happening and/or various Reds under the Polish and Lithuanian beds.

Regardless of how short-lived Saunders' time was with the Lithuanian air service it is nevertheless clear that Crozier was back in Ireland by March/April 1920, and was to ultimately resign in February 1921 when several dozen Auxiliaries he had suspended for looting were re-instated by the British authorities. Years later Crozier was to write "A Brass Hat in No Man's Land" [Cape Publishing, 1930], which was quite frank in many respects, e.g. it dealt with the issue of him supervising the execution of a young Belfast private in a 'pour encourage les autres' manner. (I have not encountered "Impressions and Recollections" [T Werner Laurie, 1930], "Five Years' Hard" [1932], "Ireland Forever" [J Cape, 1932] or "The Men I Killed"

---

331 Flight magazine of 13 May 1920 (p.535).

[Michael Joseph Publishing,1937] but I gather that they are of varying quality, although it is understood that "Impressions and Recollections" makes reference to Crozier's service in Lithuania but does not make specific reference to Saunders). Crozier was to become an unlikely international peace campaigner in his later years, so it should perhaps be expected to some extent that his memoirs would talk up the blood, guts, and the horror of war and so forth in the context of his potential new readership. Of Crozier's henchmen in Lithuania it would appear that their numbers were quite small, perhaps no more than half a dozen, and it would appear that Saunders served alongside Pranas 'Frank' Hiska, a Lithuanian with RAF training, and a small number of RAF pilots. However, I do not have sufficient documentary material to reliably state anything in respect of the RAF's "civilian" presence in Lithuania or Saunders' particular role in respect of same.

On 06 February 1923 the Air Ministry announced that Flying Officer Alfred William Saunders DFC, had been transferred to the Class "A" Reserve with effect from 05 February 1923.[332] However, on 16 December 1924 the Air Ministry announced that Saunders was one of a number of officers transferred from Class "A" reserve to Class "C" reserve with effect from that date.[333]

There is a notice in the London Gazette on 05 November 1926 to the effect that an Alfred William Saunders had been appointed Attendant at the British Museum without competition, and it is generally suggested that the Irish ace was the individual in question. However, I am not convinced that that this is so. For example, I am aware of the existence of at least one other Alfred William Saunders who served in the RAF (a chair-maker from Buckinghamshire who was a rigger in the RFC and RAF, service record AIR 79/630). Further, there was an Alfred William Saunders mentioned in the London Gazette of 03 February 1920 who had been appointed under the reconstruction scheme—without competition—as a labourer in the

---

332 London Gazette, Issue 32793, p.912.
333 London Gazette, Issue 33002, p.9156.

Admiralty's dockyards, i.e. not every military appointment of former civilian or military personnel need necessarily relate to the Irish ace.

On 25 February 1927 the Air Ministry announced that Saunders was one of a number of officers who had relinquished their commissions upon completion of their service in the RAF Reserve.[334]

Saunders died in an air crash involving a de Havilland Gipsy Moth over Auckland, New Zealand on 22 May 1930. According to the media reports Saunders attempted to spin too close to the ground. An Alfred W Minchin was also killed in the crash. The media reports of the time stated that Saunders' mother, brother and sister resided in Auckland.

✦ ✦ ✦

---

334 London Gazette 25 February 1927, Issue 33251, p.1257.

TIDMARSH, DAVID MARY

(**7 aerial victories**)

Born: 28 January 1892, Co Limerick
Died: 27 November 1944
Awards: Military Cross
Religion: Roman Catholic

Captain David Mary Tidmarsh was born in Co Limerick to David Aloysius and Elizabeth 'Lillie' Tidmarsh, of Lota, North Circular Road, Limerick. David's father was from Kilkenny City, his mother from Nenagh, Co Tipperary.

The Tidmarsh family were a well known drapers in Limerick, with James Moriarty Tidmarsh having acquired Cannock & Co in 1869 from Peter Tait and George Cannock. James' son David James Tidmarsh succeeded him in January 1877.[335] David Aloysius Tidmarsh succeeded him in September 1896. The "History of Cannocks" by Finbarr Crowe provides plenty of additional information on the expansion of the Limerick department store and the termination of its relationship with the Clerys family and their Dublin department store.

The Irish Census 1901 records the family as being resident at Kilrush Little. David's father is described as being a draper. Neither David nor his brothers John and Gerard are present at the family

---

[335] Limerick City Council have extensive records of Cannocks, which survived until 1984, although its days were numbered when it relinquished its O'Connell St premises in 1980.

home but his sisters—Ethel, Lillie and Mary—are all resident there, as is a governess, a servant, a coachman and a nurse. In the UK Census 1901 both David and his brothers Gerard and John are recorded as being boarders at a school in Eton, Berkshire. Superficially this would appear to be quite surprising given the Tidmarsh's religious background: Ampleforth, Downside or Stonyhurst would have been more appropriate for wealthy Catholic family. However, a quick glance at the detail of the Census form reveals it to be Baylis House, Berkshire, which was a Roman Catholic school owned and run by the Butt family until they went bankrupt in 1907. Of the 30 scholars present in 1901 there were 12 Irish, 3 Spanish, 1 Bolivian and 1 French, i.e. quite a shortage of English Roman Catholics, not to mention the presence of an Irish priest, Rev James Shore.

The Irish Census 1911 records David and the family as being resident at an address on Circular Road, Limerick City. David's cousin, Mary Hamilton, is also present, as a housemaid and a cook, but David's older brother Gerard and his three sisters are no longer living at the family home. David is working as a draper with his father.

Tidmarsh joined the colours with the Royal Irish Regiment. He was promoted from 2nd Lieutenant to Lieutenant on 23 April 1915, which was gazetted on 22 April 1915.[336] According to his service record[337] Tidmarsh transferred to the Royal Flying Corps in August 1915. He was initially posted to Shoreham for training, then to South Harrow on 27 August 1915.

Flight magazine of 15 October 1915 (p.783) reports that Tidmarsh was awarded Royal Aero Club Aviator's Certificate No.1833, qualifying on a Maurice Farman biplane at the Military School, Ruislip, on 07 October 1915. This was only 3 days after Joseph Cruess Callaghan had obtained R.Ae Certificate No.1829 at Norwich. It would appear that the Irish were well represented among the early aviators of the war.

---

336 London Gazette Supplement, Issue 29139, p.3937.
337 AIR 76/507 David M Tidmarsh, UK National Archives.

TIDMARSH, DAVID MARY

In December 1915 Tidmarsh trained with 4 R.A.S. (Reserve Aircraft Squadron) and subsequently 11 R.A.S. before being posted to No.24 Squadron upon appointment as Flying Officer on 27 January 1916. However, some records date Tidmarsh's appointment as Flying Officer to 13 January 1916.[338]

In Jon Guttman's *Bristol F2 Fighter Aces of World War I* (pp.10-11) (London: Osprey, 2007) and *Pusher Aces of World War I* (p.32) (London: Osprey, 2009) Tidmarsh is credited with several victories in which the enemy casualty is specifically identified. I try not to follow the "who got who" rounds of speculation, as often a plane may crash quite a distance from the original combat, or there may be several competing claims, but in some instances there are matching records. On 02 April 1916 Tidmarsh opened up No.24 Squadron's account when he shot down an Albatros between Grandcourt and Albert, killing Uffz Paul Wein and Leutnant Karl Oskar Breibisch-Guthmann of FFA32. RFC Communiqué No.34 of 1916, which covers the period 13-30 April 1916, records that Tidmarsh survived a close call on 21 April 1916 when an anti-aircraft shell went through the nacelle of his D.H.2 (5924) without exploding or causing any injury.

On 30 April 1916 Tidmarsh engaged a Fokker Eindecker over Péronne, which was being flown by Ltn Otto Schmedes of Kampfeinsitzer Kommando (KEK) Bertincourt, attached to FFA32. The German aircraft disintegrated when diving in combat and Tidmarsh didn't actually open fire in the course of the maneuvering when he dived from 4,000 feet at Schmeckes' aircraft. The Germans record their man as having been lost when his control wires were shot away! It still counted as an aerial victory for Tidmarsh.

On 20 May 1916 Tidmarsh scored his third victory, which is described in RFC Communiqué No.37 of 1916:

"An Albatros was attacked by three of our machines over Poziere; a Martinsyde of No 22 Sqn, pilot, Capt Summers, and two De Havillands of 24 Sqn, pilots Lt Wilson and 2nd Lt Tidmarsh. Lt Wilson attacked first, opening fire at 50 yards range, and turned aside owing

---

338 London Gazette, Issue 29458, p.1243.

to his gun jamming. Capt Summers on the Martinsyde then attacked, firing half a drum at 30 yards range, apparently without effect. Second Lt Tidmarsh then dived on to the hostile machine from above and fired a drum at 40 yards from behind it. The hostile machine burst into flames and fell between Poziere and Contalmaison".[339]

According to Guttman (2009, p.33) those killed were Franz Patzig and Georg Loenholdt.

The Irish Times of 24 May 1916 reported that Tidmarsh's parents, of Lota, Limerick "had received official intelligence" that their second son, 2nd Lieutenant David M Tidmarsh, 4th Battalion, Royal Irish Regiment and Royal Flying Corps, had been awarded the Military Cross "for gallant and distinguished service at the front".

It was an open secret, however, and on 31 May 1916 Tidmarsh's Military Cross citation was gazetted:

"2nd Lt. David Mary Tidmarsh, 4th Bn., R. Ir. R. (Spec. Res.) and R.F.C.

For conspicuous gallantry and skill when attacking hostile aircraft on several occasions, notably on one occasion when he dived at an enemy machine and drove it down wrecked to the ground".[340]

Also gazetted on that day was Robert Verschoyle Walker, a Donegal man who had served with the Connaught Rangers before joining the RFC.

Temporary promotions came rapidly thereafter. Tidmarsh was promoted from 2nd Lieutenant to temporary Lieutenant with effect from 01 July 1916, which was gazetted on 08 August 1916.[341] Tidmarsh was then appointed Flight Commander with effect from 16 August 1916. This was gazetted on 01 September 1916, with Tidmarsh being described as 2nd Lieutenant (temporary Lieutenant) but serving as temporary Captain whilst employed as Flight Commander.[342] It was not uncommon for pilots to serve at several grades above

---

339 Christopher Cole (ed) "Royal Flying Corps Communiqués 1915-1916", p.151 [Tom Donovan, 1990]
340 London Gazette Supplement, Issue 29602, p.5410.
341 London Gazette Supplement, Issue 29702, p.7896.
342 London Gazette Supplement, Issue 29730, p.8596.

their home grade without actually being promoted up the intermediate grades. On 14 October 1916 Tidmarsh was returned to Home Establishment, and was assigned to the School of Aerial Gunnery on 03 November 1916, where he served as Wing Commander. Tidmarsh was an instructor there, as part of 6th Wing, until 04 March 1917, when he was assigned to No.48 Squadron.

Tidmarsh became a Flight Commander in No.48 Squadron, which was the first squadron to fly the Bristol F.2a Fighter in combat. Tidmarsh achieved 4 victories in April 1917 using the new fighter, with Tidmarsh being generally attributed with the killing of the 20-victory German ace Wilhelm Frankl of Jasta 4 on 08 April 1917.[343] It would appear that Frankl's aircraft suffered structural failure when trying to maneuver clear from Tidmarsh's attack. Tidmarsh's squadron, however, had gotten off to a shaky start: on 05 April 1917 one of its Flight Commanders, Captain William Leefe Robinson, was shot down and—just days later, another Flight Commander—Tidmarsh himself, was shot down by Leutnant Kurt Wolff of Jasta 11 on 11 April 1917. In Tyrrel Mann Hawker's biography of Major Lanoe George Hawker, "Hawker VC" (Mitre Press, 1965), Tidmarsh is described as going to the rescue of a companion in distress and consequently shot down whilst facing hopeless odds (p.217).

Tidmarsh spent the rest of the war in a POW camp in Germany. However, he was notionally kept on secondment from the Royal Irish Regiment to the Royal Flying Corps, being promoted from 2nd Lieutenant to Lieutenant with effect from 01 July 1917, which was gazetted on 04 March 1918.[344]

David's younger brother John, a Lieutenant with the Duke of Wellington's Regiment, transferred to the RAF in 1918. However, John never got to avenge his brother, as he died in a training accident on 03 September 1918. The funeral took place at St Munchin's

---

343 Frankl was—prior to the Israeli Air Force's foundation—one of only a handful of Jewish aces. Frankl, together with Fritz Beckhardt, Berthold Guthmann and Willi Rosenstein had won numerous honours but were expunged from history by the Nazis.
344 London Gazette Supplement, Issue 30553, p.2706.

Parish Church on Wednesday 10 September 1918, with burial at Mount St Lawrence Cemetery. The Commonwealth War Graves Commission records his surname as "Tidmarch".

Frances Twomey, in writing "Cannocks—a Social and Economic History of the Limerick Company from 1840 to 1930", engaged in extensive correspondence with members of the Tidmarsh family. Twomey received a number of letters from David's sister Maureen, (Sister Mary Fidelis), a nun in the Priory of Our Lady of Good Counsel, Hassocks, West Sussex, in which she discusses her memories of David's experiences as a POW in Germany.

Sister Mary Fidelis' account of David being shot down and captured is somewhat different from the heroic-melodramatic versions of against all odds which feature in the various RAF pilots' memoirs:

"After he War I asked him what happened and as far as I remember he told me that he was pursuing a German trying to escape back to his base, and as he got near the aerodrome, their ground fire was intensified. His right wing was hit and immediately burst into flames; knowing that he couldn't return home and that he and his companion were soon to be burnt to death, like a flash he let the plane do a dead drop from a great height, hoping that this might extinguish the fire, and just when the watching Germans expected it to crash to the ground in flames, David "with marvelous skill and courage" as his companion told us [??] flattened out and just managed to land safely—the Germans rushed forward and helped them out of the now blazing wing, and apart from some nasty burns they were both alive. The Germans did all they could to help them because a living English pilot could give them information, or might have useful papers on him, whereas a dead body wasn't much use!

David said that they were quite decent to their prisoners, but they were not given nearly enough to eat, so were nearly starving until his letters home arrived, which was about 3 weeks or a month later. After that he and the others always received the many parcels or food and clothing sent through the Red Cross by their relations. David said that we must not blame the Germans for the scant rations of the prisoners, because it was nearly the end of the war and Germany being blockaded on all sides was herself desperately short of food.

The prisoners amused themselves getting up concerts, giving lectures, learning French and German, sketching and of course sports. In a letter home dated 28-5-1918 he said that 2 prisoners were shot dead for trying to escape. Because David twice drew pictures of an English pilot shooting down several German planes he was told that he would be shot at dawn. They made him stand before a wall while 5 Germans pointed guns at him, but at the command "fire", only empty cartridges [??] doing no harm. He said it was a "nasty experience"".[345]

Following the armistice, in the course of repatriation Tidmarsh arrived at Hull on 30 December 1918, being returned to serve with the RAF. In March 1919 he was assessed and deemed fit for light duties with flying. On 13 July 1919 Tidmarsh was assigned to 33 Training Squadron, and was attached to RAF Witney. On 09 August 1919 Tidmarsh was assigned to "S.S. Weston". This would appear to be RAF Weston-on-the-Green in Oxfordshire, which had a role in both the training squadrons and in acting as a satellite to RAF Brize Norton, much like the base at Witney did. Several months after rejoining the RAF, Tidmarsh was transferred to the Unemployed List with effect from 28 October 1919, which was gazetted on 18 November 1919.[346] Tidmarsh relinquished his commission on 01 April 1920, retaining the rank of Lieutenant. This was gazetted on 20 December 1920.[347]

Tidmarsh was one of the few Irish aces to return to Ireland after the war. According to Thomas Toomey's *War of Independence in Limerick*, this decision nearly cost Tidmarsh his life: on the night of 2nd/3rd December 1920 he was caught in an IRA ambush. Their intended target had been Colonel Michael Williamson, the local magistrate.

---

345 Letter dated 01 September 1979 from Sister Mary Fidelis to Frances Twomey. Special thanks to Limerick City Archives for making Frances' research material available.
346 London Gazette, Issue 31646, p.13917.
347 London Gazette Supplement, Issue 32168, p.12478.

In the summer of 2012 the Bureau of Military History published accounts of IRA volunteers who fought in the War of Independence. There are two separate accounts of the wounding of "Tidmarch". The first is by Volunteer Thomas Moynihan, Ahane Company, 3rd Battalion, Mid-Limerick Brigade:

"Our next attempt at an ambush was at Ballinacourtney, near Castleconnell. In this case we had been informed that a District Inspector of the R.I.C. [Royal Irish Constabulary] was to be entertained to dinner one day by Sir Stephen Quinn. On this particular day we again waited in ambush. When dinner was over a motorcar which had been observed to leave Quinn's residence was attacked by our party; one occupant in the car was wounded and the car put out of action. The wounded man turned out to be a man named Tidmarch. The D.I. was not in the car, but had returned to Limerick by a different route from that in which he came to dinner. The man Tidmarch had been mistaken for the D.I. Eight members of the IRA took part in this attack".[348]

Company Captain Seán Ó Ceallaigh gives a slightly different version of the ambush:

"On another occasion, Sean Carroll, with a number of his men, waited in ambush positions to attack a district Inspector of the R.I.C. They opened fire on a private motorcar in which they thought he was travelling, but it appears that the D.I. had travelled in a different car. The occupant of the car was wounded he was a man named Tidmarch".[349]

David's father died on 21 December 1920, just weeks after the incident.

Tidmarsh re-joined the RAF to serve in World War II. Initially re was commissioned as a Pilot Officer on probation, dated 16 May 1939 and gazetted on 23 May 1939.[350] He was subsequently pro-

---

348 Bureau of Military History 1913-1921, No. WS 1452, 07 July 1956, File No. S.2785.
349 Bureau of Military History 1913-1921, No. WS 1476, 28 August 1956, File No. S.2805.
350 London Gazette, Issue 34628, p.3482.

moted to Flying Officer on 31 August 1939, under the service number 73434, which was gazetted on 26 September 1939.[351] He was promoted from Flight Lieutenant to temporary Squadron Leader on 01 September 1942, which was gazetted on 10 November 1942.[352] Tidmarsh retired on ill-health grounds on 20 January 1944, retaining the rank of Squadron Leader, which was gazetted on 01 February 1944.[353]

His brother, Major Gerard David Tidmarsh, Royal Artillery, died on 09 November 1944. (Gerard had married Elizabeth Mary Shiffner on 20 March 1915 in Steyning, Sussex; the Shiffner were a minor Baronetcy. However, this was no the family's only link to Sussex: his sister was a nun there). David only outlived his brother by 18 days: he died in a Dublin nursing home on 27 November 1944.

The Tidmarsh family's link to Cannocks of Limerick survived until 1975, when Sister Mary Fidelius and Lilian (David's sisters) and their nephew Group Captain Thunder disposed of their shares.

Note: Limerick City Council have extensive material on Cannocks, specifically the research material of Frances Twomey used in writing "Cannocks—a Social and Economic History of the Limerick Company from 1840 to 1930", including letters from Maureen Tidmarsh (Sister Mary Fidelis), a nun in the Priory of Our Lady of Good Counsel. I am grateful for their assistance regarding Sister Fidelis' memories of David's experiences as a POW in Germany.

✦ ✦ ✦

---

351 London Gazette, Issue 34694, p.6508. Further clarification on 06 February 1940, Gazette Issue 34786, p.722.
352 London Gazette Supplement, Issue 35784, p.4933.
353 London Gazette Supplement, Issue 36354, p.586.

TYRRELL, WALTER ALEXANDER

(**17 aerial victories**)

Born: 23 August 1898, Belfast

Died: 09 June 1918

Awards: Military Cross

Commemorated: Beauvais Communal Cemetery, Oise, France;

Great War Memorial, Bangor, Co Down

Religion: Presbyterian

Captain Walter Alexander Tyrell was one of two brothers to serve with the Royal Flying Corps and Royal Air Force. Another brother was to serve with the Royal Air Force in World War II.

His father was John Tyrrell, an alderman, merchant (an army contractor) and justice of the peace. His mother was Jeanie Tyrrell (née Todd). They had 9 children.

The Irish Census 1901 records the family as being resident on the Crumlin Road, in the Court Ward of Belfast, Co Antrim. Also present with the family were a seamstress, a domestic nurse and a servant. Walter is the second youngest in the family. His eldest brother, William and his brothers Jason Mandeson, Herbert and John Marcus Tyrrell are all present, as are his four sisters. (One of his sisters, Jennie Ethel Tyrrell, died on 26 May 1910, aged 16 years). By the time of the Irish Census 1911 the family had moved to the Antrim Road in the Clifton ward of Belfast. Walter had another brother by this stage, Charles Frederick Gerard Tyrrell. His eldest brother—William—was a medical student at Queen's University Belfast, whilst his brother Herbert was helping out in the father's business.

He attended "Inst" and the Belfast Municipal Technical Institution. Tyrrell enlisted with the Royal Naval Air Service but did not see aerial service with them, as he fought in France with the Armoured Car Section as a Petty Officer (Motor Mechanic). According to some sources, Tyrrell was injured when an armoured car crushed his foot, and he used a specially made boot.

Tyrrell's naval service record in respect of the Royal Naval Air Service, however, does not indicate that he was discharged on account of his injuries.[354] It states that he was 5'11", a motor mechanic and had signed up on 30 December 1914 for the duration of the hostilities. His initial posting was to Pembroke III, a shore establishment, from 30 December 1914 to 31 March 1915. Tyrrell would have been based at Eastchurch in Kent. He was then placed on the notional strength of another shore establishment (HMS President II), from 01 April 1915 to 14 December 1915, by which stage the RNAS Armoured Car units on the Western Front were disbanded for being unsuitable in the context of the static trench warfare conditions. Tyrrell's RNAS service record indicates that he was stationed in France from 28 April 1915 to 29 October 1915. However, there is a note to the effect that on 07 December 1915 approval was granted for the discharge of Tyrrell from the RNAS Armoured Car Division.

Tyrrell joined the Royal Flying Corps on 09 April 1917. He had been a member of the Queen's University Belfast OTC and was working as an apprentice motor engineer when commissioned. Initially he was posted to 2 School of Aeronautics at Oxford but was subsequently transferred to 7 Reserve Squadron at Netheravon in June 1917. On 06 July 1917 Tyrrell's promotion to temporary 2nd Lieutenant on probation was gazetted.

On 01 August 1917 Tyrrell was posted to 43 Training Squadron, which was based at Tern Hill. On 30 August 1917 Tyrrell was appointed Flying Officer (2nd Lieutenant), which was gazetted on 19

---

354 ADM 188/565 Walter Alexander Tyrrell, UK National Archives.

September 1917. The 43 Training Squadron had metamorphosed into No.13 TDS, and was to form the nucleus of No.95 Squadron at Ternhill, but Tyrrell's service records indicate that the was flying the Airco D.H.5 at the time of his posting to the front on 03 October 1917.

Tyrrell was appointed to No.32 Squadron. Despite the many failings of the D.H.5 and its deep unpopularity with pilots, Tyrrell scored 5 victories on the type between 30 October 1917 and 05 December 1917, flying the same D.H.5 (B4916). Of these 5 victories, 4 were shared. Note: in 1989 and 1990 several sets of papers from AIR 1/1222/204/5/2634, which contained many of the records of No.32 Squadron, were found to have been missing. Although a member of staff was convicted on charges of theft and criminal damage not all of the papers were recovered. Some of the digitized records are consequently fragmentary in nature. However, one of the reports for 05 December 1917 has survived. A patrol of 4 D.H.5s were on Southern Offensive patrol at 4,000 feet near "K.3 Central (Sh.28)", a reference point, when they encountered two German AGO two-seaters:

"Pilots dived from 7,000 feet on to EA two seaters – all pilots attacking the rear machine. Captain Pearson attacked EA, firing a burst of 100 rounds at close range, and then he had to pull out to clear a No.3 stoppage. Lt Tyrrell got on the tail of this EA, which had turned south after Captain Pearson's dive, and fired 100 rounds at very close range. He then saw the observer throw up his arms, and collapse in the cockpit. EA fell down out of control, patrol getting good bursts into it. Meanwhile the second EA attacked Lt Howson, who attacked EA, firing a long burst into him. EA was last seen still diving, very low down over K3 Central (Sh.28).

770 rounds were fired by patrol in the two combats".

However, despite the ammunition expended, only the Tyrrell combat was awarded to the patrol as a decisive 'out of control' aerial victory, the other AGO being counted as 'driven down'.

No.32 Squadron re-quipped with the S.E.5a. Although disliked by some, (e.g. Mannock), and highly praised by others, (e.g. Molesworth),

IRISH AVIATORS OF WORLD WAR I

it's clear that Tyrrell became one of its premier experts. On 07 April 1918 Tyrrell scored a triple victory, destroying a Fokker Dr.I and an Albatros DV north-east of Lamotte and sending another Albatros DV down out of control. He went on to score 2 further victories in April, including an AGO in flames.

RAF Communiqué No.1 of 1918, which covers the period 01 April 1918 to 07 April 1918, describes his first victory flying the S.E.5A:

"2nd Lt W.A. Tyrrell, 32 Sqn, fired 150 rounds into an EA triplane which was attacking one of our machines; the EA went down in a fast spin, pulling out at 2,000 feet. 2nd Lt Tyrrell, who followed the EA down, got onto its tail again and fired 100 rounds at close range; the EA then fell vertically and crashed into the ground north-east of La Motte".[355]

The corresponding 'Combats in the Air' report states that Tyrell's patrol encountered 10 Fokker Dr.I Triplanes over Villers-Brettonneux at 10,000 feet. Tyrrell, who was still only a 2nd Lieutenant, managed to shake off a triplane and then get onto its tail when it attacked Captain Simpson. Tyrrell followed it down to 2,000 feet when finishing it off. The report continues:

"Pilot then made west, climbing, and observed 4 Albatros D.Vs shooting p our troops in the neighbourhood of Thiennes-Hangard. Pilot dived on rearmost EA and fired 100 rounds at close range, whereupon EA went east in a steep dive. Last seen at 200 feet. Pilot unable to observe result owing to large numbers of EA being in the vicinity".

RAF Communiqué No.2 of 1918, which covers the period 08 April 1918 to 14 April 1918, describes his victory of 11 April 1918 in which the German went down in flames:

"2 Lt W.A. Tyrrell, 32 Sqn, attacked an EA two-seater and opened fire at moderate range; the EA immediately turned and went east, and was followed by 2 Lt Tyrrell, who this time got to close range and fired 500 rounds into it in short bursts. The EA went down

---
355 Christopher Cole [ed] "RAF Communiqués 1918", p.25 [Tom Donovan, 1990].

in flames and was last seen at 500 feet completely ablaze".[356] The 'Combats in the Air' report indicates that his victim was identified as an AGO two-seater, and that Tyrrell "followed, sitting on tail of EA", which – after 500 rounds – went down in a steep dive "with flames gushing from fuselage".

On 03 May 1918 Tyrrell achieved his second triple-victory, sending down 2 Fokker Dr.Is down out of control over Frelinghem and succeeding in bringing down an LVG, which was captured near Poperinghe. The forcing down and capturing of the German LVG aircraft took place on 03 May 1918, which is described in RAF Communiqué No.5 of 1918:

"Lt W.A. Tyrrell, 32 Sqn, was attacked by two EA two-seaters. He maneuvered onto the tail of one EA and fired 50 rounds into it at point blank range. The EA turned west, followed by Lt Tyrrell, who prevented it from turning east again by firing short bursts, and the EA was finally forced to land in our lines about a mile W.S.W. of Poperinghe".[357]

The crew, Uffz Nievitecki and Uffz Priehs of FAA 266, were both captured alive and taken POW.

Tyrrell was to obtain one further victory that month, on 08 May 1918, destroying a Pfalz DIII, into which he fired 100 rounds at point blank range. It went into a steep spiral and afterwards a vertical nosedive, and was seen to crash in the neighbourhood of Sailly en-Ostrevent.

On 18 May 1918 he was appointed temporary Captain (Flying), which was gazetted on 04 June 1918. On 06 June 1918 Tyrrell managed the almost unprecedented: he scored three victories, which entailed a double victory in the evening following a dawn patrol victory in which he sent his opponent down in flames. In fact two of his victims went down in flames that day. The 'Combats in the Air'

---

356 Christopher Cole [ed] "RAF Communiqués 1918", p.31-32 [Tom Donovan 1990].
357 Christopher Cole [ed] "RAF Communiqués 1918", p.57 [Tom Donovan, 1990].

report for the first of these states that Captain W.A. Tyrrell was on offensive patrol duties with Lt. J.W. Trusler at 5:50 am. Tyrrell was in S.E.5a (B8374), at 10,000 feet, when they sighted two Pfalz scouts, one at 10,000 feet with another at 17,000 feet:

"Captain Tyrrell and Lt Trusler manoeuvred and dived from the sun on the lower EA, both pilots getting in a burst of 100 rounds at close range. EA went down in a steep dive on fire".

At 18:45 Tyrrell was on the evening offensive patrol duties, flying his S.E.5a (B8374) at 9,000 feet over Montdidier when the aircraft of No.32 Squadron were attacked by 7 Fokker biplanes. The 'Combats in the Air' report states the following:

"Pilot attacked EA which was attacking Lt Hooper, firing a burst of 100 rounds into EA at point blank range, whereupon EA burst into flames and went down.

Pilot was then attacked by two other EA, and turning he opened fire at close range, firing a burst of 150 rounds into EA, whereupon EA went down in a spin, out of control, being last seen still out of control at 6,000 feet.

Two more EA attacked pilot. No results were observed".

Major Russell of No.32 Squadron counter-signed the claim, with the Lt Colonel of 9th Wing confirming a double victory for Tyrrell, one of the aircraft being described as 'out of control', the other as 'destroyed in flames'.

He was awarded the Military Cross on 19 May 1918, which was gazetted on 16 September 1918:

"T./2nd Lt. Walter Alexander Tyrrell, Gen. list, attd. R.A.F.

For conspicuous gallantry and devotion to duty. On one day this officer attacked two enemy triplanes, destroying one and driving down the other out of control. After this he was attacked by two other machines, one of which he forced to land, taking the occupants prisoners. On various other occasions he has destroyed or driven down out of control enemy machines".[358]

---

358 London Gazette Supplement, Issue 30901, p.11027.

However, Tyrrell was dead by the time the citation was gazetted—he had been killed on 09 June 1918 by ground fire. According to one source[359] Walter was shot in the chest, but managed to get back behind his own lines before crashing. His brother Captain John Marcus Tyrrell was killed on 20 June 1918.

Flight magazine of 20 June 1918 (p.692) and 04 July 1918 (p.752) contained a brief obituary for the two brothers, but also making reference to the fact that their eldest brother, Lt Col William Tyrrell, DSO, MC, MB, RAMC, had been on active service on the Western Front since the commencement of the war.

William had been a former Irish rugby international (later President of the IRFU in the 1950s) and was to become a highly respected Principal Medical Officer in the RAF, a significant contributor to the 1920 War Office Committee of Inquiry into "shell shock" and later an Air Vice Marshal.

From the information to hand it would appear that Walter's brother was a member of Richmond Masonic Lodge No.262 in Belfast. Their father, John, was chosen by Belfast Lodge No.977 to unfurl a memorial banner to the 36th (Ulster) Division. However, I have not identified a Freemason membership record in respect of Walter.

Their mother Jennie died on 14 May 1922 aged 59 years. Their father John died on 28 October 1925, aged 61 years.

✦ ✦ ✦

---

359 Michele Barrett "Casualty Figures: How Five Men Survived the First World War", pp.109-111 [Verso 2007]

TYRRELL, WILLIAM UPTON

(6 aerial victories)

Born: 03 May 1896, Co Kildare

Died: 1979

Religion: Church of Ireland

William Upton Tyrrell was born on 03 May 1896 to William Jonathan Haughton Tyrrell and Elizabeth Tyrrell. He is often confused with William Tyrrell (b.20 November 1885), the brother of John Marcus and Walter Alexander Tyrrell.

The Irish Census 1901 records the Tyrrell family as being resident in the townland of Ballindoolin in the district electoral division of Carrick, in Co Kildare. In addition to his parents and his sister, there are 2 visitors and 3 servants present at the time of the census. His father was a "farmer and land agent" from Co Kildare. His mother was Canadian. The Census records William as having been born in Co Kildare but the Civil Registration Indexes indicate that his birth was registered in Edenderry, King's County (Co Offaly). However, Edenderry was most likely the nearest sizeable town to the Tyrell's corner of north Kildare. William was no longer residing with his parents by the Irish Census 1911, but I have been unable to identify the location at which he was residing, i.e. as a boarder in a school in England or Ireland.

Tyrrell joined the colours with the 3rd Reserve Battalion of the Royal Irish Rifles. On 10 August 1915 his appointment from Gentleman Cadet from the Royal Military College [Sandhurst] to 2nd Lieutenant was gazetted.[360]

---

360 London Gazette, Issue 29258, p.7905.

Tyrrell was promoted from 2nd Lieutenant to Lieutenant with effect from 10 December 1916, gazetted on 27 December 1916. This was revised, with the London Gazette of 05 January 1917 reporting that his promotion from 2nd Lieutenant to Lieutenant had been antedated to 24 November 1916.[361]

He transferred to the Royal Air Force and, on 19 May 1918, was returned to Home Establishment for training. Initially Tyrrell was posted to the school of aerial gunnery but was subsequently transferred to 1 Flight School Tunberry on 03 August 1918. By 22 August 1918 he was completing his training at WT School, Chattis Hill. It is my understanding that at this time 'WT' would have stood for 'wireless telegraphy' but was later to mean 'wireless telephony'. Tyrrell was posted to the British Expeditionary Force on 01 September 1918 as a fighter reconnaissance observer. On 17 September 1918 his appointment as temporary 2nd Lieutenant (Honorary Lieutenant), Observer, was gazetted, with the promotion being dated as 29 August 1918.

Tyrrell served with No.22 Squadron. Another Irish ace, George McCormack, had also served with the squadron but there were plenty of pilots there with an Irish connection, e.g. the American-born, English-raised Owen Tudor Hart had married in Ireland, in 1911, to Anne Cecilia Stoney, daughter of Bindon Blood Stoney (scion of 2 very prominent Irish families) and Susanna Frances Walker (of Grangemore, Raheny, Dublin). Similarly there was Yorkshireman Frederick Williams, killed on 02 April 1918, whose father had worked with Gallahers in Belfast. Of the Irish casualties with No.22 Squadron, Gilbert Watson Webb was killed on 01 July 1916, one of the squadron's earliest casualties.

Tyrrell's first victory came on 05 September 1918, just days after joining the squadron. In a Bristol F.2b (D7998) piloted by Lt Herbert Beddow they drove down a Fokker D VII out of control over Douai. Throughout the month of September 1918 he was observer to a succession of pilots, achieving some success, including 2 double victories. His final aerial victory came on 27 September 1918 in a Bristol

---

361 Gazette Issue 29881 (p.12635), Gazette Issue 29892 (p.285).

TYRRELL, WILLIAM UPTON

F.2b (E2517) piloted by Lt LC Rowney they shared in the destruction of a Fokker D VII with Lt Chester William McKinley Thompson and Lt R James.

Jon Guttman's *Bristol F2 Fighter aces of World War I* (London: Osprey, 2007) does make reference to Tyrrell (p.33) but only in the context of Thompson sharing victories with the two ex-Royal Irish Rifles members, McCormack and Tyrrell.

RAF Communiqué No.26 of 1918 records the following with regard to Thompson and Tyrrell's actions of 26 September 1918:

"Lts C.W.M. Thomson and W.U. Tyrrell, 22 Sqn, when returning from escort duty to the above raid [an attack on Lieu St Amand Aerodrome by No.203 Sqn] became engaged with a number of Fokker biplanes, two of which they shot down out of control and were observed to crash by other pilots".[362]

The London Gazette of 17 September 1918 reported Tyrrell's re-grading as Honorary Lieutenant in the RAF as an observer officer, with effect from 29 August 1918.[363] In common with many late-war observer aces, Tyrrell did not win the Military Cross or Distinguished Flying Cross

Tyrell was briefly posted to No.205 Squadron. This was the former 5 (Naval) Squadron and had evolved from the RNAS role of bombing Belgian port installations and German airfields to more of an army cooperation role with aerial photography but essentially it continued with its previous activities in bombing railways, bridges and other strategic targets. The squadron's Operations Record Book (UK National Archives AIR 27/1217) does not make any specific reference to Tyrrell but it would appear to have been a short-lived posting in December 1918. Tyrrell had returned to No.22 Squadron by late December 1918, and was transferred to Home Establishment on 14 March 1919. On 18 April 1919 he was transferred to 11 (Irish) Group.

---

362 Christopher Cole [ed] "RAF Communiqués 1918", p.200 [Tom Donovan 1990].
363 London Gazette, Issue 30905, p.11096.

On 24 June 1919 Tyrrell relinquished his commission, which was gazetted on 11 July 1919.[364] Tyrrell's forename initials were misdescribed as 'W.V.' instead of 'W.U.' and therefore it can give rise to confusion. However, we do know that Tyrrell reported to the 3rd Battalion of the Royal Irish Rifles at Ruxley.

On 07 October 1919 the Air Ministry announced that Tyrrell had been promoted to Lieutenant, which was backdated to 30 August 1918. Once again he was gazetted as "W.V. Tyrrell".[365] Indeed, the letter "U" on his RAF service record is the subject of some elaborate artwork, which suggests that someone thought it was a "V" and others a "U".

He married Alice Helen Ennice Tyrrell in the parish of St Mary the Virgin, Twickenham on 10 April 1920. The marriage was registered in Brentford, Middlesex in the 2nd quarter of 1920. Unusually they both had the same surname pre-marriage, Helen being the daughter of a Joseph Henry Tyrrell of Cumberland and Alice Tyrrell, of Guernsey, Channel Islands. William and Helen had two children. Desirée Helen Tyrrell was born on 11 February 1921 and died on 02 April 1974.

Tyrrell was not directly affected by the disbandment of the Irish regiments of the British Army that had recruited in the geographical area of what had since become the Irish Free State, as the Royal Irish Rifles simply became the Royal Ulster Rifles. However, throughout the 1920s Tyrrell was to transfer through a number of regiments. At the time of his application for war medals in November 1922 Tyrrell's correspondence address was "1st Division Signals, McGregor Barracks, Aldershot".

On 11 March 1924 Tyrrell was seconded from the Royal Ulster Rifles to the Royal Corps of Signals.[366] On 08 April 1924 Lt Tyrrell relinquished the appointment of Adjutant of 10 October 1923.[367] On 12 July 1924 Lieutenant Tyrrell transferred from the Royal

---

364 London Gazette, Issue 31449, p.8854.
365 London Gazette, Issue 31587, p.12421.
366 London Gazette, Issue 32917, p.2135.
367 London Gazette, Issue 32925, p.2921.

Ulster Rifles to the Royal Corps of Signals. On 05 August 1924 the War Office announced that Tyrrell's date of transfer was effective from 27 February 1924 and that he had been promoted to Captain from the same date.[368]

Given the sheer number of adjutant and staff appointments I do not propose to traverse them all in detail. Captain Tyrrell was seconded for employment as a Temporary Adjutant from 14 August 1925, which was gazetted on 18 September 1925. He served with Anti-Aircraft Signals (Artillery Zones) as Adjutant, to which he was seconded on 03 October 1925. Tyrrell vacated this position on 01 November 1926.[369]

On 29 October 1926 he was granted Regimental seniority from 11 January 1920, but this did not count for Army seniority, nor for pay and allowances, for pay increases or for retirement pay. On 11 January 1927 Captain Tyrrell was restored to the establishment with effect from 23 December 1926.[370]

Tyrrell seems to be irrepressible. He was seconded to be a student at the Staff College from 21 January 1930.[371]

Following his training, on 04 May 1934 Tyrrell was appointed as Staff Captain, Eastern Command with effect from 28 April 1934. On 28 April 1934 he was seconded for service on the Staff of the Royal Corps of Signals. He was serving at the rank of Captain at the time, so a Staff Officer position would have been an appropriate move for a man of his age. This appointment was also gazetted on 22 May 1934.[372]

On 20 March 1936 Major W.U. Tyrrell, Royal Signals, was promoted from Staff Captain in Eastern Command to be General Staff Officer, 3rd Grade, at the War Office. This promotion was dated to 16 March 1936. However, he was only a year at the position. On 02 July 1937 it was announced that Tyrrell had relinquished his appointment

---

368 London Gazette, Issue 32955, p.5321; Issue 32962, p.5890.
369 Gazette Issues 33085 (p.6087), 33089 (p.6348), 33222 (p.7479).
370 London Gazette, Issue 33216 (p.6887), 33238 (p.215).
371 London Gazette, Issue 33575, p.649.
372 London Gazette, Issues 34047 (p.2859), 34052 (p.3301).

as General Staff Officer at the War Office with effect from 01 March 1937, which had also been gazetted on 02 March 1937.[373]

The Supplement to the London Gazette of 28 May 1948 reported that Major (War Subs Lieutenant-Colonel) W.U. Tyrrell, Royal Corps of Signals, having exceeded the age limit for retirement was placed on retired pay, 27 May 1948, and granted the honorary rank of Colonel.[374]

On 18 March 1955 2nd Lieutenant William Upton Tyrrell—under the service number 13536—was promoted to Captain in the Territorial Army with effect from 12 February 1955. He was described as Major (Honorary Colonel) of the Royal Signals (retired).

His wife died in 1967 in Cleethorpes, Lincolnshire but I can find no record of a will. However, on 26 September 1967 William Upton Tyrrell is reported as having a claim on the estate of Harry Abraham of "Oakdene", Walesby, Lincolnshire, a retired farmer who had died on 03 September 1967.[375]

William Upton Tyrrell died in Lincolnshire in the 2nd quarter of 1979. The Caistor registration district recorded his date of birth as 03 May 1896, which corresponds to that of the Irish ace although undoubtedly most who knew him would have associated Tyrrell with the army rather than the flying services given his lengthy career with the former over his short but glorious one with the latter.

❖ ❖ ❖

---

373 London Gazette, Issues 34266 (p.1818), 34376 (p.1413), 34414 (p.4249).
374 London Gazette Supplement, Issue 38301, p.3182.
375 London Gazette, Issue 44416, p.10506.

WALLER, ALBERT GREGORY

(**11 aerial victories**)

Born: 15 October 1890, Co Galway
Died: 1967
Awards: Military Cross
Religion: Church of Ireland

Captain Albert Gregory Waller was born in Co Galway on 15 October 1890, the youngest of nine children to Francis Albert Waller and Frances Otway Waller. In 1892 Waller's father drowned in a boating accident on the Shannon, near the family home. Waller's teenage sister Georgina Charlotte Waller (1873-1892) also drowned in the incident.

Waller was raised in Banagher, King's County (Co Offaly). The next-of-kin address on his service record[376] is 'Shannon Grove, Banagher'. This address may give rise to the erroneous impression that Waller's family owned the Shannon Grove estate near Rathkeale in Co Limerick. (Indeed the Landed Estates Database of the National University of Ireland Galway seems to suggest the Wallers of Castletown, Co Limerick and the Wallers of Prior Park, Tipperary were one and the same).

According to the excellent churchrecords.irishgenealogy.ie website, Waller's parents were married on 07 September 1872 in St Peter's Church of Ireland, Dublin. Waller's mother's address at the time was 23 Pembroke Rd, Dublin. Waller's sister Elizabeth Eva Waller

---

376 AIR 76/527 Albert Gregory Waller, UK National Archives.

(1875-1968) married Abraham Chatterton, of Enniskerry Co Wicklow on 08 November 1898 in St Stephen's Church of Ireland, Dublin. Elizabeth's address at the time was 102 Lower Mount St, Dublin, which suggests that the family moved quickly to ensure the women in the family were not left on the shelf in a widow's estate.

Of Waller's other siblings, his next eldest sister, Selina Frances Otway Waller (1878-1919) married Percy Watson, Dublin. His sister Elizabeth Hannah Waller (1879-1963) married Colonel Jacynth d'Ewes FitzGerald Coke in 1902. His sister Dorothy Waller (1882-1915) married Morgan Franks. His brother Caesar James Loftus Otway Waller (1884-1950) was a Captain in the RASC. His sister Katherine de Warrenne Waller (1886-1958) married Captain Guy Landon, RFC in 1914. His brother, William Hastings de Warrenne "Billy" Waller (1888-1971) won the AFC in 1918 and was a Wing Commander in the RAF in World War II. (Billy's son Edward served in the Royal Navy).

The Irish Census 1901 records Waller as being resident at Dovegrove, Birr, King's County (Co Offaly), as a boarder. Birr, or Parsonstown, was probably best known for once having the largest telescope in the world, which had been built for the 3rd Earl of Rosse in the 1840s and was not surpassed in size until 1917—although it had long since been surpassed by improvements in lens technology. The name Parsonstown did not derive from the presence of clergy but from being largely owned by the Parsons family—the Earls of Rosse—at one stage of its existence. Birr was a garrison town, the home of the 3rd Leinster Regiment, but the schoolchildren boarding are largely from rural areas of Munster and Connacht that would probably not have had the population to support a local Protestant school. Among the more notable of the 17 students recorded in the 1901 census was Harold Frederick Balleine de Caen, later a Captain with the Royal Field Artillery.

In the Irish Census 1901 Waller's mother is recorded as being resident at a house in the townland of Kilnaborris, Kilmacshane, Co Galway, together with her daughter Dorothy, and a parlour maid and a cook. Waller's mother Frances is described as being a widow, and originally from Co Donegal. Waller's sister Dorothy was born in Co Galway. In the Irish Census 1911 Waller is resident with the rest of the family in Co Galway. His sister Dorothy has moved out but some of his other sisters—Kathleen Waller and Elizabeth Coke—are present, as are Elizabeth's two children. There are also a governess, a housemaid, a cook and a parlourmaid present, which would suggest that the Co Galway estate was a profitable one. Albert is described as being a "farmer". Interestingly his sister Elizabeth was born in the King's County but his sisters Kathleen and Dorothy were born in Co Galway, which would suggest at least some land ownership on either side of the river Shannon, as Shannon Grove is variously described as being of Galway and of Banagher, King's County. It would appear that this arises from the Waller estate being located on both sides of the river Shannon. Leet's Directory records the Shannon Grove of the District Electoral Division of Kilmacshane, Townland of Kilnaborris, Co Galway as the residence of Hon. B. Yelverton in 1814 and which had been leased to a Hubert Moore in 1855. This Shannon Grove is also a mile from Banagher, King's County (Co Offaly).

It is therefore more accurate to describe the Wallers as being from the branch of the Wallers of Prior Park. Waller's father was in fact the Francis Albert Waller (1846-1892) that had established himself as a supplier of barley to his brother George Arthur Waller (1835-1923) who was Chief Brewer of Guinness at the time. The maltings of F.A. Waller Ltd of Banagher existed up until the 20th century, when it combined with D.E. Williams Ltd of Tullamore to become Williams-Waller Ltd, one of Ireland's largest suppliers to the Guinness brewery. According to many sources, Francis Waller was drowned on Lough Derg on the Shannon, together with his teenage daughter Georgina (1873-1892). This would accord with the census data of 1901 and 1911.

Waller was commissioned as an officer in the Army Service Corps, and served in France from 06 November 1914 until he transferred to the Royal Flying Corps. It has been suggested that Waller served as an observer for a number of months prior to being sent for pilot training. Initially he was posted to the School of Aeronautics at Reading on 04 September 1916. Waller was transferred to 31 Reserve Squadron on 25 October 1916, where he received training on the Farman Longhorn and Shorthorn trainers. Waller was subsequently posted to 10 Reserve Squadron at Joyce Green, where he earned Royal Aero Club Certificate No.4015 on 03 December 1916.

Flight magazine of 08 March 1917 (p.235) quotes the London Gazette of 27 February 1917 regarding Temporary Captain A.G. Waller's appointment as Flying Officer and his transfer from Army Service Corps to General List with effect from 10 February 1917. Upon appointment as Flying Officer Waller was transferred to St Omer on 10 February 1917. From 21 February 1917 to 15 November 1917 Waller received further training before being posted to No.55 Squadron. Waller spent the winter of 1917/1918 with No.55 Squadron, being appointed Flight Commander on 12 February 1918 and transferred to No.18 Squadron.

On 06 March 1918, flying a D.H.4 (A7798), with Sergeant M.V. Kilroy as observer, they sent down an Albatros DV out of control near Carvin. The 'Combats in the Air' report states that they were returning from a bombing and photography raid when they saw six German aircraft attack a RFC aircraft. Both Waller and Kilroy, using the Vickers and Lewis guns respectively, fired on three different Germans. Waller sent one down in a spin and Kilroy could see from his tracer bullets that he had hit the fuselage of two others but from 250 yards it was difficult for a decisive combat to be awarded, notwithstanding the fact that one of the Germans hit by Kilroy also went down in a spin. Only one aerial victory was awarded for this encounter. However, Sergeants McCleery and Dyke, in another D.H.4 (A7833) were also awarded an aerial victory in respect of this aerial mêlée that involved 30 aircraft at one stage.

Waller and Kilroy teamed up for a further victory on 10 March 1918 in a D.H.4 (A7770), sending another Albatros DV down out of control. Waller's report, in 'Combats in the Air' for No.18 Squadron, refers to the Pfalz as 'Phalz' throughout his report:

"I led a formation of six D.H.4s to bomb dump in C.20d and C.18a. We dropped some of our bombs on the former dump and four on the latter. At once a large formation of EA attacked two of my rear machines. I turned and dived on 2nd Lt McKim, who had 2 EA attacking him and was going down under control. I fired a long burst into these 2 EA and they left him. My observer got a long burst into another EA when I was climbing away. I saw the EA turn over, dive, stall and go down completely out of control. I then saw another EA diving in front of me. I got two bursts into him and a lot of smoke came out of the fuselage but I had to 'zoom' to avoid a collision and could see no more. Sergeant Kilroy, my observer, was firing at another higher machine. I then was alone, so I climbed going West. I came up with six Camels with red noses, and we went around together as all the former EA had gone down. Then 8 EA came from the east at about 12,000 feet. I got into the sun and then behind the EA I dived on the highest of the EA with the Camels beside me, but they left me and did not dive. I got a long burst into this EA which was a Phalz, but could see no result. I found 2/Lt Stewart and 2/Lt Darvill over La Bassee. We then followed the 8 EA to NE of the Bois de Biez. We all three dived on various EA. 2/Lt Stewart shot one down which crashed. I then got a burst into another EA on 2/Lt Stewart's tail. The EA at once turned over and went under my wing. We all three then came home.

My observer fired 300 rounds; I fired 250 rounds with front gun".

Despite such a lengthy sequence of combat actions only one aerial victory was awarded to Waller and Kilroy. The reference to "McKim" should have been to Lieutenant Harry William Mackintosh Mackay, who was the son of William Mackay, the editor of the "North British Agriculturist". Harry had served with the 6th Bn of the Gordon Highlanders before transferring into the Royal Flying Corps. Although Waller shook the two Germans off Mackay's tail he was probably doomed at that stage and they merely abandoned the crippled prey. One superficial impression from the report would be that Sopwith Camel fighter pilots were reluctant to enter the fray, but in reality they would have thought they were escorting a lone, vulnerable D.H.4 bomber to safety, and were probably not expecting it to go on the offensive against German fighters.

On 15 March 1918 Waller achieved a further aerial victory, over a Pfalz DIII over Avelin. He was flying a D.H.4 (A8076) with Lt J. Brisbane as his observer at a height of 14,000 feet when the following series of engagements took place:

"I crossed the lines near Fromelles at 14,000 feet at 12 noon to 12.15 pm. My formation was attacked by 8 EA. I turned the formation and several observers fired on them. I saw no results.

I climbed to 16,000 feet and led the three remaining machines to Avelins which we bombed – except 2/Lt Stewart, who went on an dropped his bombs on or near Pont-a-Marcq. I waited fro him, doing S turns. He was quite alone and at least 100 feet above me, when I dived on 2 EA with 2/Lt Atkey and 2/Lt Mayne. I fired 50 rounds at the first machine and 150 at the second. The first my observer saw spin and stall and go down. He, and 2/Lt Atkey's observer, also fired at him. They both state he went down out of control, but I did not see this.

I then climbed to the lines where I found 2/Lt Stewart alone, about 1,000 feet above me facing West. He joined me and we went home".

A separate combat report filed by 2nd Lieutenant D.A. Stewart and Sergeant Pollard in D.H.4 (A8038) claim they fired 30 rounds into a Pfalz at 50 yards' range but that they actually saw the aircraft crash.

The next day Waller led a six aircraft bombing mission, consisting of two flights. Waller led one whilst the other was led by Captain D. Ogden. Several aircraft crew were awarded a shared 'out of control' victory for the following incident:

"Just after dropping our bombs on Wavrin Station we were attacked by eight scouts. 2/Lt R.A. Mayne, who was on my left, started smoking and went under me with one EA on his tail. He was under control, and the smoke went out. I dived but only fired a small burst of about 50 rounds as my tail was hit, and elevator working wrongly. My observer fired 300 rounds odd, and all the other observers fired 800 rounds between them, making 1,150.

Then one EA was fired at by 2/Lt Atkey's observer – Sgt M Kilroy – and all the other observers fired, and drove all the EA below us. One EA I saw, and also 2/Lt Atkey saw, going down out of control, but it was not seen to crash".

However, Waller was not awarded an aerial victory in respect of that particular aerial combat engagement. As one may note, Sergeant MV Kilroy features heavily in the air combat reports as a formidable Lewis gunner. Michael Vincent Kilroy's father was from Co Roscommon, although Michael is not generally considered to be an Irish ace.

In March 1918 Waller was briefly seconded from No.18 Squadron to Biggin Hill for training in wireless telegraphy. *Flight* magazine of 21 March 1918 (p.323) quotes the London Gazette of 15 March 1918, which reported that Waller had been promoted from Temporary Captain to Flight Commander.

By April 1918 Waller was back with No.18 Squadron, achieving two shared aerial victories on 12 April 1918, one of these going down in flames over Estaires. RAF Communiqué No.2 of 1918 reports Waller bringing down in flames one enemy aircraft from a swarm of 20 attackers on that date. In the actual 'Combats in the Air' report, submitted by Waller as leader of the formation, he actually attributes it in terms of "all observers fired on them, and one EA was seen by 2/Lt A Atkey MC and Sergt. H Hammond to go down in flames and one was seen by all to go down out of control".

RAF Communiqué No.7 of 1918 reports Captain Waller and a Lt Kempster firing several bursts into a formation of eight enemy aircraft, one of which went down out of control and was later confirmed by A.A. to have crashed. According to Waller's 'Combats in the Air' report of 14 May 1918, however, he was on a photography mission in D.H.4 (A8000) and that between the front and back gun they fired 500 rounds in all.

On 16 May 1918 Waller and Kempster led a formation of six D.H.4s on a bombing mission over Estaires. On their return four Fokker triplanes and two Pfalz scouts intercepted the D.H.4s. Kempster's gunnery is credited with sending one Fokker Dr.I down out of control but the other five observers combined to drive off another. One D.H.4 observer (2/Lt E. Walker) was in a position to confirm the 'out of control' descent of the Fokker triplane attacked by Waller's D.H.4 (A8041). By this stage of the war it was extremely rare for an 'out of control' aerial victory to be mentioned in the RAF Communiqués, although they still featured in the air combat reports and were still credited to particular pilots and/or observers.

On 19 May 1918 Waller shared in an 'out of control' aerial victory though he also recorded in the 'Combats in the Air' report that another Albatros had been driven down: it appeared to go down out of control but was not seen for very long.

In a somewhat different encounter on 25 May 1918 Waller's D.H.4s were being protected by eight Bristol F2bs from No.22 Squadron when they were attacked by a large formation of German aircraft of assorted types, including "a new two-seater machine with a long span, narrow wings very much swept back". (One hopes Waller hadn't actually seen an RAF two-seater, e.g. D.H.4 bomber or Bristol F2b fighter, in the process of destruction and thus looking like it had swept-back wings). Waller would not appear to have actually needed the escort, reporting that "I dived on one triplane and fired about 50 rounds into him: he went down vertically as far as I could see, and other members of the formation confirmed his having gone right down out of control". In a hand-written note to the combat report it was recorded "this has since been confirmed by pilot of No.22 Squadron". In fact all of Waller's aerial victories came against German fighter aircraft, e.g. the Albatros DV, Pfalz DII, the excellent Fokker DVII and Fokker Dr.I. Although his victories were scored with a variety of observers all were secured when flying the Airco de Havilland D.H.4 bomber, a remarkable achievement considering this machine's many failings and the appalling losses the Independent Force (the forerunner of RAF Bomber Command) was to suffer when using the D.H.4 in the bombing campaign over Germany from July 1918 onwards.

Waller's final victories are recorded as having taken place on 30 May 1918. He was flying D.H.4 (A8018) with Lt B.J. Blackett as his observer on reconnaissance duty over Bac st Maur when they encountered seven German aircraft.

"I dived on one and fired a short burst. He rolled over and I followed him down a little way, firing about 70 rounds. I then lost sight of him. (This EA is confirmed to have ultimately gone down in flames).

Three Camels then joined us and my observer saw them drive one down.

I then dived on another EA and fired a short burst. He went down and I dived firing. Something fell off his top plane and my observer saw him go straight down, and I am practically certain he must have crashed".

However, Waller's claim for two 'destroyed' would not appear to have been granted as such, with one being regarded as having gone down 'out of control'.

Waller returned to Home Establishment on 24 June 1918. From his service record it would appear that the original intention had been to post Waller to 3 Flying School in July 1918, but instead Waller was posted to Irish Group, 55 Wing, on 25 July 1918. Waller transferred to the Air Ministry (CAS) on 03 August 1918, for duty as a communication pilot. I have presumed that CAS denotes the Chief of the Air Staff rather than the Casualty unit of the RAF.

Waller was awarded the Military Cross, which was gazetted on 16 September 1918:

"T./Capt. Albert Gregory Waller, Gen. List, and R.A.F.

For conspicuous gallantry and devotion to duty. He has led fifteen successful bombing raids, twenty-two low bombing and reconnaissance flights and eight successful photographic flights. In addition he has destroyed five enemy machines. As a flight commander he has shown initiative and enterprise both in the air and on the ground, and the excellent work done by the flight under his command is entirely due to his fine example and untiring energy".[377]

Flight magazine of 21 November 1918 (p.1335) stated that the London Gazette of 29 October 1918 had incorrectly reported Captain Waller's promotion to Acting Major as being that of Walker. A correcting notice issued on 15 November 1918.

According to Waller's service record he had returned to 11 (Irish) Group on 23 October 1918, from which he was assigned to 22 T.D.S. as Second in Command. This Training Depot Station was RAF Gormanston. The RAF's 11 (Irish) Group never reached its intended strength, although the Training Squadrons (TS, formerly RS—Reserve Squadrons) had been restructured into Training Depot Stations (TDS) by this stage of the war. They were organized as follows:

No.22 TDS Gormanston
No.23 TDS Baldonnell
No.24 TDS Collinstown
No.25 TDS Tallaght

Additionally, 11 (Irish) Group had No.19 TS at Curragh Camp, but at various stages had the following units in Ireland:

Medical HQ Ireland—Baldonnell
No 11 (Dublin) Stores Distributing Park—Dublin
Care and Maintenance Party—Rathmullan, County Donegal
Irish Stores Centre—Baldonell
Meteorological Station—Baldonell

---

377 London Gazette Supplement, Issue 30901, p.11030.

Wireless Station—Baldonell
Wireless Station—Castlebar
Wireless Station—Fermoy
Wireless Station—Oranmore

Of the actual frontline squadrons attached to 11 (Irish) Group their disposition was as follows:

No. 2 Squadron: -
 HQ—Oranmore
 1 Flight—Castlebar
 1 Flight—Fermoy
No.4 Squadron:-
 'A' Flight was stationed at Aldergrove from Nov 1920 to May 1921
 'A' Flight was stationed at Baldonnel from 04 May 1921 to 18 January 1922
 No. 100 Squadron, which was re-formed at Baldonnel on 01 February 1920 from remnants of No.117 (Gormanston) and No.141 Squadron (Baldonnel);
 No. 105 Squadron;
 No. 106 Squadron;
 No.244 Squadron (briefly stationed at Tallaght from Aug to Nov 1918).
 No.22 TDS Gormanston was originally intended to form on 01 August 1918 through the transfer of 26 TS and 69 TS from Norfolk to form 'A' Flight of 130 Squadron and 'C' Flight of 137 Squadron. However, this did not evolve as originally intended. At the time of the Armistice No.22 TS was to withdraw through A Flight of 130 Squadron evacuating to Bracebridge, Lincolnshire on 08 November 1918 and C Flight of 137 Squadron to Chingford, Essex on 04 December 1918. Similarly, No.23 TDS Baldonnel, No.24 TDS Collinstown and No.25 TDS Cookstown had various grandiose plans which came to little: various flights of 135, 163 and 164 Squadrons

were formed and evacuated at a range of stages of completion. The 4 TDS bases remained active for training purposes throughout much of 1919. The Flying Instructors School at the Curragh disbanded in May 1919. The Irish Aircraft Repair Depot at Lucan was also disbanded in 1919. It was not just the Irish units who disbanded in Ireland, e.g. No.149 Squadron arrived in Tallaght on 26 March 1919 for disbandment, being dissolved on 01 August 1919.

Regardless of all the foregoing it should be noted that the primary aerial activity against German submarine threat was effected via the US Naval Air Service, which operated from a number of coastal bases in Ireland during the final year of the war. This American force was assisted by the Royal Navy but there were also RAF actions against German submarines, e.g. the protection of Dublin to Holyhead and other Irish sea shipping routes had been organized from a temporary airship base at Malahide. (Bad weather had prevented the airships flying on 10 October 1918, which gave rise to the sinking of the SS Leinster 7 miles off the Kish Light vessel by U-123 and the loss of 176 civilian casualties and over 350 military personnel).

Waller's service in Ireland during the winter of 1918/1919 would have coincided with the UK General Election of November 1918 and the formation of Dáil Éireann in January 1919. By the time Waller had been transferred to the Unemployed List on 03 February 1919 the 11 (Irish) Group was well on the way to being downsized.[378]

Although Waller had not been named in the New Year's Honours List, *Flight* magazine of 30 January 1919 (p.136) reported that it was announced by the Air Ministry on 22 January 1919 that Waller was

---

378 It was to later be redesignated No.11 (Irish) Wing in April 1920 but retained Command status in the RAF. By July 1920 No.100 Squadron had moved one Flight to Castlebar from Baldonnell, whilst No.2 Squadron had moved its HQ from Oranmore in Galway to Fermoy in Co Cork even though it maintained Flights at Fermoy and Oranmore. No.11 (Irish) Wing was further reorganized as RAF Ireland on 17 February 1922 and disbanded by February 1923. In the area of Ireland that had since become Northern Ireland under the Government of Ireland Act 1920, No.12 Wing was still based at Aldergrove near Belfast.

one of those who had been brought to the notice of the Secretary of State in respect of the valuable services rendered in connection with the war and that a record to this effect was being made in the Official records. This would appear to have been the "press mention" equivalent of being "mentioned in despatches".

Flight magazine of 06 March 1919, (p.320), reports that Waller had been transferred to the Unemployed List.

It is suggested that Waller served with 6 (Naval) Squadron of the Royal Naval Air Service, which later No.206 Squadron of the RAF. However, I believe this to be a case of mistaken identity: there was an Albert Waller who served with the RNAS, but it was not the Irish ace. All Waller's victories came with No.18 Squadron of the Royal Flying Corps and Royal Air Force. This was a reconnaissance and bomber squadron but several Irishmen scored at least some of their victories with No.18 Squadron—see also Blennerhasset, Cruess-Callaghan and Huston—although Belfast man Victor Huston was the only other pilot to became an ace with No.18 Squadron.

In 1920 Waller married Marjorie Harrison of Cirencester, Gloucestershire. They had four children: Jocelyn de Warrenne Waller (b.1921), Heath Otway Waller (b. 1923), Oswald Francis Waller (b. 1928) and Christopher James Waller (b. 1934).

A cousin of Waller, Hardress de Warrenne Waller, was lost on 21 February 1920 when his Bristol Fighter, along with two others, disappeared when flying from Shotwick to Baldonnel. Shortly after leaving Shotwick (near Chester) they were sighted between Denbigh and Rhyl in Wales, flying in formation. One of the aircraft crashed several hundred miles off course, near the Scilly Isles but it was lost before it or the pilot could be identified. No trace was found of Hardress de Warrenne Waller.

The Bureau of Military History includes an account by an Irish Volunteer Lieutenant (and later IRA Captain) James M Roche (WS1225) from Co Limerick in May 1920, in which he describes the outcome of a raid in Kilmallock RIC Barracks. On their return they commandeered a car owned by a "Major Waller" near Pallaskenry,

Co Limerick. Albert Gregory Waller was living at Bell Isle at the time, so it is undoubtedly his car they confiscated. Waller was lucky to only lose his car and not his life: one of the IRA men, Liam Scully, had been mortally wounded when he went to take the surrender of the RIC forces in the barracks when they waved a white flag. (Apparently the IRA had managed to set the roof on fire but when the RIC officers realized the localized nature of the blaze they retreated to another part of the building and continued to fight). Roche's men would still have been in the mood for revenge. Then again Roche would appear to have been quite humane: when Brigadier Lucas was captured when on a fishing trip Roche's Limerick unit were sent to assist the North Cork IRA on prisoner guard duties, and Lucas was well treated. However, weeks later a captured British spy by the name of Crowley (alias Peader Clancy) was executed by Roche's men in July 1920.

On 06 January 1921 Waller resigned his commission in the British Empire's Indian Army reserve of officers, which was gazetted on 12 April 1921.[379]

In an incident in early 1921, described by Martin Needham (WS 1323) of the North Tipperary IRA, that "a levy of sixpence per acre was imposed on every farmer" but that there were four defaulters: Major Waller, Bell Isle, Captain Stoney, Portlaw, Eric Kenny, Kilcarron and Mrs French, Redwood. "I raided and searched these houses, and warned the owners that this action was being taken because of their failure to pay the levy. In Waller's and Stoney's, we seized a number of British army uniforms and two cameras".

It's unlikely that Waller's parade ground finest or his "mess dress" would have been any use to the IRA and Waller would not have had service/battle dress of much use for infiltration or ambushes. The intention may have been to take something he valued. However, this area of North Tipperary and East Galway was relatively quiet, with a Sinn Féin court operating in the absence of any justice system following the abandonment of Lorrha RIC barracks by Crown Forces. The

---

379 London Gazette, Issue 32288, p.2903.

IRA seemed interested in keeping the area peaceful so as to facilitate training of personnel, and Crown Forces were largely restricted to the garrison towns of Portumna and Birr. "Loyal Irishmen" like Waller, abandoned by Ulster Unionists in 1919/20, had to grin and bear it as they were in effect left to make their own arrangements to accommodate themselves with the emerging new Irish state as the decaying UK one ceded control of territory long before any formal Treaty.

It is suggested that Waller served in the Irish Air Corps as one of its instructors. However, I believe this to have been his brother Billy. I cannot find a service record for either, though it is known that a Waller served temporarily as a reserve in the Irish Defence Forces during the early stages of "the Emergency", being stationed at Rathkeale, Co Limerick.

On 12 December 1940 Waller returned to duty with the Administrative and Special Duties Branch of the RAF, at the grade of probationary Pilot Officer (88991). This was gazetted on 07 January 1941.[380] Waller was discharged on ill health grounds on 08 November 1943, retaining the rank of Flight Lieutenant, (i.e. there is no acknowledgement that Waller had earned that rank in his previous wartime service). This was gazetted on 23 November 1943.[381]

Waller lived at Beechmount, Rathkeale, Co Limerick. His only daughter, Heath Otway Waller, married Lt-Cdr Terence Vincent Aylmer Cleeve on 10 May 1946. Waller is described as being Master of the East Galway Hunt, but I have been unable to confirm this: the East Galway Hunt was established in 1791 it has been disbanded on numerous occasions throughout the 19th and 20th centuries. However, it was disbanded in 1956 and not resurrected until 1970, which would put Waller's Mastership in the 1950s. Despite his father's death on the Shannon, Albert was a yachtsman and fly fisherman. He was a member of the Lough Derg Yacht Club. As mentioned previously, Waller lived at Bell Isle, Portumna, later moving to Beechmount near Rathkeale, Co. Limerick. He died in 1967.

---

380 London Gazette, Issue 35037, pp.154-155.
381 London Gazette Supplement, Issue 36258, pp.5138-5139.

PART II – UNCONFIRMED IRISH ACES

CASEY, ROBERT FRANCIS

(**4 aerial victories**)

Born: 1896, Ireland
Died: 1966, New Forest, Hampshire, UK
Awards: Distinguished Flying Cross
Religion: Roman Catholic
Also: William Russell Patey (2 aerial victories)

The Independent Force was the forerunner of RAF Bomber Command. It was founded in July 1918 with the intention of conducting strategic bombing operations on Germany independently of any army support function. It was beyond the technological capabilities of the time to construct aircraft with a sufficient range or payload to be an effective force for the task envisaged. However, this did not prevent the RAF expending hundreds of lives. The Germans organised a communications network that encompassed forward observation posts, anti-aircraft batteries, observation balloons and special home defence *Kampfeinsitzer Staffeln* ('Kest') units. The Kest units flew with a variety of aircraft but they usually had a DFW 2-seater equipped with a wireless set, from which it could redirect the interceptors to track the RAF bombers, based upon the data being received from the communications network. Consequently RAF losses were quite high. Of the squadrons involved in day bombing operations, (55, 99, 104 and 110) in the Independent Force there were several Irish casualties, e.g. Benjamin Johnson (No.104 Squadron); Patrick J Cunningham, William Henry Currie, Herbert Blennerhasset Mercier, Stanley Nixon (No.55

Squadron); and Wilfred Hodge (No.99 Squadron). Lt AJC Gormley (No.55 Squadron) was taken POW.

Of those Irish who served with distinction in the Independent Force there was London-born William Russell Patey. He was the son of Frank and Jeannette Patey (née Carson). His father was English, his mother from Derry. Patey was raised in Belfast. (The Irish Census 1901 Census indicates that they were resident with Jeannette's parents, Robert H and Bessie W Carson, of Coolsaragh, Inniscairn, Derry. The 1911 Irish Census gives an address as Magheragall, Co Antrim). Patey won the Distinguished Flying Cross with No.55 Squadron, shooting down at least one German scout on a long-range bombing raid. According to RAF Communiqué No.7 of 1918 Patey accounted for two enemy aircraft, together with Lt A.S. Keep.

Another DFC winner with the Independent Force was Lt Robert Francis Casey, formerly 8th Battalion Royal Inniskilling Fusiliers. Casey is the only credible claim for being an Irish ace with the Independent Force. Casey's wartime RAF officer's file is not publicly available, as he served with the RAF in the postwar years. Consequently, there is confusion as to Casey's place of birth, and several competing claims regarding his background. A Private Robert Casey of the Royal Inniskilling Fusiliers was born in Co Antrim. The UK Census 1911 records this particular Casey as being garrisoned at Mandora Barracks, Aldershot. His birthplace is recorded as Ballymoney, Co Antrim. However, he was killed in action on 26th May 1915. The Robert Casey of the 8th Battalion of the Royal Inniskilling Fusiliers who served with the RAF is more likely to have come from Co Tyrone, as the 8th Bn was formed at Omagh in October 1914 and the surviving leftovers of it were amalgamated with the 7th Bn in August 1917, but there are at least two other Robert Caseys from Co Antrim who match the age and profile of RF Casey.

Regardless of the origins of Casey's enlistment to the 8th Battalion of the Royal Inniskillings it would appear that his appointment as temporary 2nd Lieutenant was dated to 06 November 1915. Upon transfer to the RAF, on 16 April 1918 Casey was granted a temporary commission as a 2nd Lieutenant (Observer Officer). He was assigned to No.110 Squadron.

In November 1917 this squadron was formed at Rendcombe, originally intended to proceed to the front in March 1918 but was retained at Sedgeford as a training squadron. It was re-equipped with the D.H.9A bomber, which was a variation of the D.H.9 but powered by the Liberty engine. It was anticipated that the improved range, payload, altitude capability and armament would make it a formidable opponent. According to the squadron records[382] the aircraft were presented by "His Serene Highness the Nisam of Hyderabad" and each machine bore this inscription. The D.H.9A was not to prove much more successful than the D.H.9, but mainly due to how predictable the routes back to Allied lines could be ascertained from the outward flights. No. 110 Squadron only became operational on frontline duties in September 1918 and it is therefore extremely unlikely that Casey could have achieved 5 aerial victories.

On 14 September 1918 No.110 Squadron targeted Boulay Aerodrome, near Metz. No enemy aircraft were encountered in the raid. Casey was observer/gunner in F993, which was piloted by Lt RP Brailli. The following day No.110 Squadron were assigned a bombing mission against Buhl Aerodrome. Once again Casey was teamed with Brailli, and once again the formation was not engaged by enemy aircraft. (However, German interceptors were active on this day: No.104 Squadron was devoured by Jasta 15 at the same time).

However, on 16 September 1918 it was the turn of No.110 Squadron to take casualties. In an attack on the *Badische Aniline und Soda Fabrik* (BASF) chemical works near Mannheim the squadron were unfortunate to have the slower D.H.4s of No.55 Squadron also involved in an attack on Mannheim, their target being the Lanz Aero Works. Several aircraft from both squadrons were lost. Lt W.E. Johns – later the author of the *Biggles* books – was wounded and

---

[382] AIR 27/857 UK National Archives, 110 Squadron ORB summary, 1917-1939.

taken POW[383]. However, there are only a handful of claims in respect of the German Jasta and Kest units that had attacked No.55 and No.110 Squadron. I can find no record of Casey having been identified as sharing in any of the aerial victories claimed.

On 25 September 1918 No.110 Squadron sent 13 D.H.4 aircraft on a mission to bomb railways and factories at Frankfurt. Of the 26 pilots and observers there were 5 killed, 3 wounded and 4 taken POW. Amidst all the slaughter Casey claimed 2 German aircraft on the outward leg at Mannheim, and although he lost consciousness after being wounded over the target zone, Casey came around on the return leg and claimed 2 further German scouts.[384] Despite a claim of 4 aerial victories on a single mission I have been unable to find another verified claim for Casey. Although sometimes counted as an ace I have insufficient information to corroborate this claim.

Despite being so badly mauled, No.110 Squadron nevertheless managed to participate in an attack on Cologne railway yards and junctions on 01 October 1918. Casey was not listed among the crew, which suggests that his wounds were serious. Similarly, on 05 October 1918 the squadron attempted a further bombing of Cologne and Kaiserslautern. In this attack No.110 Squadron lost 3 killed, 1 wounded and 4 taken POW. Casey was not listed among the crew. (Lt Brailli continued to fly F993, but with a 2nd Lt Stephenson as his observer. This new pairing flew reconnaissance missions on 18 and 21 October 1918).

On 21 October 1918 No.110 Squadron were largely annihilated, losing 2 killed and 12 POW, one of whom died of wounds. Casey was

---

383 Although his Irish airman Biggles was generally presumed to have been assigned that nationality to avoid regional dialect problems or a requirement that the character have a particular local knowledge of an area of Great Britain, W.E. Johns actually served with numerous Irish officers in No.55 Squadron and, without wishing to be facetious, it is entirely conceivable that there were plenty of Irish characters upon which he could have drawn inspiration. Group Captain Quinnell from Co Kerry was the CO of No.104 Squadron.

384 London Gazette Supplement, Issue 31046, p.14319. Douglas Hugh Moffat Carbery's DFC is also gazetted in this edition.

not among the crew. For the next number of weeks the only offensive duties of No.110 Squadron related to reconnaissance missions by single aircraft. Casey was not involved in any of these. Eventually, on 05 November 1918 a repopulated No.110 Squadron was involved in a mission to bomb Morhange Aerodrome, following this up with a further raid on 10 November 1918. Casey is not listed among the crew on either of these missions.

Casey's medal index card gives his correspondence address as of 07 March 1921 as being the School of Naval Co-Operation and Aerial Navigation at Calshot, Hampshire, with a further address as "288 Whitehouse Road, West Croydon" also being supplied. *Flight* magazine of 16 February 1922 reports Casey as among those attending the King's Levee, held on 10 February 1922 at St James' Palace. In 1926 Casey transferred to No.99 Squadron, which were based at Bircham Newton. In 1927 Casey transferred to No.39 Squadron, at Spittlegate, Lincolnshire. On 05 April 1927 the Air Ministry announced that Flying Officer Casey had been placed on the retired list at his own request.[385]

However, it is clear that, despite claims to the contrary regarding Casey, there were no Irish aces serving with the Independent Force.

❖ ❖ ❖

---

385 London Gazette, Issue 33263, p.2215.

CATHIE, ARCHIBALD JAMES

(3 aerial victories)

Born: 1888, Gosport, Hampshire, UK

Died: 11 July 1917

Commemorated: Cirencester Cemetery, Gloucestershire; Great War Memorial, St Patrick's Church, Dalkey, Co Dublin

Religion: Anglican

Archibald James ("AJ") Cathie was the son of Annie Barker Cathie and Comdr Richard Archibald Cathie of Corrig House, Convent Road, Dalkey, Co Dublin. His mother was English and his father was Irish-born of Scottish/Irish parentage.

The Irish Census 1901 records the family as being resident in Co Mayo. Archibald's father was in charge of the Coastguard Station at Bunatrahir Bay near Ballycastle, Co Mayo. However, AJ is not present with the family. He is present in the UK Census at an address in Newgate Street, London.

The Irish Census 1911 records the family as being resident in Bayview, Pembroke district of Dublin. Richard Archibald and Annie Cathie are present at that address, together with their daughters Annie Kathleen and Gwendoline Maria Cathie. Also present are four boarders and one servant. AJ is not present. Interestingly, Richard Archibald describes himself as having been born in Scotland. However, an examination of the UK Census 1891 records Lieutenant Richard Archibald Cathie as being present at the Royal Naval

Barracks at Keyham, Devonport, Devonshire. In the 1891 Census he is described as being from Ireland. Similarly, the UK 1881 Census records Richard A Cathie, then a Gunner's Mate, serving with the Royal Navy at sea. He is also described as being from Ireland. Further, his naval records and the births, deaths and marriages records identify R.A. Cathie as being born in Queenstown (Cobh), Co Cork on 02 February 1852 to Archibald Cathie and Johanna Coghlan. Queenstown was the naval equivalent of a garrison town, and thus likely that RA Cathie's alternation between Irish and Scottish nationality may have related to the geographical fact of birth in Ireland to an Irish mother and Scottish father. Conversely, AJ's birth in the naval garrison port of Gosport to an Irish father and English mother would also be describable as an accident of geography. However, AJ's family were raised in Ireland.

RFC Communiqué No.53 of 1916 indicates that on 09 September 1916 Cathie was involved in an engagement in which about 20 German aircraft were in combat with the RFC's 3rd Brigade, near Miramount. Lieutenant Harvey and 2nd Lieutenant AJ Cathie of No.11 Squadron drove down two hostile machines, which were damaged. Another aircraft flown by 2nd Lieutenant Molloy and Sergeant Allen sent another German aircraft out of control. Consequent to these engagements a German machine was seen to make a forced landing near Bapaume.

The most optimistic reading of the foregoing would attribute 2 shared aerial victories to Cathie, with the possibility of a number of No.11 Squadron aircraft sharing a further victory for the forced landing (assuming of course it was not one of the aircraft sent down in the other engagements).

RFC Communiqué No.54 of 1916 records that, on 15 September 1916, Cathie was observer in a plane flown by Lt Harvey. They were acting as top cover for a low flying formation of No.12 Squadron's bombers, which were targeting Bapaume Station. Five RFC aircraft brought down four German aircraft. The RFC aircraft were crewed by the following pilots and observers: Lt Harvey with 2nd Lt

CATHIE, ARCHIBALD JAMES

Cathie, 2nd Lt Bowman with Sgt Walker, 2nd Lt Molloy with Sgt Morton, Captain Foot with Lt Welsford, and Lt Quested with Corporal Monk.

Once again, the most wildly optimistic reading of the foregoing would attribute four shared victories to Harvey and Cathie, but this would not accord with any standard claims procedure for that period of the war.

However, on 17 September 1916 No.11 Squadron were devoured: 4 aircraft were shot down; missing were Captain D Gray, Lt LB Helder, 2nd Lt LBF Morris, Lt T Rees, 2nd Lt H Thompson, Sgt JE Glover, 2nd Lt TPL Molloy and Sgt GJ Morton. Two days later the leftovers of No.11 Squadron sent several F.E.s on reconnaissance, with No.60 Squadron as escort. They were attacked by a large formation of German aircraft. Harvey and Cathie's aircraft went to the assistance of a Captain Hugh Christopher Tower of No.60 Squadron, who was being badly shot up by a Roland. They managed to drive it off but were themselves the subject of heavy enemy fire. Cathie was wounded, as was a Corporal Monk in another No.11 Squadron F.E., which was flown by Lt Bowman. Both F.E.s made it back to Allied lines. (However, No.60 Squadron's Captain Tower's aircraft went down and he was killed).

Cathie's service history[386] confirms that he was wounded in France on 19 September 1916. Medical board examinations indicate that he was unfit for frontline duties for several months. Cathie was formally appointed as a Flying Officer (Observer) on 27 October 1916 with effect from 10 October 1916.

On 27 January 1917, after recovering from injury, Cathie was assigned to No.51 (Home Duties) Squadron. However, he was not fit for flying duties at this stage. Cathie was assigned to a number of Reserve Squadrons (27, 1) over the March to May 1917 period. He transferred to 38 Reserve Squadron on appointment as Flying Officer on 25 June 1917.

Cathie never got to return to frontline squadron duties: he was killed in an aeroplane accident on 11 July 1917.

---

386 AIR 76/80 AJ Cathie, UK National Archives.

The *Irish Times* of 21 July 1917 and *Weekly Irish Times* of 28 July 1917 both make reference to Cathie's death. Although his family moved around Ireland quite a lot – as evidenced in the 1901 and 1911 Irish census returns – it would appear that their closest association was with Dalkey, Co Dublin. AJ is commemorated there. On account of being commemorated in the war memorial of St Patrick's Church, Dalkey he is recorded in the Earl of Ypres' commission volumes, *Ireland's War Memorials*.

Given his Irish-English parentage, the absence of any personal link to Gosport, and the fact of being raised in Ireland for a substantial part of his life, his family's lengthy period of residence in Ireland, and his commemoration in an Irish war memorial I would count Cathie as an Irish aviator. However, I remain to be convinced that he could ever have reached 5 aerial victories as an early war observer ace. The facts simply do not accord with any standard reading of shared aerial victory claims.

✦ ✦ ✦

DE BURGH, DESMOND HERLOUIN

(4 aerial victories)

Born: 05 August 1897, Co Monaghan
Died: 18 January 1943
Awards: Air Force Cross
Commemorated: Alamein Memorial, Egypt
Religion: Church of Ireland

Air Commodore Desmond Herlouin de Burgh was the son of Colonel Ulick George Campbell de Burgh and Anna Blance Constance Paget, of Scarva House, Co Monaghan. On his father's side he was the grandson of Thomas de Burgh of Oldtown, Naas, Co Kildare. On his mother's side he was the grandson of Baroness of Donoughmore of Knocklofty, Co Tipperary.

The de Burgh clan of Oldtown, Co Kildare claim a direct descent from Emperor Charlemagne. They have provided Ireland with bishops, parliamentarians and generals over the generations. The musician Chris de Burgh and his daughter, the model Rosanna Davison, are perhaps the most prominent family members from recent generations.

Desmond was educated at West Downs School, Winchester. He served with the Royal Field Artillery before transferring to the Royal Flying Corps. Initially de Burgh served as a Flying Officer (Observer), from 01 April 1916 onwards. However, I have been unable to identify an aerial victory attributed to de Burgh when serving as an observer.

In biographies of George Bernard Shaw it is generally agreed that in the debut performance of his play *O'Flaherty VC* in February 1917 it was de Burgh who performed the role of Mrs O'Flaherty, with the Irish ace Robert Gregory taking on the part of Tessie the Maid and Captain Denis Osmond Mulholland taking the lead character role. For such a risible play it is amusing to note just how many decorated Irishmen of No.40 Squadron featured in its debut performance.

Desmond is also mentioned as Mick Mannock's sparring partner and debating partner in most accounts of No.40 Squadron.

According to a series of articles in *Cross & Cockade (Great Britain)*[387] journal, de Burgh is credited with 2 aerial victories with No.40 Squadron and 4 other wartime aerial victories. However, there are a number of competing accounts as to de Burgh's tally with the squadron.

According to the No.40 Squadron "Combats in the Air" submissions[388] to the claims board, on 29 January 1917 de Burgh was flying an F.E.8 (6428) at 11,000 feet on escort duty to a photography mission. The F.E.2b aircraft on the reconnaissance mission were intercepted by 8 Halberstadts, which soon had the attention of de Burgh. An F.E.2b was diving with a Halberstadt on its tail when de Burgh dived on it and fired three-quarters of a drum at a range of 150 yards. The German fled east. The F.E.2b also lived to tell the tale. The Germans broke off. However, de Burgh reported that there were "no casualties observed on either side", which would not have helped his case for a claim, as 150 yards was within killing range. Unsurprisingly, de Burgh was not awarded an aerial victory for the riddled Halberstadt. However, RFC Communiqué No.73 of 1917 records that the three F.E.8s of No.40 Squadron and the five F.E.2bs of No.25 Squadron were awarded aerial victories against two of the German attackers, with two other Germans being described as being forced to land. No.25 Squadron had suffered casualties, though no

---

387 Cross & Cockade (Great Britain), Vol. 4 No.4 [Winter 1973], Vol.5, No. 1 [Spring 1974].
388 AIR/1/1222/204/5/2634, UK National Archives.

loss of aircraft: a 2nd Lieutenant A.V. Blenkiron of No.25 Squadron had been wounded in the encounter.

On 09 April 1917 de Burgh attacked two Albatros two-seaters between Lens and Lievin. de Burgh was in his usual Nieuport (A6781). He "gave combat and fired a burst at a range of 150 yards. HA turned east, disappeared in clouds and was not seen again". He then engaged another Albatros, this time at a more effective range of 100 yards. However, the German "turned East and Nieuport was forced to break off fight owing to gun stoppage". This would appear to suggest two indecisive encounters.

On 14 April 1917 de Burgh, in a Nieuport (A6781), shared the destruction of an Albatros DIII with Lt Ian Napier. (In RFC Communiqué No.84 of 1917 the incident is recorded as having taken place on 15 April 1917, with the enemy aircraft crashing in a field and bursting into flames). However, an examination of the "Combats in the Air" files submitted by No.40 Squadron[389] indicates that de Burgh and Napier also engaged 3 German aircraft at 5.20 pm and 2 Albatros aircraft at 5.30 pm, neither engagement being decisive. It is likely that a large number of these indecisive encounters have been mistakenly added to de Burgh's tally.

On 22 April 1917 de Burgh is credited with the destruction of a German kite balloon, although RFC Communiqué No.85 of 1917 indicates that he hit the balloon with Le Prieur rockets, which started to smoke, but the Germans managed to haul it down in a deflated state before it could ignite.

Overall one may gather than the award of only two aerial victories in respect of de Burgh's efforts with No.40 Squadron would not have precluded a large number of anecdotal tales of German aircraft being engaged and driven off. Perhaps some of these have fed into the tale of de Burgh as an ace with No.40 Squadron?

de Burgh was appointed temporary Captain with effect from 30 April 1918. In January 1919 de Burgh was awarded the Air Force Cross for his wartime service.

---

389 AIR/1/1222/204/5/2634, UK National Archives.

On 04 November 1920 de Burgh's engagement was announced and on 05 January 1921 de Burgh married Norah Dorothy Sharpe, but they divorced in 1939. It is suggested that he remarried, with the Commonwealth War Graves Commission recording his spouse as Betty Herlouin de Burgh, of Chiswick, Middlesex. de Burgh served with the RAF during the interwar years, being promoted from Flying Officer to Flight Lieutenant in 1922 and receiving training at the Electrical and Wireless School, and later Cambridge University. As a Flight Lieutenant de Burgh served at the School of Photography at Farnborough in August 1930. He was promoted to Squadron Leader, subsequently being posted to India as the Chief Signals Officer at the RAF HQ, New Delhi from 1931 to early 1935.[390] He was subsequently promoted from Squadron Leader to Wing Commander in the half-yearly promotions list of January 1937. In January 1938 Flight magazine carries a report of discussions on the Lorenz system, with de Burgh making several contributions on the effectiveness of such a marker beacon system. de Burgh served with the RAF in World War II, as did his son Ulric Campbell de Burgh. Desmond was promoted from Wing Commander to Group Captain in 1940 and to Air Commodore in 1943. He was killed in an air crash in January 1943 and is recorded on the Alamein Memorial in Egypt. In the London Gazette of 05 December 1944 his solicitors give de Burgh's former address as being c/o Lloyds Bank Ltd, 68 Warwick Square, London SW1, and "formerly of Tankards Wonersh, Guildford Surrey". (This is a Grade II listed building in the village, between Gerald's Wood and Blackheath Cemetery).

At no stage during the post-war years have I encountered an article that described de Burgh as an ace in which there was any attempt to detail the precise basis of that assertion. The reference to 6 aerial victories would appear to be based upon shared claims that were not necessarily described as such in the summary of claims forms. Pre-

---

390 For example see *Flight* magazine of 07 March 1935 re his observations on the merits of electrical cables being placed underground or carrying neon markings to be more visible to aircraft.

sumably some of these aerial victories would relate to his time as an observer whilst others would relate to his years as a pilot. However, in the absence of specific details I cannot include de Burgh as a confirmed ace. I do not have a copy of *Air Aces of the 1914-1918 War* by Bruce Robertson (Harleyford, 1959), the original work on aces, but gather that this publication is the source of some misunderstandings on the allocation of claims. It may well be the basis for de Burgh being attributed 6 aerial victories but a large body of research has superseded it over the subsequent decades.

✦ ✦ ✦

DICKEY, ROBERT FREDERICK LEA

(**3 or 4 aerial victories**)

Born: 27 July 1895, Co Derry

Died: UNKNOWN

Awards: Distinguished Service Cross with Two Bars, Mentioned in Despatches (twice), Croix de Guerre with Bronze Palm.

Religion: Presbyterian

Captain R.F.L. Dickey is forever associated with the destruction of the Zeppelin L43: indeed the *Cross & Cockade* calendar of 2006 featured an image of this iconic event. However, Dickey was a distinguished submarine hunter and is known to have also won a number of air-to-air combat engagements. However, it is unclear as to whether he reached ace status.

Dickey was the son of Mary Jane Smith Dickey and Professor Robert Henry Frederick Dickey of Magee College, Derry. His father was originally from Co Donegal and his mother from Co Tyrone. In the Irish Census 1901 the family are resident at College Avenue, Derry. Robert's father is described as "Reverend Professor of Oriental Literature and Biblical Criticism". Robert is listed by an abbreviated name, which looks like "Eric".

In the Irish Census 1911 the family are resident at College Avenue, Derry. Robert's older brother John Smith Porter Dickey is still present, as are his sisters Ethel Mary and Annie Maud Steele Dickey. John Smith is described as a student of medicine at the University of

Edinburgh and a graduate of Oxford. Annie Maud is described as being a teacher of drawing and design. His other sister Mabel is not present but is still described as being alive in the census return form.

Dickey enlisted with the RNAS as a Petty Officer Motor Mechanic. His first set of service records[391] indicate that Dickey was a student engineer when he enlisted on 19 April 1915. From 01 September 1915 he served as an Air Mechanic (1st Class). Dickey was based at RNAS Detling, which was near Maidstone in Kent. Dickey was appointed Temporary Probationary Flight Sub-Lieutenant on 10 June 1916. His officer's service record[392] states that Dickey was initially based at Chingford, from where he obtained Royal Aero Club Certificate No.3950 on 06 December 1916 and was confirmed in his rank as Flight Sub-Lieutenant on 14 February 1917. Dickey is described as a "first class pilot" and a good officer. He was recommended for seaplane training and was posted to Felixstowe in April 1917. Dickey finished the seaplane course on 15 April 1917, being described as "quite a good pilot. Keen but rather slow. Should improve with experience. Recommended for seaplane patrol".

The L43 was the second 'S' type *Luftschiffbau Zeppelin* to be built. This type had an improved operational ceiling, around 20,000 feet – some 4,000 feet higher than the standard design, and was essentially an improved version of the successful 'M' class Zeppelin. On 04 May 1917 the L43 had a distinguished duel with the Australian light cruiser *HMAS Sydney*, an event celebrated in painting by Charles Bryant. The Australian ship was leading a British ship *HMS Dublin* and four destroyers (*Nepean, Obdurate, Pelican, Pylades*) on a sweep off the Scottish coast when lured into an attempted ambush by German submarines, which they easily evaded. However, the L43 appeared on the scene, and subjected the cruisers and destroyers to a sustained bombing. The duel continued for two hours, resulting in minor damage to several ships, most of which had expended all their high alti-

---

391 ADM 188/568, p.76 RFL Dickey. (UK National Archives).
392 ADM 273/9, p.124 RFL Dickey. (UK National Archives).

tude munitions ineffectually against the Zeppelin. Clearly the L43 would be a danger to slower, less well-armed shipping.

On 14 June 1917 the L43's Kaptainleutnant Kraushaar embarked on a further naval reconnaissance mission. The signal was intercepted. In a Curtiss H-12 flying boat (designed by Irishman and RNAS Felixstowe station chief John Cyril Porte) Dickey was part of the duty crew ordered by "James the One" Owen Hugh Knox Maguire (another Irishman) to intercept and destroy the German airship. Maguire plotted the likely course on their 'spider web' grid.

W.G. Carr's *Good Hunting* and T.D. Hallam's *Spider Web* both feature detailed accounts of this aerial victory. Hallam describes Dickey as being "a good shot, a capable navigator, a fine observer, always keen on going forward and loath to turn back". Interestingly, Hallam suggests that Dickey had been out on eight missions prior to that date, without success, i.e. there are no aerial victories prior to this event. Apparently Dickey only used 15 cartridges of Brock & Pomeroy explosive ammunition to ignite the L43. However, Dickey was "only" awarded the Distinguished Service Cross (DSC) for the action. The pilot of the flying boat, Billiken Hobbs, was awarded the Distinguished Service Order (DSO), which is second only to the Victoria Cross as the highest ranking bravery award. The Germans could not believe their loss: throughout the day the German wireless stations frantically called to the L43.

Dickey was awarded the DSC on 29 June 1917. According to his service record, Dickey was "very keen, courageous to a fault", which suggests that a higher award may have been envisaged but not awarded. In terms of further aerial engagements, Dickey's file contains an entry dated 13 July 1917 "Expression of TL's [the Lordships'] appreciation of services, respecting engagement with enemy seaplane, after an anti-Zeppelin patrol of 405 miles in Seaplane 8677 on 17 June". However, this does not suggest that the German seaplane was destroyed in the incident on 17 June 1917, merely that it was a noteworthy and praiseworthy occasion.

On 13 June 1917 Dickey was awarded a Bar to his DSC for the destruction of a U-Boat on 28 June 1917. In August 1917 Dickey was mentioned in despatches for anti-Zeppelin patrols, which was gazetted on 11 August 1917 together with the Bar to his Distinguished Service Cross. Dickey's subsequent bar to his Distinguished Service Cross was awarded for attacks on enemy submarines. Although U-boat kills were notoriously difficult to verify, Dickey claimed three further U-boats destroyed: on 03 September 1917, 13 September 1917 and 30 September 1917.

However, although there were several indecisive aerial engagements over the course of 1917 I have not seen an incident in which Dickey is specifically credited with the destruction of an enemy aircraft. The H-12 seaplanes could take a lot of punishment and it may be presumed that their German counterparts could also survive heavy damage. (Indeed an aircraft seen going down could well manage to land at sea for emergency repairs or to send carrier pigeons to the nearest naval establishment). Consequently I am reluctant to regard Dickey as having achieved anything more than the destruction of the L43 Zeppelin and the damaging of a German seaplane in June 1917.

On 20 October 1917 Dickey was admitted to Chatham hospital, requiring treatment for "urethral fistula". On 19 October 1917 he was discharged from Chatham hospital and admitted to Greenwich college hospital. On 25 January 1918 Dickey was admitted to Peebles hospital, not being discharged until late February 1918. Clearly Dickey could not have been a party to any aerial engagements during this period. During this time the award of a 2nd Bar to the DSC was gazetted on 30 November 1917, and his second mention in despatches was gazetted on 19 December 1917. Only a handful of people received a Second Bar to the Distinguished Service Cross during World War I.

However, it is known that on 30 April 1918 Dickey's flying boat was engaged by five German attackers, one of which he shot down in flames. On 09 May 1918 Dickey was recommended for promotion to Captain in the RAF. Approximately one month later, on 05 June 1918, Dickey's flying boat suffered mechanical failure and although it is possible that his aircraft succeeded in shooting down one opponent the crippled H-12 was forced to land in neutral Dutch waters. It is claimed that his crew (Russell and Hodgson) shot down 2 enemy aircraft from their static position after landing. Dickey was interned for the remainder of the war. The RAF would not appear to have credited any of these three victories to the flying boat, but in any event two of these were sea-to-air gunnery from the crippled plane and therefore could not count as aerial victories.

Dickey served in Iraq during the interwar years. He also served in World War II, being recalled to the Royal Naval Volunteer Reserve, retiring in March 1941 at the rank of Lieutenant-Colonel. He would appear to have earned service medals rather than gallantry awards for this period.

It is likely that Dickey died in winter 1959 at Uckfield, Sussex.

In 1988 Dickey's medals were auctioned at Sotheby's. In July 2003 a set of eleven miniature dress medals were auctioned by Dix Noonan Webb, reaching a hammer price of £250 – far in excess of the estimate range of £80-£120 for the lot. In December 2006 the same set were sold at auction for £210. In December 2012 Dix Noonan Webb sold Dickey's gallantry and service medals at auction: the estimate was £20,000 to £25,000 but the hammer price was only £21,000, which included Dickey's original aviator's certificate, flying log books and letters of appointment and recommendation in the auction lot.

✦ ✦ ✦

DODD, WALTER DE COURCY

(4 aerial victories)

Born: 1896, Co Kerry

Died: 31 October 1917

Commemorated: Honourable Artillery Company Cemetery, Ecoust-St. Mein, Pas de Calais, France

Religion: Roman Catholic

Walter was the son of Dr William Henry Dodd and Ellen Mary Dodd, of Ballymacprior Lodge, Killorglin, Co Kerry. This address is associated with the Blennerhasset family, from where the Sligo-born ace Giles Noble Blennerhasset's father originates.

Walter was one of three brothers to serve in World War I, all three of whom were killed. In the Irish Census 1901 the family are resident at Ballymacprior Lodge. Present are Walter's parents, his two sisters (Mary Josephine and Mabel), four of his brothers (George, Francis, Arthur and Alfred), and three servants. Walter is present but his eldest brother, John O'Connell Dodd, is not.

On 29 January 1916 Walter was appointed 2nd Lieutenant, on probation, with the Royal Munster Fusiliers.[393] According to Walter's service record[394] he transferred from the Royal Munster Fusiliers to the Royal Flying Corps on 15 May 1917. Initially Walter was sent to the School of Aerial Gunnery at Hythe for a month long course as an aerial observer. On 16 July 1917 Walter was appointed 2nd Lieutenant,

---

393 London Gazette, Gazette Issue 29454, 28 January 1916, p.1138.
394 AIR 76/136, p.411. Walter de Courcy Dodd, UK National Archives.

Flying Officer (Observer), which was gazetted on 02 August 1917. On 29 July 1917 he was promoted to Lieutenant in the Royal Munster Fusiliers, which was gazetted on 18 February 1918.[395]

On 26 June 1917 Dodd was posted to No.11 Squadron as an observer. He made an immediate impact. The *Combats in the Air* files of No.11 Squadron reveal the extent of the aerial engagements in which Dodd was involved. For example, on 10 July 1917, in a Bristol F2b (A7140) piloted by McKeever and with Dodd as observer, they were patrolling at a height of 13,000 feet over Sailly when they joined a mêlée of 7 Nieuports and 8 Albatros scouts. McKeever had the Vickers gun, firing forwards, with Dodd on the harder-hitting Lewis gun. Dodd engaged an Albatros and fired 50 rounds at a range of 75 yards range, causing the German to break off and head eastwards. However, despite the close range, apparently it was undamaged. Dodd then trained his gun on another. He fired 75 rounds at 200 yards range, resulting in the Albatros diving away from the combat, but under control. McKeever then got to engage a third Albatros, firing 75 rounds at 50 yards, i.e. the ideal effective killing range. Dodd could verify that the German was still spinning down out of control at a very low altitude when last observed. Major C.T. Maclean, Commanding Officer of No.11 Squadron, submitted one "out of control" aerial victory to the claims board. However, it does understate the effectiveness of the observer in breaking up enemy combat formations and driving them from the fight. RFC Communiqué No.96 of 1917 duly credits McKeever and Dodd with one aerial victory.

According to No.11 Squadron's combat reports[396] of 13 July 1917, in a Bristol F2b, McKeever and Dodd were patrolling at a height of 14,000 feet over Haneycourt when they engaged a large formation of German aircraft. McKeever opened fire at 200 yards with the Vickers, firing 50 rounds. The Albatros disappeared east, losing height but apparently undamaged. Dodd then opened fire on another Albatros

---

395 Dodd was dead by this stage. London Gazette Supplement, Issue 30531, p.2182.
396 11/com/120. Contained in AIR/1/121920452634, UK National Archives.

from a distance of 150 yards, firing 70 rounds, sending the German aircraft down in a steep nosedive, but it appeared to be still under control as it disappeared from view. McKeever then dived on another enemy aircraft and opened fire at 150 yards. The German fell, spinning downwards out of control, but it was not possible at that altitude to see it crash. Dodd trained his Lewis gun on an incoming Albatros, firing 75 rounds at 100 yards distance. The German broke off and turned eastwards. McKeever then closed in on another, firing 75 rounds from 100 yards range. The German fired a red light – presumably a distress signal or perhaps there were fragments of incendiary material igniting as the Albatros leaked fuel – but the aircraft dropped from the sky out of control. Dodd then fired 50 rounds at 200 yards, which resulted in the Albatros having enough and turning east. Similarly McKeever fired 50 rounds on another at 250 yards, but the German went east without any apparent damage being inflicted. Overall, Major Maclean, the C.O. of No.11 Squadron, submitted two "out of control" aerial victories to the claims board. In RFC Communiqué No.97 of 1917, which dates the combat to 14 July 1917 due to reporting conventions regarding late evening flights, McKeever and Dodd are duly credited with a further "out of control" aerial victories.

On 21 September 1917, this time with a Bristol F2b piloted by Captain Geoffrey Herbert Hooper, a famous Australian ace, they recorded an indecisive combat.[397] They were part of a patrol of 4 Bristol Fighters when, just south of Cambrai at a height of 13,000 feet, they were attacked by 9 Albatros scouts. The Germans dived from a height of 2,000 feet above. In a single-seat aircraft combat this should prove decisive but the Bristol F2b observer/gunners could direct intersecting arcs of fire if flown well. Just prior to combat one Bristol fighter had to break off the engagement and return, suffering with magneto trouble. The other three fighters fired about 850 rounds at the enemy. No observable damage was recorded, with all 9 Germans retreating east.

---

397 11/combat/197. Contained in AIR/1/121920452634, UK National Archives.

According to No.11 Squadron's *Combats in the Air* (11/com/204), on 24 September 1917, McKeever and Dodd were once again paired. At a height of 12,000 feet over Vis-en-Artois they spotted a formation of 5 Albatros scouts. They dived on one of the enemy, firing about 100 rounds from 100 yards away. The atmospheric conditions were not favourable, and no obvious damage was observed in the hazy conditions. The German escaped eastwards and it was not possible to pursue the others. This was adjudged to be yet another indecisive combat.

However, No.11 Squadron's *Combats in the Air* (11/com/205), of 25 September 1917 McKeever and Dodd shared in the destruction of a two-seater. It was painted white and green but was a type unknown to the RFC attackers. Lieutenant George Eric Miall-Smith's Bristol F2b swooped but timed the attack badly, overshooting their target due to the differential in speed and altitude. The German observer hit the Bristol fighter several times and it went into an uncontrollable spin, disintegrating as it plummeted earthwards. (Miall-Smith and his observer Charles Cowley Dennis are buried at Warlincourt Halte British Cemetery). McKeever got in close, firing 25 rounds at 25 yards. The German aircraft went down out of control. Another Bristol F2b also fired on the German two-seater but from a distance of 100 yards range. On an army messages and signals "O" Form, No.41 Squadron reported that a Captain Hall of their squadron had seen the German crash. However, it was initially awarded as an "out of control" aerial victory to McKeever and Dodd. RFC Communiqué No.107 of 1917, however, credits McKeever and Dodd with the destruction of an Albatros on 25 September 1917, which suggests that due cognisance was taken of No.41 Squadron's report.

On 31 October 1917 2nd Lieutenant SW Randall and Dodd were shot down. Dodd died in German custody. It is implied that he may have died by his own hand. However, I believe this to be a case of mistaken identity: of the three Dodd brothers who died in the war it was actually his brother Francis Joseph Dodd who may have committed suicide. (2nd Lieutenant F.J. Dodd enlisted with the Royal Dublin

Fusiliers in September 1914 and was serving with the Machine Gun corps at the time of his death on 31 October 1918. He is buried at Grantham Cemetery, Lincolnshire, but is also commemorated on the Clongowes Great War Memorial).

Dodd would therefore appear to have four confirmed aerial victories, but no more than this. Ironically for a Kerryman, his shared victories with the Canadian ace, Andrew Edward McKeever, involved a chap who hailed from Listowel, Ontario, not Listowel, Co Kerry.

His eldest brother, John O'Connell Dodd, who like Walter also served with the Royal Munsters, is recorded in the UK 1901 Census as being resident at 67 Chestnut Grove, Streatham, working as a clerk in an insurance office. According to the London Irish rugby club supporters' website, in 1909 John was the joint winner of the Starkey Cup at the first London Irish Athletic meeting, when he won the mile race and came second in the 440 yards and relay, and third place in the 100 yards. He was killed in action on 07 November 1918 and was buried in Monceau St. Waast Communal Cemetery, France.

It is suggested that all three brothers are commemorated on a plaque at the parish church in Killorglin, Co Kerry but I have no confirmation of this.

Unhappily for Dodd's family his effects were only worth £28 16s. 8d., for which his mother Ellen was named the beneficiary when probate was granted in October 1918.

❖ ❖ ❖

GRATTAN-BELLEW, WILLIAM ARTHUR

(**4 aerial victories**)

Born: 15 September 1893, Co Galway

Died: 24 March 1917

Awards: Military Cross, Mentioned in Despatches.

Commemorated: Avesnes-le-Comte Communal Cemetery Extension, Pas de Calais, France.

Religion: Roman Catholic

Major William Arthur Grattan-Bellew served with No.16, No.25 and No.29 Squadrons in the early stages of the war. In many accounts he is attributed ace status. However, the extensive body of research over the past number of decades would suggest that Grattan-Bellew may well have achieved only four shared aerial victories rather than the seven or eight suggested. Grattan-Bellew would therefore fall into a category similar to Desmond Herlouin de Burgh, i.e. of a once-established but now an unconfirmed ace.

William was the son of Sir Henry Christopher Grattan Bellew, 3rd Baronet, and Lady Sophia Maria Elizabeth Grattan-Bellew (née Forbes), who was the daughter of the 7th Earl of Granard. The Forbes family were converts to Roman Catholicism and thus William's grandparents' side of the family had many of the trappings of the devout RC such as membership of the Sovereign Military Hospitaller Order of St John of Jerusalem of Rhodes and of Malta.

The surname Grattan-Bellew arose from the marriage of Thomas Arthur Bellew, 2nd Baronet, to Pauline Grattan, who was the daughter of the Irish statesman Sir Henry Grattan. The original de Bellews were an Anglo-Norman family, from which towns such as Beleawe, Co Meath, Bellewstown, Co Louth and Mount Bellew, Co Galway. They were the subject of the dispossession and displacement of the Cromwellian period, hence the Galway branch of the family coming into being. Despite being a Roman Catholic family they managed to escape the penal law restrictions on land ownership and gradually rebuilt over the centuries. By William's time the various branches of the family held several thousand aces in Co Louth and at least 25,000 acres in Co Galway. Unlike Robert Gregory's family, however, the Grattan-Bellews participated in the various Land Act tenant purchase schemes throughout the 1880s, 1890s and 1900s. Politically they supported the Act of Union but to describe them as Unionist would obviously relate to political beliefs rather than the sectarian definition more commonly associated with the term, e.g. as Roman Catholics they would have been ineligible for membership of the loyal orders such as the Orange Order or Royal Black Preceptory. In fact the Grattan-Bellew family remained in Ireland as Galway landowners in the post-Independence period, with another branch of the family supplying a member to the Senate of *Saor Stát Éireann*. (Contrary to expectations, the member was not Sir Thomas Henry Grattan Esmonde, Baronet, whose mother was Louisa Grattan, but was actually Bernard Arthur William Patrick Hastings Forbes – 8th Earl of Granard – who served in the Senate from 1922 to 1934).

William's family do not appear in the Irish Census 1901. However, as Sir Henry had served with the 5th Dragoon Guards and ultimately was a Lieutenant-Colonel in the Connaught Rangers. William's brother Arthur John was born in Gravesend, Kent in 1901, which suggests an overseas posting with the family temporarily resident in England.

The Irish Census 1911 records William's parents and his five sisters and brothers as being resident at Mount Bellew Demesne, Mount

Bellew, Co Galway. Also present is a governess and twelve servants. William's aunt, Eva Mary Margaret Forbes, was also present as a visitor. William is recorded in the UK Census 1911 as a boarder at Downside, Somerset. (William's brothers were also Old Gregorians). His other brother, Charles Christopher Grattan-Bellew, is recorded as being a Lieutenant with the 3rd Battalion of the King's Royal Rifle Corps, which were stationed at Dagshai, India. (He was to become the 4th Baronet but had not originally been destined to be such until William's eldest brother, Herbert Michael Grattan-Bellew, died in 1906). William went from Downside to Cambridge.

William joined the colours with the Connaught Rangers. He transferred into the Royal Flying Corps in January 1915, being sent to the Central Flying School on 28 January 1915. According to his service record[398] Grattan-Bellew's appointment as temporary 2nd Lieutenant was dated to 17 January 1915. (The London Gazette of 01 February 1915 reports Grattan-Bellew's confirmation as 2nd Lieutenant, together with another Irishman, Stanislaus Cruess-Callaghan – the brother of ace Joseph Cruess Callaghan). On 24 April 1915 Grattan-Bellew was assigned to No.16 Squadron, and was subsequently appointed as a Flying Officer with effect from 09 April 1915. However, Grattan-Bellew saw hardly any service with No.16 Squadron, being hospitalized with hernia in June 1915. The Medical Board assessments of 23 June and 26 July 1915 certify him as unfit for one month and two months respectively. However, a further assessment on 28 July 1915 – did he request a second opinion, one wonders – found Grattan-Bellew fit for light duties. Subsequently a Medical Board assessment on 25 September 1915 found Grattan-Bellew fit to resume duties. Mike O'Connor, in his excellent *Airfields and Airmen: Arras*, which was published as part of the 'Battleground Europe' series, suggests that the hernia was a consequence of an appendix operation.

As one may gather, it is simply impossible for Grattan-Bellew to have recorded any aerial victories in respect of his time at No.16

---

398 AIR 76/33, p.299 (UK National Archives).

Squadron. There are no combat reports available for April and May 1915 in respect of No.16 Squadron but I have examined the available combat reports for June, July, September and October 1915: Grattan-Bellew is not mentioned in these. However, it should also be mentioned that the first RFC Communiqué did not issue until July 1915 and therefore it is possible for the various conflicting reporting mechanisms of April and May 1915 to have begged reference to some contribution of Grattan-Bellew's in respect of aerial combat. I have not been presented with any evidence of this, and so must operate on a working assumption that any aerial victories obtained were those which occurred with No. 25 and No.29 Squadrons.

Grattan-Bellew did not actually return to No.16 Squadron in late September 1915 but was posted to No.25 Squadron on 05 October 1915 as a founder member. He was promoted to Lieutenant with effect from 01 December 1915, which was gazetted on 17 January 1916. On 24 March 1916 Grattan-Bellew was promoted to Flight Commander (Captain).

Grattan-Bellew was awarded the Military Cross, which was gazetted on 27 July 1916:

"22nd Lt. (temp. Capt.) William Arthur Grattan Bellow, Conn. Rang, and R.F.C.

For conspicuous gallantry and skill on several occasions, notably the following: —

With three other machines he attacked and drove off eight enemy machines, forcing one to the ground.

He attacked four Fokkers, forcing one down to 2,500 feet. Another was seen to crash to the ground during the fight.

When on a bombing raid two of the machines got behind owing to clouds, and were attacked by Fokkers. Capt. Grattan Bellew returned and attacked three Fokkers, one of which his Observer shot down and the others made off".[399]

However, a more detailed reading of the RFC Communiqués does not necessarily attribute three aerial victories to Grattan-Bellew,

---

399 London Gazette Supplement, Gazette Issue No.29684, p.7437.

e.g. the incident on 27 April 1916 is covered in RFC Communiqué No.34 of 1916 reports that four F.E.s teamed up to attack a formation of eight Aviatiks. The Germans scattered. A running fight ensued, which lasted 10 minutes. "Captain Bellew drove one to the ground near Illes under control. Lt Maxwell drove one to the ground near Herlies, where it was seen to land in a ploughed field, apparently under control. Of the remainder, two landed at Don and the others disappeared south, flying very low".

Essentially the foregoing indicates Grattan-Bellew and Maxwell obtaining one "forced to land" (FTL) victory each, with the two Aviatiks escaping to Don and landing under control being mere moral victories of having been forced from the skies. In the early war years it may have been possible to harbour delusions of two aerial victories each for Grattan-Bellew and Maxwell but even by the mid-war era the "forced to land" aerial victory was no longer being awarded. In this regard, the highest case that can be made from the first incident is one aerial victory for Grattan-Bellew.

The second incident mentioned in the London Gazette is detailed in RFC Communiqué No.37 of 1916. On 18 June 1916 the following combat incident occurred:

"Two F.E.s of 25 Sqn, pilots Captain Grattan Bellew and 2nd Lt Armstrong, observers Lt Lewes and Sgt Chapman, working together encountered two Fokkers east of Lens at 4.14pm at about 9,000 feet. The F.E.s chased the Fokkers down, diving steeply in small circles and firing all the time. Capt Bellew left his opponent diving vertically at about 2,500 feet, being short of petrol. The other Fokker was shot down by Sgt Chapman and crashed to earth from 4,000 feet".

Once again it may be noted that Grattan-Bellew was involved in an incident in which he did not specifically destroy or damage an enemy aircraft: his opponent was "driven down" but at 2,500 feet it would be difficult to describe it as an "out of control" aerial victory. The diplomatic use of the phrase "another was seen to crash to the ground during the fight" in his medal citation is one that skilfully evades mention of the fact that it was the observer Sgt Chapman who shot it down, not Grattan-Bellew. The highest case that can be made in this scenario is one shared aerial victory between Grattan-Bellew and Chapman, with another driven down, this latter outcome not counting for aerial victory purposes.

However, the third incident in the medal citation is detailed in RFC Communiqué No.40 of 1916 is one in which Grattan-Bellew's contribution is understated. On 26 June 1916 Grattan-Bellew was involved in an exceptionally brave battle to help extricate four other F.E.s of No.25 Squadron from a swarm of Fokkers. The fuel tank of Captain Tedder's F.E. was punctured and he was lucky to make it back without being immolated. 2nd Lieutenant G.R. McCubbin was "severely wounded in the arm" although it is suggested that his observer, Corporal J.H. Waller, may have either driven one off or sent it down out of control. (It may well have returned to the fray in the course of the aerial combat engagements: McCubbin had to land near Beauvray and so is not in a position to definitively claim a kill). Of the three surviving F.E. aircraft Grattan-Bellew "engaged a Fokker which was following up Lt Sherwell's machine and drove it off. He then attacked another that was coming up, and his observer fired two drums into it at 10 yards range. The Fokker heeled over and went down vertically, crashing behind the enemy's lines". However, Lt Sherwell's aircraft crash-landed, with his observer, Aircraftman 2nd Class H.L. Chadwick bleeding to death. The other F.E., flown by 2nd Lieutenant R.G. Riley, made a hard landing near Mazinegarbe, hitting barbed wire defences and being wrecked. Riley suffered concussion and was "severely wounded in combat". His observer, Lt E.H. Bird, suffered a broken wrist and is described in the communiqué as being "dangerously wounded in combat". (Eric H. Bird died days later). With 4 of the 5 F.E.s knocked out it would be reasonable to assume that Grattan-Bellew's interventions had saved the lives of some of the crew. After shooting down one and driving off another "Captain Bellew was then at 2,600 feet. He could see three Fokkers going east at 1,000 feet over La Bassee. He waited about, but nothing came within reach, so he came come … From the accounts of spectators in the Loos Salient, two Fokkers certainly crashed behind the enemy's lines".

A Hollywood version of this scenario could well imagine having Grattan-Bellew circling the scene, roaring "who's next? Come back here. I'll take on all of you" as the Germans disappeared but the reality is that Tedder's damaged aircraft could conceivably have brought down one of the two crashed Fokkers. In the circumstances it is reasonable to suggest that the highest case to be made for Grattan-Bellew was two shared aerial victories from this aerial combat incident. McCubbin, a South African, and G.H. Waller, his observer, had – on 18 June 1916 – claimed the destruction of the Fokker E.III Eindecker of the great German ace Max Immelmann. It is suggested that Immelmann's interrupter gear malfunctioned, resulting in his machine gun shooting off his own propeller blades. Norman L.R. Franks suggests that McCubbin and Waller were attempting to save a machine being shot up by Immelmann when his aircraft went down.[400] For propaganda purposes it was essential to award the claim to the RFC, and so McCubbin and Waller were awarded the DSO and DCM respectively. It is therefore clear that Grattan-Bellew's colleagues in No.25 Squadron were experienced pilots and battle-hardened observer/gunners. It is therefore difficult to award both crashed Fokkers to Grattan-Bellew.

Grattan-Bellew was promoted from Flight Commander (i.e. Captain) to Squadron Commander (i.e. Major) with effect from 05 September 1916. He took command of No.29 Squadron. Numerous claims are made of Grattan-Bellew's months with No.29 Squadron, but as Officer Commanding he would not have had even a fraction of the combat opportunities attributed to him.

On 21 March 1917 Grattan-Bellew was delivering a D.H.2 to an aircraft depot in exchange for a Nieuport when his engine failed. He crashed, suffering severe injuries. His left leg was amputated and his

---

[400] The F.E.2 in question was flown by a pilot of Irish ancestry, Lt John Raymond Boscawen Savage, who was killed and his observer, TNU Robinson, taken POW.

right leg was fractured. Three days later Grattan-Bellew died. Several months later a mention in despatches was gazetted in respect of Grattan-Bellew, on 01 June 1917.

McCudden, in *Five Years in the Royal Flying Corps*, attributes Grattan-Bellew's actions as helping save his life in January 1917 through sidetracking a Fokker when McCudden suffered engine trouble and propeller damage due to spent cartridges falling into it during combat. On 02 February 1917 McCudden and Grattan-Bellew shared the destruction of a German two-seater. McCudden's account is as follows:

"I was leading my patrol over Monchy-au-Bois at about 11,000 feet and saw a Hun two-seater flying towards the lines at about 3,000 feet. We dived and caught up with the Hun, who at once turned off east.

I opened fire at about 200 yards range, and had closed to about 100 yards when I almost collided with another D.H.2 on my left who was also firing at the Hun, so I had to turn away from the target to avoid a collision. I made up my mind to strafe the pilot of the other D.H.2 when I got home for nearly colliding with me, but when I landed I found the other pilot was Major Grattan-Bellew, who had joined in the patrol, so I at once forgot the strafing.

The Hun went down and crashed, and was credited between Major Bellew and me, although I am positive that the C.O. got the Hun".[401]

RFC Communiqué No.73 of 1917 reports this as a shared "out of control" victory for McCudden and Grattan-Bellew.

McCudden also said "I was very sorry to leave 29 Squadron and all the good fellows it contained, and was most of all sorry to bid adieu to my O.C., Major Grattan-Bellew, one of the very best C.O.s that it has ever been my good fortune to serve under". Charles G. Grey, the editor of *Aeroplane* somewhat dramatically opined in the footnotes to McCudden's book that "Major Grattan-Bellew was one of the most gallant pilots and best beloved commanding officers in

---

[401] *Flying Fury: Five Years in the Royal Flying Corps*, p.126 (Casemate reprint, 2009).

the RAF. He was another splendid example of the fighting Irishman, and his death in an accident was as a great calamity to the Corps as Major McCudden's".

In recent years Grattan-Bellew's gallantry awards and service medals were available at auction from Fraser Medals of Ontario, but no additional documentary evidence is disclosed in relation to any claims to him being an ace.

As one may note from the foregoing I have no evidence that Grattan-Bellew achieved any aerial victories with No.16 Squadron and have a number of incidents with No.25 Squadron that could amount to no more than 3 plausible claims on any realistic reading of the material. Further, there is only one confirmed claim relating to Grattan-Bellew's time with No.29 Squadron. Accordingly I believe his downwards adjusted score of four aerial victories to be correct and that Grattan-Bellew was not an ace.

✦ ✦ ✦

HARVEY-KELLY, HUBERT DUNSTERVILLE "BAY"

(**3 or 4 aerial victories**)

Born: 09 February 1891, Teignmouth, Devon, UK

Died: 29 April 1917

Awards: Distinguished Service Order, Mentioned in Despatches (08 October 1914, 30 April 1916 and 09 April 1917).

Commemorated: Brown's Copse Cemetery, Roeux, France

Religion: Anglican

Major Harvey-Kelly was one of those flamboyant individuals about whom many apocryphal tales have hung, but there is a grain of truth in at least some of them.

The Harvey-Kelly family are generally associated with Co Roscommon and Co Westmeath. On his mother's side of the family, his mother was Constance Harvey-Kelly (b.1855, Hyderabad, India) and his grandfather was Lt General Lionel D'Arcy Dunsterville (b.1831, Bombay, India). His father was Colonel Harvey Hamilton Harvey-Kelly, who was the son of Robert Hume Vandeleur Kelly (who served in the Royal Field Artillery) and grandson of Robert Vandeleur Kelly, Justice of the Peace for Co Westmeath and Lieutenant-Colonel of the New South Wales Army Medical Corps and of Grouse Lodge, Moate, Co Westmeath. (It is now a well known music recording studio). Hubert's father died in Madras, India on 13 March 1903. The Vandeleur branch of the Harvey-Kelly family still owned lands near Wardenstown, Co Westmeath at this time.

Hubert's eldest brother, Harvey St George Hume Harvey-Kelly, served in World War I and World War II, ultimately at the rank of Lieutenant-Colonel, retiring to Ireland in the 1950s. He married Ellen Louisa Stephenson in India on 23 December 1914. Hubert's other brothers, Charles and Gilbert, both also served in the military, Gilbert in World War I. During the war Gilbert Isdell Harvey-Kelly married Rosamund Gertrude Nuttall, the daughter of a wealthy Lancashire businessman, in Bombay on 30 December 1914, but they eventually also returned to Ireland and lived near Mullingar, Co Westmeath. To the best of my knowledge Charles Hamilton Grant Hume Harvey-Kelly (b.15 June 1885, India) served in the pre-war years with the Indian Army but I do not have a corresponding wartime service record for him.

From the several generations of military service on both sides of the family, it would be expected that Hubert would be born in a military environment. However, he was actually born in Teignmouth, Devon, but his family's links to Australia, India and Ireland would have allowed Hubert to declare any nationality he wished among these. On 24 September 1893 Colonel Harvey-Kelly, his wife and two of his children travelled on the *Clan MacPherson* from Liverpool to Madras, destined for Calcutta. It's most likely that one of the two unnamed children was Hubert, as by this stage the older two brothers would be of school-going age.

In the UK Census 1901 Hubert was recorded as being at the house of his widowed aunt, Leonora Howard-Vyse at Welton Cottage, Daventry, Northamptonshire. His birthplace is recorded as Totnes, Devon.

Hubert joined the Royal Irish Regiment in October 1910. In the UK Census 1911 he is recorded as being based at Fort George, Guernsey, Channel Islands. Harvey-Kelly was a 2nd Lieutenant with the 2nd Battalion of the Royal Irish Regiment. In the UK Census 1911 his mother was resident in Dulwich with Hubert's brother Charles. His mother Constance is described as being a widow, as was his grandfather Lt-General Lionel D'Arcy Dunsterville. Hubert's brother Charles is described as being a Lieutenant in the Indian Army and was born in India.

Hubert transferred from the Royal Irish Regiment to the Royal Flying Corps in 1913. Upon joining the Royal Flying Corps he was assigned to No.2 Squadron. As one may gather, however, there were only a handful of squadrons in existence at this point in time. Harvey-Kelly was awarded Royal Aero Club Certificate No.501 on 30 May 1913.

On 26 January 1914 Harvey-Kelly, with a Captain Dawes, took delivery of a Maurice Farman 214 from the factory at Aldershot to fly to Montrose, Scotland. According to an article in *Cross and Cockade (International)* in Winter 1992, it is suggested that they encountered mechanical failure and had to land at York. A further attempt to reach Montrose saw them forced to land near Whitley Bay on 02 February 1914. After at least one further forced landing they reached Montrose but the Maurice Farman was left behind when the squadron went to war!

The diaries of General Lionel Dunsterville have been made publicly available online through the Great War Primary Documents Archive. The entry for 20 March 1914 noted that "Bay, Connie's fourth son in the Royal Irish Regt. arrived yesterday from Montrose to which place he had just flown his aeroplane from Aldershot". Similarly, the entry for 28 May 1914 indicates that the general took an interest in the aerial achievements of "Bay" Harvey-Kelly, noting that his aero squadron was leaving for Aldershot.

However, the entry for 01 July 1914 reads as follows:

"I am now numbered among those few individuals who have flown in the air! Bay arrived and took me for a splendid flight all over the country about half an hour, sensation splendid, but you feel death at your elbow. No notion of sickness or giddiness. As I had implicit confidence in my pilot Hubert Harvey-Kelly, my gallant nephew, it was just unalloyed pleasure to me. One of the eventful days of my life".

Quite how "Bay" would have been authorised to take the general on an aerial excursion remains a mystery but is entirely consistent with the tales surrounding Harvey-Kelly.[402]

---

402 Harvey-Kelly's uncle, Major-General Lionel Charles Dunsterville, was to command British forces in the battles between Baghdad and Baku during the

Lord Douglas of Kirtleside (aka 'Sholto' Douglas) served with No.2 Squadron. In his autobiography *Years of Combat* his impressions of Harvey-Kelly are recorded:

"But the outstanding pilot in the squadron was undoubtedly H.D. Harvey-Kelly. With fair hair topping a rubicund complexion, he was one of the most likeable men, and he was already famous for his great sense of humour and his lighthearted and gay approach towards everything that he ever did. Even in the zestful company of the Flying Corps he was a noted individualist".[403]

In August 1914 Harvey-Kelly flew a B.E.2 from Montrose, Scotland to France. However, two other Irishmen contest the feat of being the first Royal Flying Corps aircraft to reach France, e.g. Francis Fitzgerald Waldron of Co Kildare and Charles James Burke of Co Armagh. As none of the three men survived the war there is a tendency for some aviation historians towards diplomacy and cite the relevant French aerodromes to which these three men first reached. Burke was the squadron commander and is generally recorded as being furious with Harvey-Kelly for reaching France first. Air Vice-Marshal Sefton Brancker suggests that Harvey-Kelly ignored an instruction from Burke for the squadron to navigate via the French coast and then follow the Somme to Amiens, and that instead Harvey-Kelly flew cross-country from Boulogne to Amiens. Walter Raleigh, in his lengthy volumes on the early years of the RAF, states that "the first machine of No. 2 Squadron to start left at 6.25 a.m., and the first to arrive landed at Amiens at 8.20 a.m. This machine was flown by Lieutenant H. D. Harvey-Kelly, one of the lightest hearted and highest spirited of the young pilots who gave their lives in the war".[404]

On 26 August 1914 Harvey-Kelly gained the first Royal Flying Corps aerial victory. He led three B.E.2s in hunting down a German

---

1918-1920 period. *The Adventures of Dunsterforce* (London: Edward Arnold, 1920) does not mention his nephew.
403 Quoted in O'Connor, Mike *Airfields and Airmen: Somme* (Pen & Sword, 2002), p.56.
404 Raleigh, Walter *The War in the Air; Being the Story of the Part Played in the Great War by the Royal Air Force, Volume I* (Oxford University Press, 1922), p.286

Taube 2 reconnaissance plane. With a combination of aggressive flying and Harvey-Kelly's pistol they forced it to land, whereupon Harvey-Kelly landed beside the Taube and set it alight as the hapless crew fled. There are several competing accounts of similar aerial victories but it would appear that Harvey-Kelly and his observer Lt WHC Mansfield can legitimately claim the first victory. (Mansfield was to later serve on Home Defence duties against the Zeppelin raids and was to later reach the rank of Lieutenant Colonel. He always vouched for the account of Harvey-Kelly's piloting skills in the encounter).

General Dunsterville's diary of 18 September 1915 indicates that, unlike many other generals, he travelled close to the frontline positions. However, there is an air of unreality about the situation, collecting acorns whilst the hundreds of wounded are passing through:

"Nobody can say I have not been within sound of the guns! Train pulled up in doubt this morning at 5.30 a.m. outside Fere Entardenois, all Supply lorries and vehicles halted on road and an appalling thunder of big guns – must be a huge battle in progress and sounds like our left being turned, but I prefer to hope it is the German right. They are all concentrated between Laon and Reims and we ought to get them in the end, but they are very strong on the line of the river Aisne. Arrived 6.45 a.m. Our wounded pour in looking ghastly. Collected 2 acorns from a very pretty wood near here because I think this will be a historic battle and the oaks in England may commemorate it. Walked around the country and found the Aeroplane H.Q. After a bit Bay came down out of the sky and we passed the time of day. He was looking well and cheery. Col. Mackinnis R.E. is railhead officer here and General French is here. Left at 4 p.m. to go at last beyond railhead to Braisne which is really on the battlefield to pick up wounded. Arrived 6.30 p.m. just behind the firing line. Everything later in pitch darkness as all the gear, telegraph lines etc., has been destroyed by the Germans. It was rather weird in the dark at night with the constant booming of the guns. Took in 296 wounded. Left at 10.15 p.m. How soon one gets accustomed to big figures like

300 wounded – seems a very small affair. The hospital at Braisne have sent down 1,120 in these last 24 hours."

At least "Bay" Harvey-Kelly was still cheery: by this stage the RFC had suffered seven fatalities and dozens wounded. On 23 September 1914 the general once again made a point of visiting "Bay", who was based at Fére en Tardenois, with Harvey-Kelly coming to the general's carriage for lunch.

On 09 December 1914 Harvey-Kelly's mention in despatches was gazetted in respect of actions of 08 October 1914. More significantly, he was awarded the Distinguished Service Order, which was gazetted on 18 February 1915 and 24 March 1915. Gallingly for Lieutenant-Colonel Burke, who also had been awarded the DSO at his time, both notices were published together.

From these early months of the air war there were only a handful of squadrons operational, and perhaps no more than a hundred enemy aircraft at this area of the Western Front. Accordingly, the haphazard nature of recording aerial encounters would often entail the use of terms "driven down" or "driven off". The emphasis was upon preventing the enemy from interfering with one's work or preventing the enemy from remaining in the vicinity to conduct its own aerial reconnaissance or artillery ranging work. Accordingly it is difficult to classify aerial victories as being the equivalent of those later in the war, when aircraft were armed and tasked with aerial interdiction duties.

On 17 March 1915 Harvey-Kelly was appointed temporary Captain (Flight Commander, which was gazetted on 26 March 1915. On 26 May 1915 Harvey-Kelly was appointed substantive rank of Captain, which was gazetted on 19 June 1915. According to his service records[405], Harvey-Kelly was transferred to No.4 Reserve Aeroplane Squadron on 12 July 1915. However, from the material available I have only one confirmed aerial victory for Harvey-Kelly, i.e. that of 26 August 1914.

On 19 August 1915 Harvey-Kelly was transferred to No.18 Squadron. Subsequently he was posted to No.14 Squadron on 12 October 1915, which was based at Gosport.

---

405   AIR 76/270 HD Harvey-Kelly, UK National Archives.

HARVEY-KELLY, HUBERT DUNSTERVILLE "BAY"

Harvey-Kelly entered France with No.3 Squadron as Flight Commander. The squadron were flying the Morane Parasol. (Cecil Lewis, author of *Sagittarius Rising*, gives a useful account of the reconnaissance role using the type). One young mechanic making his way up the ranks was James McCudden. In his autobiography his main reference to Harvey-Kelly occurs in the context of the troublesome nature of the spark plugs in his Morane parasol. However, McCudden also mentions having to act as observer to Harvey-Kelly as part of his selection test to qualify for the role. (Harvey-Kelly approved McCudden for observer training). The squadron had a number of notable pilots but Harvey-Kelly seems to have made an impression with several others. Robert Raymond Money was a colleague of Harvey-Kelly but was shot down in 1916 and taken POW. His autobiography, *Flying and Soldiering* (Nicholson & Watson Ltd, 1936), has this to say of Harvey-Kelly:

"Morane squadrons specialized in Flight-Commanders who were full of character; Harvey-Kelly was one: he had a custom of spitting over the side of his machine if a burst of Archie made very near, and one day he returned because, he said, he had no spit left. He went on leave from France on one occasion, and was told to report to London Headquarters at the expiration of his leave. He did not turn up, so a kindly Staff sent him orders by post. He did not acknowledge these, nor did he report for duty; so the kind Staff, rather worried, sent someone else in his place and posted fresh orders to Harvey-Kelly. For three weeks they tried to find him, and telegrams and orders were waiting for him in every well-known hotel and bar in London. Eventually he turned up at the War Office one day in a highly aggrieved state, and flung a handful of contradictory telegrams and letters on the table, asking how in the name of O'Brien Óg could he go to all of those places at once, and anyway, he was fed up with England and wanted to go back to the war. They let him.

He lived to command a Squadron and to be killed in the air, and I have always been of the opinion that he was one of the "mad Majors" whose doings became almost mythical among the infantry".[406]

---

[406] Quoted in O'Connor, Mike *Airfields and Airmen: Arras* (Pen and Sword, 2004), p.72.

On 20 January 1916 Harvey-Kelly was promoted from Flight Commander to Squadron Commander, i.e. from Captain to Major, which was gazetted on 08 February 1916. In October 1916 Harvey-Kelly was posted to 1 Reserve Squadron but by December 1916 had been posted to No.56 Squadron. This was a short-term posting, however, and he was sent to the School of Aerial Gunnery in January 1917.

On 01 February 1917 Harvey-Kelly returned to France in command of No.19 Squadron. Jon Guttman's *SPAD VII vs Albatros D III: 1917-1918* (London: Osprey, 2011), p. 57 and his *SPAD VII Aces of World War I* (London: Osprey, 2001) pp.41-42, mentions some of Harvey-Kelly's aerial encounters during his months in command of No.19 Squadron.

On 17 March 1917 attacked a two-seater and an Albatros scout. Harvey-Kelly opened fire at about 200 feet but the Vickers gun jammed. Less than an hour later Harvey-Kelly attacked another Albatros but the gun jammed again and could not be freed. It is therefore clear that Harvey-Kelly did not open the squadron's account.

On 23 April 1917 Harvey-Kelly attacked an Albatros over Graincourt and after firing 50-60 rounds at a range of 50 yards, reported that it crash-landed about a mile from Cambrai. This incident is mentioned in RFC Communiqué No.85 of 1917. In the Squadron Operations Record Book for No.19 Squadron[407] it is also recorded that Harvey-Kelly and Lt J.M. Child both accounted for enemy aircraft that day. On 24 April 1917 Harvey-Kelly is credited with the destruction of another Albatros.

On 29 April 1917 Harvey-Kelly led a two-aircraft flight on an interception mission. There were only a handful of operational SPAD VIIs available to the squadron and, as a Squadron Commander, Harvey-Kelly should not actually have been conducting normal pilot duties in offensive operations. Nevertheless Harvey-Kelly and Lt William Norman Hamilton took off, being joined later by 2nd Lt Applin, who was an inexperienced pilot. They encountered eighteen aircraft

---

407 AIR 27/252, p.5, UK National Archives.

of Richthofen's circus. Both Manfred and Lothar were in the circus that day. Most accounts suggest that Harvey-Kelly was shot down by Kurt Wolff of Jasta 11. As may be recalled from Part I, Wolff was a highly successful ace, who had shot down David Mary Tidmarsh on 11 April 1917.

Floyd Gibbons' *Red Knight of Germany* (1927) gives Hamilton's account of events (pp.242-243) in which he claims that six RNAS Sopwith triplanes were in the vicinity but sheered off, leaving the three SPADs to their fate. It would appear that Richthofen shot down Applin. However Hamilton says "I carried out my original plan of attacking the centre machine, noticing, as I did so that Harvey-Kelly had apparently accounted for two Huns and was pretty busy with four or five more".

Hamilton's gun jammed and in a running fight he was brought down and taken POW. According to Gibbons' book Hamilton is attributed the following quote:

"I heard later that Applin was dead and that Harvey-Kelly died in a hospital three days later from head wounds. I also understand, but could never get authentic confirmation, that Harvey-Kelley and myself accounted for five of the Huns before we were shot down. Applin, of course, was killed before he could fire a shot".[408]

This is the point of contention as to the likelihood or otherwise of the Germans losing any, let alone that many, of Richthofen's circus in the circumstances described. Although Gibbons is often characterized as a "headline hunter" he was also a responsible war correspondent from Chicago, who lost an eye in World War I. His collection of the various accounts cannot be simply consigned to the category of 'hell in the heavens' melodramatic military fiction. On the other hand the loss of three RFC SPADs could well influence a "you should have seen the other guy" mindset and so Hamilton may simply have believed what he wanted to see, i.e. five enemy fall in the encounter. The German records do not have any corresponding matches for that level of claimed losses, though this does not preclude

---

408 Floyd Gibbons *Red Knight of Germany* (Doubleday,1927), p.244.

German aircraft being damaged in the encounter. Harvey-Kelly's death is briefly mentioned by Franks and Giblin in *Under the Guns of the German Aces* (London: Grub Street, 1997), p.174, but it is more about Wolff than his victims.

Maurice Baring was the eighth child of Baron Revelstoke, of the Baring banking family, and the author of numerous books. In World War I Baring served as the aide to General 'Boom' Trenchard, and describes their visit to RFC squadrons on 29 April 1917:

"We went to Vert Galand to see Harvey-Kelly, who commands No.19 Squadron. When we got there we were told he had gone up by himself and one other pilot for a short patrol. We stayed there all the morning. By luncheon time he had not come back. He was due and overdue. When we went away the General said "Tell Harvey-Kelly I was sorry to miss him", but I knew quite well from the sound of his voice he did not expect this message would ever be delivered. Nor did I".[409]

Flight magazine of 10 May 1917 and 05 July 1917 contained a cursory obituary to Harvey-Kelly, as did the *Irish Times* of 05 July 1917, which suggests that at the time his fame (notoriety) was not as great as it was to later become in the post-war years, perhaps when men were no longer in uniform and so could recount freely the various tall tales of Harvey-Kelly's life. Indeed the sombre McCudden memoir was published before his death and is devoid of any scandalous comment on any of the officers under which McCudden served.

One strange situation, however, is that we are to believe that between his aerial victories in August 1914 and April 1917 Harvey-Kelly did not add a single further claim, despite being mentioned in despatches on several occasions and winning the DSO. However, I am inclined to believe that, regardless of the outcome of his final combat, Harvey-Kelly may well have been an ace but for the pur-

---

[409] Baring, Michael *Flying Corps Headquarters 1914-1918* (London 1920). Quoted in O'Connor Mike *Airfields and Airmen: Somme* (Pen & Sword, 2002), p.57.

HARVEY-KELLY, HUBERT DUNSTERVILLE "BAY"

poses of this book I cannot include him as anything more than an unconfirmed ace.

Hubert's next-of-kin address on 30 April 1917 was that of his mother, at Barham Lodge, Buckinghamshire. Harvey-Kelly's B.E.2 hangs in the Imperial War Museum in London.

✦ ✦ ✦

MULHOLLAND, DENIS OSMOND

(**3 aerial victories**)

Born: 06 September 1892, Donaghadee, Co Down

Died: 12 April 1949

Awards: Air Force Cross (1919), Mentioned in Despatches (1937), CBE (1943)

Religion: Presbyterian

Also: George Philip Mulholland (2 aerial victories)

Wing Commander Denis Osmond Mullholland was an early war pilot of some renown. However, it is unlikely that he reached ace status.

Denis was the son of James Henry Mullholland and Jeannie Mulholland of Strathclyde, Donaghadee, Co Down. Denis' father was English and his mother Irish. The Irish Census 1901 records the family as being resident at New Street, Ballycross, Co Down. Denis' parents are present, as are his two sisters and his three brothers.

Denis' brother, George Philip Mulholland, (born 04 January 1898) was also to serve as a Flying Officer in World War I. Most of the boys in the family were educated at Campbell College, Belfast.

In the UK Census 1911 there is a Denis Mulholland stationed on board the HMS Gloucester as an ordinary seaman, but that individual was from Co Cork.

Mulholland actually joined the Connaught Rangers and served with the 4th Battalion from 07 November 1914.[410] It is implied that he may have been an O.T.C. cadet. On 24 November 1915 Mulholland was awarded Royal Aero Club Certificate No.2111, graduating on a Maurice Farman biplane at the Military School, Farnborough. On his aviator's certificate index card the next-of-kin address is recorded as Strathclyde, Donaghadee, Co Down.

On 25 February 1916 Mulholland was seconded from the Connaught Rangers to the Royal Flying Corps as a Flying Officer (2nd Lieutenant). On 10 August 1916 Mulholland was promoted temporary Lieutenant with the Royal Flying Corps, with effect from 01 June 1916. However, days later it was reported that Mulholland had been promoted to Flight Commander (temporary Captain) with effect from 25 July 1916.[411]

Mulholland served with No.40 Squadron in its early years, when the squadron was equipped with 'pusher' aircraft. No.40 Squadron's "Combats in the Air" submissions contain a number of aerial combats involving Mulholland. On 22 September 1916, at 8.20 am, Captain D.O. Mulholland was flying F.E.8 (6384) on escort duties at 14,000 feet when they saw an F.E.2b being attacked by a Fokker at about 6,000 feet. However, the Fokker dived, apparently having been hit by the gunfire of the F.E.2b. Mulholland fired a continuous burst, emptying half a drum into the Fokker as it went into a spinning nosedive. The Fokker crashed in a field west of Douai. RFC Communiqué No.55 of 1916 also confirms this as an aerial victory for Mulholland. On 20 October 1916 Mulholland, flying an F.E.8, shared 3 aerial victories with another pilot of 40 Squadron (2nd Lieutenant EL Benbow) and a two-seater of No.25 Squadron crewed by 2nd Lieutenant ESP Hynes and Sapper LN Smith. This was mentioned in RFC Communiqués No.58 and 59 of 1916.

---

410 London Gazette Supplements of 06 November 1914 (Issue 28965, p.9024) and 24 April 1915 (Issue 29141, p.4042) both confirm this appointment with various qualifications.
411 London Gazette Supplements of 10 August 1916 (Issue 29702, p.7896) and 12 August 1916 (Issue 29705, p.7978).

MULHOLLAND, DENIS OSMOND

RFC Communiqué No.65 of 1916 records the following incident on 04 December 1916:

"Captain D.O. Mulholland and Lt E.L. Benbow, 40 Sqn, when on patrol, saw three hostile aeroplanes manoeuvring for position to attack a B.E.2c. Capt Mulholland attacked and destroyed one of the German machines. Lt Benbow got to within 50 feet of a second and fired twenty rounds. The hostile machine turned over and fell to earth in a slow spinning nose dive".[412]

This is the last wartime aerial victory I can locate that is attributed to Mulholland.

According to Gale K. Larson[413] it would appear that in February 1917 Mulholland was one of the cast in G.B. Shaw's debut performance of *O'Flaherty VC*. Mulholland was known as "Little Mull" and would have been quite a comical contrast to the tall, angular de Burgh. According to various Gregory family legends it was Mulholland, also a Connaught Rangers officer, who was responsible for Robert getting promotion in the RFC.

It would appear that some of the potential confusion in relation to a Mulholland being regarded as an ace might have arisen between Denis and his brother, George Philip (or "Philip George" in his RFC personnel records), who served with a number of squadrons. However, they are clearly identifiable as distinct records on the RFC subsection of the Army lists. On the other hand, with the same next-of-kin address and with the younger brother moving through a number of squadrons there is nevertheless the potential for the Mulholland brothers' aerial victories to be the subject of some misunderstandings. For the record George trained at Oxford with 27 Reserve Squadron, later with 55 Training Squadron at Yatesbury, entering France with No.28 Squadron. RFC Communiqué No.110 of 1917 records that on 20 October 1917 2nd Lieutenant PG Mulholland, flying a Sopwith Camel, was one of four pilots with No.28 Squadron to shoot down

---

412 Cole, Christopher (ed) *Royal Flying Corps Communiqués 1915-1916* (London: Tom Donovan Publishing, 1990), p.325.
413 Larson, Gale K *Shaw and History – the Annual of G.B. Shaw Studies* (Penn State Press, 1999), p.91, also p.96 passim.

an enemy aircraft that day, all of which either broke up in the air or were seen to crash. There's a further Mulholland aerial victory on the Italian front, shared between Lt Arthur Jarvis (B2303), Lt PG Mulholland (B5183) and Lt OW Frayne (B6345) of No.28 Squadron, and either Silvio Scaroni or Antonio Riva of 76a *Squadriglia*. This incident occurred on 26 December 1917 near Camalo, as part of the "Air Battle of Istrana" in which the Germans suffered heavy losses on the Italian front. There are conflicting accounts of what transpired on that day: apparently an RAF bomber made an authorised raid on the German aerodrome on Christmas Day, violating an unofficial truce. In retaliation the Germans sent two waves of bombers the next day, nearly all of which were shot down or crashed, the vast majority being accounted for by the Italian aircraft defending the base. Many of the German POWs were apparently still quite drunk or hungover. (On the other hand some British accounts cite the death of Sergeant Charles William Henry Roberts on 26 December 1917 from a previous day's bombing by the Germans as the basis for the tit-for-tat bombings that gave rise to the heavy German losses).

George Mulholland was to transfer to the No.2 Flying School in July 1918 as an instructor on the Sopwith Camel. He was transferred to No.50 Squadron and later No.143 Squadron for the remainder of the war. In the post-war era he served as Vice Chairman of the 28 Squadron Old Boys' Association.

It would therefore appear that between the two brothers there were only 5 confirmed aerial victories.

On 16 July 1918 Denis was promoted from Captain to Major. On 03 June 1919 it was announced that Captain (Acting Major) Denis Osmond Mulholland had been awarded the Air Force Cross.[414]

On 16 September 1919 the Air Ministry announced that Mulholland had been granted a short-service commission as a Flight Lieutenant. However, on 14 November 1919 it was announced that Mulholland was among a number of officers who had their short service commissions cancelled.

---

414 London Gazette Supplement, Gazette Issue 31378, p.7034.

However, the RAF retained Mulholland as a Flight Lieutenant and he served with No.100 Squadron until 21 April 1922, when he was posted to Iraq. Mulholland had to serve in a ground-based capacity for a number of months in the Middle East, being transferred from HQ, Iraq Command, to No.5 Armoured Car Company (Iraq Command) for duty as Adjutant with effect from 03 November 1922.

On 03 July 1923 the Air Ministry announced that Mulholland had been promoted from Flight Lieutenant to Squadron Leader.[415] However, he did not remain in frontline service for long: on 16 July 1925 Mulholland was appointed to the Cadet College, Cranwell as an instructor.

Mulholland served with No.16 Squadron from 1928 to 1931 as Squadron Leader. He was appointed to the squadron on 25 September 1928, at which time they were based at Old Sarum.

On 13 June 1929 his engagement to Felice was announced. Felice Grant McIntyre was Scottish, originally from Glasgow. Felice Grant married a Belfast man, W Herbert McConnell, of Dundesart, Belfast.

On 01 September 1931 Mulholland was transferred from No.16 Squadron to Station HQ, RAF Manston. In the interwar upheavals it is difficult to track Mulholland's career, as his brother had by this stage upstaged him, but on 23 July 1937 Mulholland was among those Mentioned in Despatches for actions undertaken in Palestine during the period April to October 1936.[416]

On 06 October 1937 Mulholland was posted to Air Staff HQ of the RAF Middle East, which was based at Cairo, Egypt. Mulholland, still a Squadron Leader, was to serve on Air Staff duties.

According to the passenger lists of the *Derbyshire*, Denis Osmond and Felice Grant Mulholland arrived on 20 June 1938 in London from Rangoon, Burma. Their address was given as Brunswick Square, Hove, Sussex. Denis is described as being an RAF officer and

---

415 London Gazette, Issue 32841, p.4621.
416 London Gazette, Issue 34420, p.4742.

that his last permanent address was Egypt. On 01 November 1938 Mulholland was promoted from Squadron Leader to Wing Commander:

On 10 June 1943 Flight magazine carried notice of Group Captain Mulholland being conferred with the Commander of the British Empire in the King's Birthday Honours List.[417] :

He died on 12 April 1949. The address of his widow, Felice Grant Mulholland, is given as The Lodge, California Lane, Bushey Heath, Hertfordshire. Mulholland's effects were worth £4,589 17s. 7d.

✦ ✦ ✦

---

417 *Flight*, 10 June 1943, p.611.

ORR, JOHN RICHARD

(2 to 6 aerial victories)

Born: 15 January 1892, Co Down

Died: 09 August 1918

Commemorated: Beacon Cemetery, Sailly-Laurette, Somme, France.

Religion: Church of Ireland

John Richard Orr was born in Downpatrick, Co Down. In both his service records and his medal card his next of kin address is given as Samuel Orr, Justice of the Peace, and Mary Jane Orr, of Ballyrenan, Downpatrick, Co Down.

Orr enlisted in Canada. His attestation papers state that he was a bank clerk who had previous service with the 30th Simcoe Foresters. The Simcoe Foresters were to form the core of the 157th and 177th Battalions of the Canadian Expeditionary Force. He was certified fit for overseas service on 04 April 1916. Orr served with the 177th Battalion of the Canadian Infantry at the rank of Lieutenant.

Initially Orr served with No.94 Squadron before being posted to No.80 Squadron.

Because Orr's service in the RAF was towards the end of the war there is a difficulty in tracing all aerial victories accorded to him: by this stage the RAF Communiqués had dispensed with reporting 'out of control' aerial victories, although they still featured in each squadron's air combat reports and were still attributed to individual pilots. Accordingly I have only two certain aerial victories recorded in respect of Orr, although it is likely that his score is somewhat higher.

On 18 July 1918 Lt JR Orr crashed a 2-seater in French Lines at Buission de Hauthisson. The occupants survived: Ltn. P Barber and Uffz G Ellert of Schlasta 20 were taken PoW on this day.

On 30 July 1918 Orr was involved in a large-scale dogfight near Fismes, initially taking on 7 Fokkers, which were subsequently reinforced with a further flight of 3 aircraft. Orr sent one down out of control, whilst Captain Whilster accounted for two of the Fokkers – one apparently smoking – and the former Royal Dublin Fusilier Lt L.D. Baker sent down another.

On 08 August 1918 Orr was shot down by ground fire. He was flying a Sopwith Camel (D4425) on a low bombing mission near Etinegem supporting III Corps advance. The Camel was not a suitable aircraft for ground attack duties, as it had no armour and was vulnerable to ground fire. An initial attempt to convert it to this role had seen a TF1 ("Trench Fighter" 1) being prototyped but this led to the development of the Sopwith Salamander from the Sopwith Snipe. The Camel was not the appropriate aircraft for the role deployed, but the pressures of war saw many good fighter pilots squandered on ground-attack duties which their aircraft could not perform.

He was initially reported as missing on 08 August 1918, and as killed on 09 August 1918. Perhaps because he was killed and buried by the Germans, on the Commonwealth War Graves Commission website his death is erroneously recorded as being with the Canadian Infantry. The Amiens offensive began on 08 August 1918, and this particular part of the front involved a large number of Australian and Canadian units, hence the likelihood of Orr being misclassified as having been killed in the Northern sector offensive, which stretched from Morlancourt to La Neuville.

Orr's death receives a passing mention from Lt Victor Maslin Yeates, the author of the disillusioned and disenchanted war novel/autobiography, *Winged Victory* (1934). Given that Yeates alternates between accounts of combat in the Sopwith Camel with fiction is it often difficult to credit specific historical events as having been accurately portrayed but Yeates described the situation as follows:

"It had been impossible lately with all the casualties to have days off; to take a lot of raw pilots among the Fokkers would be murder; the experienced men had to stick to it. The squadron would have to be rested soon or go back north, else the experienced men would be dead or gibbering. Yet they had only been ten days on the Somme front. The horrors of ground-strafing, of continually fighting machines by which they were altogether outclassed, had made this time as wearing a time as the previous three months."

Yeates, who had spent most of the war with No.46 Squadron, left No.80 Squadron on 31 August 1918.

However, the Canadian Bank of Commerce, in their publication ***Letters from the front. Being a record of the part played by officers of the Bank in the great war, 1914-1919 (Volume 2)***, actually refers to Orr in the following terms:

"+Orr, John Richard — Lieutenant. Born 10th January 1892, at Downpatrick, County Down, Ireland. Father, Samuel Orr, J.P., Farmer. Educated at Ballyculter National School and Skerry's Academy, Ireland. Entered the service of the Bank, 27th May, 1911. Enlisted, June, 1916, from Hamilton branch, in 177th Canadian Battalion, with the rank of Lieutenant. Transferred to Royal Flying Corps, June, 1917. Service: With 80th Squadron, Royal Air Force in France, from January to August, 1918.

Killed in Action, near Amiens, 9th August, 1918.

Note: Lieutenant Orr succeeded in bringing down six enemy machines, and, according to a letter from his Squadron Commander, was recommended for promotion and decoration on the morning of his death, for his work during the German Offensive in the Spring of 1918.

"He was one of my most gallant and reliable officers, and loved by everybody. His loss to the Air Force and to the older officers is a heavy one; he was always so bright and so cheery. He was shot from the ground, and must have been killed instantly, as he came down out of control and crashed. He was too good a pilot to lose control unless unconscious. His wrecked machine is still on the other side of the lines. I had hoped to get him a decoration before long in recognition of his splendid work, but now his only reward is a gap which cannot be filled in the hearts of all of us."

— His Squadron Commander."

The foregoing suggests that No.80 Squadron regarded Orr as having accounted for six German aircraft. On the other hand I have examined similar volumes relating to Bank of Ireland and Guinness; there are often a number of erroneous entries. However, when there is a suggestion that his squadron commander "had hoped to get him a decoration" it is quite likely that the requisite number of aerial victories had been reached for the award of the Military Cross or Distinguished Flying Cross.

It is known, however, that three pilots with the surname Orr achieved well over a dozen aerial victories between them, all of the three flying the Sopwith Camel for the majority of their aerial victories. Two of these men enlisted via Canada (the Irishman John Richard and the American Osborne John Orr). Another potential point of confusion lies in the fact that two of the three were killed in August 1918 (Robert Sefton Scott Orr and John Richard Orr).

Robert Seton Scott Orr served with No 201 Sqn RAF and claimed six victories between 16 May 1918 and 01 August 1918; he was killed in action on 08 August 1918 in a Sopwith Camel (D9645). As noted earlier John Richard Orr was killed in action on 08 August 1918 in a Sopwith Camel (D9429). Osborne John Orr (DFC) served with No 204 Sqn RAF and claimed five victories between 12 August 1918 and 14 October 1918; he was killed in action on 23 October 1918 in a Sopwith Camel (D9613).

According to the Squadron Operations Record Book, No.80 (Fighter) Squadron was primarily engaged in ground strafing operations and low-level bombing raids. It had originally been envisaged as a fighter squadron but was switched to ground attack duties as part of the "backs to the wall" period of halting the German advance. Sopwith Camels were unsuited to ground attack duties. The squadron claimed 21 enemy aircraft destroyed, and 29 aircraft and 2 balloons driven down out of control. The kill: loss ratio was not a positive one, however, as they lost 34 killed/missing, 13 POW and 16 wounded.

On 01 February 1920 the squadron was renumbered 56 Squadron as its remnants were merged into that squadron. The only confirmed ace with No.80 Squadron was Group Captain Harold Alfred Whistler, who accounted for 23 of their 52 aerial victories.

In the light of all the foregoing I am inclined to disregard the Canadian Bank of Commerce account of six aerial victories for Orr. I do not entirely discount the possibility that he reached ace status but I do not have sufficient evidence to hand to support such a contention. In the circumstances I cannot include Orr as an Irish ace.

✦ ✦ ✦

SCUTT, GEORGE HOWARD HOMER

(**5 aerial victories**)

Born: Jun 1898, Wilton, Somerset, UK

Died: 15 February 1924, Folkestone, Kent, UK

Awards: Military Cross

Commemorated: Great War Roll of Honour, St Mary's Church, New Ross, Co Wexford, Ireland.

Religion: Church of Ireland

George Howard Homer Scutt was raised in Ireland, his siblings were born in Ireland, the majority of his family died in Ireland, but he is not generally considered to be an Irish ace. On the one hand I have effectively excluded the Irish community in Britain from inclusion as Irish aces and therefore am open to the charge of inconsistency if I do not then include those non-Irish aces from Ireland, i.e. "Ireland's aces" rather than "Irish aces". I accept the charge of inconsistency, however, as my overriding concern has been to avoid any grave robbing activities: this volume on Irish aces takes the ultraminimal approach to allow for any further evidence to be adduced. Scutt would appear to be an ace from Ireland of English origin, who therefore remains unconfirmed as an "Irish ace" for the purposes of this volume.

George was the son of George Decimus Homer Scutt and Emmie Scutt. George's parents were both English. They married in 1897 in Kensington. In the Irish Census 1911 Scutt is resident in Craywell, New Ross, Co Wexford with his parents, his younger brother (Rodney

Owen, aged five) and his younger sister (Gwyneth Emmaline, aged 8 months) together with two servants. George's father was a brewer. George himself was also born in England, but his brother was born in Dublin and his sister in Wexford. The Scutts have been characterised as an English family living in Ireland. However, all three children were raised in Ireland, two of whom were born in Ireland.

During the early stages of the war Scutt was commissioned as a 2nd Lieutenant in the Liverpool Regiment.[418] In December 1917 he transferred to the Royal Flying Corps.

Scutt claimed five victories with No.48 Squadron, all with 2nd Lt L.A. Payne as pilot:

26 February 1918 – an LVG in flames;
08 March 1918 – two Albatros scouts out of control;
12 March 1918 – a Fokker Dr.I triplane out of control;
21 March 1918 – a LVG out of control.

The aerial victories of 08 March 1918 are referenced in RFC Communiqué No.130 of 1918. One of these is detailed by Scutt in Air Combat report No.464 of No.48 Squadron. Payne and Scutt were in Bristol F2b (A7298) on reconnaissance over Mont d'Origny aerodrome when the following occurred:

"Whilst on reconnaissance a DIII Albatros attacked us from a height of 8,000 feet. I engaged same with my rear gun firing two long bursts at 300 yards. The E.A. [enemy aircraft] went down completely out of control, but I could not observe whether it crashed, owing to haze. Last seen going down in a vertical nose-dive 6,000 feet below us and then disappearing into the haze".

Their commanding officer annotated the report with the comment "considered decisive".

Scutt was awarded the Military Cross, which was gazetted on 22 June 1918:

"Lt. George Howard Homer Scutt. Gen. List, and R.F.C.

---

418 London Gazette Supplement, Issue 29537, p.3683, 06 April 1916.

For conspicuous gallantry and devotion to duty. He has destroyed one hostile machine, and driven down three others out of control. He carried out an important single-machine reconnaissance, frequently descending to a height of 100 feet under heavy rifle and machine-gun fire, and obtained valuable information. While returning, he attacked 5 enemy machines, and ably assisted his pilot in driving them back over their lines. He has carried out many successful photographic reconnaissances, and has at all times proved himself to be a keen and daring officer".[419]

Scutt's medal index card gives his address as " 28 Squadron, RAF, Ambala, India" as of 18 January 1921, when Scutt applied for his service medals. His address is "Creywell, New Ross, Co Wexford, Ireland" on 20 July 1921.

In January 1924 he was promoted from Flying Officer to Flight Lieutenant. Of Irish interest, also in the promotion list were Francis Joseph Fogarty on promotion from Flying Officer to Flight Lieutenant, as were future Air Vice-Marshals George Dermot Daly DFC and William Munro Yool; Edward Dawson Atkinson DFC AFC from Flight Lieutenant to Squadron Leader; and William Foster MacNeece CBE, DSO, DFC from Wing Commander to Group Captain.[420]

Scutt was killed in an air crash in February 1924 at Hawkinge, Folkestone, Kent. However, his death falls outside the 1914-1920 period for commemoration as a World War I death and so the Great War memorial at St Mary's Church in New Ross, Co Wexford is correct to include him in its Roll of Honour rather than in the Casualty section of the memorial.

Flight magazine reports Scutt's death:

An inquest was held several months later, which absolved the other pilots of responsibility for Scutt's death:

"An inquest was held at Hawkinge Aerodrome, near Folkestone, on the body of Flight Lieutenant George Howard Homer Scutt M.C, 25th Squadron, R.A.F. who was killed in an aeroplane accident.

---

419 London Gazette Supplement, Issue 30761, p.7422.
420 London Gazette Supplement, Issue 32893, p.9

Flying-Officer C. E. Maitland said that three machines were flying in formation.

At about 1,500ft the witness gave the order to dive to 500ft. When he got to 400ft. down he noticed that Flight Lieutenant Scutt's machine was very nearly behind him. The high wing bent up and the machine nosed down to the ground. The witness was of opinion that Flight-Lieutenant Scutt got out of formation, and by the fact of his being immediately behind the witness he came into disturbed and eddying air caused by his (the witness's) machine.

He was certain his machine did not touch the other.

Medical evidence was that death was due to fracture of the skull, and the jury returned a verdict of 'Death from misadventure.'".[421]

A related article concerns the theory that an air pocket was the cause of the fatal crash at Croydon Aerodrome that killed Lieutenant-Colonel James Lindsay Travers. Travers had served in Chile with Victor Huston as an Aeronautical Adviser to the Chilean government. At his inquest the coroner held that "it was quite evident that inexperience was not the cause of the accident. He recorded' a verdict of 'Accidental death'."

Probate was granted on 03 July 1924. Scutt left £ 956 7s. 2d., with his father administering his estate. George's parents continued to live in Ireland. George Decimus Homer Scutt died in Tramore, Co Waterford on 28 December 1956. Probate was dated 12 March 1957; Scutt left £2,808 18s. 3d. to his daughter Gwyneth Emmaline Homer Whiteside.

✦ ✦ ✦

---

421 Archive of *West Australian* newspaper (Perth, W.A.: 1879-1954), 11 June 1924, p.10.

WORKMAN, CHARLES SERVICE

(4 aerial victories)

Born: 1897, Belfast, Co Antrim or Glasgow, Scotland

Died: 20 July 1917

Awards: Military Cross

Commemorated: Kortrijk (St Jan) Communal Cemetery, West-Vlaanderen, Belgium; University of Glasgow Roll of Honour, Glasgow, Scotland.

Religion: Presbyterian

Lieutenant Charles Service Workman was the son of Dr Charles Workman (b.1853) and Jessie Downie Workman (née McNeill, b.1855). Both of Charles' parents were Irish and two of his sisters (Evelyn and Winifred) were also born in Ireland. However, Charles and his sister Jessie may both have been born in Glasgow; another sister (Karoline) was born in Germany.

In the UK Census 1901 the family are resident at 5 Woodside Terrace, Glasgow, Scotland. In this particular census Charles is listed as having been born in Glasgow. However, the UK Census 1911 records Charles Workman MD and wife Jessie Downie visiting Rua Lachhead McNeill (surgeon and brother of Jessie) in Wolverhampton. In this census Charles and his parents are all listed as being from Belfast, Co Antrim.

When the war came Charles enlisted with the local Cameronians (Scottish Rifles) and not an Irish regiment. His medal index card indicates that he served with the 5th Battalion of the Scottish Rifles, disembarking in France on 05 November 1914. Workman transferred to the Royal Flying Corps in August 1916, serving initially as an observer with No.25 Squadron. On 03 October 1916 his appointment as Flying Officer (Observer) with effect from 11 September 1916 was announced. Workman is credited with several aerial victories during his time with No.25 Squadron.

On 09 August 1916 Workman was observer/gunner in an F.E.2b (4839) piloted by Noel Webb when they forced an Albatros C to land after an engagement over Beaumont.

RFC Communiqué No.52 of 1916 records that on 01 September 1916 Webb and Workman attacked and destroyed or damaged two balloons:

"2 Lt N.W. Webb and Lt C.S. Workman, in an F.E.2b of 25 Sqn, attacked tow hostile balloons. They crossed the line in clouds, and after flying for about 10 minutes, descended and found themselves about 2 miles from one of the balloons. 2 Lt Webb dived, and his observer [Workman] fired five drums of tracer ammunition at the balloon, and also dropped 4 bombs on it when it was nearly on the ground. Tracers were observed to hit the balloon. The bombs fell very close. They then attacked the second balloon, which was about a mile distant. The balloon was also hit, and drawn down. They then recrossed the lines at 1,200 feet, their machine having suffered considerable damage from A.A. fire".

One problem, however, resides with the system (or absence of a standardized system) by which credits were awarded for attacks on balloons. It would appear from any normal reading of the Communiqué that the balloons were at the very least damaged. However, this is not sufficient for aerial victories to be awarded in some instances, notwithstanding that it may count for the award of gallantry medals on occasion.

On 07 September 1916, in a well-documented hunt for the German ace Max von Mulzer, Workman, in an F.E.2b (6993) piloted by Welsh ace Captain Alwyne Loyd, they shared with two others in sending a Fokker Eindecker down out of control near Pont a Vendin.

RFC Communiqué No.55 of 1916 reports that on 25 September 1916 Workman was in a F.E.2b piloted by Lt Woolvern on a bombing mission against the German troop transportation station at Libercourt. The aircraft of No.25 Squadron were escorted by F.E.8s of No.40 Squadron, who got to engage in diversionary attacks on the adjacent German aerodromes. An F.E.2b flown by Captain Chadwick hit a German train, causing major loss of life and forcing a second train to a halt. According to the Communiqué:

"The other F.E.2b, pilot Lt Woolvern, with Lt Workman, attacked it with six 20-pound bombs, two of which hit the train and one the engine. Troops also began to descend and were fired on. They ran towards Envin village".

As remarkable and successful this attack had proven to be, it was actually only a diversion from the main attack on Libercourt station, which also caused significant damage but probably less in terms of loss of life than the two train wrecks.

Workman returned to Home Establishment on 10 November 1916, serving brief periods at Netheravon, the School of Aeronautics and 34 Reserve Squadron. The citation for Workman's Military Cross was gazetted on 14 November 1916:

"2nd Lt. (temp. Capt.) Charles Service Workman, Sco. Rif. and R.F.C.

For conspicuous gallantry in action. He and his pilot dived down to a low altitude, attacked a train, causing many casualties, and displayed great courage and determination".[422]

Although Workman received pilot training I cannot identify the corresponding Royal Aero Club certificate. However, there was an ex-Royal Irish Rifles Lieutenant Franz Workman, of Newtonbreda Manse, Belfast (b.15 May 1886) who obtained RAeC 3335 on 05 August 1916. Given that Charles had a sister born in Germany I would not be surprised if the Germanic-sounding Belfast man was also related. The Irish Census shows Franz to be the son of Robert (a Doctor of Divinity) and Anna (German-born) Workman from Belfast.

---

422 Supplement to London Gazette, Issue 29824, 14 November 1916, p.11071.

Charles was appointed Flying Officer with effect from 30 March 1917. He transferred from 34 Reserve Squadron to No.70 Squadron, entering France on 05 May 1917. It would appear that Workman served initially as a pilot in the two-seater Sopwith 11/2 Strutter (A8230) with AM2 S.A. Groves as his observer before becoming a Sopwith Camel pilot.

According to Trevor Henshaw's *The Sky Their Battlefield* (Grub Street, 1995) Workman was shot down in a Sopwith Camel (B3779) on 17 July 1917 whilst patrolling the Roulers-Isseghem-Courtrai area with No.70 Squadron. Apparently Workman left Liettres aerodrome at 19:30. He was shot down east of Comines by Ltn Robert Tüxen of Jasta 6 for Tüxen's first victory. Workman was initially reported as POW. Although he was taken to a German hospital he died from his wounds on 20 July 1917.

Given that Workman flew as an observer in two-seaters any attempt to compile scores is fraught with difficulties: sometimes aerial victories are credited to the front or rear gun, on other occasions they are shared between pilot and observer. Further confusion arises on account of several of his aerial victories being with the English ace Noel William Ward Webb, which was often abbreviated to N.W. Webb and thus often confused with the notable Irish pilot G.W. Webb (Captain Gilbert Watson Webb of No.22 Squadron). Coincidentally N.W. Webb also ended up in No.70 Squadron with Workman. However, I am reasonably satisfied that Workman only obtained four aerial victories with No.25 Squadron, and that there remains the prospect that the two balloon kills may even have been disallowed. Further, I have been unable to identify any aerial victories for Workman with No.70 Squadron but am open to correction on this matter.

The *Weekly Irish Times* of 29 September 1917 reported Workman's death as having died of wounds. It sated that Charles was "the younger son of Dr Charles Workman, 5 Woodside terrace, Glasgow, and was a first-year student in medicine in 1914 at Glasgow University … and was a grandson of the late Mr Robert Workman, Ceara, Windsor, Belfast, and nephew of Mr Frank Workman, DL, Belfast".

Charles' sister Evelyn Jane Lochhead Workman (b.08 March 1881, Belfast, d.1968) was the Irish painter and artist of minor fame, who married the academic and medic Robert Buchanan Carslaw. On 13 June 1921 Charles' mother was still living at 5 Woodside Terrace, Glasgow, as this date is recorded as that upon which Jessie made an application for Charles' service medals.

✦ ✦ ✦

APPENDIX I

IRISH AVIATORS OF WORLD WAR I

Table I: 'Pusher' Aerial Victories

Date	Time	Pilot	Squadron	Aircraft (Serial No)	Opponent (Category of victory)	Location
02-Apr-16	06:55	D.M. Tidmarsh	24	D.H.2 (5924)	Albatros C (DES)	Grandcourt-Albert
26-Apr-16	09:45	J. Cruess-Callaghan	18	F.E.2b (5232)	Fokker Eindecker (DES)	Mencourt
30-Apr-16	10:45	D.M. Tidmarsh	24	D.H.2 (5965)	Fokker Eindecker (DES)	Bapaume
04-May-16	09:00	S.E. Cowan	24	D.H.2 (5966)	2-seater (DES)	Hem-Clery
20-May-16	04:15	D.M. Tidmarsh	24	D.H.2 (5965)	2-seater (DESF)	S Pozieres
01-Jul-16	07:45	S.E. Cowan	24	D.H.2 (5964)	2-seater (OOC)	Pys Morval-Vaux
29-Jul-16	14:00	S.E. Cowan	24	D.H.2 (6000)	Roland CII (DES)	Wood
03-Aug-16	15:30	S.E. Cowan	24	D.H.2 (5904)	LVG C (OOC)	Sailly
09-Aug-16	07:30	S.E. Cowan	24	D.H.2 (5998)	2-seater (DES)	Le Sars
31-Aug-16	18:00	P.A.L. Byrne	24	D.H.2 (6010)	HA (FTL)	N Bapaume
02-Sep-16	19:35	P.A.L. Byrne	24	D.H.2 (6010)	2-seater (OOC)	Beaulencourt
15-Sep-16	08:30	P.A.L. Byrne	24	D.H.2 (7911)	2-seater (DESF)	NE Morval
16-Sep-16	10:15	S.E. Cowan	24	D.H.2 (5964)	Fokker DII (DESF)	Sailly-Saillisel
16-Sep-16	19:00	P.A.L. Byrne	24	D.H.2 (7911)	Fokker DII (DES)	Achiet
21-Sep-16	17:45	P.A.L. Byrne	24	D.H.2 (7911)	LVG C (FTL)	N Miraumont
22-Sep-16	11:40	P.A.L. Byrne	24	D.H.2 (7911)	EA (FTL)	Velu
22-Sep-16	18:00	P.A.L. Byrne	24	D.H.2 (7911)	Rumpler C (FTL)	Grandcourt
23-Sep-16	08:05	P.A.L. Byrne	24	D.H.2 (7911)	Rumpler C (FTL)	E Combles
28-Sep-16	17:10	P.A.L. Byrne	24	D.H.2 (A2538)	LVG C (FTL)	Rocquigny
16-Oct-16	10:30	P.A.L. Byrne	24	D.H.2 (5925)	Albatros DI (FTL)	Biefvillers

APPENDIX I

Date	Time	Pilot	Squadron	Aircraft (Serial No)	Opponent (Category of victory)	Location
09-Nov-16		W.R. Gregory	40	F.E.8	Roland C (OOC)	N of le Sars
17-Nov-16		S.E. Cowan	29	D.H.2 (A2555)	Halberstadt DII (OOC)	-
04-Feb-17	16:00	G.N. Blennerhasset	18	F.E.2b (A5640)	Albatros DIII (OOC)	
09-Feb-17		W.R. Gregory	40	F.E.8	Albatros C (OOC)	Grevillers
15-Feb-17	10:15	V.H. Huston	18	F.E.2b (A5455)	2-seater (DES)	Givenchy
06-Mar-17	10:50	W.R. Gregory (pilot) + G.N. Blennerhasset (observer)	40	F.E.8 (6384)	Halberstadt C (OOC)	
05-Apr-17	12:00	V.H. Huston (pilot) + G.N. Blennerhasset (observer)	18	F.E.2b (4969)	Albatros DIII (OOC)	Inchy
05-Apr-17	12:00	G.N. Blennerhasset	18	F.E.2b (4969)	Albatros DIII (OOC)	Inchy Beámetz-
06-Apr-17	10:00	G.N. Blennerhasset	18	F.E.2b (A5468)	Albatros DII (DES)	Beugny
16-Apr-17	08:30	G.N. Blennerhasset	18	F.E.2b (A5461)	Albatros DII (OOC)	Gaincourt Baralle-Bour-
24-Apr-17	08:15	V.H. Huston	18	F.E.2d (4998)	Albatros DIII (DES)	lon
30-Apr-17	09:45	F. Leathley	57	F.E.2d (A1966)	Albatros DIII (OOC)	Buissy
03-May-17	18:30	G.N. Blennerhasset	18	F.E.2b (A5506)	Albatros DIII (OOC)	Bourlon Wood
05-May-17	17:10	J.J. Cowell	20	F.E.2d (A6400)	Albatros DIII (OOC)	Poelcapelle
13-May-17	17:45	V.H. Huston	18	F.E.2b (4998)	Halberstadt D (DES)	NW Cambrai
13-May-17	10:40	J.J. Cowell	20	F.E.2d (A6412)	2-seater (DES)	Reckem
20-May-17	09:20	J.J. Cowell	20	F.E.2d (A6412)	Albatros DIII (OOC)	Menin
23-May-17	13:25	G.N. Blennerhasset	18	F.E.2b (7003)	Albatros DIII (DES)	E of Eswars

419

IRISH AVIATORS OF WORLD WAR I

Date	Time	Pilot	Squadron	Aircraft (Serial No)	Opponent (Category of victory)	Location
23-May-17	13:25	G.N. Blemmerhasset	18	F.E.2b (7003)	Albatros DIII (OOC)	E of Eswars
25-May-17	08:50	J.J. Cowell	20	F.E.2d (A6415)	Albatros DIII (OOC)	Wervicq
26-May-17	20:10	J.J. Cowell	20	F.E.2d (A6415)	Albatros DIII (DESF)	SE Ypres
26-May-17	00:30	J.J. Cowell	20	F.E.2d (A6415)	Albatros DIII (OOC)	Comines
27-May-17	07:45	V.H. Huston	18	F.E.2b (4998)	Albatros DV (DES)	N Havrincourt
02-Jun-17	09:45	J.J. Cowell	20	F.E.2d (A6480)	Albatros DIII (DES)	Gheluvelt
29-Jun-17	16:10	J.J. Cowell	20	F.E.2d (A6376)	Albatros DV (OOC)	Beccelaere E Ploegsteert
12-Jul-17	17:00	J.J. Cowell	20	F.E.2d (A6376)	Albatros DV (DES)	Wood E Ploegsteert
12-Jul-17	17:15	J.J. Cowell	20	F.E.2d (A6376)	Albatros DV (OOC)	Wood
17-Jul-17	19:50	J.J. Cowell	20	F.E.2d (A6468)	Albatros DV (DES)	28Q_28
17-Jul-17	19:45	J.J. Cowell	20	F.E.2d (A6468)	Albatros DV (DESF)	Polygon Wood
20-Jul-17	09:55	J.J. Cowell	20	F.E.2d (A6376)	Albatros DV (OOC)	Wervicq Menin
22-Jul-17	16:50	J.J. Cowell	20	F.E.2d (A6376)	Albatros DV (OOC)	Wervicq
28-Jul-17	18:45	J.J. Cowell	20	F.E.2d (A6376)	Albatros DV (OOC)	E Messines

APPENDIX I

Table II: Bristol F2 Fighter Aerial Victories

Date	Time	Pilot	Squadron	Aircraft (Serial No)	Opponent (Category of victory)	Location
08-Apr-17		D.M. Tidmarsh	48	F2a	Albatros DIII (DES)	Vitry-Sailly
10-Apr-17		D.M. Tidmarsh	48	F2a (A3338)	1-seater (OOC)	Remy
11-Apr-17	08:30-09:00	D.M. Tidmarsh	48	F2a (A3338)	Albatros DIII (DES)	Fampoux
11-Apr-17	08:30-09:00	D.M. Tidmarsh	48	F2a (A3338)	Albatros DIII (DES)	Fampoux
13-Jan-18	14:25	H.G. Crowe	20	F2b (B1122)	2-seater (DES)	N Moorslede
22-Jan-18	11:15	H.G. Crowe	20	F2b (A7256)	Albatros DV (DESF)	S Moorslede
22-Jan-18	11:10	H.G. Crowe	20	F2b (A7256)	Albatros DV (OOC)	W Roulers
28-Mar-18	08:30	H.G. Crowe	20	F2b (B1191)	Fokker DrI (OOC)	Albert
21-Apr-18	11:00	H.G. Crowe	20	F2b (C4749)	Albatros DV (OOC)	N Wervicq
03-May-18	17:30	H.G. Crowe	20	F2b (C4749)	Albatros DV (OOC)	SE Ypres
03-May-18	17:20	H.G. Crowe	20	F2b (C4749)	Fokker DrI (DESF)	SE Hollebeke
08-May-18	16:50	H.G. Crowe	20	F2b (C4749)	Fokker DrI (DES)	Comines-Wervicq
09-May-18	16:50	A.S. Mills	20	F2b	Fokker DrI (DESF)	W Lille
22-May-18	18:40	A.S. Mills	20	F2b (C856)	Albatros DV (OOC)	Warneton
22-May-18	07:05	A.S. Mills	20	F2b (C856)	LVG C (DES)	Wytschaete-St Eloi
29-May-18	18:30	A.S. Mills	20	F2b (C951)	Albatros DV (OOC)	Bac St Maur
30-May-18	17:20	A.S. Mills	20	F2b (C951)	Pfalz DIII (DES)	NW Lille
30-May-18	17:20	A.S. Mills	20	F2b (C951)	Pfalz DIII (DES)	W Macquart

IRISH AVIATORS OF WORLD WAR I

Date	Time	Pilot	Squadron	Aircraft (Serial No)	Opponent (Category of victory)	Location
31-May-18	18:50	A.S. Mills	20	F2b (B1168)	Pfalz DIII (DESF)	Armentières
31-May-18	19:50	T. Proctor	88	F2b (C821)	Albatros DV (OOC)	Ostende
31-May-18	07:40	A.S. Mills	20	F2b (C951)	Pfalz DIII (DES)	SW Armentières Middlekerke
02-Jun-18	19:35	T. Proctor	88	F2b (C821)	Albatros DV (DESF)	Ostende
24-Jul-18	20:00	A.S. Mills	20	F2b (C4672)	Fokker DVII (DES)	N Comines
29-Jul-18	20:10	J.J. Cowell	20	F2b (E2471)	Fokker DVII (OOC)	NW Wervicq
11-Aug-18	11:45	T. Proctor	88	F2b (C852)	Fokker DVII (DES)	NW Péronne
11-Aug-18	11:45	T. Proctor	88	F2b (C852)	Fokker DVII (DES)	NW Péronne
19-Aug-18	10:25	T. Proctor	88	F2b (E2153)	Fokker DrI (OOC)	Bauvin-Douai
03-Sep-18	17:45	A.S. Mills	20	F2b (E2470)	Fokker DVII (DES)	Havrincourt Wood
03-Sep-18	07:00	G. McCormack	22	F2b (F5820)	Pfalz DXII (DES)	Sailly-Saillisel
05-Sep-18	17:00	W.U. Tyrrell	22	F2b (D7998)	Fokker DVII (OOC)	Douai
05-Sep-18	17:00	G. McCormack	22	F2b (F5820)	Fokker DVII (OOC)	Douai
06-Sep-18	08:30	A.S. Mills	20	F2b (E2470)	Fokker DVII (DES)	Cambrai-Péronne
06-Sep-18	08:50	A.S. Mills	20	F2b (E2470)	Fokker DVII (OOC)	St Quentin
15-Sep-18	17:50	A.S. Mills	20	F2b (E2470)	Hannover CL (DES)	Harly, SE St Quentin
17-Sep-18	18:30	G. McCormack	22	F2b (C1045)	Fokker DVII (DES)	SW Douai

422

APPENDIX I

Date	Time	Pilot	Squadron	Aircraft (Serial No)	Opponent (Category of victory)	Location
17-Sep-18	18:40	G. McCormack	22	F2b (C1045)	Fokker DVII (OOC)	Brebieres
20-Sep-18	10:30	A.S. Mills	20	F2b (E2246)	Fokker DVII (DES)	Rouvroy
20-Sep-18	10:32	A.S. Mills	20	F2b (E2246)	Fokker DVII (DES)	Rouvroy
24-Sep-18	17:00	G. McCormack	22	F2b (C1035)	Fokker DVII (OOC)	Cambrai
24-Sep-18	17:00	W.U. Tyrrell	22	F2b (F5823)	Fokker DVII (DES)	Mesnieres-Grevecourt
24-Sep-18	17:00	W.U. Tyrrell	22	F2b (F5823)	Fokker DVII (OOC)	Mesnieres-Grevecourt
26-Sep-18	13:00	W.U. Tyrrell	22	F2b (C1035)	Fokker DVII (DES)	Cambrai-Arras Road
26-Sep-18	13:15	W.U. Tyrrell	22	F2b (C1035)	Fokker DVII (DES)	Cambrai-Arras Road
27-Sep-18	07:30	W.U. Tyrrell	22	F2b (E2517)	Fokker DVII (DES)	Oisy-le-Verger

Table III: Nieuport Aerial Victories

Date	Time	Pilot	Squadron	Aircraft (Serial No)	Opponent (Category of victory)	Location
04-Mar-17	16:10	T.F. Hazell	1	(A6604)	HA (OOC)	Westhoek
25-Mar-17	17:00	E.D. Atkinson	1		Balloon (DES)	Warneton-Wervicq
30-Mar-17	14:15	W.R. Gregory	40	(A6680)	Halberstadt C (OOC)	Bailleul-Arras
22-Apr-17	07:05	E.D. Atkinson	1	(A6624)	Albatros DII (OOC)	Lille
22-Apr-17	17:20	W.E. Molesworth	60	(B1569)	Albatros DIII (OOC)	Vitry
24-Apr-17	12:00	T.F. Hazell	1	(A6738)	Albatros C (DESF)	Bois Grenier
24-Apr-17	10:40	W.E. Molesworth	60	(B1569)	Balloon (DES)	Boiry Notre Dame
29-Apr-17	17:40	E.D. Atkinson	1	(A6678)	Albatros C (OOC)	Armentières
06-May-17	18:40	W.R. Gregory	40	(B1548)	Albatros C (OOC)	Lens
07-May-17		W.R. Gregory	40		Albatros D (FTL)	Quierry la Motte
07-May-17	09:35	E.C. Mannock	40	(A6733)	Balloon (DES)	Houthem
09-May-17	07:40	T.F. Hazell	1	(B1632)	Albatros C (OOC)	Hénin-Liétard
10-May-17	16:40	W.R. Gregory	40	(B1548)	Albatros C (OOC)	

APPENDIX I

Date	Time	Pilot	Squadron	Aircraft No	Opponent (Category of victory)	Location
27-May-17	18:45	W.R. Gregory	40	(B1548)	Albatros C (OOC)	Hénin-Liétard
04-Jun-17	07:00	T.F. Hazell	1	(B1649)	Albatros DIII (DES)	E Hollebeke
04-Jun-17	07:02	T.F. Hazell	1	(B1649)	Albatros DIII (DES)	E Hollebeke
05-Jun-17	09:00	T.F. Hazell	1	(B1649)	2-seater (DES)	Houthem
05-Jun-17	06:30	T.F. Hazell	1	(B1649)	Albatros DIII (DES)	E Ypres
07-Jun-17	07:15	E.C. Mannock	40	(B1552)	Albatros DIII (OOC)	N Lille
08-Jun-17	06:40	T.F. Hazell	1	(B1649)	Albatros DIII (OOC)	E Becelaere
08-Jun-17	07:45	S.L.G. Pope	60	(B1652)	Albatros C (OOC)	Vitry
09-Jun-17	20:00	T.F. Hazell	1	(B1649)	Albatros DIII (OOC)	Zandvoorde
20-Jun-17	11:40	S.L.G. Pope	60	(B1679)	Albatros DV (OOC)	Equerchin
29-Jun-17	18:00	W.E. Molesworth	60	(B1652)	Albatros DIII (DES)	Douai Estrees
11-Jul-17	14:10	W.E. Molesworth	60	(B1652)	Albatros DIII (OOC)	Queant
12-Jul-17	10:10	E.C. Mannock	40	(B1682)	DFW C (CAPT)	Avion
12-Jul-17	20:20	T.F. Hazell	1	(B3455)	Albatros DIII (OOC)	Menin
12-Jul-17	20:30	T.F. Hazell	1	(B3455)	Albatros DIII (OOC)	Dadizeele
13-Jul-17	09:20	E.C. Mannock	40	(B1682)	DFW C (OOC)	Sallaumines
22-Jul-17	19:00	T.F. Hazell	1	(B3455)	Albatros DV (DES)	Wervicq

425

Date	Time	Pilot	Squadron	Aircraft (Serial No)	Opponent (Category of victory)	Location
22-Jul-17	19:20	T.F. Hazell	1	(B3455)	Albatros DV (DES)	Houthem
22-Jul-17	08:20	T.F. Hazell	1	(B3455)	DFW C (DES)	Houthem-Amerika Farm
05-Aug-17	16:10	E.C. Mannock	40	(B3554)	Albatros DV (OOC)	Avion
10-Aug-17	14:20	T.F. Hazell	1	(B3455)	Albatros DV (OOC)	Bousbecque SE Petit-
12-Aug-17	15:15	E.C. Mannock	40	(B3554)	Albatros DV (CAPT)	Vimy
13-Aug-17	09:20	T.F. Hazell	1	(B3455)	Albatros C (OOC)	Houthem
13-Aug-17	07:10	T.F. Hazell	1	(B3455)	Rumpler C (DES)	Becelaere
14-Aug-17	19:10	T.F. Hazell	1	(B3455)	Albatros DV (DESF)	S Moorslede
14-Aug-17	19:15	T.F. Hazell	1	(B3455)	Albatros DV (OOC)	S Moorslede
15-Aug-17	12:15	E.C. Mannock	40	(B3554)	Albatros DV (OOC)	Lens
15-Aug-17	19:30	E.C. Mannock	40	(B3554)	Albatros DV (OOC)	N Lens
16-Aug-17	19:45	T.F. Hazell	1	(B3455)	Albatros DV (OOC)	Houthulst
17-Aug-17	10:50	E.C. Mannock	40	(B3554)	DFW C (OOC)	NE Sallaumines
04-Sep-17	16:30	E.C. Mannock	40	(B3607)	DFW C (CAPT)	Petit-Vimy
04-Sep-17	11:30	E.C. Mannock	40	(B3607)	DFW C (OOC)	E Lens-Lievin

APPENDIX I

Date	Time	Pilot	Squadron	Aircraft (Serial No)	Opponent (Category of victory)	Location
11-Sep-17	11:15	E.C. Mannock	40	(B3607)	DFW C (OOC)	Thelus-Oppy
20-Sep-17	17:35	E.C. Mannock	40	(B3607)	DFW C (OOC)	Hulloch
23-Sep-17	16:45	E.C. Mannock	40	(B3541)	2-seater (DESF)	Oppy
25-Sep-17	15:10	E.C. Mannock	40	(B3607)	Rumpler C (OOC)	Sallaumines Houthoulst
08-Nov-17	16:00	W.E. Molesworth	29	(B6812)	2-seater (DESF)	Forest E Westroose-
08-Nov-17	15:15	W.E. Molesworth	29	(B6812)	Albatros DV (DESF)	beke S E
26-Nov-17	14:50	W.E. Molesworth	29	(B6820)	Albatros DV (OOC)	Houthoulst S Moor-slede
03-Jan-18	15:30	W.E. Molesworth	29	(B6812)	Albatros DV (OOC)	NE Stadlen
22-Jan-18	12:35	W.E. Molesworth	29	(B6812)	Albatros DV (DES)	NE Roulers
24-Jan-18	12:00	W.E. Molesworth	29	(B6812)	2-seater (DES)	NE Roulers
24-Jan-18	13:10	W.E. Molesworth	29	(B6812)	2-seater (DES)	NE Roulers E Moor-
29-Jan-18	12:55	W.E. Molesworth	29	(B6797)	Albatros DV (DESF)	slede Moorslede-
05-Feb-18	10:20	W.E. Molesworth	29	(B6812)	2-seater (OOC)	Roulers

Date	Time	Pilot	Squadron	Aircraft (Serial No)	Opponent (Category of victory)	Location
21-Feb-18	14:10	W.E. Molesworth	29	(B6812)	2-seater (CAPT)	Ypres-Zonnebeke
26-Feb-18	11:00	W.E. Molesworth	29	(B6812)	2-seater (DES)	SE Becelaere
18-Mar-18	11:45	W.E. Molesworth	29	(B6812)	Pfalz DIII (DES)	SE Rumbeke

APPENDIX I

Table IV: Sopwith Camel Aerial Victories

Date	Time	Pilot	Squadron	Aircraft (Serial No)	Opponent (Category of victory)	Location
17-Jul-17	20:55	E. Gribben	70		Albatros DV (OOC)	S Gheluvelt, E Polygon Wood
24-Jul-17	20:30	E. Gribben	70	(B3813)	Albatros DIII (OOC)	Roulers
10-Aug-17	19:45	E. Gribben	70	(B3840)	Albatros DIII (DES)	Menin-Roulers
10-Aug-17	19:45	E. Gribben	70	(B3840)	Albatros DIII (OOC)	Menin
13-Aug-17	19:30	E. Gribben	70	(B3840)	DFW C (DES)	E Dixmude, St Cite
05-Dec-17	13:50	G.W. Price	8 (Naval)	(B6311)	Albatros DV (DES)	Auguste
05-Dec-17	13:55	G.W. Price	8 (Naval)	(B6311)	Albatros DV (OOC)	Wingles, NW Wen-
05-Dec-17	15:05	M.L. Cooper	13 (Naval)	(B6407)	2-seater (DES)	duyne, SE Loison
06-Dec-17	10:45	G.W. Price	8 (Naval)		DFW C (OOC)	Lens, Henin-Lie-
27-Dec-17	14:35	G.W. Price	8 (Naval)		DFW C (OOC)	tard
28-Dec-17	11:00	G.W. Price	8 (Naval)	(B6229)	DFW C (OOC)	Vitry Cite, St
02-Jan-18	11:13	G.W. Price	8 (Naval)	(B6312)	Albatros DV (DESF)	Auguste Oppy -
06-Jan-18	12:55	G.W. Price	8 (Naval)	(B6371)	2-seater (DES)	Fresnes
19-Jan-18	12:15	G.W. Price	8 (Naval)	(B6371)	Albatros DV (OOC)	Sailly-S Vitry
22-Jan-18	11:20	G.W. Price	8 (Naval)	(B6379)	Albatros DV (OOC)	Vitry

IRISH AVIATORS OF WORLD WAR I

Date	Time	Pilot	Squadron	Aircraft (Serial No)	Opponent (Category of victory)	Location
24-Jan-18	12:25	G.W. Price	8 (Naval)	B6379	Albatros DV (DES)	La Bassee
28-Jan-18	11:05	G.W. Price	8 (Naval)	B6379	2-seater (DESF)	La Bassee
29-Jan-18	14:00	M.L. Cooper	13 (Naval)	B6410	Seaplane (DES)	Blankenberghe Pier
16-Feb-18	11:15	G.W. Price	8 (Naval)	B6379	Albatros DV (DESF)	Pronville
12-Mar-18	09:05	M.L. Cooper	13 (Naval)	B6410	2-seater (DESF)	Ostend-Wenduyne
01-Apr-18	14:30	M.L. Cooper	213	B6416	Seaplane C (DESF)	Zeebrugge
09-May-18	13:15	R. McLaughlin	201	B3884	Albatros DV (DES)	Bapaume
15-May-18	06:45	R. McLaughlin	201		Albatros DV (DES)	Bapaume Achiet le
30-May-18	19:55	R. McLaughlin	201	B7191	Albatros DV (OOC)	Grand
30-Jun-18	20:40	O.A.P. Heron	70	D6492	Albatros DV (DESF)	E Bray
30-Jun-18	20:35	O.A.P. Heron	70	D6492	Albatros DV (OOC)	E Bray
07-Jul-18	11:40	M.L. Cooper	213	B3326	Albatros DV (OOC)	Middelkerke
30-Jul-18	11:50	M.L. Cooper	213	D3326	Albatros DV (OOC)	Bruges
12-Aug-18	11:00	R. McLaughlin	201	B6398	Fokker DVII (DES)	St Christ
12-Aug-18	11:00	R. McLaughlin	201	B6398	Fokker DVII (DES)	St Christ Houthem
19-Aug-18	19:55	O.A.P. Heron	70	C3306	Fokker DVII (DES)	Hollebeke
16-Sep-18	17:35	R. McLaughlin	201	C195	Fokker DVII (OOC)	SE Cambrai NE Passchendaele
28-Sep-18	11:45	O.A.P. Heron	70	D6696	Fokker DVII (DES)	
01-Oct-18	16:30	O.A.P. Heron	70	E7201	LVG C (DES)	SW Ardoye
07-Oct-18	08:45	O.A.P. Heron	70	D6696	Fokker DVII (DESF)	Lichtervelde

430

APPENDIX I

Date	Time	Pilot	Squadron	Aircraft (Serial No)	Opponent (Category of victory)	Location
07-Oct-18	08:45	O.A.P. Heron	70	(D6696)	Fokker DVII (DESF)	Lichtervelde
09-Oct-18	09:45	O.A.P. Heron	70	(E7277)	Fokker DVII (CAPT)	W Mayerneine
09-Oct-18	09:40	O.A.P. Heron	70	(E7277)	Fokker DVII (DES)	E Roulers
09-Oct-18	09:41	O.A.P. Heron	70	(E7277)	Fokker DVII (DES)	Roulers
26-Oct-18	15:15	O.A.P. Heron	70	(C8201)	Fokker DVII (DES)	S Monchau Montroelau
26-Oct-18	15:15	O.A.P. Heron	70	(C8201)	Fokker DVII (OOC)	Bois
28-Oct-18	11:40	O.A.P. Heron	70	(B7883)	Fokker DVII (DESF)	Quatres

Table V: Airco D.H.4 bomber Aerial Victories

Date	Time	Pilot	Squadron	Aircraft (Serial No)	Opponent (Category of victory)	Location
28-Jul-17	18:30	F. Leathley	57	(A7537)	Albatros DV (DES)	Ingelmunster
28-Jul-17	18:30	F. Leathley	57	(A7537)	Albatros DV (OOC)	Ingelmunster
16-Aug-17	17:45	F. Leathley	57	(A7563)	Albatros DV (OOC)	Houthulst
17-Aug-17	07:30	F. Leathley	57	(A7563)	Albatros DV (OOC)	Menin
17-Aug-17	07:30	F. Leathley	57	(A7563)	Albatros DV (OOC)	Menin
17-Aug-17	07:32	F. Leathley	57	(A7563)	Albatros DV (OOC)	W Menin
20-Aug-17	11:15	F. Leathley	57	(A7564)	Albatros DV (OOC)	E Ypres
02-Oct-17	13:40	E.P. Hartigan	57	(A7568)	Albatros DV (DES)	Houthulst
02-Oct-17	13:36	E.P. Hartigan	57	(A7568)	Albatros DV (DESF)	Roulers
02-Oct-17	13:35	E.P. Hartigan	57	(A7568)	Albatros DV (OOC)	Roulers
02-Oct-17	13:37	E.P. Hartigan	57	(A7568)	Albatros DV (OOC)	Roulers
28-Oct-17	12:30	E.P. Hartigan	57	(A7568)	Albatros DV (OOC)	W Roulers
06-Mar-18	11:25	A.G. Waller	18	(A7798)	Albatros DV (OOC)	Carvin
10-Mar-18	12:15	A.G. Waller	18	(A7770)	Albatros DV (OOC)	Fromelles
15-Mar-18	12:45	A.G. Waller	18	(A8076)	Pfalz DIII (OOC)	Avelin
12-Apr-18	10:25	A.G. Waller	18	D.H.4	Pfalz DIII (DESF)	Estaires
12-Apr-18	10:25	A.G. Waller	18	D.H.4	Pfalz DIII (OOC)	Estaires
14-May-18	18:00	A.G. Waller	18	(A8000)	Fokker DVII (DES)	Merville
16-May-18	13:50	A.G. Waller	18	(A8041)	Fokker DrI (OOC)	Neuf Berquin
19-May-18	12:00	A.G. Waller	18	D.H.4	Albatros DV (OOC)	Douai
25-May-18	11:30	A.G. Waller	18	D.H.4	Albatros DV (OOC)	Courrieres

APPENDIX I

Date	Time	Pilot	Squad-ron	Aircraft (Serial No)	Opponent (Category of victory)	Location
30-May-18	20:30	A.G. Waller	18	(A8018)	Fokker DVII (DESF)	Bac St Maur
30-May-18	20:50	A.G. Waller	18	(A8018)	Fokker DVII (OOC)	Bac St Maur
05-Jun-18	12:00	E.B.C. Betts	202	(A7446)	Pfalz DIII (DES)	NE Eassen
09-Jun-18		E.B.C. Betts	202	(A7446)	Albatros D (DES)	Maria-Aalter
10-Aug-18	14:25	E.B.C. Betts	202	(A7446)	Fokker DVII (OOC)	Bruges
16-Sep-18	11:25	E.B.C. Betts	202	(A7446)	Fokker DVII (DESF)	Dudzele
16-Sep-18	11:05	E.B.C. Betts	202	(A7446)	Pfalz DXII (DES)	Benkemaere

433

APPENDIX II – ACES OF IRISH PARENTAGE AND IRISH DESCENT

18 Aces of Irish parentage

Gottfried Freiherr [Baron] von Banfield (9 aerial victories)

Banfield was born to an Irish father and Austrian mother. Banfield, "the Eagle of Trieste", was quite remarkable insofar as the majority of his aerial victories were secured using a flying boat and he is well respected by naval historians. The Austro-Hungarian Empire's victory confirmation system was complex, and it is difficult to make like-for-like comparison with the British system but his 9 confirmed and 11 unconfirmed kills would probably have equated to 20 aerial victories by RFC, RNAS or RAF standards. Although he died in September 1986 I cannot find an English-language account of his life in which Banfield ever expressed being Irish, even though he emigrated from Austria-Hungary to the UK briefly following the annexation of Trieste by Italy. Consequently I do not include him as an Irish ace.

2nd Lieutenant Fergus Grey Craig (5 aerial victories)

Craig was born on 10 October 1899 to Gavin and Matilda Craig. However, it is difficult to trace Craig, as although he is apparently Scottish of Irish parentage there are nevertheless quite a number of Irish-Scottish families with these names. For example: there is a Matilda Craig (née Finlay) who was born at Kilcranny, Coleraine,

Co Londonderry; married to a Gavin who was born in 1858 at Banbrook, Coleraine, Co Londonderry. In the Scottish Census 1901 the family are recorded as being resident at Alexandra Place, Muiredge Road, Bothwell, Scotland. Fergus' parents are recorded as Irish but Fergus, his brother Jason and his sister Charlotte are all recorded as having been born at Whitburn, Wigtown. However, that particular Fergus Craig died of diphtheria as a child.

What is known is that Fergus Craig enlisted in 1917 with the 5th Bn Scottish Rifles, transferring to the RAF in 1918. He flew with a variety of pilots in No.57 Squadron, as an observer/gunner in the DH4 bombers. In August and September 1918 Fergus chalked up five aerial victories. Transferring between a number of squadrons in the immediate post-war era, Craig was transferred to the unemployed list in late 1919. In World War II he served as an Aircraftman Second Class, becoming a Leading Aircraftman during the war. Despite having two Irish parents I cannot however find any reference in the material to hand on No.57, No.25 and No.18 Squadron that would indicate Craig had ever identified himself as being Irish. Consequently I cannot include him among the Irish aces.

Lieutenant Robert James Cullen (5 aerial victories)

Kent-born Cullen was the son of James Cullen (b.1866, Scotland) and Mary Jane Cullen (née Cuthbert, b.1868, Ballinskelligs, Co Kerry). His mother was not a typical Kerrywoman, however, as the Cuthberts were originally a Scottish Presbyterian family who moved to Ireland with the introduction of the trans-Atlantic telegraph service and lived on the islands off the Co Kerry coast. Robert Cullen came from hardy Irish-Scottish stock even though he is invariably counted as an English ace. Typically, he enlisted with a Scottish regiment instead of his native Buffs (East Kent) regiment. Robert became an ace with No.88 Squadron, with 5 victories in May and June 1918.

APPENDIX II—ACES OF IRISH PARENTAGE AND IRISH DESCENT

Lieutenant-Colonel Jack Armand Cunningham (10 aerial victories)

Liverpool-born Cunningham was Son of David Cunningham (b.1842, Lancashire) and Augusta A Cunningham (b.1863, Co Tyrone, Ireland). The UK Census 1901 sees Jack A recorded as being resident with them at Eddisbury, Haymans Green, West Derby, Liverpool, Lancashire. David Cunningham was a wealthy cotton merchant, but although several of the servants are from Ireland this would not have been unusual for Lancashire and would not imply any temporary period of residence in Ireland.

Captain John Edgcumbe Doyle (9 aerial victories)

Doyle was born in the Cape Colony, South Africa. His father, Rev Ralph W Doyle, was from Ireland, his mother Eleanor M Doyle was from Hampshire. Rev Ralph Doyle was the chaplain to the Governor of Cape Province. In the UK Census 1901 the family are living at Warkworth St, Cambridge. His older brother George (b.1891) was also born in South Africa but his sister Julia (b.1896) was born in Rutland and Dorothy (b.1899) was born in Cambridge. In the UK Census 1911 he was living with his grandparents in Somerset. His grandfather was George Phillips, a retired Colonel of the Royal Engineers. Doyle served with 56 and 60 Squadrons, being most closely associated with the latter. He was shot down and badly injured, his right leg requiring amputation. Doyle became a POW but was awarded the DFC. In the interwar years Doyle worked at a variety of jobs, including that of tour bus organiser, and suffered severe financial hardship. In World War II he secured a training role in the RAF. He contributed to numerous publications, his accounts being of varying quality. Although Doyle mentions his South African birth –and his Irish and English parentage– he would not ever appear to have regarded himself as being Irish.

Captain Maurice Michael Freehill (7 aerial victories)

Maurice was the son of Eugene (b.1869, Trim, Co Meath) and Lilian (b.1868, Selborne, Hants). Because he served with No.46 Squadron and No.80 Squadron it is easy for a passing reference to an Irish parent to become a means through he would be lumped with Frank Jonynt Milligan, Albert James Moore, John Richard Orr and so forth. I have not seen any account in which Freehill indicated that he was Irish and so I do not include him with the Irish aces.

Captain Charles Robert Hickey (21 aerial victories)

Canadian-born Charles Hickey was from British Columbia. His father was Anglo-Irish, the Indian-born Major Robert Hume Fayrer Hickey of the 11th Canadian Mounted Rifles, who also served in World War I.

His mother was Irish-Canadian, Charlotte Emily Hickey (née Reeves), who was the daughter of Charles Robert and Charlotte Reeves, an Irish family. However, some sources—including her marriage certificate—identify Charlotte as also having been Irish-born, in Caledon, Co Tyrone.

Hickey was one of eight children, and joined the Canadian "Mounties" just like his father. He was discharged to enlist with the Royal Naval Air Service. Hickey is credited with 21 aerial victories and was awarded the DFC and Bar. Notwithstanding the fact that neither of his parents would appear to have been Canadian, and perhaps both were actually Irish, Hickey didn't survive the war and so cannot be identified as anything other than Irish-Canadian.

Michael Vincent Kilroy (5 aerial victories)

Michael was born in St-Anne's-on-the-Sea, the Fylde, Lancashire. There are two dates of birth recorded on his service records (08 April 1894 and 25 January 1895). Either one or both of his parents were from Co Roscommon. Michael does not appear on the UK Census

APPENDIX II—ACES OF IRISH PARENTAGE AND IRISH DESCENT

1901. However, by the UK Census 1911 he is resident at 10 Park Road, St Annes-on-the-Sea, the Fylde, Lancashire. He was one of several servants to the Smith and Whiteside families, who ran a cab and carriage company.

In Michael's service record one next-of-kin address given is for his uncle, John Kilroy, of 202 St David's Road North, St Annes-on-the-Sea. Tracing this link via the UK Census 1911 we find an Irishman, John Kilroy (b.1879, Co Roscommon), his English wife Catherine (b.1881, Barrow in Furness) together with their children Kathleen and Franklin at that address, along with two lodgers. One further link in the UK Census 1911 to Co Roscommon, the Kilroy surname and the Fylde is a Bridget Kilroy (b.1871). She was a servant at the Bethel family household of 48 Gilda Brook Road, Barton upon Irwell, Eccles, Lancashire. Back in the UK Census 1901 Bridget was a servant at the Hargreaves family household of 24 Glen Eldon Road, St Anne's-on-the-Sea, the Fylde, Lancashire. It is therefore somewhat possible that Bridget was Michael's mother, and thus unmarried if retaining the surname of Michael's uncle. However, I cannot definitively link the two and it is far more likely that this was another sister of John Kilroy and an aunt of Michael. Regardless of the foregoing, given the Irish uncle it is likely that Michael had one Irish parent, and probably two.

Kilroy enlisted on 03 February 1915, under the service number 3510, as an Aircraftman 2nd Class. He was promoted to Sergeant and ultimately served with No.18 and No.19 Squadrons. Michael features in Albert Gregory Waller's aerial victories with No.18 Squadron, several claims being attributed to Michael's gunnery.

In the interwar years Kilroy returned to work as a cab driver in his native Lancashire. He married a Dinah Singleton in 1923 and is recorded as being resident at 10 Church Road, St Anne's on Sea. Kilroy re-enlisted on 15 February 1939 and saw limited action in World War II on the home front.

Kilroy continued to live in Lancashire after the wars, his death being recorded in Fylde in the third quarter of 1956, but I cannot find a single local history in which Kilroy is recorded as being Irish.

Air Vice-Marshal Edgar James Kingston-McCloughry (21 aerial victories)
Captain Wilfred Ashton McClaughry (non-ace, 3 aerial victories)

The Kingston-McCloughry brothers were under different variations of their surname to distinguish themselves from one another. Their mother was Charlotte Rebecca Ashton, an Australian. Their father was James Kingston-McCloughry from Larne, Co Antrim.

Wilfred served in the 9th Light Horse, and was wounded twice at Gallipoli. He flew in home defence squadrons against Zeppelins and with No.100 Squadron on night bombing missions. He was to command No.4 Squadron of the Australian Flying Corps, winning the MC, DFC, DSO and being mentioned in despatches several times. He was killed in World War II.

Edgar served in World War I and World War II, winning the DSO, the DFC and Bar. He was knighted, becoming a Companion of the Order of the Bath (i.e. a "C.B.") in 1950 and a Commander of the Order of the British Empire (i.e. a "C.B.E.") in 1943. He wrote several books on aerial strategy but I have not found a reference to him being considered Irish.

Captain Samuel Marcus Kinkead (43 aerial victories, 35 in World War I)

South African-born Samuel had an Irish father. He was born in Johannesburg on 25 February 1897. His father Samuel was from Ballykelly, Co Derry. His mother, Helen Calder, was Scottish.

After World War I he served with the RAF campaign in South Russia, which led to the temporary capture of Tsaritsyn (Stalingrad) by White Russian forces. He was a member of the Schneider Trophy team in 1927 but the British team were not successful. Kinkead was killed in an RAF high-speed test flight on 12 March 1928 at Calshot.

Dr Julian Lewis MP (Conservative, New Forest East) has written a biography "Racing Ace—the Fights and Flights of 'Kink' Kinkead DSO DSC and Bar DFC and Bar". It is reasonably clear

APPENDIX II—ACES OF IRISH PARENTAGE AND IRISH DESCENT

that Kinkead, though of his Irish and Scottish heritage, was a South African ace.

Captain Denis Latimer (28 aerial victories)

Denis was born in Withington, Manchester on 31 August 1895 to James Davies Latimer from Drogheda, Co Louth, and Ida Lottie Latimer of London. He was christened on 30 March 1896 at Holy Trinity Church, Oswestry, Shropshire.

Latimer is recorded in the UK Census 1901 and 1911 as being resident with his parents at the Corbett Arms Hotel, Corbett Square, Towyn, Merioneth, Wales. His father was the "hotel proprietor" or "inn keeper". In 1911 Denis was still a student at Towyn County School.

However, the family was not simply a product of England, Ireland and Wales: Denis' sister (Ethel Maud) and brother (Hugh) were both born in the USA. Ethel was born on 10 January 1892 at Oakland, Alameda, California. Hugh was born in San Francisco. Hugh was resident at 21 East Bank, Stamford Hill, North Hackney at the time of the UK 1911 Census, living with his granduncle James Rutherford and working as a butcher. (Contrary to some accounts, Denis' brother Hugh was not killed at the Somme, although there is a Hugh Latimer, 15th Bn Royal Irish Rifles, who is commemorated at the Thiepval Memorial).

With the family having moved around a lot, well at least for a decade or so, it is not easy to categorize Latimer or his brother and sister as being American, English, Irish or Welsh: although all these would have had a bearing on the family. Ultimately it would appear that the children identified with the nationality of their parents. In that regard would seem reasonable to include Latimer among the Irish aces if there was any evidence of him as having been identified as Irish.

However, Norman J Roberson's "The History of No.20 Squadron, Royal Flying Corps—Royal Air Force" [1987] does not disclose any particular detail on Latimer. There are numerous articles in 'Cross & Cockade', for example 'Lethal Company—Lt William Mackenzie Thompson MC DFC, 2nd Lt Harold Leslie Edwards MM DFC' by Stewart K Taylor in Cross & Cockade International (Spring 2012, 41.047), a Canadian pilot Edwin Albert McGee makes passing reference to flying with Latimer, but his nationality simply does not arise.

The official records of No.20 Squadron are better than most, e.g. they include a list of claims in the Squadron Operations Record book. (The UK National Archives have selected and compiled documents into AIR 27/258, but the organization is somewhat haphazard, e.g. some of the dates are not visible in the scanned material. Further, the material on what is described as the "Mohmand War" is slightly out of sequence). There were 44 aces who obtained some or most of their victories with No.20 Squadron. Of the other Irish aces that served with the squadron, both Air Commodore Henry Crowe and John J Cowell scored all of their victories with No.20 Squadron—the latter both as pilot and observer. (He is recorded as JJ Cowell in the squadron's list of claims). However, these records do not refer to nationality.

Latimer's service record[423] states that he was a university student in Manchester from 1912 to 1914. It also records his first name as "Dennis", and therefore in many publications on military history he is recorded under that name. Although he survived being shot down and taken POW I have not seen any post-war memoirs in which Latimer is specifically identified as Irish, although numerous secondary sources identify him as Irish.

Captain James Thomas Byford McCudden (57 aerial victories)
John Anthony "Jack" McCudden (8 aerial victories)

The McCudden brothers are a contentious battleground. Irish military historians (e.g. Richard Doherty) include James as Irish in any

---

423 AIR 76/289 Dennis Latimer, UK National Archives.

APPENDIX II—ACES OF IRISH PARENTAGE AND IRISH DESCENT

Victoria Cross tally. Equally, English aviation historians (e.g. Alex Revell) provide mountainous volumes of detail of the lives of the McCudden brothers, much of which suggests an English Catholic working class family from which James rose from the ranks of the Royal Engineers to become an air mechanic and eventually one of the most outstanding pilots in the Royal Flying Corps.

What is known is that the McCudden's father was from Co Carlow. His family were not originally from south Leinster however, having migrated south from Ulster. Several members of that family served in the British army, and consequently the McCudden brothers not only have an Irish father but numerous Irish uncles, many of whom had British-born children who regarded themselves as being Irish. Their mother, whose maiden name was Byford, was English of Scottish ancestry.

One further aspect to all this is the good friendship between James McCudden and 'Mick' Mannock. In one incident in January 1918 McCudden, Mannock and George "McIrish" McElroy are out on the tear together with William "McScotch" MacLanachan. McScotch and others describe McCudden as Irish, but I have not seen any record of any of the four McCudden brothers describing themselves as Irish. (There were two non-ace brothers, W.T.J. McCudden, killed in a crash at Gosport Flying School, and Maurice Vincent McCudden). McCudden and Mannock though had many common background characteristics, e.g. both had an Irish parent, both were self-educated and not part of the Officer Training Corps intake of gentlemen cadets, both came from the Royal Engineers as non-commissioned officers to break in to the rarefied atmosphere of the Royal Flying Corps whilst being considerably older than the others. Also, Mannock and McCudden were team players, developing formation flying and tactics in contrast to the early war aces, who have been typified as having the perspective of combat in the air as being an aerial jousting contest of some description. Overall there's much to link McCudden and Mannock besides the claim "ah sure they were both Irish".

443

James McCudden wrote an autobiography of sorts, called *Five Years in the Royal Flying Corps*. In later years the publishers tried to sex-up the title and re-named it "Flying Fury" and subtitled it "Five Years in the Royal Flying Corps". In this book McCudden steers clear of questions of Britishness and Irishness, simply trying to explain the evolving tactics and strategies of aviation and aerial combat. The preface by the editor of *Aeroplane* magazine, C.G. Grey, however, in an early edition of the book stated that:

"James McCudden was born on March 28, 1895, at Gillingham, Kent, the son of Mr W.H. McCudden, R.E., an Irishman from the County Carlow, but of North of Ireland descent. One of his grandmothers was French, and the combination of Northern and Southern Irish, and French blood explains James McCudden's character. He possessed the intensity of purpose of the Northerner, with the ingenuity and quickness of mind of the Frenchman. That dispassionate and disillusioned outlook which is so evident in his writing is typical of both the Southern Irish and of the French, as also is his lightness of heart, and his enthusiasm for people and things whom he admired. And his habit of switching over suddenly from a straight narrative to a brief sadly reflective mood, and back again to a funny story or a plain military was pure Southern Irish ...

... even the eternal Irish question did not interest him, although, or perhaps because, he was so essentially Irish. He was first, foremost, and all the time, a soldier of the King".

Actually, being able to say things without meaning them and maintaining a reasonably pleasant disposition when having to negotiate any military censorship were probably closer to his Irishness. He certainly avoided the contentious issues regarding the failure of high command to act on the issuance of parachutes and so forth.

McCudden was probably Irish to people who were Irish, e.g. Mannock, McElroy and so forth, and was probably otherwise English.

However, when at a function in Ireland in 1963 Air Marshal Lord Douglas of Kirtleside, aka 'Sholto' Douglas, was asked who

APPENDIX II—ACES OF IRISH PARENTAGE AND IRISH DESCENT

he regarded as the greatest Irish pilot of all time. He replied "James McCudden". Douglas was an Englishman who was no stranger to Ireland, having lived there—his father was Professor Robert Langton Douglas, Director of the National Gallery of Ireland—and in later life 'Sholto' was to lay down the basis for modern Irish aviation when he established airstrips at Aldergrove, Baldonnel, Collinstown and so forth when recuperating in Ireland in May 1917. He would not have chosen McCudden as an Irishman without being cognisant of the authority his voice would have for his Irish audience.

Further, the McCudden brothers' cousin E.J. McCudden, in 1995 wrote a book called "Barrack Rat: an Architect's Story". In it he detailed the family history of the McCudden clan. E.J. McCudden was the son of Christopher Joseph McCudden, the brother of James and Jack's father. C.J. McCudden was actually born in Hampshire but his son E.J. was born in Co Cork, a variation on James and Jack's situation. E.J. regarded his English-born father as being Irish. Overall, there would appear to be quite a number of English-born "Irish" McCuddens and therefore it is not impossible for family records to show that James and Jack regarded themselves as Irish, although any such material would undoubtedly have come to light by this stage.

As one may gather from all the foregoing, given the absence of a consensus on the McCudden brothers I have excluded them from the list of 37 Irish aces.

Lieutenant Archibald William Buchanan Miller (6 aerial victories)

There are conflicting accounts of Miller's place of birth. However, the UK Census 1901 records Archibald W.B. Miller (b.1897) as being Edinburgh-born. He was resent at Kirkurd Manse with his older brother Thomas and his parents. Their father was the Reverend Thomas Miller (b.1852, Perth, Scotland) and their mother was Margaret J Miller (b.1856, Cork, Ireland).

Archibald served as an observer with No.1 Squadron before undergoing pilot training. He was posted to No.29 Squadron in May

1917, becoming quite proficient in aerial combat with the Nieuport. Miller scored 6 aerial victories in June and July 1917 before being shot down and killed on 13 July 1917 by Leutnant Hans Adam of Jasta 6.

Despite having an Irish mother, I can find no account in No.29 Squadron, or indeed in any contemporary newspaper coverage, that would suggest that Miller ever considered himself Irish.

Lieutenant Hugh Fitzgerald Moore (6 aerial victories)

Hugh Fitzgerald Moore was born on 17 February 1897 in Glasgow to George (b.1870, Scotland) and Daisy (b.1873, Ireland) Moore. In the UK Census 1901 the family are recorded as being resident at St George's Road, Glasgow.

The family emigrated from Ireland to Canada in 1907. Moore enlisted in Canada, but there is a hand-written note on his attestation papers to the effect that his parents' consent was refused and so he was discharged on 08 July 1915. Moore re-enlisted. There is nothing, however, in the general material to hand to suggest that Moore was regarded as Irish. He died in Vancouver, British Columbia on 05 March 1974.

Captain James Anderson Slater (24 aerial victories)

James Anderson Slater was born on 27 November 1896 at Paignton, Devonshire to John (b.1859, Bolton, Lancashire) and Rose Anne Slater (b.1857, Ardmore, Co Waterford, née Cunniffe). In the UK Census 1901 the family are resident at Polsham Park, Paignton, Devonshire. James was the youngest of 5 children. In the previous census of 1891, before he was born, the family were also resident at that address, together with Rose's mother, Mary E Cunniffe, a widow. In the UK Census 1911 James is in school at Merton House, Roman Road, Southwick, Sussex. His parents are resident at Old Shoreham Road, Southern Cross, Portslade, Shoreham, Sussex in the same census.

APPENDIX II—ACES OF IRISH PARENTAGE AND IRISH DESCENT

Unsurprisingly Slater enlisted with the local Royal Sussex Regiment as a private. However, Slater obtained his commission with the Royal Irish Rifles.

"Jimmy" Slater started his RFC career with No.1 Squadron but really came into his own with No.64 Squadron, becoming one of the highest-scoring aces on the S.E.5a and was awarded the Military Cross and Bar, and the Distinguished Flying Cross.

Slater ended the war as a flying instructor and was killed in a flying accident at the Central Flying School, Upavon on 26 November 1925.

Although he joined an Irish regiment and had an Irish mother he was not generally considered to be Irish.

Constantine Falkland Cary "Conn" Smythe (non-ace, 0-6 aerial victories)

"Conn" Smythe was born on 01 February 1895 in Toronto to an Irish father, Albert Smythe, from Co Antrim, and an English mother, Mary Adelaide Constantine.

The Smythe family had immigrated to Canada in 1889, and Conn's sister Mary may not have been born in Canada. (She died in 1903, aged 13). Conn's family moved around Toronto to lodgings of varying quality, as Albert's earnings were limited and irregular. Conn's mother died in 1906, having a troubled relationship with alcohol, which made Conn a lifelong abstainer like his father Albert.

Smythe was a basketball, hockey and rugby player. Conn and most of his hockey teammates enlisted together in 1915. He served in the artillery, fighting at the Somme as part of the 40th (Sportsmen's) Battery and being awarded the Military Cross.

He transferred into the Royal Flying Corps in July 1917. This is where the point of contention arises as to whether he reached ace status. He was shot down and taken POW on 14 October 1917. It's my opinion that Conn Smythe is being confused with a C.R. Smythe of No.11 Squadron. The latter character appears in various RAF communiqués, as achieving a number of victories in the Bristol 2-seater fighter with a 2nd Lt W.T. Barnes. As late as 03 October 1918 their Bristol F2b (B8941) sent a Fokker DVII down out of control near Cambrai for one of that squadron's last victories of the war. In the circumstances it is likely that Conn Smythe never reached ace status. (Incidentally the unfortunate William Thomas Barnes chap won the DFC and ultimately was to die on 28 November 1920 in an IRA ambush at Kilmichael, when serving as an Auxillary in the Irish War of Independence).

Conn certainly had a larger-than-life existence in the post-war years, selling a homestead plot to fund a sand-and-gravel business, whilst coaching ice hockey teams in the evenings. He built up a sporting empire that included thoroughbred horses but is most closely associated with the Toronto Maple Leafs; the Conn Smythe Trophy is still awarded annually to the player judged most valuable to his team in the Stanley Cup.

Overall it is not surprising that some myths and legends would surround his life. I would remain to be convinced that he was even a Canadian ace, let alone an Irish one.

Captain Edmund Roger Tempest (17 aerial victories)
Wulstan Joseph Tempest (non-ace, 3 aerial victories)

Edmund Tempest was born on 30 October 1894 in Pontefract, West Yorkshire to Wilfred Francis Tempest (b.1847, Ackworth, North Yorkshire) and Florence Helen O'Rourke Tempest (b.1868, Dublin, Ireland). In the UK Census 1901 he is present as a pupil at the Convent of Mercy school, Abingdon, Berkshire. (Three of the teachers there were Irish, as were 4 of the non-academic staff, but just 2 pupils). In the UK Census 1911 his parents are living in Yorkshire but in the UK 1901 Census they were not present in the UK. However, prior to Edmund's birth the UK Census 1891 records the family as being present in the UK at Ackworth Grange, Doncaster Rd, Ackworth, Yorkshire. (Some of their servants are Irish, but this doesn't imply that the family ever resided in Ireland).

APPENDIX II—ACES OF IRISH PARENTAGE AND IRISH DESCENT

Edmund was living in Canada prior to enlistment. Tempest, together with his brother Wulstan, joined the King's Own Yorkshire Light Infantry, and not a Canadian or an Irish regiment. Both brothers transferred to the RFC early in the war. Edmund won the Military Cross and the DFC during the war, whilst Wulstan is credited with the destruction of Zeppelin L31 on 01 October 1916, winning the DSO in the process, and killing the leading Zeppelin commander Heinrich Mathy (who jumped rather than burn to death, making a deep impression in the ground in a field at Potter's Bar).

Edmund Tempest died in a crash near Baghdad on 17 December 1921. He lived in the UK and Canada prior to World War I but there is nothing to suggest that he ever identified himself as Irish in either country or during his wartime service. Given that his brother Wulstan was to become a reasonably famous wartime celebrity, with a Tempest Avenue and a Wulstan Park named after him, it would be impossible for the Irish angle to remain uncommented upon had either brother regarded themselves as Irish. Wulstan died in 1966.

Lieutenant William Wheeler (6 aerial victories)

William Allan Wheeler was born in Coventry on 05 April 1888, the son of James (b.1860, Wiltshire) and Elizabeth (b.1859, Derry). His father was a draper. In the UK Census 1891 the family are resident at Broad Gate, Coventry St Michael, Coventry. There are 10 drapers assistants present, including James' brother Edwin, which suggests a reasonably large business operation. In the UK Census 1901 William is no longer resident with the family but in the UK Census 1911 William and his brothers (Ernest and Alfred) are running a drapers business on Foleshill Road, Coventry. Their housekeeper is a 66-year-old Margaret McIlroy from Aghadowey, Co Derry, which would suggest that their mother may have sourced servants from her native Derry.

Wheeler became a late-war ace with No.88 Squadron, scoring 6 victories in the July to October 1918, although this should not be taken as Wheeler accounting for 4% (6/147ths) of the squadron's wartime total, as the individual pilot tallies included whole numbers for shared victories whilst the overall squadron total discounted these when compiling the figures. However, Wheeler does not feature in any memoirs of or articles about the prominent members of No.88 Squadron, e.g. the Australians such as Wing Commander Allan Hepburn (who appears in Wortley's "Letters of a Flying Officer") and Edgar Johnston (descendant of Marshall Clifton of Western Australian Land Company fame/notoriety), the Canadian Kenneth Burns Conn, Scottish ace Group Captain Charles Findlay and so forth.

In the circumstances he cannot be identified as an Irish ace.

Aces of Irish descent

In addition to the 18 aces of Irish parentage there a further 13 aces of Irish ancestry who are occasionally identified as being Irish (not including dozens of Irish-American aces such as Thomas Cassidy, James Connelly, J.A. Keating, E.G. Tobin, Sydney MacGillvary Brown, L.K. Callahan, J.A. Healy and Ralph O'Neill, and Irish-Australian aces such as Jerry Pentland, P.J. "Ginty" McGinness, Geoffrey Hooper, G.F. Hughes, H.J. Larkin, Edward Patrick Kenny, G.F. Malley, Francis Ryan Smith, Arthur O'Hara Wood and so forth).

The 13 people of Irish ancestry who are often identified as being Irish aces:

Lovell Dickens Baker (5 aerial victories)

Californian-born Lovell Dickens Baker was the son of a Minnesotan mother, Ida May (née Fletcher) and John Ridley Baker, who is variously described as being Irish or Irish-American. (There is a John Ridley Baker born in Newington to a Welsh mother in 1856 and recorded in the UK Census 1871 as being resident in Newington. However, the Criminal Registers for England and Wales would appear to show that particular individual serving a 15 month sentence in 1877 for larceny whilst a servant. This would remove him from a matching timeframe for being the spouse of Ida May Fletcher). There was a Lovell Dickens Baker baptised in Southwark, London, on 05 June 1898, but he would have been nine years of age by that stage. (Then again his Californian-born brother John Baker is recorded in some accounts as having been born on 16 April 1897 and christened on 24 May 1899 at Holy Trinity, Gainsborough, Lincoln. However, a British Columbia death record for him records his DOB as 16 August 1900 and his death as 26 April 1945). Lovell's father died when he was young. The UK Census 1901 records Lovell as being a student at Christ's Hospital, Newgate St, London. The UK Census 1911 indicates that he was 22, residing with his brother and three sisters at 6 Ormiston Road, New Brighton, Wallasey, Birkenhead, Cheshire. Lovell was born at San Francisco but his siblings were all born at Alameda. Significantly, Baker joined an Irish regiment (the Royal Dublin Fusiliers) rather than a British one in the years before he transferred into the Royal Flying Corps. However, I can find no record of him being specifically identified as Irish. On 03 August 1918 he married into a French family, a Renée Madeleine Brocvielle, youngest daughter of Camille Brocvielle of Amiens. In May 1923 his medal index card records Lovell's address as "19 rue Montegny, Dieppe, France". On 12 October 1923 Lovell is recorded as a passenger on the 'Montrose', sailing from Liverpool to Montreal. His address was given as "Bank of Montreal, Waterloo Place, London". His place of permanent residence was recorded under the 'other parts of the British Empire' category and he intended to live in Canada. Overall, despite the probability of an Irish-American father (and possibly an Irish one) and despite Lovell joining an Irish regiment I cannot justify including him among the Irish aces.

John Bernard "Don" Brophy (5 or 6 aerial victories)

Canadian-born Brophy was from an Irish-Canadian family, with both his father's and mother's sides of the family being of Irish origin. His father, John Byrne Brophy, was the son of John Brophy and Jane Byrne. His mother was Isabella Hearn.

"Don" Brophy was raised in Ottawa, in a 'lace curtain Irish' Bytown environment, becoming a distinguished athlete. He attended

St Patrick's School, Ottawa and Ottawa (Lisgar) Collegiate Institute. Upon the death of his mother, Brophy's father and two sisters moved to Capre Breton Island. Brophy attended McGill University in 1913, on the strength of his football skills. However, he failed first year and had taken a position with the Department of the Interior prior to the outbreak of the war.

Brophy's service record[424] indicates that he was initially assigned to 5 Reserve Aeroplane squadron before being transferred to 8 Reserve squadron on 26 November 1915. He initially served with home defence units, e.g. No.33 and No.19 Squadron, but upon qualifying as a pilot Brophy was assigned to No.21 Squadron in April 1916. He entered France with the squadron on 04 May 1916. It was truly a baptism of fire: the squadron's role as a bomber and long-range reconnaissance force was attempted using the obsolete RE7 and later the BE12, a wholly unsuitable type; Brophy is the only recorded ace with the squadron. Even with the bombing raids Brophy did end up making an attempt at an aerial engagement with a German observation balloon on 15 July 1916, but his bombs failed to ignite it. On 08 August 1916 Brophy was wounded when his aircraft struck a parked lorry. He was thrown 50 feet from the crash. He recovered and within weeks had recorded several aerial victories. On 07 September 1916 Brophy had an indecisive encounter with German scout near Bapaume. Brophy's guns jammed during the chase and the German apparently got away. On 09 September 1916 there was a further indecisive encounter, in which Brophy fired several rounds at an LVG that was attacking some FE2b on reconnaissance duties. Brophy's gun jammed and when turning he encountered a further three German aircraft, which he proceeded to face with his revolver. However, several DH2s came to the rescue. Once again, on at least the third occasion, Brophy had been recorded as driving down at least one German aircraft, but yet again it was not a decisive combat outcome. Later that day Brophy encountered a formation of Germans over Le Transloy but couldn't induce a group of BE12s of

---

424   AIR 76/57 JB Brophy, UK National Archives.

APPENDIX II—ACES OF IRISH PARENTAGE AND IRISH DESCENT

No.19 Squadron to follow him down. With the assistance of a French Nieuport they engaged and drove off the Germans but Brophy's gun had jammed in the encounter. The BE12 was armed with a Vickers gun firing through the propeller via an interrupter gear but it was notoriously prone to jamming. However, Brophy appears to have been particularly unlucky. On the other hand, when one considers that the B.E.12 was actually just a single-seat version of the obsolete B.E.2c it was quite remarkable that it could function in any sort of air-to-air combat role. To paraphrase Samuel Johnson the BE12 in aerial combat is like a dog walking on its hind legs: it is not done well but one is surprised to find it done at all.

On Friday 15 September 1916 Brophy had two further indecisive encounters, helping drive off two German aircraft:

"I was on patrol for three hours in the afternoon. We took bombs along [and] I bombed a village. I saw several Huns about and one of our machines was being attacked lower down. I turned and dived at the Hun, and a French Nieuport also joined in, and the Hun went into the low clouds and disappeared. Klingenstein was in the BE 12 and has not returned.

Later I saw a Hun attack three FEs and as one FE got behind him and was attacking him I dived to head the Hun off. He saw he was cornered and immediately did a loop and almost hit the FE, and went on diving until he got into the clouds".

On Saturday 16 September 1916 Brophy's first aerial victory was recorded:

"There were no Huns in sight, so I climbed above the clouds and crossed the lines to peep through the holes and see what was doing.

Spotted two observation balloons which I reported. Saw a lonely Hun come up to the clouds. Fired about seventy rounds at him, and he turned over and dived through. Went under clouds and saw no sign of him. This was put in [the] Flying Corps Communiqué, as a 'believed brought down' (my first appearance in Communiqué).

[The] Major 'chided' me for going across when I'm supposed to be doing defensive patrol, and grinned broadly".

RFC Communiqué No.54 of 1916 records Brophy as "JW Brophy" of 21 Squadron, which sometimes gives rise to confusion regarding the number of aerial victories attributed to him. On 17 September 1916 Brophy attacked a German aircraft over Bois de St Pierre Vaast, sending it down in flames. Brophy also attacked another over Pozieres, hunting him down to 2,000 feet until his gun jammed. Another pilot, Lt Watkins, observed the German continue downwards, levelling out near the ground. However, it is disputed as to whether this was officially recorded as a 'forced to land' aerial victory.

RFC Communiqué No.56 of 1916 records Brophy as having destroyed a German machine over the Bois du Dessus on 29 September 1916, whilst also forcing another German to land. Brophy's own account of these two aerial victories is as follows:

"In the afternoon four of us went on a patrol at 3:30. Bombed a dump of goods and ammunition at Rocquigny. We saw ten Huns flying on their side, below St. Pierre Vaast Wood. Waited for a big cloud to get into position, and then got near to them behind it and came out and dived onto them. Got in about ninety shots and one Hun fell into the wood. The rest went away like a flock of ducks. Later on attacked them again, and away they went. The archies put up some shrapnel at us. Attacked Huns again later, and one went down, and landed away behind, too far to see whether he crashed or not".

On 01 October 1916 Brophy suffered from a jammed gun, probably on account of firing whilst diving at speed, but he still managed to drive off a German who was attempting to engage a FE reconnaissance aircraft. Similarly, on 10 October 1916 Brophy had several indecisive engagements with German aircraft.

On Friday 20 October 1916 Brophy destroyed a German balloon, which was either his fifth or sixth aerial victory, depending upon the standard applied. He described the encounter as follows:

"Got up at 8:30 after another night of freezing and went and engulfed breakfast. Went on a patrol at one o'clock.

I espied a balloon as I got over Thiepval, coming from hunland at a height of 14,000 ft. I was 13,800 and couldn't get any higher. Aha,

APPENDIX II—ACES OF IRISH PARENTAGE AND IRISH DESCENT

says I, what's this? And I went and looked it over. I then saw it was a balloon and it had two big bundles hanging from it. I wasn't sure whether they were people or parcels, but decided to have a closer look, and as I couldn't get up to it, I thought the thing to do was to bring it down. So I flew under it and opened fire with my back gun.

It was evidently hit as it began to lose height after I had put a drum into it.

When it got down to my height I checked it over closely and saw the bundles were parcels. I wanted to see what they were so I got above it and dived into it and fired a few dozen shots so that it caught fire and went down. I immediately shut off and went after it.

It landed in a field. So did I. I found the parcels had fallen off, so I packed up the balloon which had only the top burnt off and put it in my seat and sat on it. It made it rather awkward to fly but I got up all right and went home. The balloon was then sent up to the Brigade by the Colonel".

The next day Brophy came to the assistance of a French Nieuport near Courcelette but the German fled and Brophy was unable to close in sufficiently to get in a fatal shot, and abandoned the chase near Miraumont. Similarly, on 22 October 1916 and 10 November 1916 Brophy had several other encounters in which he was unable to get a telling shot.

Brophy returned to Home Establishment on 23 November 1916, being reassigned to No.33 (Home Defence) Squadron. They were deployed to counter the Zeppelin raids. On the night of 27/28 November 1916 Brophy engaged in a patrol lasting three hours, chasing a Zeppelin for 40 miles before losing it in the darkness. However, on 24 December 1916 Brophy was killed in a flying accident when his BE 12 failed to recover from a loop during a routine Christmas Eve non-combat test flight. He was buried at Gainsborough General Cemetery, Lincolnshire.

Brophy was mentioned in despatches on 13 November 1916 for his successes with No.21 Squadron. However, by the time this was gazetted on 04 January 1917 he was dead.

455

Brophy kept a diary from 08 December 1915 to 12 November 1916, one of only a handful of Canadian war diaries relating to the flying services. Upon entering France in May 1916 the diary takes a less lighthearted tone, as Brophy expresses a confused range of emotions, from anger, frustration, fear, despair, fatalism yet also sporting bravado. One constant in it all is an attempt at flippancy, though the ongoing death toll he records does convey the reality of the situation. Brophy is very Irish yet unmistakably Canadian, e.g. in his diary entry for 19 December 1915 when passing the Irish coast it was the land of "our forefathers", i.e. of all the Canadian troops, rather than "my forefathers". He details the deaths of many colleagues, e.g. in a raid against Marcoing station (near Cambrai) on 09 July 1916 Brophy records the death of 2nd Lt Charles Victor Hewson of Gore Bay, Ontario: "I let my bomb go and had to turn off quickly to dodge a bomb from another youth who was above me … As soon as our bombs were dropped we turned and lit out for home, divil take the hindmost. He did, as poor old Hewson was picked off by a bunch of Huns, who attacked us from behind".

Brophy's diary was reproduced along with that of Harold Price in Brereton Greenhouse's *A Rattle of Pebbles: The First World War Diaries of Two Canadian Airmen* (Ottawa: Directorate of History, DND; 1987). As one may gather, Greenhouse quotes WB Yeats "Though the great song return no more/ There's keen delight in what we have – /A rattle of pebbles on the shore/ Under the receding wave". Overall Brophy remains an important early-war aviator but I cannot include him as Irish on foot of a couple of Irish grandparents, as it would adversely impact upon the credibility of the book: there are hundreds of pilots and observers who would qualify on that criterion. Although he is Irish-Canadian I cannot include him in this book as an Irish ace.

Verschoyle Philip "Shanachie" (Seanachaí) Cronyn (5 aerial victories)

Shanachie Cronyn's autobiography "Other Days" takes it's title from the Irish poet Thomas Moore's "Oft in the stilly night/ Ere slumber's chain has bound me/Fond memory brings the light/ Of other days around me". (For a warrior it's surprising that Cronyn didn't quote Moore's "Minstrel Boy", or indeed as a man in his eighties writing about his life perhaps "The Last Rose of Summer" would have been appropriate). Cronyn's great-grandfather, William Hume Blake QC, was born at Humewood Castle, Kiltegan, Co Wicklow, Ireland. Cronyn's grandfather was also Irish, though not actually born in Ireland: the family set sail from Ireland some months before his birth and so Verschoyle had numerous Irish-born granduncles but his grandfather was, technically-speaking, the first Canadian generation of Cronyns, even if he always features in the various Cronyn memoirs as their Irish grandfather. Contrary to expectations, the forename 'Verschoyle' does not arise as a forename from an adaptation of the Norman-Irish surname on his mother's side of the family; it was actually the surname of his great-grandfather's best friend in Trinity College Dublin. Cronyn's grandmother was Sophia Eliza Blake. Cronyn's father was Hume Blake Cronyn and his mother was Frances Amelia Labatt of the brewery family. Verschoyle served as a director of Labatt's. Cronyn was involved in the famous dogfight in which the great German ace Werner Voss was shot down and killed, Voss fighting single-handedly against 9 British attackers, of whom 7 were hit; Cronyn was particularly badly shaken by the experience, being taken off frontline duties. His autobiography "Other Days" does reference his Irish ancestry, and he often makes reference to various aspects of his contrarian character in terms of being Irish, e.g. in a court martial case in World War II he angrily refused to use a man as an example to others – "my Irish temper" and so forth – but he is very much a Canadian war hero. Consequently I do not include him, as to extend the term "Irish" to those of Irish grandparents would require the inclusion of a large number of Irish-American and Irish-Australian aces.

Samuel Hollis Alfred D'Arcy (5 aerial victories)

A descendant of the Wild Geese. Several of his great great great grandparents were Irish, i.e. Hyacinth D'Arcy (d.1743) of

Kiltullagh, Co Galway, also Jane Martin (d.1730) of Dangan, Co Galway. Richard D'Arcy (b.05 August 1729, d.09 April 1781) was 1st Baron D'Arcy in 1780, a Colonel in the Irish Brigade in France. Samuel's uncle Francois was son of the 4th Comte D'Arcy, was also killed in 1918. However, Samuel Hollis Alfred D'Arcy was the son of the 5th Count D'Arcy. He flew with the RAF, not the French air service, and was awarded the DSO, but was killed on 08 June 1918. To include the "Wild Geese" descendants would render the whole exercise meaningless, as it would be impossible to exclude those of Irish parents or grandparents.

Rowan Daly (7 aerial victories)

Rowan Heywood Daly was born on 30 March 1898 in Austria to an English mother and a Manx father from an Irish family. Rowan's father, Charles Valentine Daly, was born at Onchan, near Douglas in 1858, and appears in the UK 1871 Census as a 12 year old ship's boy on the *HMS Conway*, which was anchored off the Wirral peninsula. (Checking the Isle of Man parish registers it would appear that Charles was born to John Hickman Daly and Elinor Daly (née Heywood), being born on 06 March 1858 and christened on 01 May 1858).

Charles Day next appears in the UK Census 1891, as a 'Master Mariner', residing with his London-born wife (Kate) and one child, (Frank, b.1890). They were resident at 4 Howard Drive, Garston, West Derby, Lancashire. Curiously, in this census Charles describes himself as having been born in Ireland.

However, by the UK Census 1901 Rowan's father has reverted to being described as born on the Isle of Man, not Ireland. Rowan's mother, Kate, was born at Brockley in London. The family are resident at Cavendish Road, Sutton, Surrey. Rowan's siblings are Frank (b.1890, Lancashire), Brian (b.1892, Lancashire), Nora (b.1894, Lancashire) and Denis (b.1896, Lancashire). Rowan is the only one born outside the UK, his birthplace being given as Austria. His father would appear to describe himself as some sort of superintendent in a shipping company.

APPENDIX II—ACES OF IRISH PARENTAGE AND IRISH DESCENT

Similarly in the UK Census 1911 Rowan's father describes himself as being from the Isle of Man, not Ireland. Rowan and his sister Nora are still resident with their parents, joined by a Guglielmo Daly (b.1905, Essex). The family are resident at Ilma, Cliff Avenue, Leigh on Sea, near Rochford, Essex.

Attestation papers suggest Rowan Heywood Daly served with the Territorial Force, enlisting in the 14th County of London Regiment in 1914, and was assigned regimental number 2288. However, the British Postal Service Appointment Books suggest that Rowan was employed there from October 1915 as a certified wireless operator, but with his father's long association with maritime service it was no surprise that Rowan ended up in the Royal Naval Air Service. He was awarded Royal Aero Club certificate 4450 on 08 February 1917 at the Royal Naval Air Station, Chingford. In July 1917, flying a Sopwith Triplane, he was on Home Defence duties when he famously shot down a German Gotha GIII bomber near Ostend, having chased the raiders from the English coast. His gun jammed before he could finish off another. In France, flying a Sopwith Camel with 10 (Naval) Squadron he obtained two further aerial victories. Over the USSR in 1919 he scored four victories with No.47 Squadron, which were based in South Russia.

Rowan's DSC citation was gazetted on 11 August 1917 and the award of the DFC on 12 July 1920. He was known as 'Bill' Daly, and features fleetingly in accounts of the lives of Collishaw and Kinkead, but I find no account in which he is identified as Irish. He was killed in an air crash at Grantham, Lincolnshire in 1924.

Henry Eric Dolan (7 aerial victories)

Because of his close association with 'Mick' Mannock in No.74 Squadron it is often suggested that Dolan was another second-generation Irishman of Catholic background. However, the reality is somewhat different: his father Alfred Archer Dolan was English-born "mining engineer" from Clapham, whilst his mother Violet Edgeworth Hanrick, was notionally of Milan, Italy but of an Irish family and born at Bayswater in London, not Ireland as is often stated. The UK Census 1911 records Henry as being a student at Downside, Somerset, whilst his parents are boarders at 40 Langham St, Marylebone, London. Eric's date of birth is generally given as 20 January 1896, which features in his service records. Dolan was shot down by 11-victory ace Raven Freiherr [Baron] von Barnekow, a friend of Ernst Udet who—like Udet—went on to commit suicide early in World War II in an apparent protest against the folly of declaring war on the USSR. Dolan's brother, Gerald Roberts "Mickey" Dolan (10 July 1900 to 14 October 1981), was a senior Royal Navy officer, finishing his post-World War II career as Director of the Naval Armaments Inspectorate in India. Gerald was born in Durban, South Africa, according to the UK Census 1911. (He was also an Old Gregorian like his brother Eric). It can be expected that if the family moved between several countries and the children were born in several different jurisdictions then the parental influence on ethnic or cultural origin or affinity would have a greater bearing on identity than geographical location of birth, but I have not seen a single account that recounts an incident in which Dolan stated that he was Irish.

Stearne Tighe Edwards (19 aerial victories)

Captain Stearne Tighe Edwards was born in Ontario, Canada on 13 February 1893 to Edwin Dennis Edwards and Annie Caroline Vincent Tighe. His grandfather Stearne Tighe was born in Ireland in 1836 and is recorded on Canadian Immigration records as having entered Canada in 1859 and although some of his children may have been Irish-born his daughter Annie was not. Stearne Tighe Edwards is therefore of Irish grandparentage. Perplexingly, in the Canadian Census of 1901 the grandfather is recorded as "Stearns Edwards", and is resident with Edwin, Annie and their three children. This may have helped add to the confusion surrounding Edwards' Irishness. One may be curious as to why the family inflicted the name Stearne on their child. Apparently, the use goes back several generations: one account claims the first Stearne being actually Sterling Tighe, who married Abigall Ward on 31 December 1763 in St Michael's (Church of Ireland), in Dublin. However, this is incorrect: that particular individual was actually the second son of Stearne Tighe and Dorothy Blundell of Co Westmeath. (That particular Stearne Tighe was born on 30 June 1733 and baptised on 15 July 1733 at St Audoen's in Dublin).

Regardless of how many generations carried the name Stearne Tighe, it is clear that Stearne Tighe Edwards' mother was Canadian-born and therefore he is of Irish grandparentage. Edwards served with the RNAS, being good friends of fellow Canadians Roy Brown (credited with killing the Red Baron) and Dan Murray Galbraith (who married an Irish-Canadian, Maureen Kathleen Bergin). There are numerous accounts of how the three friends went from Canada to the USA and trained at their own expense to become pilots. Edwards had a remarkable career with 9 (Naval) Squadron, becoming a Flight Commander towards the end of the war. He was badly injured in a serious crash when serving as a flight instructor, dying on 22 November 1918 from his injuries. There are occasional references to Edwards' Irish ancestry but I have not seen a single account in which Edwards was actually claimed as Irish. Even if there were I could not justifiably include him among the Irish aces, as he is of Irish grandparentage and not Irish parentage as is sometimes claimed.

Desmond Fitzgerald Fitzgibbon (8 aerial victories)

The Fitzgibbon are known as the "White Knight", a prominent Anglo-Norman Irish family who settled mainly in Tipperary and Limerick. In the mid-17th century David FitzGibbon was Governor of Ardfinnan Castle. However, Desmond is quite a few generations on from this family: his great grandfather was Philip Fitzgibbon, of Mount Eagle, Kilworth, Co Cork. His great grandmother was Elizabeth Coates, of Killinure, Co Wicklow. His great-great-grandfather, Gerald Fitzgibbon, owned Castle Grace, Co Tipperary. It would appear that Fitzgibbon's father, Gerald, was a moderately successful English journalist, in respect of whom I can find no reference to his Irish grandparents and so I would therefore regard Desmond's connection to be far too remote for him to be considered Irish. (On his mother's side Margaret Mary Matthews was the daughter of Thomas Matthews, a very English family). The only reason why he would even be considered Irish is because he served with the Royal Naval Air Service, and as one may be aware, the RNAS stuck to the Royal Navy traditions in many respects; it takes three generations to make a gentleman and therefore presumably as long to shed being Irish.

William Charles Kennedy-Cochran-Patrick (21 aerial victories)

In nearly several major publications on aces of the Great War, e.g. *Above the Trenches* and many subsequent publications, Major Kennedy-Cochran-Patrick is identified as being Irish.

This would not be unusual given his complex family tree. He was the son of Sir Neil James Kennedy and Eleonora Agnes Cochran-Patrick, of Woodside and Ladyland. His grandfather, John Kennedy of Underwood, was Scottish of Irish ancestry, and his mother Eleonora Kennedy-Cochran-Patrick, was from a prominent Scottish family of Irish ancestry within which there had been a few bouts of cousin-marrying at various branches of the complex family tree. Eleonora was the granddaughter of Robert Caldwell Hunter (of Larne, Co Antrim) and Christian MacKnight Crawford (of Ayrshire, Scotland).

Over the course of the war he won the Distinguished Service Order, and Military Cross and Bar. He was mentioned in despatches. He has generally been identified as the "Patrick" character who was Lewis' mentor in *Sagittarius Rising*, although he is not explicitly identified as such in the book.

William was killed near Johannesburg, South Africa, on 26 September 1933 in a crash. However, he had married Natalie Bertha Tanner. Their child, Neil Aylmer Kennedy-Cochran-Patrick, adopted his grandmother's surname and became Neil Aylmer Hunter. He was a

APPENDIX II—ACES OF IRISH PARENTAGE AND IRISH DESCENT

Scottish soldier, winning a Silver Medal in the Olympic Games at Melbourne in 1956 for sailing.

Even if one were to step back a generation from Neil and claim that his father identified as Irish it would be a strange identity. William had 3 sisters: Eleanora Hunter Kennedy-Cochran-Patrick, and twin sisters Margaret Hamilton Kennedy-Cochran-Patrick and Kathleen Agnes Kennedy-Cochran-Patrick. Their published accounts of a journey to South Africa disclose nothing more than a longing for Scotland.

Given all the foregoing, and no matter how many Irish crop of on both sides of the Kennedy-Cochran-Patrick family tree, I cannot include him as an Irish ace.

Conrad Tolendal Lally (5 aerial victories)

Toronto-born Conrad was the grandson of Thomas Arthur Lally, who famously lost France's Indian colonies to the British during the Seven Years War. He was the great grandson of Trophime Gérard de Lally, Marquis de Lally Tollendal, who led a large contingent of the Galway 'Wild Geese' into the French army following the Siege of Limerick.

Many Irish people would hold the Lally name in high esteem due to the regiment de Lally of the Irish Brigade helping sweep the Hanoverian British forces from the field at Fontenoy in May 1745. Given that it involved the defeat of the Duke of Cumberland, later "the Butcher Cumberland" of various Scottish massacres infamy, presumably many a Scottish person would have bought Conrad a dram had they known of his distinguished Jacobite ancestry.

Before the war Lally had served as Mayor of Wainwright. He returned there after the war, disfigured from a bad crash that had fractured his jaw in three places, but went on to serve a further term as mayor after becoming the town's postmaster in 1923. However, whilst it is reasonably clear that Conrad was proud of his Irish and French ancestry, he is a Canadian war hero, winning the Military Cross and Bar, and the Air Force Cross.

Patrick Sarsfield Manley (5 aerial victories)

Manley was born in Coteau-du-Lac, Quebec on 04 October 1895. His father, Edward J Manley (25 July 1861 to 22 January 1928) was born in Thorold, Ontario, to Edward Manley (b.15 March 1819, Glencastle, Co Mayo) and Margaret Dixon (1821-1881), who also hailed from Co Mayo. Manley's grandparents travelled to Canada in May 1846 from Killala, Co Mayo, on the 'coffin ship' the "Elizabeth and Sarah", a 74-year-old barque of 330 tones, which carried 279 passengers but only had 36 berths (4 of which were reserved for the crew). Many of the passengers would appear to have been the subject of a mass clearance from Lord Sligo's lands around Westport, Co Mayo. Their real surname of the Manleys was most likely 'Munnelly'.

Patrick Sarsfield's mother, Margaret Anne Boylan, would appear to have been also born in Canada (on 01 November 1861, died May 1928) to another Irish family, (Edward Boylan and Margaret O'Brien).

Patrick Sarsfield's father—Edward J Manley—worked for many of the Irish construction firms, e.g. Larkin & Connolly, (who built the Louise Basin at Québec City) and MJ Hogan (railroad construction). Edward worked on the Panama Canal at one stage and his own firm, the Manley Company, became the Frontenac Dredging Company Ltd when it became a ltd stock company.

Manley served with No.62 Squadron. He scored all his victories in a 2-seater Bristol F2 Fighter, with Sgt George Hines as his observer. They were shot down and taken POW on 27 September 1918. Although he is mentioned in Jon Guttman's excellent *Bristol F2 Fighter Aces of World War I* (London: Osprey, 2007) it is in the context of his achievements and not any particular ethnic background to his Canadian nationality.

However, despite a good Irish pedigree, Patrick Sarsfield's wartime letters to Niagara University make quite a number of references to his Catholic faith, indeed some of his letters have an awful Irish Catholic fatalism "if God wills, I am happy to die", but none of

Patrick's letters refer to his Irish ancestry. He moved to the US on 01 March 1941 and was drafted to the US military in 1942. Patrick died 30 October 1952, Cleveland, Ohio, USA.

Despite his Irish-Canadian parents, and several Irish grandparents, I cannot include him as an Irish ace.

Guy Borthwick Moore (10 aerial victories)

Guy was born on 28 May 1895 at Mattawa, Ontario to Edward Hamilton Moore (b.12 September 1856, Quebec) and Emma Jane Borthwick (b.1866, Ottawa). Guy's grandfather, Benjamin George Moore, was Irish.

Significantly, Guy joined the Irish Fusiliers of Canada. He transferred to the Royal Flying Corps in December 1916. He was awarded the Military Cross for leading a mission to destroy 3 well defended German balloons. Moore was killed by German anti-aircraft fire on 07 April 1918. Moore died intestate. Looking at the probate records for Saskatchewan of 1925 I find nothing in the letters of administration to suggest that any Irish-Canadian veterans fund or any other ethnically identifying material arises in the papers, e.g. there's a property worth $1,200 and some securities upon which interest and repayments of $633 were earned, which the parents apply to split equally between themselves, but that Emma Jane Moore had died on 21 October 1920 and so therefore Guy's father was to be sole beneficiary.

Despite having joined an Irish-Canadian regiment I cannot justify including him as an Irish ace, without having the Irish casualty list multiply to unjustifiably large figures on foot of a grandparent being the criterion for inclusion.

Desmond Percival Fitzgerald Uniacke (13 aerial victories)

Desmond was born on 18 December 1895 at Chelsea to Richard Gordon Fitzgerald Uniacke (b.19 August 1867, d.1934) and Cecilia Monica Lambert. He was grandson of Rev Robert FitzGerald

Uniacke, of the Uniackes of Uniacke and Castleton, Co Cork. Desmond's great great grandfather was Richard John Uniacke, Attorney-General of Nova Scotia.

Desmond's father Richard published *Some Old County Cork Families: the Uniackes of Youghal* in 1895 but was better known in Ireland as a Fellow of the Royal Society of Antiquaries of Ireland. Richard was also a genealogist in the modern sense of the term, i.e. family histories were charted without resorting to the traditional fabrication of a link to some famous ancient nobility.

It would appear that Desmond joined either the Royal Irish Rifles or the Royal Inniskilling Fusiliers. (The London Gazette and the Medal Cards do not fully reconcile). Unusually, he did not join the Royal Munster Fusiliers, which would have been the most likely destination for a prominent Cork family.

Uniacke transferred to the Royal Flying Corps in May 1917. He served as observer/gunner in the Bristol F2.b fighter, achieving 13 victories with the English ace Ralph Luxmore Curtis. On 21 September 1917 they were shot down by Hermann Goring, with Curtis being killed and Uniacke being taken POW.

After the war Uniacke became a wine salesman. He died on 25 March 1933, aged 37.

Despite Desmond joining an Irish regiment and having Irish grandparents I cannot extend the definition of the term "Irish ace" this far without consequences for the many thousands of non-ace aviators of Irish grandparents.

SELECTED BIBLIOGRAPHY

Barrett, Michele *Casualty Figures* (London and New York: Verso, 2007)

Bowyer, Chaz (ed) *Royal Flying Corps Communiqués 1917-1918* (London: Grub Street, 1998)

Boyle, Andrew *The Riddle of Erskine Childers* (London: Hutchinson, 1977)

Coates, Tim (ed) *Tragic Journeys* (London: HMSO, 2001)

Cole, Christopher [ed], *Royal Flying Corps Communiqués 1915-1916* (London: Tom Donovan Publishing, 1990)

Cole, Christopher [ed], *Royal Air Force Communiqués 1918* (London: Tom Donovan Publishing, 1990)

Committee of the Irish National War Memorial, *Ireland's Memorial Records, World War I 1914-1918, Volumes I-VIII* (1923; Republished by Eneclann, 2005)

Crane, David *Scott of the Antarctic* (New York: Alfred A. Knopf, 2005)

Dungan, Myles *Distant Drums* (Belfast: Appletree Press, 1993)

Fanning, Ronan et al [eds] *Documents on Irish Foreign Policy, Volume I: 1919-1922* (Dublin: Royal Irish Academy, 1998)

Franks, Norman *Nieuport Aces of World War I* (London: Osprey, 2000)

Franks, Norman *SE 5/5a Aces of World War I* (London: Osprey, 2007)

Franks, Norman *Sharks Among Minnows* (London: Grub Street, 2001)

Franks, Norman *Sopwith Camel Aces of World War I* (London: Osprey, 2003)

Franks, Norman *Sopwith Pup Aces of World War I* (London: Osprey, 2005)

Norman Franks, Hal Giblin & Nigel McCrery *Under the Guns of the Red Baron* (London: Grub Street, 1995)

Norman Franks, Russell Guest & Gregory Alegi *Above the War Fronts* (London: Grub Street, 1997)

Grayson, Richard *Belfast Boys* (London: Continuum, 2009)

Guinness, Arthur & Son *Roll of Employees who served in His Majesty's Naval, Military and Air Forces, 1914-1918* [Guinness, 1920; Reprint by Naval & Military Press]

Guttman, Jon, *Bristol F2 Fighter Aces of World War I* (London: Osprey, 2007)

Guttman, Jon *Balloon-Busting Aces of World War I* (London: Osprey, 2005)

Guttman, Jon *Pusher Aces of World War I* (London: Osprey, 2009)

Guttman, Jon, *SPAD VII Aces of World War I* (London: Osprey, 2001)

Guttman, Jon, *SPAD VII -vs- Albatros DIII: 1917-1918* (London: Osprey, 2011)

Hallam, Theodore Douglas *The Spider Web* (London: Leonaur, 2009)

Hennessy, Thomas *The Great War 1914-1918, Bank of Ireland Staff Service Record* [Dublin: Alex Thom 1920; Reprint by Naval & Military Press]

Henry, William *Forgotten Heroes, Galway Soldiers of the Great War 1914-1918* (Cork: Mercier, 2007)

Hill, Judith *Lady Gregory: An Irish Life* (London: Sutton, 2005)

Larson, Gale *Shaw and History* (Pennsylvania: Penn State Press, 1999)

MacCarron, Donal *A View from Above: 200 Years of Aviation in Ireland* (Dublin: O'Brien Press, 2000)

McCudden, James *Five Years in the Royal Flying Corps* (London: J. Hamilton, 1922)

O'Connor, Mike *Airfields & Airmen: Arras* (Barnsley: Pen & Sword Military, 2004)

O'Connor, Mike *Airfields & Airmen: Cambrai* (Barnsley: Pen & Sword, 2003)

O'Connor, Mike *Airfields & Airmen: Somme* (Barnsley: Pen & Sword, 2002)

O'Connor, Mike *Airfields & Airmen: Ypres* (Barnsley: Pen & Sword, 2001)

SELECTED BIBLIOGRAPHY

O'Connor, Mike *Airfields & Airmen of the Channel Coast* (Barnsley: Pen & Sword Aviation, 2005)

O'Malley, Michael *Military Aviation in Ireland, 1921-45* (Dublin: UCD Press, 2010)

Oughton, Frederick [ed] *The Personal Diary of 'Mick' Mannock VC, DSO (2 bars, MC (1 bar)* (London: Spearman, 1966)

Partridge, Michael *Maverick Airman—the Extraordinary Life of Frederick Frank Reilly Minchin* (Eastbourne College Arnold Embellishers, 2010)

Quinn, Anthony *Wigs & Guns, Irish Barristers in the Great War* (Dublin: Four Courts Press, 2006)

Rennles, Keith *Independent Force* (London: Grub Street, 2002)

Revell, Alex *British Single-Seater Fighter Squadrons in World War I* (Pennslyvania: Schiffer, 2006)

Revell, Alex *No.60 Squadron RFC/RAF* (London: Osprey, 2011)

Ross, David *A Critical Companion to William Butler Yeats: A Literary Reference to His Life* (New York: Infobase Publishing, 2009)

Sandford, Jeremy [ed] *Mary Carbery's West Cork Journal, 1898-1901* (Dublin: Lilliput Press, 1998)

Scott, AJL *Sixty Squadron RAF—A History of the Squadron from its Formation* (London: William Heinemann, 1920)

Christopher Shores, Norman Franks & Russell Guest *Above The Trenches* (London: Grub Street, 1990)

Christopher Shores, Norman Franks & Russell Guest *Above The Trenches Supplement* (London: Grub Street, 1996)

Smith, Adrian *Mick Mannock Fighter Pilot: Myth, Life and Politics* (London: Palgrave, 2001)

Smythe, Colin (ed) *Robert Gregory 1881-1918* (London: Colin Smythe Ltd, 1981)

Swanzy, Rev Henry Biddal *The Families of French of Belturbet and Nixon of Fermanagh and their Descendants* (Dublin: Alex Thom & Co Ltd, 1908)

Udet, Ernst *Ace of the Iron Cross* (New York: Doubleday, 1970)

Warner, Guy *World War I Aircraft Pioneer: The Story and Diaries of Jack McCleery, RNAS RAF* (Barnsley: Pen & Sword Aviation, 2011)

Gerry White and Brendan O'Shea [eds] *A Great Sacrifice: Cork Servicemen who died in the Great War* (Cork: Echo Publications, 2010)

Journals, Periodicals, Newspapers

Cross & Cockade (Great Britain)
Cross & Cockade (International)
Flight/Flightglobal [especially their digitized online archive]
History Ireland
Irish Sword—Journal of the Military History Society of Ireland
Irish Times
London Gazette

Miscellaneous

I have examined several hundred service records and squadron operations record books from the UK National Archives. It would be wholly impractical to list them all here: references are cited in respect of individual aviators in their biographies. (My thanks to the staff of the UK National Archives in efficiently providing information requested). The reference to AIR 76 is to those records generated up to 1922 in respect of Royal Flying Corps and those who transferred to the RAF in April 1918. The reference to ADM is to a file of the Royal Naval Air Service. A reference to AIR 79 is to that of a file relating to one of the first 329,000 people who served in the RAF from April 1918 onwards. Many of these served in the inter-war years and World War II. Consequently these records have not been digitized; some of the information is appearing in print for the first time. The WO file references are the service medal card indexes and the reference to AIR 27 is to a Squadron Operations Record Book.

The Imperial War Museum also has an extensive publicly accessible collection of audio recordings, including many conducted with former RFC, RNAS and RAF personnel. References are cited in the biographies of individual aviators.

SELECTED BIBLIOGRAPHY

Of the numerous genealogy websites I have found FamilySearch to be particularly useful as a starting point for further research and would like to thank the Church of Jesus Christ of the Latter-Day Saints accordingly.

Of the sites with particular relevance to Ireland, the www.irishgenealogy.ie site is excellent for many Church of Ireland records. Similarly, the www.census.nationalarchives.ie is a good starting point for tracing the early years of many Irish servicemen via the 1901 and 1911 census returns.

For cross-checking the records of the Earl of Ypres' commission and/or squadron histories I found the following site to be invaluable in identifying any Irish memorials for the fallen:

http://www.irishwarmemorials.ie/

For many searches of the UK Census and for travel records, passport application details and so forth I used ancestry.co.uk and findmypast.co.uk.

For military history and aviation history I found the following sites to be particularly useful:

www.theaerodrome.com

http://1914-1918.invisionzone.com/forums/index.php

http://www.rafweb.org/

None of the foregoing information should be taken to imply that the owners of those sites endorse in any way or form the views expressed by this author.

4711568R00293

Printed in Great Britain
by Amazon.co.uk, Ltd.,
Marston Gate.